T0214789

Lecture Notes in Computer Science 12191

More information about this series at http://www.springer.com/series/7409

Jessie Y. C. Chen · Gino Fragomeni (Eds.)

Virtual, Augmented and Mixed Reality

Industrial and Everyday Life Applications

12th International Conference, VAMR 2020
Held as Part of the 22nd HCI International Conference, HCII 2020
Copenhagen, Denmark, July 19–24, 2020
Proceedings, Part II

 Springer

Editors
Jessie Y. C. Chen
U.S. Army Research Laboratory
Aberdeen Proving Ground, MD, USA

Gino Fragomeni
U.S. Army Combat Capabilities
Development Command
Orlando, FL, USA

ISSN 0302-9743 ISSN 1611-3349 (electronic)
Lecture Notes in Computer Science
ISBN 978-3-030-49697-5 ISBN 978-3-030-49698-2 (eBook)
https://doi.org/10.1007/978-3-030-49698-2

LNCS Sublibrary: SL3 – Information Systems and Applications, incl. Internet/Web, and HCI

This Springer imprint is published by the registered company Springer Nature Switzerland AG
The registered company address is: Gewerbestrasse 11, 6330 Cham, Switzerland

Foreword

The 22nd International Conference on Human-Computer Interaction, HCI International 2020 (HCII 2020), was planned to be held at the AC Bella Sky Hotel and Bella Center, Copenhagen, Denmark, during July 19–24, 2020. Due to the COVID-19 coronavirus pandemic and the resolution of the Danish government not to allow events larger than 500 people to be hosted until September 1, 2020, HCII 2020 had to be held virtually. It incorporated the 21 thematic areas and affiliated conferences listed on the following page.

A total of 6,326 individuals from academia, research institutes, industry, and governmental agencies from 97 countries submitted contributions, and 1,439 papers and 238 posters were included in the conference proceedings. These contributions address the latest research and development efforts and highlight the human aspects of design and use of computing systems. The contributions thoroughly cover the entire field of human-computer interaction, addressing major advances in knowledge and effective use of computers in a variety of application areas. The volumes constituting the full set of the conference proceedings are listed in the following pages.

The HCI International (HCII) conference also offers the option of "late-breaking work" which applies both for papers and posters and the corresponding volume(s) of the proceedings will be published just after the conference. Full papers will be included in the "HCII 2020 - Late Breaking Papers" volume of the proceedings to be published in the Springer LNCS series, while poster extended abstracts will be included as short papers in the "HCII 2020 - Late Breaking Posters" volume to be published in the Springer CCIS series.

I would like to thank the program board chairs and the members of the program boards of all thematic areas and affiliated conferences for their contribution to the highest scientific quality and the overall success of the HCI International 2020 conference.

This conference would not have been possible without the continuous and unwavering support and advice of the founder, Conference General Chair Emeritus and Conference Scientific Advisor Prof. Gavriel Salvendy. For his outstanding efforts, I would like to express my appreciation to the communications chair and editor of HCI International News, Dr. Abbas Moallem.

July 2020   Constantine Stephanidis

Conference Proceedings Volumes Full List

38. CCIS 1224, HCI International 2020 Posters - Part I, edited by Constantine Stephanidis and Margherita Antona
39. CCIS 1225, HCI International 2020 Posters - Part II, edited by Constantine Stephanidis and Margherita Antona
40. CCIS 1226, HCI International 2020 Posters - Part III, edited by Constantine Stephanidis and Margherita Antona

http://2020.hci.international/proceedings

12th International Conference on Virtual, Augmented and Mixed Reality (VAMR 2020)

Program Board Chairs: **Jessie Y. C. Chen, U.S. Army Research Laboratory, USA, and Gino Fragomeni, U.S. Army Combat Capabilities Development Command Soldier Center, USA**

- Daniel W. Carruth, USA
- Shih-Yi Chien, Taiwan
- Jeff Hansberger, USA
- Fotis Liarokapis, Czech Republic
- Joseph B. Lyons, USA
- Phillip Mangos, USA
- Crystal Maraj, USA
- Rafael Radkowski, USA
- Maria Olinda Rodas, USA
- Jose San Martin, Spain
- Andreas Schreiber, Germany
- Peter Smith, USA
- Simon Su, USA
- Tom Williams, USA
- Kevin Wynne, USA
- Denny Yu, USA

The full list with the Program Board Chairs and the members of the Program Boards of all thematic areas and affiliated conferences is available online at:

http://www.hci.international/board-members-2020.php

HCI International 2021

The 23rd International Conference on Human-Computer Interaction, HCI International 2021 (HCII 2021), will be held jointly with the affiliated conferences in Washington DC, USA, at the Washington Hilton Hotel, July 24–29, 2021. It will cover a broad spectrum of themes related to Human-Computer Interaction (HCI), including theoretical issues, methods, tools, processes, and case studies in HCI design, as well as novel interaction techniques, interfaces, and applications. The proceedings will be published by Springer. More information will be available on the conference website: http://2021.hci.international/.

General Chair
Prof. Constantine Stephanidis
University of Crete and ICS-FORTH
Heraklion, Crete, Greece
Email: general_chair@hcii2021.org

http://2021.hci.international/

Contents – Part II

Learning, Narrative, Storytelling and Cultural Applications of VAMR

VAMR for Health, Well-being and Medicine

Contents – Part I

Gestures and Haptic Interaction in VAMR

Cognitive, Psychological and Health Aspects in VAMR

VAMR for Training, Guidance and Assistance in Industry and Business

Navigating a Heavy Industry Environment Using Augmented Reality - A Comparison of Two Indoor Navigation Designs

Alexander Arntz$^{(\boxtimes)}$, Dustin Keßler, Nele Borgert, Nico Zengeler, Marc Jansen, Uwe Handmann, and Sabrina C. Eimler

Institute of Computer Science, University of Applied Sciences Ruhr West, Bottrop, Germany
{alexander.arntz,dustin.kessler,nele.borgert,nico.zengeler, marc.jansen,uwe.handmann,sabrina.eimler}@hs-ruhrwest.de

Abstract. The fourth industrial revolution seeks to enhance and optimize industrial processes through digital systems. However, such systems need to meet special criteria for usability and task support, ensuring users' acceptance and safety. This paper presents an approach to support employees in heavy industries with augmented reality based indoor navigation and instruction systems. An experimental study examined two different user interface concepts (navigation path vs. navigation arrow) for augmented reality head-mounted-displays. In order to validate a prototypical augmented reality application that can be deployed in such production processes, a simulated industrial environment was created. Participants walked through the scenario and were instructed to work on representative tasks, while the wearable device offered assistance and guidance. Users' perception of the system and task performance were assessed. Results indicate a superior performance of the navigation path design, as it granted participants significantly higher perceived support in the simulated working tasks. Nevertheless, the covered distance by the participants was significantly shorter in navigation arrow condition compared to the navigation path condition. Considering that the navigation path design resulted in a higher perceived Support, renders this design approach more suitable for assisting personnel working at industrial workplaces.

Keywords: Augmented reality · Heavy industry · Indoor navigation · Work support · HCI · Experimental study

1 Introduction

Heavy industries, especially metal manufacturing enterprises in Germany, are facing an ever-increasing competition on a global scale. In order to compete, local metal suppliers are in need to respond with cost effective products offering

© Springer Nature Switzerland AG 2020
J. Y. C. Chen and G. Fragomeni (Eds.): HCII 2020, LNCS 12191, pp. 3–18, 2020.
https://doi.org/10.1007/978-3-030-49698-2_1

a high quality and variety. Thus, the optimization of production processes is a key factor in reaching this goal. A major element in the production process is the workforce [17]. At every point in the entire production chain and in various hierarchical levels, employees' decisions have an impact on the success of the planning and the execution of the production [26]. The introduction of digital systems in production processes can aid to connect interoperable machines, sensory communication and employees, thus increasing efficiency [8,35]. Providing a system that supports employees in their actions by offering secure, real-time and process-related data could help reducing flawed decisions and shorten reaction times [27]. This can result in an overall improved production and contributes to economic success. The goal of this project is to deliver this data in a simple, reliable and intuitive way that automatically recognizes the context, the user's role and permissions. At the same time, the system should provide information required in the current circumstance and avoid redundant data that might confuse the user [32]. For this purpose, the project DamokleS 4.0 developed a context model [18], which manages and sorts all data and sends it to a variety of mobile devices, on demand for the user. One of these mobile devices utilized in the architecture is an augmented reality head-mounted-display (HUD) [13]. Augmented reality provides an interface for embedding digital content, such as indoor navigation and context-based information, in an industrial application and allows to visualize data, i.e. navigation paths, directly into the field of view (FOV) of the employees [17]. However, due to the various safety concerns in an industrial environment (heavy machinery and hazardous materials), it is necessary to evaluate how and in what way AR-support is most effective in this kind of scenario [24]. For this purpose, an experimental setup was created that compares two AR-applications, each containing a distinct indoor navigation user interface and a set of tasks for the test participants to conduct. The project aimed at evaluating the effectiveness of different, hands-free navigational design approaches in AR to determine the benefit and the possible field of application of such technologies.

2   Related Work

While there are several AR-navigation approaches and different projects researching the usage of AR for heavy industries, few combined the aspects of context-based instructions and indoor navigation in potentially hazardous environments [22]. A crucial factor is the position localization, as only a precise implementation can help to warn the user of potentially dangerous areas or, in the case of an emergency, guide the person to the nearest exit. Mobile solutions, whether on a smartphone or HMD, cannot rely on a GPS signal alone for a calculation of the user's position, as signal strength will be diminished indoors, especially in an industrial environment [22]. Similar research projects used backpacks with additional hardware, such as a sophisticated GPS receiver, to improve results of the navigation, though the precision still highly depends on the structural components of the indoor environment [23]. Considering that additional hardware carried by the personnel is inconvenient and cumbersome, other solutions were pursuit for this project [27]. Kim and Jun proposed a vision-based location algorithm for AR-based indoor navigation, which uses an image database of prerecorded images in order to estimate the current location of the user [19]. This requires external computation, which processes the live images and compares them to a database. Rehman and Cao presented a similar app-roach using a mobile framework, which did the comparison of live information and an image database on the device [29]. Both methods require a detailed image library, a consistent environment and a network connection. Due to the limited capabilities of current, mobile, AR-compatible cameras to cope with dim lit environments, these solutions were not found suitable for an industrial context. Omitting the image-based calculation by the AR-device, beacon-based naviga-tion was evaluated as an external reference for location data, as prior research in this technology was promising. For this purpose, the experimental environment was outfitted with a set of beacon transmitters, which used a trilateration app-roach for location detection [10,33]. This technique is calculating the position based on the relative distance of three reference points. However, the structural composition of common industrial facilities caused too much interference, result-ing in a constant signal instability. Even the usage of additional filters failed to deliver reliable data for positional location. A much more reliable solution was the utilization of a camera-based detection model that can track the movement of personnel and objects in real-time and calculate their position. In case of short network interruptions that hinder the information relay to the AR-device, a backup solution was implemented. Current AR-devices, such as the Microsoft HoloLens, make use of infrared cameras to create a virtual topography of the sur-roundings, which results in a precise position detection in 3-dimensional space, even in low light or changing environments [4].

3   Research Questions

With the technical aspects figured out, the question remained how to design the user interface (UI) of the AR-application, to efficiently assist users' in their tasks within the production facilities, while securely directing them around. The first objective was to design a UI that is displayed properly within the field of view without occluding the perception of the user. The design of the AR-content is required to allow the user to focus equally on the virtual elements and the real environment. Prior research suggests that high contrast iconography is suitable for dim lit conditions [21]. Apart from the visual aspects, audio cues can be neglected due to the volume of noise in industrial areas [35].

The next important aspect is the usability of the used AR-application. Despite the design of usability aspects and overall user-experience of AR-hardware still being a challenge, AR brings the enormous benefit of seamlessly integrating information into the real-world environment, enabling the coexis-tence of virtual content next to actual surroundings. This improves Ease of Use as the usage of metaphors that need to meet the expectation of a users mental model is diminished. In addition, an application or system containing a high Ease of Use is expected to generate greater acceptance by the user, thus contributing to the overall effectiveness of the technology [20]. In order to validate the concept of an AR-based support and navigation application, a test scenario was created that compares two distinctive navigation designs. The first being a representation of an arrow giving directions to the current way-point, while the second method consists of a 3D line which augments the users view with additional data regarding the optimal path. The concept of the first design, containing the arrow, is to provide the user the freedom to choose the path desired while delivering an assistance on where to go next. In addition to this, displaying a constant visual indication towards the next point of interest helps the user to always maintain an overview of his surroundings. The second approach encourages the user to follow the optimal calculated path, which is displayed as a virtual line on top of the real-world environment. Those two techniques were chosen, as they resemble traditional navigation systems used in the automobile industry or smartphone based navigation applications. The user tasks, iconography and texts were identical in both applications. Based on the assumption that inexperienced participants will need more assistance while guiding through the scenario, it is expected that the path condition outperforms the arrow condition. Although more restrictive in movement, the path condition indicates a precise route for the user, thus reducing uncertainty in the process of finding the way. This is described in the following research questions:

- RQ1: Is the distance of the covered path longer when using the navigation path design compared to the navigation arrow design?
- RQ2: Is the time needed to navigate between two workstations longer when using the navigation path design compared to the navigation arrow design?
- RQ3: Is the perceived Ease of Use better when using the path navigation design compared to the navigation arrow design?
- RQ4: Is the perceived Support in the environmental tasks better when using the navigation path design compared to the navigation arrow design?

4   The AR-Device

Before developing the AR-application, decisions on the target platform were made. The current market offers a variety of different AR-devices, ranging from camera-based embedding of virtual content into a viewfinder to full spectrum holographic projections [3]. Most AR-headsets are based on the Android operational system, like the ODG series or Vuzix headsets [6]. Although these headsets feature a slim frame, which grants the advantage to be worn simultaneously with a helmet within an industrial environment, they lack the substantial hardware needed to render complex 3D objects. The HoloLens has a 40° field of view and uses two see-through holographic lenses combined with two high dynamic light engines, allowing for a bright, high-resolution display of information [3]. A mobile Intel chip and 2 GB of random access memory in combination with 4 infrared sensors that capture the real environment allow for high-quality holograms and positioning them within the real world [4].

5   Method and Material

In order to design the application, prior research was used as a guideline in order to design an efficient system with no interfering variables [11]. Parts of the Microsoft guidelines for mixed reality design were also applied in combination with the ISO-9241 for ergonomics of human-computer interaction, covering aspects such as visual representations, auditory outputs and interactions with the system [2,5]. Principles described in the literature [31] were incorporated into the design process of the components such as fonts and icons, animations and the overall appearance of the application [7]. Colors were bright enough to be seen in an industrial environment with low light situations, while offering enough contrast to support users with visual impairments or color-blindness. The color white was avoided in written text, as the HoloLens tends to produce strong chromatic aberration effects during quick head movements, which might distract or confuse the user. Also, the type of font used in the application was an important factor in terms of readability. Serif fonts are more visually pleasing to some, but have the problem that when displayed in AR, the small field of view of current AR-devices leads to a more compressed look of the letters and therefore makes them harder to read. In addition, certain icons are used as visual cues for the user to indicate additional functionalities (Fig. 1 and Fig. 2).

5.1   Navigation Arrow Design

The first layout condition consisted mainly of a three dimensional arrow, resembling a compass pointing in the direction of the next target (Fig. 1). The arrow was programmed to point to the destination in a line of sight, instructing the user not on the direct path but merely the overall direction. The arrow was color-coded, hence the right direction colored the arrow green and any other direction red, with a smooth transition between the two states [11].

5.2   Navigation Path Design

The second navigation implementation contained a navigation route that, based on the user's own body height, was displayed thirty centimeters below the eyes. The idea was to provide a navigation line that can easily be seen without obstructing the participants view. Projecting the path onto the ground level of the real environment would have positioned a large part of it outside of the rendering area of the HoloLens. The displayed line showed a direct path to the next target and hinted the way to the following objective, which is shown in Fig. 2.

5.3   Trial Run

A trial run was conducted to get first insights about the application and test procedure as well as to detect aspects that need optimization before conducting

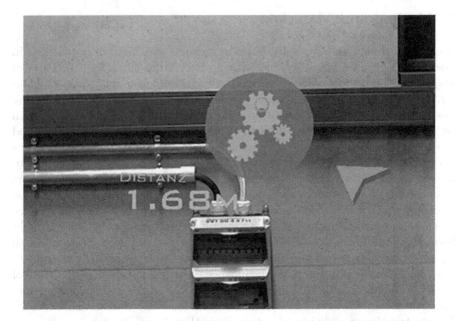

Fig. 1. The design of the arrow navigation right next to the task icon, alerting the participants that a specific machine demands their attention ("distance 1.68 m").

Fig. 2. The navigation route showing the direct path to the next target. The line hints at the next direction, similar to turn-by-turn navigation found on applications such as Google Maps ("distance 4.39 m").

the larger scale experiment. A total of ten participants took part in the test and were instructed to use both applications and compare their impressions. The participants were provided with microphones and instructed to complete the tasks while thinking-aloud. The test case with the AR-applications took about 3 min, with an average duration of $M = 157$ s $(SD = 24)$. After completing each of the two scenarios, participants of the trial run were additionally interviewed by the supervisor and asked about their positive and negative impressions of both applications, as well as about major problems or additional thoughts. Participants were students and staff from the University of Applied Sciences Ruhr West and did not receive any compensation for taking part in this research. After data collection, the voice recordings from the trial and the subsequent interviews were transcribed and analyzed. Half of the participants were male, the other half were female. Since a qualitative approach is applied for exploring the strength and weaknesses of the prototype, the comparably small number of participants was considered adequate [16]. This approach was useful to collect relevant aspects for both redesign and item generation for the actual in-depth study with the system [15]. The average age was $M = 28.9$ years $(SD = 4.3)$. Some of the remarks were due to technical and hardware limitations of the currently available AR-technology, i.e. a small FOV or chromatic aberration during fast head movements. Only minor aspects were named regarding the application itself. These included the positioning of text labels and the size of the augmented content. These aspects were adjusted for the main experimental study.

5.4   Test Procedure

Before participants took part in the industrial scenario that was staged, they were asked to fill out a pre-questionnaire. Apart from demographical questions, the survey asked participants about their previous experience with AR-technologies, their technology acceptance and their overall well-being. The latter was done to determine negative physical effects of the AR-application such as motion sickness. Then participants were outfitted with security clothing commonly found in industrial related workplaces in addition to the AR-glasses. The combination of the surroundings being enriched with loud sounds, several props acting as industrial machines and barriers deliberately structured as a maze and thus forcing the participants to follow the navigation to their respective tasks (Fig. 3), simulated a believable industrial setting. The first task was designed to replicate the maintenance of machine, in which participants were guided through the necessary steps by the AR-application. At the end of the procedure of the first task, the participants were guided to another location and were then instructed to log their actions into a console, which represented the second task. Afterwards the instruction was to follow the navigation to a simulated third station, while a simulated hot steel plate was encountered en route (Fig. 4). The AR-application recognized this hazardous area and guided the user safely around it. Once the hazardous area was passed, a fire alarm was triggered, which prompted the AR-application to notify the participants that an evacuation is necessary.

Showing the route to the nearest exit, the AR-application assisted the participants in finding their way out (Fig. 5). Once complete, the scenario was stopped, and the supervisor helped the participant out of the security clothing and AR-glasses. The participants were then asked to fill out the second part of the questionnaire, that asked about positive and negative activation, flow, immersion and augmented-reality-attitude [9]. Additionally, every task and the navigation between the tasks were assessed.

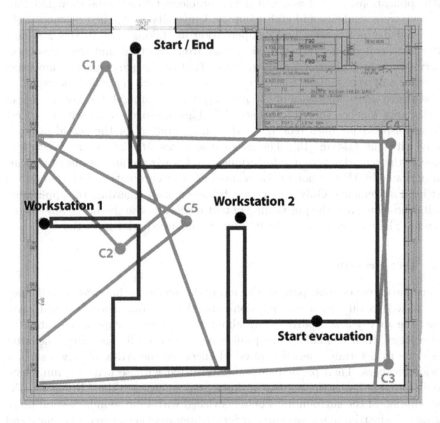

Fig. 3. The test track in the simulated industrial environment, as described in [35]. The participants follow a calculated navigation route (blue) and complete a series of tasks, which is captured by five cameras (green). (Color figure online)

5.5   Sample

In total, 52 participants took part in the study. All of them were students from the University of Applied Sciences Ruhr West. The gender distribution of the participants was 67.3% male and 32.7% female. The assignment to the respective conditions was conducted at random with 26 participants for each condition. 5.7% of all participants reported to regularly use AR-devices. Most of the participants (76.9%) stated to wear an AR-device for the first time.

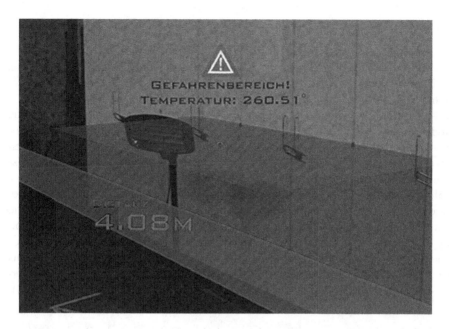

Fig. 4. The hazardous area is indicated by a red box accompanied by a warning label ("hazardous area!, temperature: 260.51°" and "distance 4.08 m") signaling to participants avoid that area. (Color figure online)

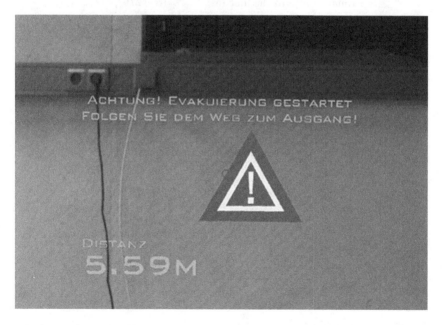

Fig. 5. The warning notification ("Attention! Evacuation initiated. Follow the path to the exit!" and "distance 5.59 m") that instructed the participants to follow the navigation to the nearest exit.

5.6   Measurements

The questionnaire used in the study contained multiple scales to evaluate the two conditions, i.e. Flow, Immersion and the Augmented Reality Applications Attitude Scale (ARAAS) [14]. Complementing to the survey, objective measurements such as the path length, based on positional data gathered either by the AR-device or the camera tracking, were evaluated as well. In order to rate the navigational design, self constructed scales were utilized in addition to established usability scales [25]. All items were rated on a 5 point Likert scale from 1 (totally disagree) to 5 (totally agree). For the evaluation of the research questions, sub-scales were used and validated with a reliability analysis. All four scales related to the covered route, each representing one task or sub-scenario, were divided into three sub-scales (Perception, Ease of Use and Support). The first scale for example contained questions like "I could perceive the content on the display well." or in case of the Ease of Use sub-scale: "The instructions provided by the device were understandable". Support was covered with questions like: "The AR-application supported me in finding the right way". All utilized sub-scales were deemed sufficient for this experiment in their reliability (Table 1).

Table 1. Reliability, means and standard deviations to the sub-scales Perception, Ease of Use and Support in every four path evaluations.

Primary route to the first task	(α)	M	SD
Perception	.83	4.15	0.76
Ease of Use	.84	4.36	0.72
Support	.90	4.25	0.75
Primary route to the second task			
Perception	.81	4.37	0.69
Ease of Use	.91	4.55	0.74
Support	.85	4.29	0.66
Primary route along hazardous area			
Perception	.89	4.27	0.82
Ease of Use	.93	4.60	0.74
Support	.91	4.36	0.65
Primary route for evacuation			
Perception	.86	3.18	0.52
Ease of Use	.94	4.62	0.72
Support	.84	4.27	0.93

6   Results

This section contains the results of an exploratory data analysis of the experiment regarding the previously established research questions. The R programming language (R version 3.6.2; RStudio version 1.2.1335) was used for statistical analyses [28, 30]. To jointly consider the relationship between the outcome variables of interest when comparing group differences, a Multivariate Analysis of Variance (MANOVA) was calculated. A robust model was conducted because both, the homogeneity of covariance matrices assumption and the multivariate normality assumption, were breached. Thus, the MANOVA was performed on the ranked data using Choi and Marden's method [12], implemented in R using the *cmanova()* function [34]. There is a significant main effect of the type of design on outcome measures, $H(16) = 45.74$, $p < .001$. Separate univariate ANOVAs on the four outcome variables systematically addressed the research questions in follow-up analyses. From these test statistics, one can conclude the nature of the effect found in the MANOVA. Figure 6 displays the error bar charts of the two navigation design groups across the found significant dependent variables.

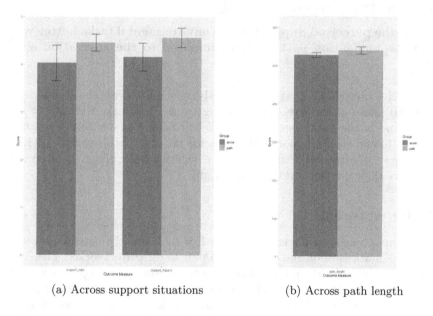

(a) Across support situations   (b) Across path length

Fig. 6. Error bar chart of navigation design groups across outcome measures.

RQ1: Is the distance of the covered path longer when using the navigation path design compared to the navigation arrow design?

Using a first ANOVA, differences in path length between the conditions were analyzed. The results show a significant difference in path length between the navigation designs, $F(1, 50) = 4.37$, $p < .05$. The path length was significantly longer for the navigation path design compared to the navigation arrow design.

RQ2: Is the time needed to navigate between two workstations longer when using the navigation path design compared to the navigation arrow design?

To examine the difference of path time between the navigation path and navigation arrow design another ANOVA was calculated. The results do not show any effect. No difference between the path time in navigation path or navigation arrow design could be noticed, $F(1, 50) = 0.028$, $p = .87$.

RQ3: Is the perceived Ease of Use better when using the path navigation design compared to the navigation arrow design?

Results of a third ANOVA indicate no effect between the designs regarding Ease of Use. However, there is a trend in group differences for specific path segments; in the hazardous area, $F(1, 50) = 2.99$, $p = .09$, and during evacuation, $F(1, 50) = 3.61$, $p = .06$. While results differed slightly, the navigation path design outperformed the navigation arrow design.

RQ4: Is the perceived Support in the environmental tasks better when using the navigation path design compared to the navigation arrow design?

The perceived system Support is significantly different between the groups during the initial phase of the navigation leading to the first task, $F(1, 50) = 4.54$, $p < .05$, and in the hazardous area, $F(1, 50) = 5.50$, $p < .05$. Further, a trend is visible in perceived Support differences for the first path segment, $F(1, 50) = 3.48$, $p = .07$. In these situations, the navigation path design is rated more supportive than the navigation arrow design.

6.1   Instructions in AR

All participants successfully completed the first task, namely matching the serial numbers of a workstation and connecting a plug to the correct socket. There were no remarks regarding the presentation of text and the general opinion was that it was useful, as participants had "no devices in the hands that would prevent them from completing the task". The second task was partially completed. A finger scanner, where participants where supposed to identify themselves was positioned right next to the workstation, which was used to enter the previously acquired serial number. None of the participants were able to find the scanner, though it was equipped with a big sign. Most of them thought, the scanner was to be found as a part of the workstation itself. Additional information regarding the location of the scanner are therefore required. Roughly half of the participants completed the input of the serial number into the workstation. Those who did not finish the task either were distracted by the overlapping of the projection of the virtual serial number and the input mask of the workstation or did not have enough time to complete the task. In this case, the form of presentation of holographic data must be adjusted and should not be similar to task 1.

6.2   Recommendations

In the following part, a short overview over the most common positive and negative characteristics of each of the two layouts is presented. Participants mentioned that the navigation using the arrow allows for a big field of view that is free from any kind of virtual display. As the arrow is relatively small and has a fixed position, it is therefore easy to see the surroundings or to adjust the head position to clear the view. In addition, the color-coding of the arrow (green vs. red) gave a fast assessment of whether the current direction of gaze is correct or not. On the other hand, the 3D-model of the arrow was not always clearly interpreted as an arrow facing exactly forwards and could be mistaken for an arrow facing backwards. In addition, as the arrow did not show a precise route to the user, once someone headed off the correct path a direction might not be enough information to get to the destination successfully. Almost all of the participants mentioned that the advantage of the route layout is the precise presentation of an exact path on the ground, which helps to orientate oneself. Especially the display of upcoming way points was evaluated positively, as the path was more transparent for the participants compared to the arrow layout. The main negative aspect was the fact that the route often overlapped with a big part of the real environment, which made it difficult to spot potential obstacles. Many participants suggested decreasing the thickness of the line while increasing its transparency to allow for a more detailed FOV. In addition, once the direction of gaze was facing away from the route augmentation, no indicator was available leading the user back to the current path. This forced the participants to look around until they found it again by themselves. The AR-devices analyzed the internal coordinates every 0.5 s and saved the current location. Locating the precise position and recording them is made possible by using the internal coordinate system of the AR-device. This data is important for future analyses, comparing the results and potential differences of the effectiveness of both navigation layouts.

7   Discussion

The results indicate, that the path length is significantly shorter in the arrow path design. Furthermore, participants rated the condition more favorably in terms of Perception, Ease of Use and Support. As these significant differences manifest in every segment of the route, the overall tendencies of the data leans towards the navigation path design. This is especially important in time critical situations, i.e. emergency evacuations, where a shorter path length reduces potential harm on personnel. Although the difference in path length was significant, the time to conduct all tasks was not. This can be argued that the staged industrial area provided insufficient space and that a larger area or a more complex setting might have provided further differences. However, this experiment showed that the navigation path approach should be considered in case these systems will be deployed in a real industrial environment. Perception and Ease of Use indicate a significant difference towards the navigation path design during the segments containing dangerous obstacles and the evacuation. One might argue that the navigation path design has a higher accommodation effect, that allows users to handle the system information more easily, thus navigating more confidently. Support during the tasks and navigation was perceived significantly better during the first stage and the evacuation process. This indicates that the navigation path design communicates its functionality more clearly for users on their first contact with the application. This situation happened again during the evacuation, where participants felt significantly more supported by the system. These results can be essential when establishing such a system in a real industrial context.

8   Conclusion

The results allow the conclusion that users benefit from the arrow path design, especially when it comes to path length and navigation efficiency. However, this needs further exploration in future studies. The path navigation received higher acceptance with regard to visual accessibility, Ease of Use and the feeling of being supported, especially in moments of insecurity, i.e. in the presence of hazardous objects or during an evacuation. It might be that, especially in these situations, users need a clearer "long term" guidance rather than the near-field micro-navigation support provided by the arrow. This might also explain why only minor or no differences occur between both designs with regard to the other measures. Further analyses are still running, including camera data and in-depth analyses of gender differences. Additional research is needed to cover more tasks, the result of trust in the system, especially in risk situations, and its application to real heavy industry environments.

Acknowledgments. This work was part of the DamokleS 4.0 project funded by the European Regional Development Fund (ERDF) [1], the European Union (EU) and the federal state North Rhine Westphalia. The authors thank Mathias Grimm, Ziyaad Qasem and Vanessa Dümpel for their preparations regarding the setup and help with data collection, as well as all participants contributing to the study.

References

1. EU regional development fund. https://ec.europa.eu/regional_policy/de/funding/erdf. Accessed 20 Jan 2020
2. HoloLens design principles. https://docs.microsoft.com/en-us/windows/mixed-reality/design. Accessed 20 Jan 2020
3. HoloLens product. https://docs.microsoft.com/en-us/windows/mixed-reality/design. Accessed 20 Jan 2020

4. HoloLens spatial mapping. https://developer.microsoft.com/en-us/windows/mixed-reality/spatial_mapping_in_unity. Accessed 20 Jan 2020
5. ISO 9241–2010. https://www.iso.org/standard/52075.html. Accessed 20 Jan 2020
6. Vuzix product. https://www.vuzix.com/. Accessed 20 Jan 2020
7. Proceedings of the 13th International Conference on Human Computer Interaction with Mobile Devices and Services (2011). https://doi.org/10.1145/2037373
8. IEEE International Conference on Emerging Technologies and Factory Automation (ETFA), 16–19 September 2014, Barcelona, Spain. IEEE, Piscataway (2014)
9. Azuma, R.T.: A survey of augmented reality. Presence Teleoperators Virtual Environ. **6**(4), 355–385 (1997). https://doi.org/10.1162/pres.1997.6.4.355
10. Baek, S.H., Cha, S.H.: The trilateration-based BLE beacon system for analyzing user-identified space usage of new ways of working offices. Build. Environ. **149**, 264–274 (2019). https://doi.org/10.1016/j.buildenv.2018.12.030, http://www.sciencedirect.com/science/article/pii/S036013231830773X
11. Billinghurst, M., Grasset, R., Looser, J.: Designing augmented reality interfaces. ACM SIGGRAPH Comput. Graph. **39**, 17–22 (2005). https://doi.org/10.1145/1057792.1057803
12. Choi, K., Marden, J.: An approach to multivariate rank tests in multivariate analysis of variance. J. Am. Stat. Assoc. **92**(440), 1581–1590 (1997). https://doi.org/10.1080/01621459.1997.10473680
13. Dörner, Ralf, Broll, Wolfgang, Grimm, Paul, Jung, Bernhard (eds.): Virtual und Augmented Reality (VR/AR). Springer, Heidelberg (2013). https://doi.org/10.1007/978-3-642-28903-3
14. Díaz Noguera, M.D., Toledo Morales, P., Hervás-Gómez, C.: Augmented reality applications attitude scale (araas): diagnosing the attitudes of future teachers. New Educ. Rev. **50**, 215–226 (2017). https://doi.org/10.15804/tner.2017.50.4.17
15. Flick, U.: Qualitative Sozialforschung: Eine Einführung, Rororo Rowohlts Enzyklopädie, vol. 55694. rowohlts enzyklopädie im Rowohlt Taschenbuch Verlag, Reinbek bei Hamburg, originalausgabe, 8. auflage edn., August 2017
16. Flick, U., von Kardorff, E., Steinke, I. (eds.): Qualitative Forschung: Ein Handbuch, Rororo Rowohlts Enzyklopädie, vol. 55628. Rowohlts Enzyklopädie im Rowohlt Taschenbuch Verlag, Reinbek bei Hamburg, 12. auflage, originalausgabe edn. (2017)
17. Hermann, M., Pentek, T., Otto, B.: Design principles for industrie 4.0 scenarios: a literature review (2015). https://doi.org/10.13140/RG.2.2.29269.22248
18. Hermsen, K., et al.: Dynamic, adaptive and mobile system for context-based and intelligent support of employees in the steel industry contact data (2019)
19. Kim, J., Jun, H.: Vision-based location positioning using augmented reality for indoor navigation. IEEE Trans. Consum. Electron. **54**(3), 954–962 (2008). https://doi.org/10.1109/TCE.2008.4637573
20. Kruijff, E., Swan, J.E., Feiner, S.: Perceptual issues in augmented reality revisited. In: Höllerer, T. (ed.) 9th IEEE International Symposium on Mixed and Augmented Reality (ISMAR), 2010. pp. 3–12. IEEE, Piscataway (2010). https://doi.org/10.1109/ISMAR.2010.5643530
21. Marín, E., Gonzalez Prieto, P., Maroto Gómez, M., Villegas, D.: Head-up displays in driving (2016)
22. Mulloni, A., Seichter, H., Schmalstieg, D.: Handheld augmented reality indoor navigation with activity-based instructions. In: Bylund, M. (ed.) Proceedings of the 13th International Conference on Human Computer Interaction with Mobile Devices and Services, p. 211. ACM, New York, NY (2011). https://doi.org/10.1145/2037373.2037406

23. Narzt, W., Pomberger, G., Ferscha, A., Kolb, D., Müller, R., Wieghardt, J., Hörtner, H., Lindinger, C.: Augmented reality navigation systems. Univ. Access Inf. Soc. **4**(3), 177–187 (2006). https://doi.org/10.1007/s10209-005-0017-5
24. Paelke, V.: Augmented reality in the smart factory: supporting workers in an industry 4.0. environment. In: IEEE International Conference on Emerging Technologies and Factory Automation (ETFA), 2014, pp. 1–4. IEEE, Piscataway (2014). https://doi.org/10.1109/ETFA.2014.7005252
25. Peres, S.C., Pham, T., Phillips, R.: Validation of the system usability scale (SUS). Proc. Hum. Factors Ergon. Soc. Annu. Meet. **57**(1), 192–196 (2013). https://doi. org/10.1177/1541931213571043
26. Pethig, F., Niggemann, O., Walter, A.: Towards industrie 4.0 compliant configuration of condition monitoring services. In: 2017 IEEE 15th International Conference on Industrial Informatics (INDIN), pp. 271–276, July 2017. https://doi.org/ 10.1109/INDIN.2017.8104783
27. Qasem, Z., Bons, J., Borgmann, C., Eimler, S., Jansen, M.: Dynamic, adaptive, and mobile system for context-based and intelligent support of employees in heavy industry. In: 2018 Sixth International Conference on Enterprise Systems (ES), pp. 90–95. IEEE (2018). https://doi.org/10.1109/ES.2018.00021
28. R Core Team: A Language and Environment for Statistical Computing. R Foundation for Statistical Computing, Vienna, Austria (2014). http://www.R-project. org/
29. Rehman, U., Cao, S.: Augmented-reality-based indoor navigation: a comparative analysis of handheld devices versus google glass. IEEE Trans. Hum. Mach. Syst., 1–12 (2016). https://doi.org/10.1109/THMS.2016.2620106
30. RStudio Team: RStudio: Integrated Development Environment for R. RStudio Inc., Boston, MA (2018). http://www.rstudio.com/
31. Salvendy, G.: Handbook of Human Factors and Ergonomics. Wiley, USA (2005)
32. Schmalstieg, D., Höllerer, T.: Augmented reality: principles and practice. In: ACM SIGGRAPH 2016 Courses, p. 1, July 2016. https://doi.org/10.1145/2897826. 2927365
33. Thomas, F., Ros, L.: Revisiting trilateration for robot localization. IEEE Trans. Robot. **21**(1), 93–101 (2005). https://doi.org/10.1109/TRO.2004.833793
34. Wilcox, R.R.: Introduction to Robust Estimation and Hypothesis Testing, 3 edn. Elsevier/Academic Press, Amsterdam (2012). http://site.ebrary.com/lib/alltitles/ docDetail.action?docID=10521171
35. Zengeler, N., et al.: Person tracking in heavy industry environments with camera images. In: S-CUBE 2019–10th EAI International Conference on Sensor Systems and Software, November 2019

A GPU Accelerated Lennard-Jones System for Immersive Molecular Dynamics Simulations in Virtual Reality

Nitesh Bhatia$^{(\boxtimes)}$, Erich A. Müller, and Omar Matar

Imperial College London, South Kensington, London SW7 2AZ, UK
{n.bhatia,e.muller,o.matar}@imperial.ac.uk
https://www.imperial.ac.uk/chemical-engineering

Abstract. Interactive tools and immersive technologies make teaching more engaging and complex concepts easier to comprehend are designed to benefit training and education. Molecular Dynamics (MD) simulations numerically solve Newton's equations of motion for a given set of particles (atoms or molecules). Improvements in computational power and advances in virtual reality (VR) technologies and immersive platforms may in principle allow the visualization of the dynamics of molecular systems allowing the observer to experience first-hand elusive physical concepts such as vapour-liquid transitions, nucleation, solidification, diffusion, etc. Typical MD implementations involve a relatively large number of particles N = $O(10^4)$ and the force models imply a pairwise calculation which scales, in case of a Lennard-Jones system, to the order of $O(N^2)$ leading to a very large number of integration steps. Hence, modelling such a computational system over CPU along with a GPU intensive virtual reality rendering often limits the system size and also leads to a lower graphical refresh rate. In the model presented in this paper, we have leveraged GPU for both data-parallel MD computation and VR rendering thereby building a robust, fast, accurate and immersive simulation medium. We have generated state-points with respect to the data of real substances such as CO_2. In this system the phases of matter viz. solid liquid and gas, and their emergent phase transition can be interactively experienced using an intuitive control panel.

Keywords: Virtual reality · GPU · Molecular dynamics

1 Introduction

Molecular dynamics (MD) is fundamentally used for studying the physical movements, interactions of molecules and phase transitions between solid, liquid and vapour states [13,34]. These concepts can be reasonably easy to understand. However, the mathematical statements and the consequences of Newtonian principles for a system of interacting molecules, where intermolecular forces relying on their potential energies as well as overall system's temperature, volume and

The original version of this chapter was revised: a video was added. The correction to this chapter is available at https://doi.org/10.1007/978-3-030-49698-2_29

J. Y. C. Chen and G. Fragomeni (Eds.): HCII 2020, LNCS 12191, pp. 19–34, 2020.
https://doi.org/10.1007/978-3-030-49698-2_2

Fig. 1. Molecular Dynamics Virtual Reality (MD VR) environment with 20,000 Lennard-Jones molecules showcasing liquid-vapour coexistence. The colour of the molecules represents the magnitude of their velocity where blue represents low and red represents the high velocity. (Color figure online)

pressure are, hard to imagine and, often daunting to the student. E.g., in [33,40], a 2D MD simulation system is presented, the former relying on Javascript and a browser and latter on Java3D. The students can develop an understanding of various MD phenomena by interactive controls and following a variety of student exercises. Educators have always explored new ways of teaching hard-to-grab MD concepts using simulations. With the advent of modern virtual and mixed reality devices such as Oculus Rift [29], HTC Vive [14] and Microsoft Hololens [26] and the improvements in computational hardware, virtual educational platforms can now offer potential benefits for training and education in a simulated setting [8]. The 3D interactive medium provided by a well designed virtual reality (VR) system for pedagogy promotes inquiry-based learning which helps in better understanding of molecular dynamics and interactions compared to a didactic approach such as classroom teaching. This kind of approach has been reported in literature [17,35,39,42]. There are two main challenges. First, the research area is inherently cross-disciplinary and therefore requires deeper exchanges between virtual reality and computational molecular engineering. Second, real-time simulations in VR require low latency both in visualisation and computations that can be a bottleneck with any MD system. Typical MD implementations involve a relatively large number of particles ($N = 10^4$) and the force models imply a pairwise calculation which scales, in case of a Lennard-Jones system, to the order of $O(N^2)$ leading to a very large number of integration steps [7]. Hence, modelling such a computational system along with a graphical intensive virtual reality rendering could be limiting in terms of the system size which may lead to a lower graphical refresh rate.

The emergence of programmable general-purpose GPU architectures such as stream processing provides one way to exploit parallelisation and achieve performance boost [22]. Hence, a fundamental difference in kind of computations best suitable for a GPU involves structural parallelisation compared to a CPU. By using high-level languages such as C and C++ and shader languages such as DirectX, HLSL, GLSL and Metal one can easily program any data-parallel algorithm over GPU [3]. A holistic review of GPU programming has already been reported in literature [30]. A general principle while programming on GPU to bake computational variables into graphics specific data structures like 2D and 3D textures [12,21]. Additionally, most modern GPUs are equipped with computational APIs and hardware to process data using shaders and shader cores [23]. Using these technologies, several academic and commercial molecular dynamics software such as GROMACS, NAMD and AMBER have already been GPU-accelerated [1,2,31]. A number of recent works have been reported on the implementation on GPU of particle systems immersed in force fields, interactions with rigid bodies or with other particles [9,18,19]. Parallel processing, therefore, plays an important role in interactive simulation as it can first, push the performance of a molecular dynamics simulation and second, the shared-memory can be directly accessed in GPU for rendering graphics in VR thereby reducing the considerable bottleneck in data-exchange as seen in CPU centric visualisations. However, the enhancement in speed, scalability and program execution time can vary among GPU hardware, VR rendering requirements and the implemented algorithms. Table 1 shows a comparison of GPU execution cores and computing performance present in recent VR devices (as of 2019). In this paper, we have tried to address the above-mentioned challenges. Our focus is on the use of virtual reality (VR) in the context of simulating immersive molecular dynamics (MD) for the enhancement of education and interactive learning experience of students. The platform is aimed at educating about dynamics of molecular systems allowing the observer to experience first-hand elusive physical concepts such as vapour-liquid transitions, nucleation, solidification, and diffusion while surrounded by jiggling molecules. This MD VR simulation system is specifically developed for PC-VR that consists of a tracked headset, a pair of hand controllers and a PC equipped with a GPU. To derive an efficient mapping of MD with VR, we have leveraged a single GPU for both data-parallel MD computations and VR rendering thereby resulting in a robust, fast, accurate and immersive simulation medium with significant runtime savings. The scope of our work is on considering a generic MD system consisting of dense, uniform, single-component fluids, where the dynamics supported by classical mechanics. Complex systems such as molecular liquids, solvent and fluids, and the interfacial phenomena are not considered. The paper is organised as follows. In the next section (Sect. 2), we describe the methodology and the implementation details are covered in Sects. 3, 4 and 5. Simulation results are discussed in Sect. 6. In

Sect. 7, we have covered a comparative analysis of performance using two different GPUs. Section 8 concludes the paper with a summary of the results and the future work.

Table 1. Performance comparison of GPUs present in PC-VR and Mobile-VR platforms in terms of core count and gigaflops (GFLOPS) compute performance.

Device	GPU	Cores	GFLOPS
Oculus Rift or HTC Vive (PC-VR)	Nvidia RTX2080	2944	8920
Oculus Rift or HTC Vive (PC-VR)	Nvidia GTX1080	2560	8228
Oculus Rift or HTC Vive (PC-VR)	Nvidia RTX2070	2304	6497
Oculus Rift or HTC Vive (PC-VR)	Nvidia GTX1070	1920	5783
Sony PlayStation VR	AMD Liverpool	1152	1843
Samsung GearVR Galaxy S10	Adreno 640	384	954
Microsoft Hololens 2	Adreno 630	256	727
Oculus Quest or Vive Focus	Adreno 540	256	567
Oculus Go	Adreno 530	256	407
Microsoft Hololens 1	Intel HD-Graphics	80	184

2 Methodology

Our goal is to simulate the classic N-body MD problem using GPU [32]. To simulate such a system in VR perceivable at a human scale, a scaled representation of the molecules and the inter molecular forces is required. In the current system, we have considered the Lennard-Jones potential for representing forces between coarse-grained spherical molecules. In a Lennard-Jones system, the molecules attract each other at long range but strongly repel one another at they come closer. This system and equations are described in Sect. 3. The primary objective for an efficient compute performance is that the MD VR simulation should run entirely on the GPU where the CPU mainly acting as a controller. We need to define positions, velocities and masses of the molecules on the GPU, update the positions according to intermolecular force influence, render the molecules in VR. The impulse on each molecule and the positions are computed on GPU with the help of a compute shader. Then using a GPU again, the molecules are rendered as spheres using a geometry shader. The compute and rendering methodology is further described in Sect. 4. For designing an interactive MD simulation framework in VR for teaching and learning, we have considered several different ingredients such as a 3D VR environment and a control panel based intuitive user interface. The design functionality is further covered in Sect. 5.

3   Scaled Lennard-Jones MD System for VR

3.1   Representation of Lennard-Jones MD System

The model consists of N spherical molecules interacting pair-wise as the system numerically resolves the step-by-step solution of the classical equations of motion. To build such a system following conditions are required to be satisfied:

Initial Condition. An initial condition acts as a starting point to begin the force and motion computations for MD simulation in a mixture of N molecules. As a convenient choice, the system is initialised with 5000 molecules at random positions in a predefined volume. The number of molecules and volume is kept modifiable by the student as described in Sect. 5.

Interaction Potential. The forces acting on molecules derive from potential functions, representing the potential energy of the system for the specific geometric arrangement of the molecules. It is given by Eq. 1.

$$F(r_1, r_2, \ldots, r_n) = -\nabla U(r_1, r_2, \ldots, r_n) \tag{1}$$

Given any two molecules i and j separated by distance $r_{ij} = |r_i - r_j|$ the potential energy U is computed pairwise for all the molecules is given by Eq. 2

$$U(r_1, r_2, \ldots, r_n) = \sum_{i<j} u(r_{ij}) \tag{2}$$

One of the most famous and commonly used pair potentials for MD systems is the Lennard-Jones potential defined in Eq. 3, which was originally proposed for liquid argon [4,16,27]. This pair potential is a sum of two inverse-power-law terms, a harshly repulsive term with exponent 12 and a softer, attractive (negative) term with exponent 6.

$$u(r) = \begin{cases} 4\epsilon \left[\left(\frac{\sigma}{r}\right)^{12} - \left(\frac{\sigma}{r}\right)^{6} \right] & r \leq r_c \\ 0 & otherwise \end{cases} \tag{3}$$

Based on Eq. 1 the resulting inter-molecular forces arising from the Lennard-Jones potential (see, Eq. 3) have the form as mentioned in Eq. 4 and shown in Fig. 2 for CO_2 molecule.

$$f(r) = \begin{cases} 48\frac{\epsilon}{r} \left[\left(\frac{\sigma}{r}\right)^{12} - 0.5 \left(\frac{\sigma}{r}\right)^{6} \right] & r \leq r_c \\ 0 & otherwise \end{cases} \tag{4}$$

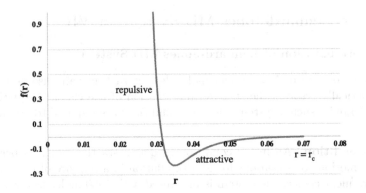

Fig. 2. Curve representing the change in Lennard-Jones force with inter molecular distance. The positive slope describes the attraction and the negative slope represents the repulsion between two molecules.

System Evolution and Motion. The evolution of the system over time can be followed by solving Newton laws of motion for all molecules in the MD system. The force is computed pairwise using Eq. 4 which results in molecular movement. The change in velocity and position is computed using verlet algorithm as shown in Eq. 5 and 6 [11].

$$v(\Delta t) = \frac{f(t)}{m} \Delta t \tag{5}$$

$$r(\Delta t) = v(t)\Delta t + \frac{f(t)}{2m}(\Delta t)^2 \tag{6}$$

Energy Conservation and Thermodynamic Equilibrium. Any system following the principle of Newtonian dynamics conserves the total energy E by maintaining a predefined temperature T for thermodynamic equilibrium [5]. The conservation of the total energy E is given by Eq. 7 where E_{KE} represents instantaneous kinetic energy given by Eq. 8 and the relation with temperature T and pressure P are given in 9 and 10.

$$E(r_1, r_2, \ldots, r_n) = E_{KE}(r_1, r_2, \ldots, r_n) + U(r_1, r_2, \ldots, r_n); \tag{7}$$

$$E_{KE}(r_1, r_2, \ldots, r_n) = \frac{1}{2}m \sum_{i=1}^{N} v(r_i)^2 \tag{8}$$

$$T = \frac{2E_{KE}}{3k_B N} \tag{9}$$

$$P = \frac{Nk_B T}{V} + \frac{1}{3V} \sum_{i=1}^{N} r_i . f(r_i) \tag{10}$$

3.2   Scaling MD to Virtual World

In scientifically correct MD simulations the Δt time steps are of the order of 10^{-12} ms [15]. Hence, the systems require a good amount of computational power for getting accurate results. For instance, simulating 1000 molecules for the equivalent of one second requires about 10^{15} floating-point operations or 10^6 GFLOPS of computing power. Modelling such system over GPU would still take months of computation time. For rendering any VR content at desired 60 to 90 frames per second, the resulting Δt time steps are of milliseconds order resulting in a reduced requirement of 10^{-3} GFLOPS [10]. This is achieved by scaling standard parameters such as mass, length and energy. While still maintaining scientifically correct results, the scaling can reduce the necessity of a high compute power thereby opening doors for existing VR systems with good GPUs. In VR, making the nanoscale objects visibly large pose another challenge. Hence, visually correct scaling of physical quantities is required for accurate physical simulations. Therefore to represent the MD system in VR so to be manipulated approximately to scale in relationship with each other, we comprised on scaling the units of length, energy, mass and Boltzmann constant. In Table 2 the sample data is shown for carbon dioxide along with the scaling parameters.

Table 2. System of units and scaling factors used in MD VR simulations.

Physical quantity	Units	CO_2 parameters	Scaling factor	Scaled CO_2 parameters for VR
Length	σ	2.8×10^{-10} m	10^8	0.028 m
Energy	ϵ	2.69×10^{-21} J	10^{18}	0.00269 J
Mass	m	7.30×10^{-26} Kg	10^{25}	0.73 Kg
Boltzmann constant	kB	1.38×10^{-23} J/k	10^{18}	0.0000138 J/k

4   Computational and Rendering Methodology

The methodology implemented is based on three modules that include data initialisation using CPU, MD processing over GPU using compute shaders and graphics rendering using surface shaders. Communication and shared data between each stage are shown in Fig. 3. The VR system is programmed in Unity 3D and the corresponding scripts are coded using C# and DirectX11 supported shader languages (HLSL). The functionality of each stage is described in the following sections.

4.1   MD Data Structure and Initialisation

The most common coarse grain model for molecules are represented by spherical balls, with radii equal to their van der Waals radii and mass equal to their molar mass [6,25]. In our model, the data structure of molecule consists of its position (as 3D Vector) in MD system, velocity (as 3D Vector), diameter (as float) and its

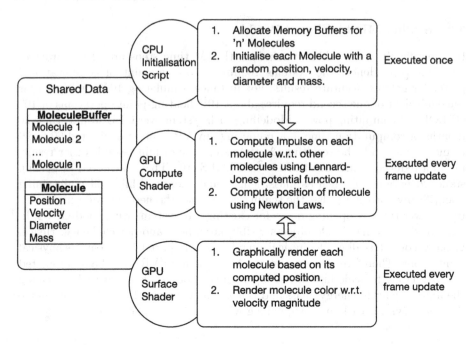

Fig. 3. Graphical representation of compute and render pipeline used in MD VR system.

molar mass (as float) as shown in Fig. 3. The molecules with random positions and velocity are initialised in CPU as an array of Unity's Compute Buffer (named as MoleculeBuffer). That is data type is responsible for transferring data to and from the CPU's memory (RAM) to GPU's memory (VRAM) which can be accessed by Compute Shaders.

4.2   MD Computations Using Compute Shaders

A compute shader in Unity is a program that is executed on the GPU regardless of the rendering pipeline [20]. For data-parallel algorithms, it can dramatically improve computational performance. For the MD computations, the compute shader consists of two kernels.

1. The first kernel calculates the total force on each molecule for every other molecule using Eq. 3. The Lennard-Jones potential exhibit strong directional forces however, at a cutoff distance, the forces become negligible and hence can be ignored. To reduce the number of pair-wise force computations we have considered a cut-off distance of 2.5 times diameter of the molecule [24].
2. The second kernel computes the position and updated velocity of the molecule using 5 and 6. The velocity is further scaled using 9 based on the temperature input selected by the user to maintain thermodynamic equilibrium. To eliminate surface effects periodic boundary conditions are used in MD [41].

In our system, moving molecules effectively wrap around the Unity's boundary limits in such a way that a molecule leaving one face enters through the opposite face.

4.3   VR Rendering Using Surface Shaders

The molecules are rendered as an instance of a single molecule modelled using spherical mesh object. A surface shader attached to the molecule runs in parallel on GPU. It locally reads the compute shader's data for each molecule and renders the mesh at its associated position. The colour of the molecule is defined over a range of velocity magnitude that varies from blue at low velocity to red at high velocity. We have utilised Unity's indirect mesh rendering technique to further speed up the rendering [37].

5   VR Environment and Controls

In this MD VR system, the molecules are rendered in a fixed volume. The volume is surrounded by a 3D model of a large room for an additional immersion. The 3D model is downloaded from Unity Asset Store [36]. In the resulting simulation, the student standing inside the room can see the molecules floating in the air and interacting with each other based on MD model. A crucial part of any VR system is how the users may interact with the system. Oculus Rift comes with handheld remote controllers. These controllers allow interaction with the VR interface using buttons. The simulation parameters can be manipulated using a control panel as shown in Fig. 4a. Using Unity's XR plug-in framework, the primary trigger is programmed to show the control interface attached to the left hand while a pointer to interact with the control panel appears on the right hand [38]. The secondary trigger is utilised for user locomotion which is programmed to be restricted inside the room. The control interface consists of following features that can be interactively modified at runtime by the user.

- **Simulation Data:** The control panel also displays the state of MD system updated every 2 s, in terms of number of molecules, computed pressure and temperature as well as the volume. A "Record Current Data" button is provided that stores the current simulation data in a text file for offline analysis.
- **Temperature:** For changing the system temperature (energy) four buttons are provided that change the temperature in the intervals of 1 K and 50 K.
- **Volume:** For changing the volume occupied by the molecules, four buttons are provided that change the volume to a cube of size $1\,m^3$, $8\,m^3$, $64\,m^3$ and the largest volume occupying the entire room of size $160\,m^3$.
- **Molecule Type:** The basic properties of a molecule such as a name, sigma, epsilon, mass and K_b is stored in as an editable JSON file as shown in Fig. 4b. The program reads this JSON file and a populated drop-down list is presented to the student for selecting different molecules during VR simulation.
- **Molecule Count:** This slider interface helps in changing the number of molecules.

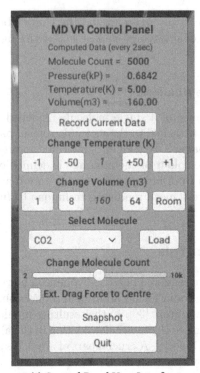
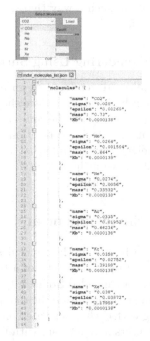

(a) Control Panel User Interface

(b) (top) Molecule list as a drop-down and the molecule properties as described in a user editable JSON file (bottom).

Fig. 4. MD VR control panel design.

- **External Drag:** For collating the molecules toward the centre, a checkbox is provided that applies a uniform radial acceleration to all the molecules towards the centre of the volume.
- **Snapshot:** Using this button, the student can capture the active viewpoint as a PNG image similar to the one shown in Fig. 1.
- **Quit:** This button is used for quitting the program.

6   Simulation Results

The primary objective of simulating a Lennard-Jones MD in VR is to have an interactive system to explore the effect of intermolecular forces concerning temperature and density of molecules on the complete phase behaviour of a molecule such as Carbon di oxide (CO_2). Any ordinary matter is found in one of three phases: vapour, liquid or solid based on the temperature. The vapour

Fig. 5. Molecules in vapour phase at low pressure and high temperature.

(gas) phase exists at high temperatures whereas the solid phase is found at low temperatures with liquid phase in between. As shown in Fig. 5 an example of gas phase where molecules overcome the intermolecular forces due to high velocity and continue to move with a kinetic energy that is proportional to the temperature.

It is possible to move continuously from the solid to the vapour phase or liquid to the vapour phase and vice versa by changing molecule density and temperature. Figure 6 shows an example of vapour to solid phase transition and the time development of kinetic and potential energies of CO_2 at low density and low temperature. As the temperature is lowered, the heat is taken out for maintaining thermodynamic equilibrium. This causes nucleation of molecules and overall the reduction of mean kinetic energy which results in transition of CO_2 from vapour to solid phase. This effect is also visible in high pressure. At the nucleation stage, the molecules being tightly packed possess a higher kinetic energy. This leads to transition of gas to liquid phase where the nucleated

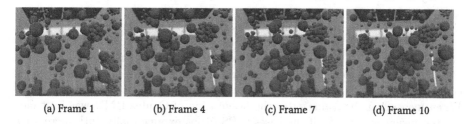

(a) Frame 1   (b) Frame 4   (c) Frame 7   (d) Frame 10

Fig. 6. Phase transition in molecules from vapour phase to the formation of solid clusters.

molecules form clusters of high potential energy molecules that move over time as shown in Fig. 7. Figure 8 an example of solid phase. At low temperature, nucleated molecules form close packed clusters. In some cases, they naturally form a hexagonally close packed structures. The clusters move slowly and vibrate proportional to their kinetic energy.

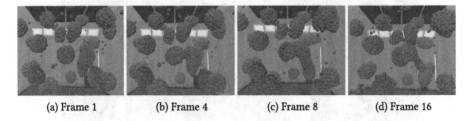

| (a) Frame 1 | (b) Frame 4 | (c) Frame 8 | (d) Frame 16 |

Fig. 7. Liquid phase and moving molecule clusters at high pressure and high temperature.

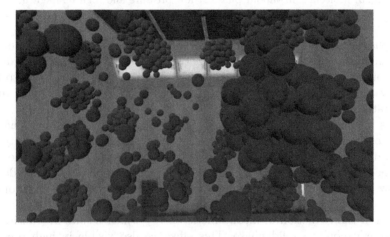

Fig. 8. Solid phase and formation of static clusters at low pressure and low temperature.

7   System Performance

We have tested the application on two machines viz. a Laptop and a Desktop both capable of rendering VR. We used HP Omen Laptop having Nvidia GTX1070 Max-Q GPU and HP EliteDesk 800 G3 Desktop having Nvidia GTX 1080 GPU. The system details are shown in Appendix A. The results show a comparison of frame-rate achieved at steady-state for the number of molecules. When measuring the frame rates the orientation of Oculus HMD was kept facing the visualisation. In all the cases, FPS drops exponentially with increasing the number of molecules. We have also included the performance comparison of running the same application without VR.

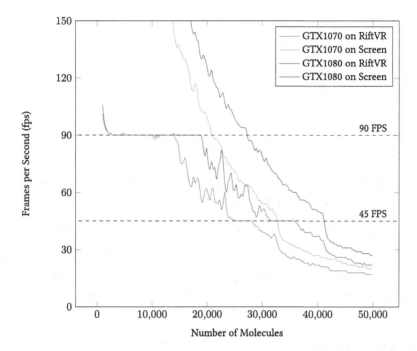

Fig. 9. FPS benchmarks using two GPUs and MD VR application running in VR and screen (non-VR) mode. The plots show a comparison of frame-rate achieved at steady-state for the number of molecules simulated in MD VR.

On Oculus Rift, a frame rate above 75 frames per second (fps) is desired for best performance. On GTX1080 with VR, MD system with up to 25,000 molecules can be rendered with up to 90 fps while on GTX1070 Max-Q this limit reduces to 15,000 molecules due to lower compute power and thermal throttling. This limit is much higher when running the same simulations without VR, i.e. on-screen. Upon increasing the number of molecules, as the computation load on GPU increases the fps starts to drop. Note that in the case of Oculus Rift, the maximum frame rate VR gets restricted to 90 fps as an upper limit. Additionally, due to asynchronous spacewarp (ASW) feature in Oculus runtime, the software tries to compensate for frame drops by introducing additional frames which are evident with jittery fps in Fig. 9 between 45 fps to 90 fps [28].

8   Conclusions

In this paper we described the design and implementation of data-parallel MD simulations using GPU, resulting in a robust, fast, accurate and immersive VR system. This modelling technique can compute pair-wise interactions of the order of $O(N^2)$ and render also a large number of molecules maintaining a respectable display refresh rate. We plan to optimise this system to leverage more advanced shader programs for GPU resource utilisation. With the introduction of newer

VR hardware, techniques such as foveated rendering can significantly unlock performance speedups. The current system is scalable from mobile GPU platforms to large scale GPU farms however, we need to test the scalability, performance and speed gains. Additionally, we plan to conduct student user-studies in future to demonstrate the effectiveness of this MD VR system in the context of teaching and learning.

Acknowledgements. Funding through Imperial College London Pedagogy Transformation programme is gratefully acknowledged.

A   Appendix: VR System Configurations Used for Performance Computations

For teaching chemical engineering through virtual reality, we acquired several Oculus VR headsets and computers under pedagogy transformation funding. For computing the performance of MD VR system, we have used Oculus Rift VR Headset tethered to two different systems, one laptop class GPU and one desktop-class GPU. The hardware and software configurations are described below.

Hardware Configuration 1

- HP Omen 15t Laptop
- Oculus Rift with Controllers
- Intel Core i7 8750H Processor
- Nvidia Geforce GTX1070 Max-Q GPU
- 16 GB RAM

Hardware Configuration 2

- HP EliteDesk 800 G3 Desktop
- Oculus Rift with Controllers
- Intel Core i7 7700 Processor
- Nvidia Geforce GTX1080 GPU
- 64 GB RAM

Software Configuration

- Microsoft Windows 10 Build 1803
- DirectX 11 supported GPU drivers
- Oculus Runtime and SDK
- Unity 2018 with Education Licence
- Microsoft Visual Studio 2017 Community Edition

B   Appendix: Demo video

Demo video is available at https://www.youtube.com/watch?v=HgkOR Eay5JY

References

1. Abraham, M.J., et al.: GROMACS: high performance molecular simulations through multi-level parallelism from laptops to supercomputers. SoftwareX **1**, 19–25 (2015)
2. Anderson, J.A., Lorenz, C.D., Travesset, A.: General purpose molecular dynamics simulations fully implemented on graphics processing units. J. Comput. Phys. **227**(10), 5342–5359 (2008)
3. Buck, I.: High level languages for GPUs. In: SIGGRAPH Courses, p. 109 (2005)
4. Buckingham, R.A.: The classical equation of state of gaseous helium, neon and argon. Proc. R. Soc. Lond. Ser. A Math. Phys. Sci. **168**(933), 264–283 (1938)
5. Callen, H.B.: Thermodynamics and an Introduction to Thermostatistics, 2nd edn., p. 512. Wiley, New York (1985). ISBN: 978-0-471-86256-7
6. Duncan, B.S., Olson, A.J.: Approximation and characterization of molecular surfaces. Biopolymers Original Res. Biomol. **33**(2), 219–229 (1993)
7. Elsen, E., Vishal, V., Houston, M., Pande, V., Hanrahan, P., Darve, E.: N-body simulations on GPUs. arXiv preprint arXiv:0706.3060 (2007)
8. Freina, L., Ott, M.: A literature review on immersive virtual reality in education: state of the art and perspectives. In: The International Scientific Conference eLearning and Software for Education, vol. 1, no. 133, pp. 10–1007 (2015)
9. Georgii, J., Westermann, R.: Mass-spring systems on the GPU. Simul. Model. Pract. Theory **13**(8), 693–702 (2005)
10. Germann, T.C., Kadau, K.: Trillion-atom molecular dynamics becomes a reality. Int. J. Mod. Phys. C **19**(09), 1315–1319 (2008)
11. Grubmüller, H., Heller, H., Windemuth, A., Schulten, K.: Generalized verlet algorithm for efficient molecular dynamics simulations with long-range interactions. Mol. Simul. **6**(1–3), 121–142 (1991)
12. Harris, M.: Mapping computational concepts to GPUs. In: ACM SIGGRAPH 2005 Courses, p. 50. ACM (2005)
13. Hirst, J.D., Glowacki, D.R., Baaden, M.: Molecular simulations and visualization: introduction and overview. Faraday Discuss. **169**, 9–22 (2014)
14. HTC: HTC Vive product page. https://www.vive.com. Accessed 20 Sept 2019
15. Jo, J.C., Kim, B.C.: Determination of proper time step for molecular dynamics simulation. Bull. Korean Chem. Soc. **21**(4), 419–424 (2000)
16. Johnson, J.K., Mueller, E.A., Gubbins, K.E.: Equation of state for Lennard-Jones chains. J. Phys. Chem. **98**(25), 6413–6419 (1994)
17. Jones, L.L., Jordan, K.D., Stillings, N.A.: Molecular visualization in chemistry education: the role of multidisciplinary collaboration. Chem. Educ. Res. Pract. **6**(3), 136–149 (2005)
18. Kolb, A., Latta, L., Rezk-Salama, C.: Hardware-based simulation and collision detection for large particle systems. In: Proceedings of the ACM SIGGRAPH/EUROGRAPHICS Conference on Graphics Hardware, pp. 123–131. ACM (2004)
19. Kruger, J., Kipfer, P., Konclratieva, P., Westermann, R.: A particle system for interactive visualization of 3D flows. IEEE Trans. Visual. Comput. Graphics **11**(6), 744–756 (2005)
20. Lammers, K.: Unity Shaders and Effects Cookbook. Packt Publishing Ltd, Birmingham (2013)
21. Luebke, D., Harris, M.: General-purpose computation on graphics hardware. In: Workshop, SIGGRAPH, vol. 33 (2004)

22. Luebke, D., et al.: GPGPU: general-purpose computation on graphics hardware. In: Proceedings of the 2006 ACM/IEEE Conference on Supercomputing, p. 208. ACM (2006)

23. Luebke, D., Humphreys, G.: How GPUs work. Computer **40**(2), 96–100 (2007)

24. Mecke, M., Winkelmann, J., Fischer, J.: Molecular dynamics simulation of the liquid-vapor interface: the Lennard-Jones fluid. J. Chem. Phys. **107**(21), 9264–9270 (1997)

25. Mezey, P.G.: Shape in Chemistry: An Introduction to Molecular Shape and Topology. Wiley-VCH, Weinheim (1993)

26. Microsoft: Microsoft Hololens product page. https://www.microsoft.com/en-us/hololens. Accessed 20 Sept 2019

27. Müller, E.A., Gubbins, K.E.: Molecular-based equations of state for associating fluids: a review of saft and related approaches. Ind. Eng. Chem. Res. **40**(10), 2193–2211 (2001)

28. Oculus: Asynchronous Spacewarp blog post. https://developer.oculus.com/blog/asynchronous-spacewarp. Accessed 20 Sept 2019

29. Oculus: Oculus Rift product page. https://www.oculus.com/rift. Accessed 20 Sept 2019

30. Owens, J.D., et al.: A survey of general-purpose computation on graphics hardware. Comput. Graph. Forum **26**(1), 80–113 (2007)

31. Purawat, S., et al.: A Kepler workflow tool for reproducible AMBER GPU molecular dynamics. Biophys. J. **112**(12), 2469–2474 (2017)

32. Rapaport, D.: Molecular dynamics simulation. Comput. Sci. Eng. **1**(1), 70–71 (1999)

33. Schroeder, D.V.: Interactive molecular dynamics. Am. J. Phys. **83**(3), 210–218 (2015)

34. Steinfeld, J.I., Francisco, J.S., Hase, W.L.: Chemical Kinetics and Dynamics, vol. 3. Prentice Hall, Englewood Cliffs (1989)

35. Stone, J.E., Gullingsrud, J., Schulten, K.: A system for interactive molecular dynamics simulation. In: Proceedings of the 2001 Symposium on Interactive 3D Graphics, pp. 191–194 (2001)

36. Store, U.A.: Paint booth UAA business. https://assetstore.unity.com/packages/3d/environments/uaa-business-paint-booth-120410. Accessed 20 Sept 2019

37. Technologies, U.: Graphics. DrawMeshInstancedIndirect function description. https://docs.unity3d.com/ScriptReference/Graphics.DrawMeshInstancedIndirect.html. Accessed 20 Sept 2019

38. Technologies, U.: XR Plugin Architecture unity. https://docs.unity3d.com/Manual/XRPluginArchitecture.html. Accessed 20 Sept 2019

39. Thorsteinsson, G., Shavinina, L.: Developing an understanding of the pedagogy of using a virtual reality learning environment (VRLE) to support innovation education. In: Shavinina, L.V. (ed.) The Routledge International Handbook of Innovation Education, pp. 456–470. Routledge, Oxford (2013). ISBN-10 415682215

40. Vormoor, O.: Quick and easy interactive molecular dynamics using Java3D. Comput. Sci. Eng. **3**(5), 98–104 (2001)

41. Yeh, I.C., Hummer, G.: System-size dependence of diffusion coefficients and viscosities from molecular dynamics simulations with periodic boundary conditions. J. Phys. Chem. B **108**(40), 15873–15879 (2004)

42. Zyda, M.: From visual simulation to virtual reality to games. Computer **38**(9), 25–32 (2005)

User Interface for an Immersive Virtual Reality Greenhouse for Training Precision Agriculture

Daniel W. Carruth[1]([⊠]) [iD], Christopher Hudson[1] [iD],
Amelia A. A. Fox[1] [iD], and Shuchisnigdha Deb[2] [iD]

[1] Mississippi State University, Mississippi State, MS 39762, USA
{dwc2, chudson}@cavs.msstate.edu, aafl03@msstate.edu
[2] The University of Texas at Arlington, Arlington, TX 76019, USA
shuchisnigdha.deb@uta.edu

Abstract. In the past 50 years, farm producers have increased use of electronic control systems for controlled environment agriculture in greenhouses and animal production. These systems use environmental sensors to automate environmental management of greenhouses and can lead to significantly larger yields. However, mismanagement of a CEA system can also lead to loss of entire crops. Due to the sensitivity of crops in CEA and potential losses, students are rarely allowed to work directly with CEA systems. In order to increase opportunities for students to interact with CEA systems, an immersive virtual greenhouse simulation was created. Implementing realistic interfaces for physical tasks and for the CEA system provides students with 'hands-on' training in the virtual greenhouse. However, there are challenges that limit implementation of physical actions and realistic interfaces in virtual reality. We consider interfaces for three types of interactions: system interactions, physical greenhouse interactions, and interactions with the CEA system. Potential interface designs are presented with a discussion of the benefits and costs associated with each design.

Keywords: Virtual reality applications · Education · User interaction in VR and MR · Design issues

1 Introduction

Since 2007 there has been an increase in the use of controlled environment agriculture (CEA) in greenhouses. Computer-automated management-controlled environments maximize production through diurnal and seasonal management of greenhouses. To support best practices and optimal outcomes in enclosed farm production, computer-based automated systems employ environmental sensors to integrate parameters such as temperature, humidity, CO_2, wind speed, wind direction, and solar intensity to make intelligent decisions. By automating high-value crop management, CEA can produce significantly larger biomass yields within a spatially limited production environment. When CEA is managed properly, biomass yields exceed the capacity of open-air

© Springer Nature Switzerland AG 2020
J. Y. C. Chen and G. Fragomeni (Eds.): HCII 2020, LNCS 12191, pp. 35–46, 2020.
https://doi.org/10.1007/978-3-030-49698-2_3

environments (conventional farms). However, mismanagement of a CEA can lead to the swift loss of an entire crop.

With the increasing integration of smart technologies into greenhouses, there is an expanding need for specialized training in the management and use of CEA systems. However, due to the sensitivity of crops within a CEA and the potential loss of yield resulting from mismanagement, students may not always be allowed to experience CEA technology and manipulate its parameters. For students, lack of real-world interaction and limited opportunities to receive hands-on experience managing CEA greenhouses reduces the likelihood of immediate and successful employment. It also limits the effective application of CEA technology, which may reduce profitability.

In order to address this need, a prototype virtual CEA greenhouse is being developed for the purpose of education and training. The virtual CEA greenhouse implements a CEA electronic control system (ECS) based on a real-world control software widely deployed in greenhouses. The virtual greenhouse is equipped with fans, curtains, sprayers, tables, and other production-enhancing instruments and tools employed in real-world CEA greenhouses. The virtual CEA systems activates and regulates fans, curtains, cooling, and heating systems to provide a realistic CEA experience. In the virtual CEA, the outdoor weather conditions affect indoor conditions and the effects of the interactions are modeled based on standard formulas.

The user interfaces for the virtual greenhouse should provide training that transfers from the virtual setting to real-world greenhouses. Recreating accurate representations of greenhouse farming and integrating a greenhouse ECS presents significant challenges. While immersive virtual reality provides an opportunity to provide training in managing a virtual CEA greenhouse without the risk of crop loss, there remain questions regarding relationships between accuracy of representations and skill transfer, and the limitations in accuracy dictated by current virtual reality technology.

2 Background

2.1 Virtual Reality Education

Post-secondary classroom technology has slowly evolved towards digital media, providing information to students using sound, photos, videos, and interactive 360 virtual media [1]. For successful conveyance of messaging in virtual media, the correct tools and visual language must be selected carefully [2, 3]. Entertainment, a secondary factor, helps capture students' attention and connects them playfully with topics and educational content [4]. Engagement is especially important when introducing trainees to high-risk environments that are unattainable in real-world environments [3]. It has been shown that immersive, episodic virtual reality (VR) training, coupled with traditional training methods increases cognitive recall, improves training outcomes, and allows users to obtain experience that may not be possible through formal experience without safety or production risks.

2.2 Virtual Reality Interfaces

Skeuomorphic designs mimic realistic representations of real, or physical world objects as interfaces to perform actions. With skeuomorphism, there is a possibility for confusion in representative design if the user is unfamiliar with the real-world object or if the actions provided in the environment do not match user expectations based on the real-world object [5]. For example, if an end-user is provided a virtual representation of a physical water sprayer but, when the trigger is pulled, all plants at the table receive water regardless of where the sprayer is aimed, the user may not comprehend this simplification and may inadvertently over- or under-spray plants. Whether a skeuomorphic design is appropriate is dependent upon the user, the environment, and the objectives of the application [6]. In this research, we consider whether matching the virtual representation to the physical interactions is necessary or helpful in teaching students how to perform tasks in a real CEA greenhouse. We further consider the relationship between system interfaces and physical interactions in a virtual reality application that mixes the two interface types.

Panels of varying sizes are often used in virtual reality applications to display interactive menus. Two common methods for user interaction with the elements of a panel are point-and-click interactions and simulated touchscreen interactions. Point-and-click interactions provide users with the ability to act on interface elements that are abstract. The operations can be performed at a distance and the user interface elements can be presented on large or small interfaces without regard to their realism. Alternatively, simulated touchscreens mimic touchscreen interactions by tracking user hand or controller positions and states and displaying a virtual hand to the user. The user can use the virtual hand to interact with menus displayed on planes in the virtual environment. Whether the plane is part of a representation of a physical object (e.g., a tablet or phone) or an abstract floating interface panel, users can leverage their familiarity with touch screen interfaces and quickly understand how to interact with the system. A comparison of a point-and-click floating panel user interface and a simulated touch tablet user interface showed that users preferred the tablet-like user interface and were better able to use the interface [7].

3 Virtual Greenhouse Application

The virtual greenhouse application consists of three major components including the:

- Virtual reality application framework including a simple learning management system (LMS),
- Virtual greenhouse, and the student-user's interaction with the greenhouse and
- ECS.

The LMS is uncomplicated and largely outside of the scope of this work. The student-user has an account managed by the LMS. An instructor-user provides the student with a list of assignments through the LMS. As the student completes and submits the assignments, the instructor is notified and can gauge student performance. The student-user's interactions within the LMS are separate from greenhouse training activities and are limited to account login and management, reviewing past assignments, completing old or new assignments, and submitting the results of a scenario to the instructor (see Table 1 for a list of student actions).

3.1 The Virtual Greenhouse

The virtual greenhouse application provides students with a model of a greenhouse complete with definitions of the structure, materials, and equipment. The greenhouse is equipped with vents (open/closed), fans (on/off), heating systems (on/off), cooling systems (on/off), curtains (open/closed), lighting systems (on/off), irrigation (on/off) and foggers (on/off) that are controlled by the ECS. Outdoor conditions that directly affect the greenhouse are based on historic or simulated weather data that include variables such as time of sunrise and sunset, low and high daily temperatures, solar intensity, cloud density, wind direction, wind speed, precipitation, and barometric pressure. Based on the outdoor condition data, greenhouse structure data, and the state of the greenhouse equipment, operational models calculate the conditions inside the greenhouse. The indoor conditions include the vapor pressure deficit, solar intensity, temperature, relative humidity, and CO_2 levels. Plant growth is calculated based on temperature, relative humidity, soil moisture, and fertilizer levels. Models of whitefly and botrytis infestation and associated plant damage provide additional challenges for students in advanced assignments.

3.2 Farming and Using the ECS

Students engaged in the virtual CEA training protocol begin by selecting the greenhouse into which a crop will be established. The VR provides students with limited choices of greenhouses classified by size, shape, and materials. Fixed equipment lists will guide students to verify that the production facility is suitable for the chosen crop. After determining the greenhouse layout, the student then determines the crop by selecting options from a varietal list. For this project, crops are limited to lettuce, spinach, and tomato. Outside of the virtual greenhouse application, students will use the USDA Virtual Grower interactive software to estimate the crop harvest date based on planting dates and relative geographic temperature averages [8].

Once the initial crop production parameters are established, students select potting and soil medium, and seed the flats on greenhouse tables. At this point, the students must engage the ECS to begin varying indoor conditions that are suited to meeting the predicted harvest date. A student will access the environmental controller and establish set points for all indoor environmental variables. When successful, the virtual growing environment begins advancing diurnally. Plants advance incrementally with daily environmental inputs. Students monitor crop growth, and review both indoor- and outdoor-logged temperatures. Scheduled water and feed consumption must ally with predicted models, and crop development must visually parallel expected norms.

During the crop growth cycle, students monitor for pests such as whitefly and botrytis infection visually by entering the virtual greenhouse and scanning for abnormalities. Students may choose to walk-through or teleport to locations. If a student fails to notice remarkable changes in crop production, biomass accumulation will reverse, and shrinkage or discoloration may replace normally healthy plants. The loss of bio-mass calculates directly against student end-profit. An entire operation may, conceivably, be lost due to non-recognition of disease and production parameters.

In advanced scenarios, at approximately 60% to harvest date, students receive a message that the desired harvest date must be changed in order to change shipping requirements (per customer demands). Students will, again, re-program the ECS to slow or speed up crop growth to meet the predicted harvest date. At the end of the entire growth season, students estimate biomass accumulation (crop gross and net weight) and calculate profit or loss from the production activities.

Table 1. Listing of the actions available to students in the virtual greenhouse.

Action	Location	Interface type
Login to the application	Main	System
Load a previous assignment	Main	System
Start a new assignment	Main	System
View and modify account details	Main	System
View and modify system settings	Main	System
Review past assignments	Main	System
Replay a past assignment	Main	System
Select a virtual greenhouse	Main	System
Select a location	Main	System
Select a date	Main	System
Quit the application	Main	System
View the greenhouse	Greenhouse	Physical
Move around within the greenhouse	Greenhouse	Physical or System
Select seeds	Greenhouse	Physical or System
Select planters	Greenhouse	Physical or System
Select soil medium	Greenhouse	Physical or System
Plant seeds in soil-filled planters	Greenhouse	Physical or System
Place plants on the greenhouse tables	Greenhouse	Physical or System
Inspect the plants	Greenhouse	Physical or System
Manually water the plants	Greenhouse	Physical or System
Manually feed the plants	Greenhouse	Physical or System
Apply insecticide to the plants	Greenhouse	Physical or System
Apply fungicide to the plants	Greenhouse	Physical or System
Discard plants	Greenhouse	Physical or System
Harvest plants	Greenhouse	Physical or System
Access the electronic control system	Greenhouse	Physical or System
View ECS main status screen	Greenhouse	ECS

(continued)

Table 1. (*continued*)

Action	Location	Interface type
Schedule watering the plants	Greenhouse	ECS
Schedule feeding the plants	Greenhouse	ECS
View data logs and graphs	Greenhouse	ECS
View equipment status	Greenhouse	ECS
Review periods and setpoints for controls	Greenhouse	ECS
Advance the calendar	Greenhouse	System
Review the outcomes of the assignment	Greenhouse	System
Submit an assignment for instructor review	Greenhouse	System
View and modify system settings	Greenhouse	System
Exit the assignment (to main)	Greenhouse	System
Quit the application	Greenhouse	System

4   User Interfaces and the User Experience

The student-user reviews the greenhouse system, model information, and makes production decisions through the virtual greenhouse user interfaces. In Table 1, we identified three types of user interfaces: System Interfaces, Physical Interfaces, and ECS Interfaces.

4.1   System Interfaces

System interfaces provide the end-user with the means to interact with the application that includes the virtual greenhouse and critical, associated actions for managing the application and the assignment LMS. System interfaces are nested in the application main menus and within the greenhouse physical environment.

The main menu is the user's first interaction with the application, and it is separate from the experience of the virtual greenhouse. The main entry point to the prototype virtual greenhouse application is the LMS. Despite its simplicity, the LMS is a key component of the application. The LMS presents the student with assignments that have been made available by an instructor. The student can select an assignment, select from available parameters, and then enter the greenhouse. However, up to the point at which the students enter a virtual greenhouse and begin a scenario, the user interface has no connection to the real greenhouse environment. In the prototype application, the main menu interface exists in a sparse abstract virtual environment with simple menus accessed with point-and-click actions (see Fig. 1).

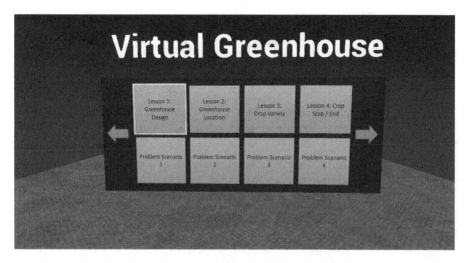

Fig. 1. User viewing the list of available assignments.

Within the greenhouse, some user actions are accessed through system interfaces. Primarily, these are user actions that are tied not to the greenhouse but to the virtual greenhouse application. For example, when inside the virtual greenhouse, the user may want to exit the scenario. To ensure that this action is readily available and easily accessed, the user accesses it by bringing up a floating user interface panel and selecting from a menu of system-level actions.

At the end of a scenario, the user harvests their crop and receives a report on the harvested biomass, rejected biomass, accumulated costs, and estimated profits. This is presented in a system menu that indicates the completion of the scenario and returns the student to the assignment context. At this point, the user can submit the results of the assignment to the LMS for assessment by the instructor.

4.2 Physical Interfaces

For other actions in the virtual greenhouse, the preference is to use physical interactions. These interfaces represent real physical actions that someone can employ in a physical greenhouse. For example, a farmer tending plants in a physical greenhouse can approach a plant and inspect it by lifting a pot, manipulating leaves, and repositioning torso and head in proximity to the plant. In the virtual greenhouse, physical actions are used whenever possible to reinforce the reality of interacting with growing plants in a greenhouse (see Fig. 2). Similarly, when watering the plants in a greenhouse, the farmer can employ a sprayer nozzle on a hose, depress a trigger, and spray water over multiple plants.

Fig. 2. User holding and inspecting a plant with a virtual hand.

The preference for interfaces that represent physical interactions with the objects in the virtual greenhouse is driven by the desire to accurately represent the reality of working in the greenhouse. It is possible that the interfaces for the user actions within the virtual greenhouse could have either a physical or a system interface (see Table 1 items labeled 'Physical or System' interface type). Whereas a physical interaction allows the user to reach out, pick up, and inspect a plant, a system interface could simplify the interaction by having the user point, select a plant, and view a panel displaying some or all of the underlying model data associated with the plant. The end result may be the same – the user accesses information about the plant status. However, only the physical interaction reifies the real-world actions of farming in the greenhouse.

The 'viewing of the greenhouse' was one action that, in the virtual reality application, had to be a Physical Interface. In the scope of the work presented here, our view is that envisioning the greenhouse is a physical activity necessary to achieve the primary objective to teach students how to use an ECS for CEA in a greenhouse. By training students in an immersive 3D virtual reality environment, we represent the virtual greenhouse as a physical greenhouse in which the students can move and observe. This perspective of the virtual greenhouse aims to engage students in making the figurative connection between the greenhouse environment, the actions of the ECS, and the outcomes for their virtual crops.

For the other actions, the costs of implementing realistic representations of the physical tools and actions must be weighed against their value in educating students in greenhouse agricultural setting. If the sole objective is training students to use an ECS, requiring students to physically plant seeds, inspect plants, or spray plants with water may not be necessary. However, training these students to perform these tasks in physically accurate ways may have more general educational benefits. For example, [9] found significant developmental growth (pre- to post-test) when employing interactive greenhouse educational materials as compared to text-based narrative teaching approaches.

4.3   Electronic Control System Interface

The ECS monitors outdoor and indoor conditions of the greenhouse and automates control of the greenhouse equipment in order to maintain indoor temperature, relative humidity, CO_2 levels, and the irrigation and/or plant feedings. The ECS uses sensor data that measures the time of day, temperature, relative humidity, CO_2 levels, wind speed and direction, barometric pressure, indoor vapor pressure deficits, and solar intensity.

The ECS user interface is provided by the CEA system manufacturer, and commercial CEA systems varies widely across the horticultural manufacturers. The ECS interface relays functions such as: (1) a review of the current status of the greenhouse and its operational systems, (2) logging of historical data, (3) ECS response to programmable inputs, and (4) setup and integration of new sensors and equipment into the ECS.

In our reference system (the Wadsworth SEED control unit [10]), a graphical user interface is presented on a touch-screen control box that is mounted in or near the greenhouse. The user interaction with the control unit is similar to using a tablet or phone touch screen. The user taps buttons to open new displays, presses and drags to move sliders or scroll on screens, etc. Several operational screens and other systems options may be used to control the CEA.

In the virtual greenhouse application, accurately representing the user interaction with the ECS will ensure skills transfer from the virtual environment to an ECS in a real greenhouse. However, there are challenges created by mimicking a touch-screen interface in virtual reality. Engagement and interaction challenges arise from the user employing a secondary controller to achieve interaction within the virtual environment.

Fig. 3. Implementations of the electronic control system interface (top left: realistic, top right: tablet-based, bottom right: large monitor, bottom left: floating user interface).

Wall-Mounted User Interface. The first option considered was a reproduction of the reference ECS interface (see top left of Fig. 3). The reference interface is a relatively small touch screen control in a plastic case mounted eye-level on an interior or exterior greenhouse wall. To interact with the ECS interface, the user must physically relocate next to the interface, lean into the display, and attempt to manipulate the interface with simulated touches. With an Oculus touch controller directing a virtual hand, users can interact with the touchscreen as they might in the real world.

While the realistic user interface accurately represents a real-world control unit, its use is cumbersome in a virtual environment. Small screen sizes are difficult to read in the limited resolutions of mainstream VR head-mounted displays and small user interface buttons are a challenge for users. In virtual reality, the display is not limited to a single fixed location, to a small display size, or to touchscreen controls. An accurate representation of the real-world control unit does not leverage potential benefits of virtual reality in exchange for realism. However, a high level of realism is not required to ensure knowledge transfer. Moreover, an intense interface interaction difficulty level in virtual reality may discourage students from regularly engaging with the ECS.

Tablet-Based User Interface. An alternative control system interaction is a tablet-based user interface (see top right of Fig. 3). The tablet-based user interface displays the ECS interface on a virtual tablet attached to one of two handheld controllers. The user employs a second controller to interact with the virtual tablet with the same simulated touchscreen actions used with the wall-mounted control unit.

The tablet user interface has multiple advantages in comparison to the wall-mounted user interface. The ECS interface is always within reach of the user. The user can quickly refer to current status and data logs available through the interface. The user interface is larger than the control unit and closer to the user's eyes, thus making it easier to read. A virtual hand makes the simulated touch controls easier to engage. However, the tablet interface is a significant departure, in form and use, from the typical wall-mounted control unit.

Large Monitor Fixed User Interface. Unlike the tablet interface, another more realistic, alternative to the wall-mounted unit is a scaled-up control unit converted into a large wall-mounted monitor (see bottom right of Fig. 3). The ECS interface is scaled up with the display size yet the user still employs a controller to interact with the display using simulated touchscreen actions.

In the wall-mounted monitor interface, the fixed location of the control unit is maintained but the increased size allows users to easily position themselves near the monitor to see and interact with the interface. A downside to the large monitor display is the user must employ larger physical movements to interact with the display, potentially leading to fatigue. This may also limit accessibility for some users.

Floating User Interface. A less realistic, alternative interface is an embedded ECS user interface in a floating panel that can be brought up by the user at any time and any place in the environment (see bottom left of Fig. 3). Rather than simulated touchscreen controls for this interface, the user interface was modified to use point-and-click interactions typically reserved for virtual environment user interface panels.

The floating panel combines ease of access to the tablet ECS interface and the large display size of the monitor. Unlike the physical interfaces that are perceived as part of the greenhouse system, the floating user interface is similar to a system interface and may be perceived by users as abstract and not part of the greenhouse. A perceived separation between the ECS interface and the control system may affect user's understanding of the relationship between the interface and the greenhouse.

5 Summary

In this paper, we describe the user interfaces associated with a virtual greenhouse application intended to instruct students in the use of an ECS interface for a CEA greenhouse. The virtual greenhouse has three distinct user interfaces: the system interfaces that allow the user to control the virtual application, the physical interfaces used to interact with tools and plants in the greenhouse, and a recreation of the ECS interface within the virtual greenhouse. While the potential benefits of physical interfaces in fostering presence and engagement in the learning task are clear, designers must consider the potential disadvantages of requiring physical interaction and the complexities of implementing physical models.

The ECS interface presents challenges when considering the tradeoff between usability and realism. A physically accurate recreation of the ECS control unit is too small in virtual reality and forgoes the benefits of virtual reality for increased realism. We consider three alternative interfaces that address weaknesses in the wall-mounted interface with varying reductions in realism.

Acknowledgments. The authors would like to thank the Patricia Dean and the team at Wadsworth Control Systems for their support. This work was supported by the USDA National Institute of Food and Agriculture (USDA-NIFA 2019-69017-29928).

References

1. Rose, D.H., Meyer, A.: Teaching Every Student in the Digital Age: Universal Design for Learning. Association for Supervision and Curriculum Development, Alexandria (2002)
2. Carruth, D.W.: Virtual reality education and workforce training. In: 15th International Conference on Emerging eLearning Technologies and Applications (ICETA), pp. 1–6. IEEE (2017)
3. Deb, S., Carruth, D.W., Sween, R., Strawderman, L.: Efficacy of virtual reality in pedestrian safety research. Appl. Ergon. **65**, 449–460 (2017)
4. Velev, D., Zlateva, P.: Virtual reality challenges in education and training. Int. J. Learn. Teach. **3**, 33–37 (2017)
5. Rose, P.: Skeuomorphism as an affordance: A principle for interaction and user interaction design. University of Plymouth, Plymouth (2013)
6. Plemmons, D., Holz, D.: Creating next-gen 3D interactive apps with motion control and Unity3D. In: SIGGRAPH 2014: ACM SIGGRAPH 2014 Studio, pp. 1–23. Association for Computing Machinery, New York (2014)

7. Bushra, N., Carruth, D., Deb, S.: A comparative study of virtual UI for risk assessment and evaluation. In: Bebis, G., et al. (eds.) ISVC 2018. LNCS, vol. 11241, pp. 226–236. Springer, Cham (2018). https://doi.org/10.1007/978-3-030-03801-4_21
8. Frantz, J.M., Hand, B., Buckingham, L., Ghose, S.: Virtual grower: software to calculate heating costs of greenhouse production in the United States. HortTechnology 20(4), 778–785 (2010)
9. Tignor, M.E.: Multi-institutional cooperation to develop digital media for interactive greenhouse education. HortTechnology 17(3), 397–399 (2007)
10. Wadsworth Control Systems: Seed. https://wadsworthcontrols.com/controls/seed/

A Comparison of Augmented and Virtual Reality Features in Industrial Trainings

Lea M. Daling$^{(\boxtimes)}$, Anas Abdelrazeq, and Ingrid Isenhardt

Chair of Information Management in Mechanical Engineering (IMA),
RWTH Aachen University, Aachen, Germany
lea.daling@ima.rwth-aachen.de

Abstract. Short-term qualification for temporary workers is a constant challenge for manufacturing companies. Cycle times of machines often have to be reduced for training processes, which demands time and financial resources. This increases the need for near-the-job trainings without manipulating cycle times of the machine. Digital visualization tools using Mixed Reality (MR) promise opportunities for application-oriented practical training. However, especially for industrial applications, where procedural knowledge has to be transferred, it is not clear which MR technology should be used for which purpose. In order to answer this question, this paper examines the underlying MR-features of the technology. In an experimental setting, the same virtual training for the assembly of a pneumatic cylinder is examined with an augmented reality/augmented virtuality (AR/AV) based application in comparison to a virtual reality (VR) based application. Based on the carried out study, there are significant differences in the evaluation of the system usability, but no differences in the evaluation of the ergonomics and the perceived task load during the task. Out of 16 test persons, 14 would choose the VR system in the final analysis. The results are discussed in the paper and recommendations for the design of MR based systems in an industrial context are given.

Keywords: Industrial trainings · Augmented reality · Virtual reality · System usability · Mixed reality features

1 Introduction

1.1 Training Procedures in Production and Manufacturing

In the course of increasingly digitalized production, the evolvement of complex, digitally networked systems also poses challenges to their operators [1]. In this context, machine operation and associated assembly processes require safe and effective interaction between man and machine [2]. This also changes the way of corresponding training procedures. Face-to-face or text-based training procedures are increasingly being replaced by more flexible digital methods such as blended-learning or virtual learning environments [3]. This becomes particularly relevant if inexperienced or temporary workers have to be trained for new (assembly) processes [4].

By using digital (i.e. virtual) near-the-job trainings, inexperienced employees can be trained in a standardized way without manipulating the cycle time of a machine [5].

© Springer Nature Switzerland AG 2020
J. Y. C. Chen and G. Fragomeni (Eds.): HCII 2020, LNCS 12191, pp. 47–65, 2020.
https://doi.org/10.1007/978-3-030-49698-2_4

This not only improves the efficiency of the training by reducing costs and time, but also increases safety and enables the consideration of different learning paces and previous knowledge [6, 7]. Such trainings play a crucial role in improving the human capital of the workforce [4]. Virtual learning environments are particularly suitable for industrial application, since they offer practicing real-life activities of manufacturing processes in a virtual environment [8]. In addition to instructional videos and learning platforms, the use of Mixed Reality (MR) technologies has become a promising procedure in order to visualize and illustrate workflows and processes near-the-job [2, 9].

Although the benefits of MR technologies are empirically proven and widely acknowledged from workers and operators [3, 10, 11], there are currently only few cautious attempts to apply these technologies in a long-term and targeted manner [7]. There is also a lack of knowledge about which technology should be used for certain tasks or how the features should be specified: "each has unique strengths and limits for aiding learning, so understanding how to choose the right medium for a particular educational situation is an important next step in realizing the potential of immersive media in learning" [12]. Neglecting these different potentials can provoke unexpected effects, e.g. that paper-based training in experimental studies leads to better results than MR technologies [13]. Possible reasons for this are missing or not optimally used features (e.g., gesture control or hand recognition) of the used technology in the respective task [14]. To determine which technology or which features are particularly suitable for a certain task, the following section presents a definition of MR as well as a brief overview of the features of the technologies and devices used in this context.

1.2   Mixed Reality

The term MR describes a continuum between reality and virtuality, involving the merging of real and virtual worlds [15]. Within the reality-virtuality continuum, a distinction is made between the real environment, Augmented Reality (AR), Augmented Virtuality (AV) and the virtual environment (Fig. 1).

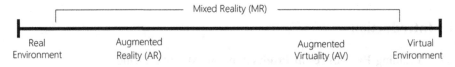

Fig. 1. Reality-virtuality continuum [15]

AR describes the immersion in reality and the handling or interaction with virtual objects. Thus, an AR system "combines real and virtual objects in a real environment; runs interactively and in real time and registers (aligns) real and virtual objects with each other" [16]. The use of AR in training of managing industrial equipment gives orientation of the correct utilization of the instruments, which in turn omits errors and production rejects [17]. AR enables the user to manage the equipment from screen or device through the recognition of current state of the equipment [17].

AV describes the immersion into a virtual world, which is extended by reality, while the user manipulates mainly virtual objects. Especially in collaborative use cases and settings AV promises to be successful. In industrial context, for example, virtual meetings can be held in which engineers can jointly manipulate or change 3D models in real time [18]. Compared to AR, immersion plays a more prominent role in AV [19]. Nevertheless, the boundary between AR and AV remains weak and depends strongly on the application and use [20].

Although not directly mentioned in the definition of Milgram and Colquhoun in 1999, Virtual Reality (VR) is a widely used technology that most closely corresponds to the virtual environment and thus is associated with the right side of the continuum [10]. In this paper, VR is understood as part of Mixed Reality. VR describes complete immersion in a virtual world, while the real environment is hidden [15]. Thus, VR offers a very comprehensive view of the structures and installations of a respective environment [21]. Providing the user with perceptive information about the structure and functioning of a real system is a cost-effective advantage of VR [8]. The advantage of using VR as industrial training is to prevent user from exposing risks of the real process equipment and familiarize with the tool and work steps at the same time through virtual immersion [22].

Many authors criticize the apparent separation of these terms in the continuum, as the boundaries of the terms become indistinct in most use cases [20]. The capabilities of technologies and devices are becoming more and more extensive and are increasingly overlapping. In the course of the discussion about the classification of Mixed Reality, suggestions came up to make the distinction rather on the basis of the technological specification (technology-centered taxonomies) [23], the preconditions of the user (user-centered taxonomies) [24], the specification of the presented information (information-centered taxonomies) [25] or the interaction between user and object (interaction-centered taxonomies) [26].

However, the applicability and usefulness of these classifications depends strongly on the use case. In the field of industrial assembly or machine operation, for example, the consideration of task characteristics is of enormous importance, which can hardly be found in any of the existing taxonomies [27]. The intransparency and overlapping of content within existing taxonomies contribute significantly to the fact that MR technologies are not yet part of the everyday tools used in the industry [14]. There is little research on when which technology (e.g. AR vs VR) is more suitable in an industrial context [6]. This impedes their implementation. Thus, companies are faced with the challenge of choosing the right methodology and the right technological tool for the respective task.

This paper aims to bridge the gap between theory-based taxonomies and practical use cases. It will answer the question which MR feature is most suitable for a specific assembly related task. Section 2 presents an industrial use case for a training process in production and defines the characteristics of the task. Based on this, the required features and specifications for the design of the based teach-in procedure are derived. Section 3 describes the study design in which two different technologies for the training process are compared. The results are presented in Sect. 4 and discussed afterwards.

2   Use Case Description

2.1   Assembly of a Pneumatic Cylinder

The Use Case describes the manual assembly of a pneumatic cylinder before its further processing in a partially automated machine. The whole assembly process consists of eleven steps. For each step it is specified whether the right or left hand shall be used. The steps are described in the following: First, the piston rod should be grasped from the colored left box and inserted into the workpiece fixture. Secondly, the piston buffer must be removed and mounted on the piston rod. Then, a piston has to be grasped from the upper left box and mounted on the piston rod. The fourth step includes taking the rod guide ring from the box. Subsequently, the ring magnet has to be grasped and a new ring magnet should be ordered via button. The ring magnet must be placed on the piston rod with the marked red side up and the rod guide ring must be mounted on the ring magnet. The mounting bush and sealing ring should then be placed on the piston rod. Then, the piston from the right box has to be mounted on the piston rod. The buffer piston must then be screwed onto the piston rod. The assembled piston rod should be inserted into the workpiece carrier and turned until it clicks. At the last step, the cylinder tube should be placed on the workpiece carrier, which will be sent to the respective station by pressing the start button.

The learning process for these steps in a face-to-face training that takes 40–70 min depending on the previous knowledge of the worker. The cycle time of the machine must then be reduced for several hours at a time.

An MR prototype has already been tested in a preliminary study. A 3D visualization of the plant was constructed and the sequence of individual work steps was visualized using Microsoft HoloLens. An overview on the virtual plant and the workspace can be seen in Fig. 2.

Fig. 2. 3D visualization of the plant

The machine was projected into real space in order to train the workers before they work on the real system. The first heuristic usability evaluation of the experts was positive. However, some important remarks concerned missing possibilities for interaction with the individual objects, as well as a possible irritation caused by an overlap of the virtual objects with the real environment in which the training was conducted. Based on the preliminary study, the required functionalities for the present use case are derived in the following section, which will define the test scenarios.

2.2 Specifications of MR Features

Based on theory-based taxonomies [20, 24–26], different characteristics should be taken into account when designing an MR-based training method. In Table 1, the features of the technologies are specified and assigned to different classifications, which are applied to the use case in the following. The first three categories (task, user, information) play an essential role in designing the training environment. The last two categories (interaction, technology) additionally contribute to the choice of the medium.

Table 1. Specification of general MR-features

Classification	Specification
Task-centered [12, 14, 27]	Procedural vs. declarative knowledge Mainly cognitive vs. physical activity
User-centered [24]	Demographic variables and prerequisites of user with regard to • the task *(Previous experiences)* • the technology *(Affinity for technology, Control beliefs while dealing with technology, Use of technology)*
Information-centered [25]	Type and dimensionality of the objects • Text-based • Images • 2D or 3D visualization
Interaction-centered [26]	Input, control, and feedback • Voice/Audio • Visual • Haptic
Technology-centered [23]	• Extension of World Knowledge (EWK) • Reproduction Fidelity (RF) • Extent of Presence Metaphor (EPM)

The task of assembling a pneumatic cylinder requires the acquisition of procedural knowledge in order to complete the work steps in the correct order. Dede and colleagues report that VR, for example, can be very effective for learning procedural tasks in which students learn a sequence of steps to complete a task that requires maneuvers in three-dimensional space [12]. With regard to the user, demographic variables such as age, gender, and educational background could play a role with regard to the success of the MR-based training procedure. Even more important, however, is the users' previous knowledge of the task. For example, inexperienced workers may need more or different instructions than experienced workers [28]. The presented use case is primarily aimed at inexperienced temporary workers who have to practice the assembly without any prior knowledge. The didactic structure of the training should take this into account by offering a modular structure, where steps can be repeated and played in different paces [7]. Furthermore, affinity and enthusiasm for technology may have an influence on the assessment of the system [29].

The objects of the virtual assembly should be displayed as realistically as possible to allow realistic orientation in the training environment. Therefore, true-to-scale 3D representations of the objects were used. Important information was additionally visualized in short, clearly arranged text fields.

In a heuristic evaluation with the MR prototype [30], the lack of possibilities for interaction was particularly criticized. Therefore, the comparison of two different media with different possibilities for interaction should contribute to evaluate the importance of e.g. haptic control. The first medium, which was also used in the preliminary study, is the Microsoft HoloLens. Here, there are possibilities for voice input as well as the possibility to use a clicker for the selection of different steps for interaction. However, the control is primarily visual, by directing the gaze at an object or field and then confirming this by voice or clicker. Since the scenario is projected into a real environment, it can be classified in the Reality-Virtuality spectrum in the middle range between AR and AV.

In contrast, the second medium is intended to offer possibilities for haptic interaction. Therefore, the same training application was implemented in a VR environment, which is related to the right end of the continuum. In the VR environment, it is possible to select steps or to move objects yourself with two controllers. Since the use case requires differentiating between using right and left hand, a feedback function for selecting objects with the right or left controller is built in.

The technical classifications are based on the preliminary work of Milgram and Kishino, to whose publication reference is made for more detailed information [23]. The first medium (AR/AV) uses a partially modelled world in the EWK dimension by virtually projecting the entire machine into the real world. The second medium (acer mixed reality glasses), on the other hand, uses a 360° view of the real environment in which the virtually modelled machine is installed. In terms of RF, both media use 3D animations with high fidelity. The extent of presence in the EPM dimension is relatively well established using Head Mounted Displays (HMDs), although it can be assumed that the VR environment allows an even higher degree of presence.

According to the feature specification with regard to the use case of the cylinder assembly, it becomes evident that the media particularly differ in the interaction possibilities with the work components. The following section presents the deduced hypotheses, from which the study design will be derived later on.

2.3 Hypothesis

The hypotheses to be examined in this study relate on the one hand to the perception and assessment of the respective medium (AR/AV vs. VR). At this point, the evaluation of usability and ergonomics is differentiated. On the other hand, hypotheses on the perception and evaluation of the training process using MR are formulated and tested in the further course of the study. Since there is no evidence for the suitability of one of the media compared to the other for such an application, the hypotheses are formulated and tested in a non-directional way (Table 2).

Table 2. Hypotheses

H_1	There is a correlation between technology affinity and the assessment of the perceived system usability
H_{2a}	The system usability of the two technologies AR/AV and VR differs significantly
H_{2b}	The evaluation of ergonomics of the two media AR/AV and VR differs significantly
H_3	The used media AR/AV and VR differ significantly in their evaluation of the training process

3 Method

3.1 Study Design

The study design consists of an experimental within subject procedure with pre- and post test. This ensures that each participant could test both AR/AV and VR training application. At first, the participants were asked to fill out a questionnaire before they were assigned to a test condition. The order of the test conditions was randomly assigned. Test condition A included the following procedure: (1) Fill out a pre-test questionnaire, (2a) conduct training with AR, (2b) fill out a post-test questionnaire on the use of AR, (3a) conduct training with VR, (3b) fill out a post-test questionnaire on the use of VR, (4) answer the question of which medium would be the best choice. In test condition B the same procedure was chosen, but at first the VR training and subsequently the AR training was performed.

The same scenario was run through with all participants. The training took place in a room outside the production hall in order to avoid disturbing influences. After a brief introduction to the use of the technology, the participants had time to inspect the virtual assembly cell. After the orientation phase, the participants were able to watch a guided exercise scenario. The participants did not have to become active themselves, but had to use the clicker to proceed with the next step. Afterwards, they were able to view the entire assembly process again in animated mode - this was possible either in real time or in a slower version. The last step included the independent execution of the assembly steps. In the AR/AV version, the components had to be selected via eye control and clicker - the animation of those components was then carried out automatically if the selection was correct. In the VR version, the participants had the task of gripping the components themselves with the controllers (a distinction was made here between gripping with the right and left hand) and placing them in the correct position. The duration of use of the devices varied between 8 and 25 min.

The description of the questionnaires used in pre- and post-tests is presented below. Subsequently, an overview of the participants of the study is given.

3.2 Questionnaires

Pre-test. In a pre-test, the participants were asked about their demographic data (age, gender, educational level) and their current job position. In order to investigate the participants' previous knowledge of the task, they were asked whether they had ever carried out pneumatic cylinder assembly on the machine before. In addition, the participants were asked whether they had ever participated in a training procedure using AR/VR.

Subsequently, the participants were asked about their technical affinity with five items (e.g., "My enthusiasm for technology is...") on a six-level scale from "very low" to "very high". To complete the data on the participants, they were also asked which media (e.g. laptop, smartphone, tablets) are available to them, how often they use them and how easy-to-use the respective medium is. In addition, we used the "locus of control" questionnaire (KUT) to assess general control beliefs while dealing with technology [31]. With its 8 items (e.g., "I feel so helpless when dealing with technical devices that I do not even touch them") on a scale of six levels from "not at all" to "absolutely", the German questionnaire achieves a reliability of Cronbach's $\alpha = .85$.

Post-test. The post-test was divided into two parts for each test condition. First, questions were answered to evaluate the training medium. First, the System Usability Scale (SUS; [32]) was used to evaluate the respective technology. A SUS score between 60–80 means that the system is marginally acceptable, scores above 80 indicate good to very good system usability and 100 points indicate an excellent rating system that fully meets the users' expectations. In order to ensure that the answer scale of the entire questionnaire is consistent, a six level scale "do not agree at all" to "fully agree" was used in this study. Accordingly, an adjusted factor was used in the calculation of the overall score in order to ensure the comparability and significance of the SUS score. This scale reached a Cronbach's alpha of $\alpha = .80$ in this study.

In order to be able to cover not only system usability but also ergonomic issues, six self-created items were used (e.g., "The field of vision of the glasses restricted me.") and assessed on the same scale. This scale reached an $\alpha = .68$ and thus has to be treated with caution. Furthermore, the questionnaire contained two open questions: "What difficulties did you encounter in the learning process with the training medium?" and "What functionalities (e.g. speech/gestural control) did you find particularly helpful?"

The second part included the evaluation of the training process. The Nasa Task Load Index (NASA TLX) was used to measure the perceived load during the task. It measures the subjectively perceived demand with a multidimensional scale that distinguishes, for example, between physical and psychological stress [33]. The German summary contains six dimensions, namely mental, physical and temporal stress as well as performance, effort and frustration. The original scale has 20 gradations from "very low" to "very high". Adapted to the German version, we have used a 10-step scale with the poles "little" and "much".

In order to capture the evaluation of the training process in depth, two open questions were asked: "To what extent do you feel prepared for the task by using the system?" and "To what extent would you prefer the system used to other training methods (please explain)? After both test conditions were carried out, a final question was asked: "Which of the two tested training media would you prefer? Please give reasons for your answer".

3.3 Participants

A total of nine men and seven women participated in the study (N = 16). Four participants were under 20, six of the participants were between 21–25 years old, one participant between 26–30 years old, four participants were between 31–40 years old and one participant was between 41–45 years old. The sample consisted of six company employees, two temporary workers, and the remaining eight were trainees, apprentices or managers. Three participants stated that they had intermediate level of secondary education, three had technical college entrance qualification. Six participants stated that their highest educational level was high school and/or university entrance qualification, the remaining eight already had an academic degree (nBachelor = 2, nMaster = 1, nPhD = 1).

Two participants stated that they already had experience with MR-based training methods. One of the participants had already conducted the MR-based training for the respective assembly, three other participants already knew the assembly, but based on manual training.

3.4 Analysis

The analysis of the collected data was conducted using SPSS. Since we are dealing with a small sample (N = 16), the inferential statistical evaluation is based on a non-parametric data level. For group comparisons, the Wilcoxon test for paired samples is used. In the following, an overview of descriptive statistics is given first. In order to comply with the SUS analysis requirements, the items on the system usability and ergonomics scales were adjusted from one to six to zero to five.

4 Results

An overview of the results of the pre-test is given below. First, descriptive statistics for the respective questionnaires in the pre- and post-test are reported. Subsequently the test results of the hypotheses are presented. In the framework of the pre-test, the use of technology, the handling of technology and the affinity of the sample towards technology are presented.

4.1 Pre-test Results

All study participants reported to have access to laptop/PC and smartphone for private or professional purposes. 14 participants work with tablets, while only three participants used Microsoft HoloLens or Oculus Rift/HTC Vive. The ease of use of these technologies was assessed on a scale from one "very difficult" to six "very easy". The Microsoft HoloLens received the lowest value with a mean value of 4.50 (Min = 4,

Max = 5, SD = .58, n = 3), the smartphone received the highest mean value with x̄ = 5.56 (Min = 1, Max = 6, SD = 1.3, n = 16).

An overview of the participants' affinity for technology is given in Table 3. The locus of control while dealing with technology in the sample had a mean value of x̄ = 4.44 (min = 3.13, max = 5.38, SD = 0.74, n = 16).

Table 3. Descriptive statistics for technical affinity.

n = 16	Mean	SD	Min	Max
Enthusiasm for technology	4.75	1.24	2	6
Interest in technology	4.69	1.30	2	6
Technological understanding	4.19	1.17	2	6
Distrust of technology	2.63	0.62	2	4
Technical skills	4.38	1.09	2	6

Hypothesis 1: There is a correlation between technology affinity and the assessment of the perceived system usability

A Spearman's correlation was run to determine the relationship between technical affinity values and SUS Index for AR/AV and VR. No correlation was found, neither for the AR/AV SUS Index (= −.12, p = .67, n = 16), nor for VR's system usability (= .25, p = .35 n = 16).

4.2   Post-test Results

The results of the post-test include an overview of the descriptive statistics for the evaluation of the media and the respective learning process. In each case, the results of the hypothesis tests are presented afterwards.

Hypothesis 2a: The usability of the two media AR/AV and VR differs significantly

Descriptive statistics (mean value, standard deviation, minimum and maximum) of the System Usability Scale are presented in Table 4. The six level scale was adjusted to zero = "do not agree at all" to five = "fully agree". The calculation of the SUS score shows that the AR/AV system has an overall score of 63.63. The SUS score for the VR system is 72.75.

The Wilcoxon test for paired samples shows a significant difference with a median of 35.5 for AR/VR and a median of 37.5 for VR (z = −2.047, p = 0.041, n = 16). Hypothesis 1a can therefore be confirmed.

Hypothesis 2b: The evaluation of ergonomics of the two media AR/AV and VR differs significantly

Descriptive statistics for the six-item scale for ergonomics is shown in Table 5. According to the Wilcoxon test for ergonomics of AR/VR (median = 23.5) and VR (median = 23.5) with z = −.596 and p = .551, it shows that the central tendencies of the respective test conditions are not different. Hypothesis H1b must therefore be rejected.

Table 4. Descriptive statistics for system usability. (The following items have been translated by the author into English for better comprehensibility.)

n = 16	AR/AV				VR			
	Mean	SD	Min	Max	Mean	SD	Min	Max
I think that I would like to use this system frequently	2.81	1.33	1	5	3.81	0.83	2	5
I found the system unnecessarily complex. (rec)	3.69	0.95	2	5	4.00	0.63	3	5
I thought the system was easy to use	3.13	1.09	1	5	3.81	0.75	2	5
I think that I would need the support of a technical person to be able to use this system. (rec)	3.06	1.18	1	5	3.19	1.11	1	5
I found the various functions in this system were well integrated	3.00	0.89	1	4	3.63	0.50	3	4
I thought there was too much inconsistency in this system. (rec)	2.81	1.22	1	4	3.88	0.81	2	5
I would imagine that most people would learn to use this system very quickly	3.25	1.00	1	5	3.31	0.95	1	5
I found the system very cumbersome to use. (rec)	3.31	1.08	1	5	4.00	0.63	3	5
I felt very confident using the system	3.00	1.21	1	5	3.25	0.86	2	4
I needed to learn a lot of things before I could get going with this system. (rec)	3.75	1.06	1	5	3.50	1.26	1	5

Difficulties Using the Media. Within the framework of the open questions, the participants reported the following difficulties in the training process with the medium AR/AV: The glasses were very heavy and/or unsuitable for wearer of glasses, limited field of vision (5), lack of integration of the hands (2), not realistic, difficulties with orientation (Where does the next step take place?) (4), difficulties with clicker operation.

When using VR, the participants reported the following problems: The field of vision flickers/is blurred (2), dizziness (2), spatial boundaries are missing, it is difficult

Table 5. Descriptive statistics for ergonomics.

n = 16	AR/AV				VR			
	Mean	SD	Min	Max	Mean	SD	Min	Max
The virtual training made me feel uncomfortable. (rec)	4.38	1.20	1	5	3.88	0.96	2	5
Wearing the glasses was pleasant	2.75	1.24	1	5	3.31	0.87	2	5
Working with the glasses was exhausting for me. (rec)	3.69	1.14	1	5	3.63	0.89	2	5
Wearing the glasses had some after-effects on me. (rec)	4.25	0.93	2	5	4.25	0.86	2	5
The field of vision of the glasses restricted me. (rec)	1.94	1.44	0	5	3.38	1.41	0	5
Wearing glasses has exhausted my eyes. (rec)	4.06	1.00	2	5	3.44	1.26	0	5
Sum	3.67	0.72	2.00	4.50	3.81	0.71	2.00	5.17

to immerse oneself in the animation, lack of intuitiveness when operating the controllers (e.g. when grasping), sound feedback is sometimes confusing.

Helpful Functionalities. The following comments were noted as helpful features for AR/AV: Clear audio instructions through the steps as a supplement to the text, pleasant wearing comfort, real environment is still visible (2), free movement in space is possible, cursor control via view, as well as clear color highlighting of the components to be used. The following features were found to be helpful when using VR glasses: Controller (possibility to grasp and move the components) (7), differentiation between right and left hand (2), color highlighting of the components to be used (2), high level of realism by imitating the real environment, and comfortable wearing comfort.

Hypothesis 3: The used media AR/AV and VR differ significantly in their evaluation of the training process

The evaluation of the NASA Task Load Index shows that the perception of the test persons regarding their load during the task does not differ according to medium. Figure 3 shows the mean values of the individual scales for the media in comparison. The Wilcoxon test shows that hypothesis 2 must be rejected with $z = -0.910$ and $p = 0.363$.

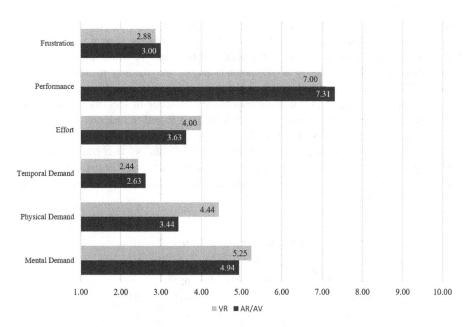

Fig. 3. NASA task load index for AR/AV and VR (n = 16).

Preparation for the Task by the System. When using the AR/AV medium, participants noted that they felt well prepared (6) because they knew the process. Some participants noted that they would repeat the exercise several times before the actual assembly (2). Others said that they felt less prepared because of the lack of orientation (3) and poor transferability to the real workplace. With the VR system, the majority of the test persons felt well to very well prepared for the upcoming task (4). One participant noticed that he felt as safe as if he had received a personal instruction to the system. Two participants also indicated that they would repeat the exercise in advance. One participant states that he feels relatively safe, but that he would not be able to answer adequately if he were asked questions.

Comparison of MR to Other Training Methods. Some participants indicate that AR/AV System is preferable to text-based process instructions (3). It is especially emphasized that the method is suitable for an initial familiarization with the process. Personal learning by another employee is still preferred by two participants. Due to the lack of haptics, the system is merely a supplement to, but not a replacement for, instructions on the physical machine. Participants positively noted that each employee can learn at his/her own pace, the training is carried out in a very standardized manner and no time or money loss is incurred due to cycle time overruns. One participant stated that he prefers a mixed form of both systems.

The VR system is described by the participants as very realistic. The participants state that it is particularly suitable for obtaining an overview and orientation of the workplace. It is preferred over text forms, but the advantage of VR over simple videos is questioned. However, when problems arise, the participants see difficulties.

Choice of Medium. The subjects rated the VR system significantly better and would choose to use it (14 for VR, 2 not quite clear, 0 for AR). The mentioned advantages of VR in this question refer to the fact that orientation is easier, the use of the hands helps to memorize procedures, the field of vision is larger and there is a higher wearing comfort. The test persons describe the experience as closer to reality.

A correlation matrix was created exploratively in order to identify the extent to which there are correlations between the decision for VR and the surveyed parameters system usability, ergonomics, and task load. Table 6 shows that there are significant point-biserial correlations between the decision for VR and system usability (= .63, n = 16, p < 0.01) as well as between VR and the evaluation of ergonomics (= .65, n = 16, p < 0.01). There seems to be no significant correlation between the task load and the decision for VR.

Table 6. Correlation matrix

n = 16	Decision_VR	Ergo_VR	SUS_VR	TLX_VR
Decision_VR		.63**	.65**	.46*
Ergo_VR			.61*	.54*
SUS_VR				.51*
TLX_VR				

**The correlation is significant (bilateral) at the level of 0.01.
*The correlation is significant (bilateral) at the level of 0.05.

5   Conclusion

5.1   Limitations

Before discussing the results of the present study, the limitations of the study are presented briefly. An essential aspect is the small size and representativeness of the sample. Especially in studies that take place outside the laboratory but directly in industry, it is difficult to acquire an adequate number of participants. The problem of the low validity of the data of such small number of participants was countered by a conservative approach to statistical analysis and additionally recorded qualitative statements. Nevertheless, any results based on such a small amount of data should be interpreted with caution. Furthermore, the composition of the sample does not fully reflect the characteristics of typical temporary workers. For this reason, we have made sure that the previous knowledge for the task should be as little as possible in order to deduce statements about inexperienced workers. Another problem is the use of a non-validated scale for the factor ergonomics. This scale should be revised and validated in larger surveys. Furthermore, the scale of system usability was evaluated in this study by a six-level item scale and not, as in the original, by a five-level scale. This could also have an influence on the reliability of the scale.

5.2 Discussion of Results

The results on the tested hypotheses are summarized in Table 7 and are discussed below, taking into account the qualitative results.

Table 7. Decision on hypotheses

Hypothesis	Statement	Decision
H_1	There is a correlation between technology affinity and the assessment of the perceived system usability	Reject
H_{2a}	The usability of the two media AR/AV and VR differs significantly	Accept
H_{2b}	The evaluation of ergonomics of the two media AR/AV and VR differs significantly	Reject
H_3	The used media AR/AV and VR differ significantly in their evaluation of the training process	Reject

The pre-test shows that the participants in the study had little or no overall experience with MR. Even though the sample has a relatively high affinity for technology and indicates that they feel confident in using technology, there seems to be no correlation with the subsequent evaluation of the systems' usability. The enthusiasm for technology seems to play a subordinate role in the training procedure for the presented use case. This leads to the assumption that people with less technical affinity could also get along well with the system - and vice versa.

The evaluation of the media was divided into the evaluation of system usability and ergonomics. Regarding system usability, both media had a rather lower score, which is described in the manual as only marginally acceptable. However, this could be due to the fact that the participants in the study were asked to closely examine both systems. The assumption that system usability scores differ can be confirmed. Data show that the VR system is rated significantly better.

Statistically speaking, there are no differences between the systems in the scale of ergonomics. This result is surprising, as the written comments mainly mention comments on ergonomically related difficulties (e.g. the restricted field of vision). This indicates that the items of the scale should be revised. The written comments on the media show that all participants prefer clear guidance through the process steps (e.g. by highlighting the objects in color or using cue arrows). When independently carrying out the assembly steps, the use of controllers in the VR system was found to be helpful. The high degree of reality provided by the 360° photo of the assembly hall is perceived as pleasant. However, some participants stated that they found the simultaneous perception of reality in AR/AV more pleasant and safer.

With regard to the evaluation of the training process through the NASA TLX, the descriptive statistics show only a small recognizable difference in the area of physical demand, which can be explained by the increased movement and interaction in VR during assembly. Overall, the load during the assembly does not seem to differ between the media. At this point it should be questioned whether the scale used is sufficiently valid for the criteria to be measured.

In the written comments it becomes evident that the participants feel well prepared for the realistic assembly through both media. Most of them note that they want to repeat the exercise before the assembly is carried out on the real system. Compared to other (e.g. text-based) instructions, the participants regard the MR procedures as superior. However, a few number (two) of the participants prefer the possibility to be trained by another person or that MR is combined with training in a real setup. Accordingly, it should be ensured that the test persons are provided with a supervisor who can answer questions if needed. The high standardization and the possibility of individual learning speed was perceived positively.

The final evaluation of the media clearly shows that the participants prefer the VR system. The main reasons are the good orientation in space, the natural field of view and the use of the controllers to interact with the work pieces. The explorative correlation matrix shows that there are correlations between the decision for VR and the system usability of VR and it's evaluation of ergonomics. Although this does not allow any conclusions to be drawn about a cause-and-effect relationship, it nevertheless confirms the importance of placing a strong focus on usability in the development of such systems and of involving users early in the development process.

5.3   Conclusion and Outlook

The findings allow drawing conclusions about the specification and importance of different MR technology features. The underlying features seem to be more important than the clear separation of the devices. Thus, for a task that requires interaction of the user with a real or virtual object, there should be appropriate possibilities for interaction in the system. This can be realized in AR/AV technologies as well as in VR. The following table (Table 8) summarizes the collected findings in preliminary guidelines for classifications, which should be reviewed and extended in further studies.

Table 8. Guideline for developing MR training systems

Classification	Guideline
Task-centered	• Task with clear focus on procedural knowledge and physical activity
User-centered	• Conducting an introduction to the technology and its control • Modular design of the training contents in order to take into account different levels of prior knowledge • In the case of videos or automatically running animations, possibilities for reducing/increasing the speed should be offered
Information-centered	• Color highlighting of the objects to be focused • Use only short texts or notes and provide the possibility for audio instructions • Clear instructions (e.g. arrows) to guide attention to the next step

(continued)

Table 8. (*continued*)

Classification	Guideline
Interaction-centered	• Parts of the task that require specific physical activities, in order to learn motor processes, should be designed as realistically as possible (e.g. gripping, moving objects) • Feedback about correct or wrong steps should include an explanation (e.g., of what has to be changed)
Technology-centered	• The more important the context is for the completion of a task, the better it should be modelled (VR) or the task should be performed directly at the machine (e.g. with instructions from AR) • HMDs are particularly suitable for tasks in which the hands are to be used. Other tasks can also be taught using hand-held devices (e.g. smartphones, tablets) • A natural or wide field of view is essential for the presence experience in the virtual or augmented world

The listed points result mainly from the qualitative results of the participants' written comments. Thus, it is evident that the collection of qualitative data is essential when evaluating new systems. In order to be able to integrate the empirical results of the quantitative survey, a further study should be conducted with a larger sample - if necessary also in a laboratory setting - and compared with the available findings. Furthermore, possible relevant user factors (such as openness to new experiences or the current mood) should be surveyed and examined for correlations with the evaluation of the systems.

Acknowledgement. This work is part of the project "'ELLI 2 - Excellent Teaching and Learning in Engineering Sciences" and was funded by the Federal Ministry of Educatio and Research (BMBF), Germany.

References

1. Benešová, A., Hirman, M., Steiner, F., Tupa, J.: Analysis of education requirements for electronics manufacturing within concept industry 4.0. In: 2018 41st International Spring Seminar on Electronics Technology (ISSE), pp. 1–5. IEEE, Piscataway (2018)
2. Chang, M.M.L., Ong, S.K., Nee, A.Y.C.: Approaches and challenges in product disassembly planning for sustainability. Procedia CIRP **60**, 506–511 (2017)
3. Kerin, M., Pham, D.T.: A review of emerging industry 4.0 technologies in remanufacturing. J. Cleaner Prod. **237**, 117805 (2019)
4. Konings, J., Vanormelingen, S.: The impact of training on productivity and wages: firm-level evidence. Rev. Econ. Stat. **97**(2), 485–497 (2015)
5. Kim, M., Park, K.-B., Choi, S.H., Lee, J.Y., Kim, D.Y.: AR/VR-based live manual for user-centric smart factory services. In: Moon, I., Lee, Gyu M., Park, J., Kiritsis, D., von Cieminski, G. (eds.) APMS 2018. IAICT, vol. 536, pp. 417–421. Springer, Cham (2018). https://doi.org/10.1007/978-3-319-99707-0_52

6. Velosa, J.D., Cobo, L., Castillo, F., Castillo, C.: Methodological proposal for use of virtual reality VR and augmented reality AR in the formation of professional skills in industrial maintenance and industrial safety. In: Auer, M.E., Zutin, D.G. (eds.) Online Engineering & Internet of Things. LNNS, vol. 22, pp. 987–1000. Springer, Cham (2018). https://doi.org/10.1007/978-3-319-64352-6_92

7. Werrlich, S., Daniel, A., Ginger, A., Nguyen, P.A., Notni, G.: Comparing HMD-based and paper-based training. In: 2018 IEEE International Symposium on Mixed and Augmented Reality (ISMAR), pp. 134–142. IEEE (2018)

8. Andaluz, V.H., et al.: Multi-user industrial training and education environment. In: De Paolis, L.T., Bourdot, P. (eds.) AVR 2018. LNCS, vol. 10851, pp. 533–546. Springer, Cham (2018). https://doi.org/10.1007/978-3-319-95282-6_38

9. Ghandi, S., Masehian, E.: Review and taxonomies of assembly and disassembly path planning problems and approaches. Comput. Aided Des. **67–68**, 58–86 (2015)

10. Choi, S., Jung, K., Noh, S.D.: Virtual reality applications in manufacturing industries: past research, present findings, and future directions. Concurr. Eng. **23**(1), 40–63 (2015)

11. Daling, L., Abdelrazeq, A., Sauerborn, C., Hees, F.: A comparative study of augmented reality assistant tools in assembly. In: Ahram, T., Falcão, C. (eds.) AHFE 2019. AISC, vol. 972, pp. 755–767. Springer, Cham (2020). https://doi.org/10.1007/978-3-030-19135-1_74

12. Dede, C.J., Jacobson, J., Richards, J.: Introduction: virtual, augmented, and mixed realities in education. In: Liu, D., Dede, C., Huang, R., et al. (eds.) Virtual, Augmented, and Mixed Realities in Education, pp. 1–19. Springer, Singapore (2017). https://doi.org/10.1007/978-981-10-5490-7_1

13. Müller, B.C., et al.: Motion tracking applied in assembly for worker training in different locations. Procedia CIRP **48**, 460–465 (2016)

14. Guo, Q.: Learning in a mixed reality system in the context of Industrie 40. J. Tech. Educ. **3**(2), 92–115 (2015)

15. Milgram, P., Colquhoun, H.: A taxonomy of real and virtual world display integration. In: Ohta, Y., Tamura, H. (eds.) Mixed reality: Merging real and virtual worlds, pp. 5–30. Springer, Berlin (1999). https://doi.org/10.1007/978-3-319-08234-9_205-1

16. Azuma, R., Baillot, Y., Behringer, R., Feiner, S., Julier, S., MacIntyre, B.: Recent advances in augmented reality. IEEE Comput. Graph. Appl. **21**(6), 34–47 (2001)

17. Chicaiza, E.A., De la Cruz, E.I., Andaluz, V.H.: Augmented reality system for training and assistance in the management of industrial equipment and instruments. In: Bebis, G., et al. (eds.) ISVC 2018. LNCS, vol. 11241, pp. 675–686. Springer, Cham (2018). https://doi.org/10.1007/978-3-030-03801-4_59

18. Regenbrecht, H., et al.: An augmented virtuality approach to 3D videoconferencing. In: Proceedings of the 2nd IEEE/ACM International Symposium on Mixed and Augmented Reality, ISMAR 2003, pp. 290–291. IEEE, Washington (2003)

19. Ternier, S., Klemke, R., Kalz, M., Van Ulzen, P., Specht, M.: AR learn: augmented reality meets augmented virtuality. J. Univers. Comput. Sci. Technol. Learn. Phys. Virt. Spaces **18**(15), 2143–2164 (2012)

20. Normand, J.M., Servières, M., Moreau, G.: A new typology of augmented reality applications. In: Proceedings of the 3rd Augmented Human International Conference, AH 2012, pp. 1–8. ACM, New York (2012)

21. Paiva Guimarães, M., Dias, D.R.C., Mota, J.H., Gnecco, B.B., Durelli, V.H.S., Trevelin, L. C.: Immersive and interactive virtual reality applications based on 3D web browsers. Multimedia Tools Appl. **77**(1), 347–361 (2018)

22. Porras, A.P., Solis, C.R., Andaluz, V.H., Sánchez, J.S., Naranjo, C.A.: Virtual training system for an industrial pasteurization process. In: De Paolis, L.T., Bourdot, P. (eds.) AVR 2019. LNCS, vol. 11614, pp. 430–441. Springer, Cham (2019). https://doi.org/10.1007/978-3-030-25999-0_35

23. Milgram, P., Kishino, F.: A taxonomy of mixed reality visual displays. IEICE Trans. Inf. Syst. **E77-D**(12), 1321–1329 (1994)

24. Lindemann, R.W., Noma, H.: A classification scheme for multi-sensory augmented reality. In: Proceedings of the 2007 ACM Symposium on Virtual Reality Software and Technology, pp. 175–178. ACM, New York (2007)

25. Tönnies, M., Plecher, D.A.: Presentation Principles in Augmented Reality - Classification and Categorization Guidelines Version 1.0. Technical Report (TUM-I1111). Technische Universität München (2011)

26. Mackay, W.E.: Augmented reality: linking real and virtual worlds - a new paradigm for interacting with computers. In: Proceedings of AVI 1998, ACM Conference on Advanced Visual Interfaces AVI, pp. 13–21. ACM, New York (2000)

27. Ortiz, J.S., et al.: Teaching-Learning process through VR applied to automotive engineering. In: Proceedings of the 2017 9th International Conference on Education Technology and Computers, ICETC 2017, pp. 36–40. ACM, New York (2017)

28. Radkowski, R., Herrema, J., Oliver, J.: Augmented reality-based manual assembly support with visual features for different degrees of difficulty. Int. J. Hum.-Comput. Inter. **31**(5), 337–349 (2015)

29. Karrer, K., Glaser, C., Clemens, C., Bruder, C.: Technikaffinität erfassen–der Fragebogen TA-EG. In: Lichtenstein, A., Stößel, C., Clemens, C. (eds.) Der Mensch im Mittelpunkt technischer Systeme. 8. Berliner Werkstatt Mensch-Maschine-Systeme, ZMMS Spektrum, vol. 22, no. 29, pp. 196–201. VDI, Düsseldorf (2009)

30. Nielsen, J.: Enhancing the explanatory power of usability heuristics. In: Adelson, B., Dumais, S., Olson, J. (eds.) Proceedings of the SIGCHI Conference on Human Factors in Computing Systems, CHI 1994, pp. 152–158. ACM, New York (1994)

31. Beier, G.: Kontrollüberzeugungen im Umgang mit Technik. Rep. Psychol. **24**(9), 684–693 (1999)

32. Brooke, J.: SUS-A quick and dirty usability scale. In: Jordan, P.W., Thomas, B., Weerdmeester, B.A., McLelland, I.L. (eds.) Usability evaluation in industry, pp. 189–194. Taylor and Francis, London (1996)

33. Hart, S.G.: NASA-task load index (NASA-TLX): 20 Years Later. In: Proceedings of the Human Factors and Ergonomics Society 50th Annual Meeting, pp. 904–908. HFES, Santa Monica (2006)

AR Assisted Process Guidance System for Ship Block Fabrication

Jiahao Ding[1], Yu Zhu[2], Mingyu Luo[1], Minghua Zhu[2],
Xiumin Fan[1(✉)], and Zelin Zhou[2]

[1] School of Mechanical Engineering, Shanghai Jiao Tong University,
Shanghai 200240, China
xmfan@sjtu.edu.cn
[2] Jiangnan Institute of Technology, Jiangnan Shipyard (Group) Co., Ltd.,
Shanghai 201913, China

Abstract. The hull structure of the ship block is complex and the number of its constituted components is very large. In order to reduce the rework of the construction process, an augmented reality (AR) assisted information visualization and process guidance system is proposed. Based on the 3D model and the fabrication process of the ship block, a fabrication process information (FPI) model of the ship block is established for the augmented reality system. With the help of the Microsoft HoloLens, the human-computer interface is designed by defining gestures and voice commands. The prototype system is developed, and case study and user test are conducted to verify the effectiveness and feasibility of the system.

Keywords: Ship block fabrication · Process information modeling · Process guidance · Augmented reality

1 Introduction

Shipbuilding is a complex process involving three different operations: hull construction, outfitting and painting. In order to improve the level of design, construction and management, new technologies have been continuously introduced and applied by leading shipyards, thereby improving overall competitiveness. In modern shipbuilding mode, a ship is subdivided into several small sections or manufacturing units, which are called blocks, for separate fabrication. The subassemblies are assembled in the final assembly stage after the completion of the ship block fabrication [1]. On-block outfitting refers to the installation of various equipment, pipelines, cables and other outfits after the hull construction of a block is completed, in order to form a more complete assembly unit to shorten shipbuilding cycle.

While performing the on-block outfitting in the fabrication of a ship block, it is common that the structure of the assembly object is complex and the number of components to be assembled is large. The process is quite complicated and occupies a considerable proportion in the ship block fabrication cycle. The parts to be assembled are usually manufactured or prepared by the material supply department according to the construction plan before assembly and stored in the material warehouse, and are

© Springer Nature Switzerland AG 2020
J. Y. C. Chen and G. Fragomeni (Eds.): HCII 2020, LNCS 12191, pp. 66–79, 2020.
https://doi.org/10.1007/978-3-030-49698-2_5

packed and delivered to the assembly site when needed. At present, the installation of parts and components is mainly based on the experience of on-site operators, and there is no fixed assembly sequence. Traditional construction guidance methods are mostly based on paper documents or electronic tablets, which require repeated comparisons by operators, resulting in a low efficiency.

Augmented Reality technology [2] is derived from virtual reality technology and is an extension of VR technology. AR technology is a technology that supplements the user's perception of the real world with the help of computer, enabling people to accept a greater amount of information, so that they can make more accurate and rapid decisions or operations. Yin et al. [3] developed an assembly assistance and monitoring system using AR technology. Through assembly behavior recognition and assembly completeness inspection, visual guidance is automatically given to the operator without any interaction.

In the field of ships, scholars have carried out researches on ship design, ship construction, and ship maintenance based on AR technology. During the construction of the ship, due to welding deformation or assembly errors, there are often deviations between the actual installation dimensions and the design dimensions, which causes the components to fail to be installed normally. Olbrich et al. [4] designed a set of software and hardware tools for this problem. AR technology was used to visualize the design dimensions of the pipes, and online adjustment functions were provided to make the produced pipes conform to the actual installation dimensions. Morikawa et al. [5] developed a piping management system to improve work productivity by associating piping with related information through the use of markers. Lee et al. [6] designed a set of spraying simulation system based on AR technology, which can be used to train workers' spraying skills. Georgel et al. [7] used the "anchor plate" as the positioning reference, and superimposed the CAD model on the finished outfit for quality inspection to see if all the components have been correctly installed. Fraga-Lamas et al. [8–10] analyzed the application scenarios of industrial augmented reality (IAR) system in shipyards, such as quality control, material positioning, warehouse management, remote assistance, etc. after proposing the concept of IAR. By comparing the software and hardware parameters of different IAR systems, an augmented reality system architecture based on micro-cloud and fog computing was proposed, and the system was tested and evaluated at the actual shipbuilding site. The results showed that by combining two computing modes, the constructed augmented reality system architecture could provide lower latency response, which was meaningful for the development of real-time augmented reality applications in shipyards.

By introducing AR technology into the on-block outfitting process, quick inspection of CAD models and process data of assembly parts can be realized at the assembly site, which will greatly facilitate operators to intuitively compare 3D models and on-site objects, so that they can find out discrepancies in time to avoid rework and thereby improve assembly efficiency.

To solve the problems mentioned above, an AR assisted process guidance system is proposed. This paper focuses on the study of data interface files obtained from 3D modeling software and process planning software. Through data extraction and transformation, FPI model is built for AR assisted system. Human-computer interface is specially designed, so that on-site operators can fulfill assembly tasks by following the instructions given by the system and interact with it through gestures and voice commends with the help of Microsoft HoloLens.

2   Overall Scheme

The overall scheme of the AR assisted process guidance system proposed is shown in Fig. 1. The system provides ship block fabricating process guidance to operators, and the system includes some key components as ship block fabrication process modeling, real-virtual scene registration and user interaction and interface.

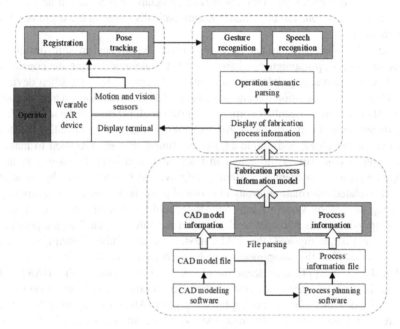

Fig. 1. Overall scheme of AR assisted process guidance system

In modern shipbuilding mode, the ship is usually modeled in 3D CAD modeling software. The 3D model of a ship block contains information such as hierarchy, geometry, and attributes. Also, it can be used for virtual verifications. Through path planning and assembly sequence planning, a reasonable assembly sequence can be obtained for each part of the ship block. In the process planning software, according to a certain assembly sequence and the process requirements of the ship construction, the process planning of the ship block fabrication can be formed at the design stage. By analyzing the data of the CAD model file and the process information file, the CAD model information and process information of the ship block can be obtained and integrated into the FPI model, which is used to describe the fabrication process of a ship block.

The use of a head-mounted display to provide operators with process guidance information has more practical application potential. Head-mounted displays can integrate motion, vision, and hearing sensors for human-computer interaction. Based on these sensors, the posture of the operator's head can be tracked and the user input can be captured. Through registration, a virtual 3D model of the ship block is superimposed on the real object.

The operator's gestures and voice commands are captured and recognized online. Human-computer interface is specially designed for better interaction. After analyzing the operation semantics, the process guidance information is displayed according to different assembly procedures.

3 Modeling of Fabrication Process Information

3.1 Information Extraction of CAD Model

A CAD model usually consists of elements that express the geometry of the model and the necessary text annotations. Each geometry element is associated with other elements to form a whole through pose constraints, as shown in Fig. 2. Information extraction includes extracting information such as part model hierarchy tree, part attributes, part geometry and so on.

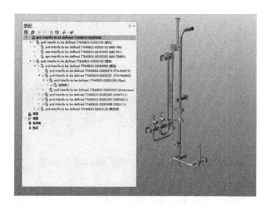

Fig. 2. CAD model of partial outfitting parts for a ship block

Analyze CAD data interface model file presented as STEP format. STEP is an open international standard that contains information such as product name, shape, and processing method. An example of the file is shown in Fig. 3. By analyzing the file in STEP format, attribute information of each part like "Part-Instance Name", "Part-Description", "Product-Part Number" and "Product-Description" are obtained, which includes the name, serial number, construction hours, construction requirements, etc. Because the STEP file cannot be used directly in the 3D virtual environment, it is converted into a model format file that can be imported into the 3D virtual environment, from which the part geometry and model hierarchy tree are extracted.

```
1   ISO-10303-21;
2   HEADER;
3   FILE_DESCRIPTION(('CATIA V6 STEP'),'2;1');
4
5   FILE_NAME('C:\\Users\\yangjun\\Desktop\\VRTest-ZZL\\sjtu-20190111.stp','2019-01-11T07:56
6
7   FILE_SCHEMA(('CONFIG_CONTROL_DESIGN'));
8
9   ENDSEC;
10  DATA;
11  #23=PRODUCT('sjtu','sjtu','',(#2)) ;
12  #61=PRODUCT('str','str','',(#2)) ;
13  #74=PRODUCT('\X2\52066BB5\X0\1','\X2\52066BB5\X0\1','',(#2)) ;
14  #87=PRODUCT('22-Deck1','22-Deck1','',(#2)) ;
15  #100=PRODUCT('222-SS1A-S13','222-SS1A-S13','',(#2)) ;
```

Fig. 3. Partial content of an example file in STEP format

3.2 Information Extraction of Fabrication Process

The 3DXML format file of the ship block is imported into the process planning software to generate process views. According to the operator's assembly experience or the calculated assembly sequence, a series of process views are made to illustrate the assembly process. In Fig. 4, the welding of pipe brackets on the ship's board is required in step one. Then, the installation of the pipe and valve in the middle part is completed in step two. In step three, another pipe and valve are installed.

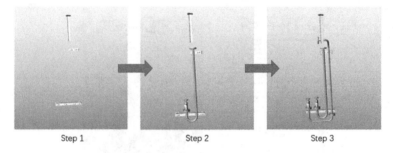

Step 1   Step 2   Step 3

Fig. 4. Sequential assembly of ship piping

The information to be extracted of the assembly process includes the operation, the name of the part displayed in each operation, and the transparency of the part. The SMGVIEW format file exported from the process planning software is indexed to extract process information. Each extracted view is ID numbered, and it is a unique retrieval flag for the process.

3.3 FPI Model of a Ship Block

As introduced above, CAD model information, including parts and their attributes, geometric shape, 3D annotation, and the part attributes like part name, part serial number, product descriptions, construction requirements and construction hours, can be obtained from the CAD modeling system through data interface. Using the same method, process information is also available. By integrating both CAD model information and fabrication process information, FPI model can be established and can be further used in AR assisted systems. The structure of FPI model is shown in Fig. 5.

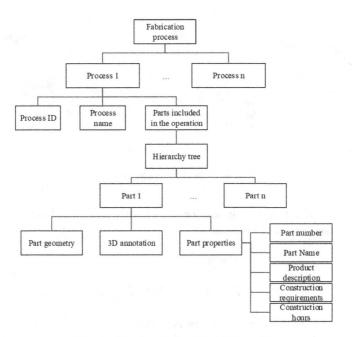

Fig. 5. Structure of proposed FPI model

4 Method for Virtual-Real Registration

In order to support operators to quickly locate the parts and intuitively compare the differences between the completed results and the design models, 3D CAD models need to be aligned with the actual object on work site.

The registration of the virtual model is carried out by means of markers, so the relative position relationship between the artificial markers and the background hull of the ship block needs to be determined in advance. In a real scene, artificial markers are placed in advance at appropriate positions near the real hull parts that need to be built to determine their relative position relationship with the real hull parts. In the designed system, P_{mar}^{Obj} indicates the coordinate of the virtual object in the marker coordinate system, which is set in advance. Simultaneous localization and mapping (SLAM) technology is used to update the 6D pose of the virtual camera relative to the real scene in real time, as shown in Fig. 6(a). When the HoloLens camera recognizes artificial markers in the real environment, the pose of artificial markers relative to the camera can be obtained through calculation (Fig. 6(b)), from which the pose of the artificial marker in the real scene can be calculated. Through the pose transformation matrix between the marker coordinate system and the real scene coordinate system, the pose of virtual model in the real scene can be obtained. After determining the pose of the virtual model in the marker coordinate system, the model can be superimposed on the real object to realize virtual and real registration, as shown in Fig. 6(c).

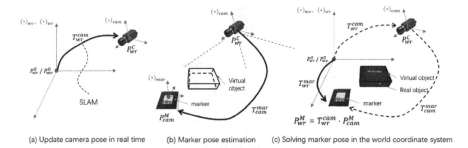

(a) Update camera pose in real time   (b) Marker pose estimation   (c) Solving marker pose in the world coordinate system

Fig. 6. Virtual-real registration

The coordinate transformation relationship of the virtual model between different coordinate systems can be expressed as:

$$P_{cam}^{Obj} = T_{cam}^{mar} \cdot P_{mar}^{Obj} \tag{1}$$

$$P_{wr}^{Obj} = T_{wr}^{cam} \cdot P_{cam}^{Obj} = T_{wr}^{cam} \cdot T_{cam}^{mar} \cdot P_{mar}^{Obj} \tag{2}$$

Where, T_{cam}^{mar} is the transformation matrix from the marker coordinate system to the camera coordinate system and can be calculated after the camera recognizes the marker; T_{wr}^{cam} is the transformation matrix from the camera coordinate system to the real scene coordinate system and can be obtained from HoloLens sensor data. P_{mar}^{Obj} is the coordinate of a virtual model in the artificial marker coordinate system and is set in advance as described above. P_{cam}^{Obj} is the coordinate of a virtual model in the camera coordinate system.

5   Design of Interaction and Display Scheme

The on-block outfitting is divided into several different processes, and the assembly is guided step by step through the selection of the processes. In each process, the operator can view the components that need to be installed in the current step, check whether the previous operation is completed, and preview the next operation. If the process number that needs to be operated is already known, operators can directly switch to the process. In addition, operators can quickly view the installed or uninstalled components by browsing the model hierarchy tree, without having to compare the complete objects with the design drawings one by one. The system provides the function of checking the attributes of parts, so that operators on site can quickly access the properties of the parts to be installed. With HoloLens, operators in the field can view process information through predefined gestures and voice commands. The user interface is designed to make the system easy to use and in line with the usage habits of field workers (Fig. 7).

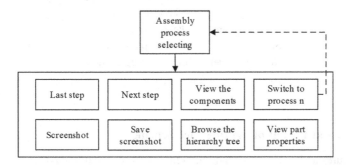

Fig. 7. Interactive reference functions of fabrication process information

5.1 Definition of Gestures and Voice Commands

Operators can interact with the proposed system through gestures. In the application, gesture state and the position of the hand can be recognized by HoloLens. Single click, double-tap, long-press, move, rotate and other operation gestures are defined. Specifically, the user can move the cursor to the button by turning the head, and then tap to click the button, thereby realizing functions such as view switching, screenshot saving, model registration, etc. In order to better view the 3D model, operators can move the cursor to a blank space, and then double-tap to show or hide the button panel. Also, operators can pinch and drag the hierarchy tree to a new position for quick comparison (Table 1).

Table 1. Defined operation gestures and corresponding functions

Operation gesture	Relative function
Single click	Click on the button to trigger the function
double-tap	Hide or show function panel
long-press	Continuously press the button
move	Move the function panel or virtual objects
rotate	Rotate a virtual object

Voice commands are also available. Table 2 lists several defined voice commands and their corresponding functions.

Table 2. Voice commands and corresponding functions

Voice command	Relative function
Next step	Go forward to next step
Last step	Go back to last step
Take a picture	Take a screenshot
Step one	Switch to process one
Register model	Virtual-real registration
…	…

5.2 Design and Layout of the Interface Scheme

Besides gestures and voice command, different interfaces are designed for users to view the different information.

Function Panel. Several buttons (as shown in Fig. 8(a), like last step, next step, screen shot, save the picture, show picture, model registration, position adjustment, show menu) are designed on the function panel. By clicking the button, operators can switch the process steps, capture and display mixed reality images and save them locally, users can perform virtual-real registration and manually adjust the model pose.

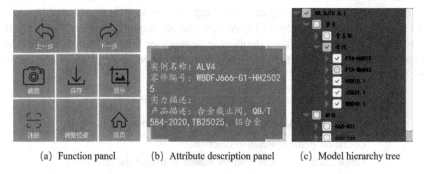

(a) Function panel   (b) Attribute description panel   (c) Model hierarchy tree

Fig. 8. Interface design for AR assisted assembly process guidance

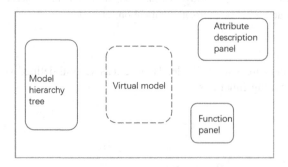

Fig. 9. Layout of the human-computer interface

Attribute Description Panel. The attribute description panel is used to display the attribute information of the component (Fig. 8(b)), operators can view the information such as the name, number, model, and material of the component.

Model Hierarchy Tree. The model hierarchy tree records the visibility of the current model components (Fig. 8(c)). Through the hierarchy tree, operators can check the current installation progress, quickly find missing components, and control the visibility of corresponding component models.

The layout of the interface is shown in Fig. 9. Where, the model hierarchy tree is fixed in the 3D space while the function panel moves with the user. The attribute description panel is fixed in the 2D screen.

6 Case Study and User Test

6.1 Preparation

There are a large number of parts and components in the on-block outfitting stage, and the installation order is not fixed. When the on-site operators perform the assembly operation, they install components based on past experience, which is prone to assembly interference. An assembly application scenario for on-block outfitting is prepared for this test. The assembly has a total of 18 iron cymbals, of which some pipes and valves have been installed, requiring operators to complete the assembly of the remaining three parts. Using the traditional method of checking drawings and comparing on-site assemblies, it would take approximately 434 s to finish the assembly operation according to the statistical data.

Before carrying out the test, the relative position of the artificial markers with respect to the background hull need to be determined (as shown in Fig. 10). After determining this relative relationship, the pose of the virtual model relative to the marker is written to the system through Unity editor.

Fig. 10. An assembly application scenario for on-block outfitting

According to the assembly experience of operators, the 3D CAD model file of the assembly is imported into Catia-Composer software to plan the assembly process, and then the process information file in format of SMGVIEW is exported. Through intermediate software, the 3D CAD model is converted into a 3D format file that can be imported into Unity software. After the two files are placed in the specific defined directory, the system is released to HoloLens via Unity, and then the system can run independently on HoloLens.

6.2   Application Test

First, the assembly 3D model is superimposed on the subassembly that has been partially assembled through virtual-real registration. Then, according to the planned process steps, operators check whether the installed components are installed correctly and follow the instructions of the system to complete the installation of the required parts. If the installed parts do not meet the design drawings, on-site operators can take a screenshot of mixed reality in the application and save it to the local computer for further processing, or adjust it on site to make the construction result meet the design model (Fig. 11).

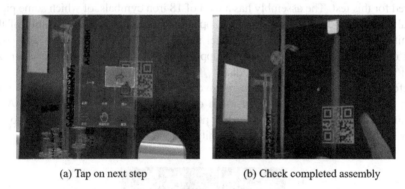

(a) Tap on next step   (b) Check completed assembly

Fig. 11.   Assembly guidance test of on-block outfitting

6.3   User Test

To verify the effectiveness of the system, six students without installation experience take the test. Before the test, all testers have received HoloLens training and are familiar with the operation of HoloLens. Starting from the first process, by comparing the 3D model registered in the space with the actual object on the site, each student first check if the assembled components are installed correctly and tried to find the components to be installed. Next, by checking the properties of the component to be installed, the student finds the corresponding component entity in the material tray. Finally, the student finishes the assembly by following the system instructions. The operating time of each student is recorded (Table 3).

Table 3. Time of assembly operation

Tester serial number	Assembly operation time
1	363 s
2	371 s
3	328 s
4	280 s
5	256 s
6	338 s
Average	323 s

It can be seen from the data that the average time for the tester to complete the assembly task under the guidance of the system wearing HoloLens is reduced by nearly 25.6% compared with the traditional method.

Questionnaires were designed to get all 6 students' experiences on system usage. Subjective evaluation of workers' workload was conducted using National Aeronautics and Space Administration-Task Loads Index (NASA-TLX) questionnaire. The statistical results show that the average workload index of the six students is 40.66. The main reason for the high workload index is that the task has a high physical requirement for the operator, and physical demand accounts for 34.4% of the total load. As can be seen from the figure, the degree of frustration has a small impact on the workload, and it can be speculated that the guidance of the system can effectively reduce the problems encountered by operators during assembly (Fig. 12).

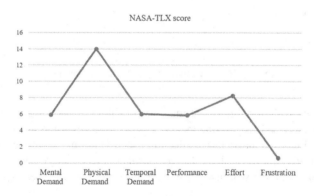

Fig. 12. Distribution of NASA-TLX scores

The questionnaire also raised 9 questions to obtain the operator's experience with the system. The nine questions are as follows (Table 4):

Table 4. Questions about user experience

Code	Question
Q1	HoloLens is very convenient to wear
Q2	HoloLens is very comfortable to wear
Q3	The system interface layout is very reasonable
Q4	The prompts given by the system are very intuitive
Q5	The tips given by the system are easy to understand
Q6	The tips given by the system are useful for task operation
Q7	I think this system works well
Q8	The field of view when wearing HoloLens for operation is not a major factor affecting the operation
Q9	I don't need to turn my head often during operation

The survey results are shown in the figure below (where a value of 1 indicates strong agreement and 5 indicates strong opposition) (Fig. 13).

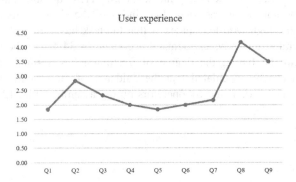

Fig. 13. Result of user experience questionnaire

It can be seen from the figure that the layout of the system is reasonable, and the prompts are intuitive and easy to understand. However, it can also be seen that the field of view of HoloLens is a major factor affecting user operations, which may cause users to turn their heads around to look for the virtual objects during the operation. In addition, wearing comfort will also have a certain impact on the user experience.

7 Conclusion

Aiming at the complex assembly problems in the on-block outfitting of ship block fabrication, a visual guidance system of fabrication process information for ship blocks based on augmented reality technology was introduced. This paper analyzes the CAD model file exported from the 3D modeling software and the process information file generated by the process planning software to establish an FPI model for the augmented reality system. The human-computer interface is specially designed by defining gestures and voice commands. With the help of Microsoft HoloLens, the proposed system can give step by step instructions on the fabrication process while 3D virtual models are superimposed on real objects. A case study was carried out to test the system feasibility and 6 students took the test. The results show that under the guidance of the proposed system, the assembly efficiency has increased by 25.6%. The results of the questionnaire indicate that the system is user-friendly but there is still room for improvement for the AR device.

Acknowledgement. The work is supported by the projects from China ((JCKY2017207A001) and (JCKY2017206B004)). The authors thank to the six students for their testing. And the authors are grateful to the editors and anonymous reviewers for their valuable comments.

References

1. Kim, D., Ko, K.H., Park, J.: Development of an AR based method for augmentation of 3D CAD data onto a real ship block image. Comput. Aided Des. **98**, 1–11 (2018)
2. Lukas, U.V.: Virtual and augmented reality in the maritime industry. In: Virtual Design and Automation: New Trends in Collaborative Product Design, pp. 193–201 (2006)
3. Yin, X., Fan, X., Zhu, W., Liu, R.: Synchronous AR assembly assistance and monitoring system based on ego-centric vision. Assembly Autom. **39**(1), (2018). https://doi.org/10.1108/AA-03-2017-032
4. Olbrich, M., Wuest, H., Riess, P., Bockholt, U.: Augmented reality pipe layout planning in the shipbuilding industry. In: 2011 10th IEEE International Symposium Mixed and Augmented Reality (ISMAR), pp. 26–29 (2011)
5. Morikawa, K., Ando, T.: Reduction of piping management person-hours through use of AR technology at shipbuilding sites. Fujitsu Sci. Tech. J. **55**(01), 20–26 (2019)
6. Lee, G.A., Jo, D., Yang, U., et al.: Virtual reality content-based training for spray painting tasks in the shipbuilding industry. ETRI J. **32**(5), 695–703 (2010)
7. Georgel, P., Schroeder, P., Benhimane, S., Hinterstoisser, S., Appel, M., Navab, N.: An industrial augmented reality solution for discrepancy check. In: Proceedings of the International Symposium on Mixed and Augmented Reality (ISMAR) (2007)
8. Fraga-Lamas, P., FernáNdez-Caramés, T.M., Blanco-Novoa, Ó., Vilar-Montesinos, M.A.: A review on industrial augmented reality systems for the industry 4.0 shipyard. In: IEEE Access, vol. 6, pp. 13358–13375 (2018). https://doi.org/10.1109/access.2018.2808326
9. Blanco-Novoa, Ó., Fernández-Caramés, T.M., Fraga-Lamas, P., Vilar-Montesinos, M.A.: A practical evaluation of commercial industrial augmented reality systems in an industry 4.0 shipyard. In: IEEE Access, vol. 6, pp. 8201–8218 (2018). https://doi.org/10.1109/access.2018.2802699
10. Fernández-Caramés, T.M., Fraga-Lamas, P., Suárez-Albela, M., Vilar-Montesinos, M.: A fog computing and cloudlet based augmented reality system for the industry 4.0 shipyard. Sensors (Basel) **18**(6), 1798 (2018). https://doi.org/10.3390/s18061798. PMID: 29865266; PMCID: PMC6022113

The Virtual Dressing Room: A Return Rate Study

Michael Boelstoft Holte[1,2,3(✉)]

[1] 3D Lab, University Hospital of Southern Denmark, Esbjerg, Denmark
Michael.Boelstoft.Holte@rsyd.dk
[2] Department of Oral and Maxillofacial Surgery,
University Hospital of Southern Denmark, Esbjerg, Denmark
[3] Department of Regional Health Science, University of Southern Denmark,
Esbjerg, Denmark

Abstract. This paper presents an evaluation of a virtual dressing room's impact on the return rate of garments purchased online. First, we introduce our recent developed prototype of a virtual dressing room. Next, we present the research and test design. This work involves a comparative study of the virtual dressing room with a traditional web shop and a real physical fitting room. Results show that, although the test participants (n = 75) preferred the real physical fitting room, the virtual dressing room showed significant (p = 0.003) better performance on delivering information on the shape/fit than the traditional web shop. While the virtual dressing room did not provide significant different performance over the web shop with respect to delivering information on the fabric, color nor size (p = 0.08), helping choosing the correct size and shape/fit were qualitatively addressed as the main advantages of the virtual dressing room. Wrong size and shape/fit were also found to be the two most important reasons for returning online purchases.

Keywords: Human-computer interaction, virtual reality, augmented reality, return rate, computer graphics, computer vision, pose estimation, gesture recognition, 3D imaging, 3D scanning · Textile industry

1 Introduction

A report shows that there is approximately a 25% return rate of the ordered goods in the online textile industry in Denmark. The reason for the returns at this moment can be speculated as, the garments do not fit the customers properly or the customers simply dislike the cloth when they actually wear it. As a result, there is an increase in the costs for the online retailers and dissatisfaction among the consumers [1–4]. The industry is beginning to recognize that new technologies like virtual reality and 3D camera-based systems have great potential to solve this problem. Hence, the virtual dressing room addresses this problem by enabling the consumers to, e.g., try the virtual version of garments on their virtual 3D avatar/profile before buying the real garments, from the convenience of their home computers, TV or hand-held devices.

© Springer Nature Switzerland AG 2020
J. Y. C. Chen and G. Fragomeni (Eds.): HCII 2020, LNCS 12191, pp. 80–90, 2020.
https://doi.org/10.1007/978-3-030-49698-2_6

1.1   Research Objective

An important aspect of a virtual dressing room is its impact on the return rate of online purchased garments, and its performance compared to traditional web shops and physical fitting rooms. Not much research has been conducted on the design and development of a virtual dressing room or virtual trying-on of garments [5]. Some solutions have been developed, e.g. [6, 7]. However, these are more commercial of nature, and do not address research related questions.

The objective of this work is to evaluate a virtual dressing room's impact on the return rate of purchased garments, and in which aspects (size, shape, color and fabric) a virtual dressing room can enhance the user's assessment of garments. The purpose of the evaluation is to analyze and discuss valuable quantitative and qualitative measurements and results for return rates in retail, and how these results can be used in a user-centered design and development of a virtual dressing room. Hence, the research is an attempt to answer the central question: how can virtual reality-based systems enhance the customer's shopping experience and assessment of garments, and thereby reduce the return rate?

1.2   Contributions

This work presents an evaluation of a virtual dressing room's impact on the return rate of purchased garments The work is targeted the human-computer interaction community, and in general for anyone with interest in interactive systems, human modeling, usability, user experience, user interaction design, virtual/augmented/mixed reality, computer graphics, computer vision etc. The contributions of this work are threefold: (1) we introduce our recent developed prototype of a state-of-the-art virtual dressing room. (2) We design a return rate test for evaluation of a virtual dressing room. (3) We conduct a return rate study to evaluate our prototype, and discuss the results with respect to the user-centered design and development of a virtual dressing room.

2   The Virtual Dressing Room

In this section we introduce our prototype of a virtual dressing room. The virtual dressing room solution can be divided into two modules: the front-end module consisting of the avatar solution, where the avatar is a close representation of the person's size and shape, targeted customers buying garments online, and the back-end module involving the 3D scanning of garments to produce digital clothing for the virtual dressing room, targeted the textile industry (see Fig. 1). This return rate study is solely based on the front-end consumer interface.

Fig. 1. The virtual dressing room prototype including the front-end interactive user interface and the back-end 3D cloth scanner.

2.1 The Front-End Avatar Solution

The front-end avatar solution consists of a user interface, where first the user's body shape is measured using a Microsoft Kinect sensor. These measurements are used to morph (adjust) the body shape and size of a predefined human model in real-time according to the actual body measurements of the user, which will become the user's avatar. Hence, the user can see an avatar, with their size and shape, and through movements captured with a Microsoft Kinect, recognize and accept this avatar as a reflection of them self. Next, the user will be able to select and try on a number of different garments using his/her avatar through a gesture-based natural user interface. Garments are applied to the model and optimized to avoid compenetration while following the body deformations. Because the avatars size and shape will be a close representation of their own, they will be able to see how the garments fit on them as a person.

2.2 The Back-End 3D Scanning of Garments

Garments are made digital by scanning real garment using a Microsoft Kinect sensor [8]. While creating digital clothing using specialized programs, e.g. Marvelous Designer 2 [9], is a time consuming process, the 3D scanning process is relatively fast. The model is acquired via registration of different views while rotating on a platform; a complete rotation is performed approximately in 60 s, however, we have achieved satisfactory results even with rotations of 15 s. The surface is textured using the RGB images acquired during the scanning process, and the color of the occluded parts is approximated via a K-Nearest Neighbors algorithm [8].

3   Return Rate Study Design

This work involves a comparative study of the virtual dressing room with a traditional web shop and a real physical fitting room. To study the impact of the developed prototype of a virtual dressing room on the return rate, we present a test design including quantitative and qualitative measurements of return rate related factors. This includes measurement of delivering information on the *size, shape/fit, color* and *fabric*, coupled with user demographics to investigate customer behavior patterns, resulting in the following questionnaire:

1. Gender.
2. Age.
3. Average annual income.
4. How frequent do you buy garments online during a year?
5. What were the reasons for returning your online purchases?
6. How well did the physical fitting room deliver information on the size?
7. How well did the web shop deliver information on the size?
8. How well did the virtual dressing room deliver information on the size?
9. How well did the physical fitting room deliver information on the shape/fit?
10. How well did the web shop deliver information on the shape/fit?
11. How well did the virtual dressing room deliver information on the shape/fit?
12. How well did the physical fitting room deliver information on the color?
13. How well did the web shop deliver information on the color?
14. How well did the virtual dressing room deliver information on the color?
15. How well did the physical fitting room deliver information on the fabric?
16. How well did the web shop deliver information on the fabric?
17. How well did the virtual dressing room deliver information on the fabric?
18. How was the experience of the virtual dressing room compared to the existing solutions?
19. Which one of the three setups for purchasing garments do you prefer (physical fitting room, web shop or virtual dressing room)?
20. Do you think the virtual dressing room can help decrease your return rate of online purchases over using a traditional web shop?
21. Do you think the virtual dressing room can help you select the desired garments for easier and faster real try-on?
22. Where would you prefer to use a virtual dressing room?

For question 6 – 18 we use a Likert scale ranging from 1 to 7, where 7 is the best score and 4 is the average score. For question 20–21, the test participants can select which of the four aspects (*size, shape/fit, color* and *fabric*) their answer is based on. Furthermore, we use interviews for detailed qualitative user statements and video observations.

Fig. 2. Test setup in the mall "Kolding Storcenter" in Denmark.

4 Experimental Results

The evaluation and data collection has been carried out in the mall "Kolding Stor-center" in Denmark. A total of 75 people took part in the experiment. The prototype was installed in a 4.5 m × 3 m black tent, which offers privacy and sufficient space for the user to move freely during virtual try-on of garments. The test setup can be seen in Fig. 1 and 2. The users where not restricted by time or number of virtual try-ons, but were given freedom to use and explore the system as they pleased while being video recorded. After, the users were asked to answer the questionnaire, and if interested, take part of a short interview.

55% of the 75 test participants were women and 45% men. The participants' age and annual income (note that the last 5% of the participants did not answer this question) can be seen in Fig. 3 and 4, respectively.

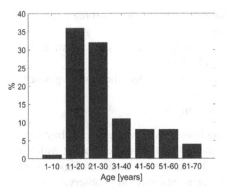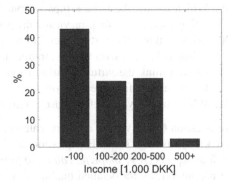

Fig. 3. The participants' age distribution.

Fig. 4. The participants' annual income distribution.

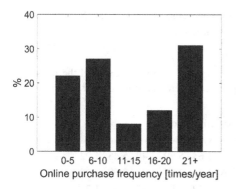

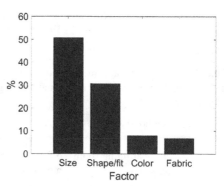

Fig. 5. The participants' annual frequency of online shopping of garments.

Fig. 6. Reasons for returning online purchases.

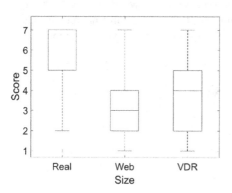

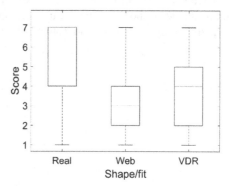

Fig. 7. Performance on delivering size info.

Fig. 8. Performance on delivering shape info.

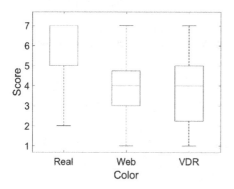

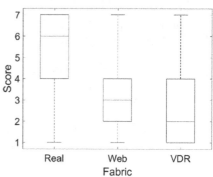

Fig. 9. Performance on delivering color info.

Fig. 10. Performance on delivering fabric info.

The participants' frequency of online purchases and their reasons for returning online purchases can be seen in Fig. 5 and 6, respectively.

Table 1. Means and standard deviations of the participants' scores on how well the physical fitting room, the web shop and the virtual dressing room delivered information on size, shape/fit, color and fabric.

Solution/Factor	Size		Shape/fit		Color		Fabric	
	$\bar{x}$	s	$\bar{x}$	s	$\bar{x}$	s	$\bar{x}$	s
Physical fitting room	5.83	1.63	5.76	1.64	5.79	1.49	5.45	1.92
Web shop	3.23	1.65	2.96	1.47	3.87	1.42	3.00	1.70
Virtual dressing room	3.81	1.76	3.83	1.72	3.82	1.67	2.81	1.71

Figure 7, 8, 9 and 10 show the participants' scores on how well the physical fitting room, the web shop and the virtual dressing room delivered information on size, shape/fit, color and fabric, and Table 1 shows the means and standard deviations.

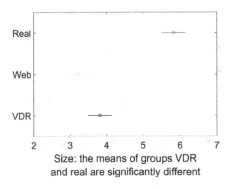

Size: the means of groups VDR
and real are significantly different

Fig. 11. Multiple comparison on the one-way ANOVA for delivering size info.

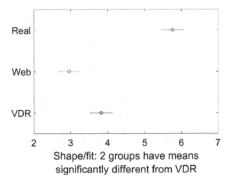

Shape/fit: 2 groups have means
significantly different from VDR

Fig. 12. Multiple comparison on the one-way ANOVA for delivering shape/fit info.

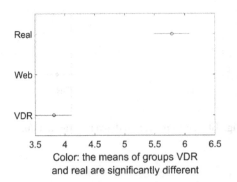

Color: the means of groups VDR
and real are significantly different

Fig. 13. Multiple comparison on the one-way ANOVA for delivering color info.

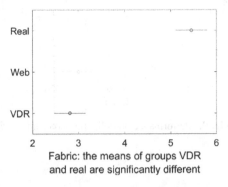

Fabric: the means of groups VDR
and real are significantly different

Fig. 14. Multiple comparison on the one-way ANOVA for delivering fabric info.

These results were tested for statistical significant differences with respect to the four aspects. Since the data fulfills the requirements of normality and homogeneous of variance, a parametric one-way ANOVA test followed by a multiple comparison using the one-way ANOVA results (to determine which estimates are significantly different) were selected for all four tests. The test results are visualized in Fig. 11, 12, 13 and 14 (VDR is an abbreviation for the Virtual Dressing Room), and show that the physical fitting room performs significantly better than the web shop and virtual dressing room in all four aspects. The virtual dressing room performs significantly better than the web shop when it comes to delivering information on the shape/fit (p = 0.003), while there are no significant difference between the virtual dressing room and the web shop in the three other aspects: size (p = 0.08), color (p = 0.98) and fabric (p = 0.80).

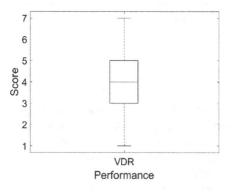

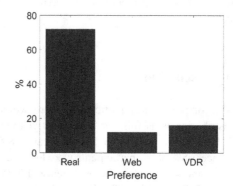

Fig. 15. The overall performance rating of the virtual dressing room.

Fig. 16. The preference of using the physical fitting room, web shop or virtual dressing room.

Figure 15 shows the test participants' overall rating of the experience of the virtual dressing room compared to the existing solutions. Resulting in a mean value, $\bar{x} = 4.29$, and standard deviation, $s = 1.61$. Figure 16 shows the participants' preference of using the physical fitting room, the web shop and the virtual dressing room. Figure 17 and 18 show the participants' opinion about, if that the virtual dressing room can help decrease their return rate of online purchases over using a traditional web shop, and can help them select the desired garments for easier and faster real try-on, respectively. Finally, it was found that 48% prefer to use a virtual dressing room at home, 13% in retail stores and 39% at both locations.

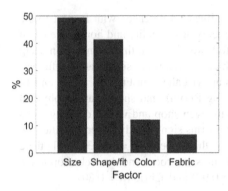
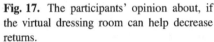

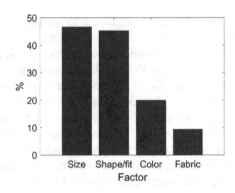

Fig. 17. The participants' opinion about, if the virtual dressing room can help decrease returns.

Fig. 18. The participants' opinion about, if the virtual dressing room can help select the desired garments for easier and faster real try-on.

5   Discussion

55% of the 75 test participants were women and 45% men. The participants' age distribution is as follows: 1% [1–10 years], 36% [11–20 years], 32% [21–30 years], 11% [31–40 years], 8% [41–50 years], 8% [51–60 years] and 4% [61–70 years]. Hence, 68% of the participants were teenagers and young adults in the age range of 11–30 years. 43% had an income below 100,000 DKK, 24% [100,000–200,000 DKK], 25% [200,000–500,000 DKK] and 3% above 500,000 DKK. 22% of the participants shop garments online [0–5 times a year], 27% [6 – 10 times a year], 8% [11–15 times a year], 12% [16 – 20 times a year] and 31% more than 20 times a year. The reasons for returning purchases were due to wrong size (51%), wrong shape/fit (31%), wrong color (8%) and wrong fabric (7%). Hence, wrong size or shape/fit were the two main reasons for returns.

The physical fitting room performed significantly better than the web shop and virtual dressing room in all four aspects, and 72% of the participants preferred to use the physical fitting room to the web shop and the virtual dressing room. However, the virtual dressing room performed significantly better than the web shop regarding delivering information on the shape/fit ($p = 0.003$), while there were no significant difference between the virtual dressing room and the web shop in the three other aspects: size ($p = 0.08$), color ($p = 0.98$) and fabric ($p = 0.80$). Although the difference in the performance of the virtual dressing room and the web shop on delivering size information was not significant, the difference in the means are noticeable. Furthermore, the qualitative measurements suggest that the participants found the virtual dressing room especially good at reducing the return rate and help them select the desired garments for easier and faster real try-on based on the size and the shape/fit. These also being the two most important reasons for returning their online purchases.

The feedback on why the virtual dressing room was lees effective at delivering information on the color was in general based on the quality of the 3D models of the garments, which were not found to be photorealistic. These results are also in line with a previous study evaluating the usability and user experience of the virtual dressing room [10]. The participants obviously could not feel the fabric in the virtual dressing room and the web shop in comparison to a realm physical fitting room, why the fabric ratings were lower.

Overall, the performance of the virtual dressing room was rated above average ($\bar{x} = 4.29$), and the participants preferred to use it a home or both at home and in the retail stores. Especially teenagers and young adults found the virtual dressing room of high interest, and showed sign of excitement. However, there is still need for improvements on all four aspects, to make the performance of the virtual dressing room come closer to the experience of the real physical try-on of garments.

6 Conclusion

This work presented an evaluation of a virtual dressing room's impact on the return rate of garments purchased online. First, we introduced our recent developed prototype of a virtual dressing room. Next, we presented the research and test design. This involved a comparative study of the virtual dressing room with a traditional web shop and a real physical fitting room. Results showed that, although the test participants (n = 75) preferred the real physical fitting room and it was rated highest in delivering information in all fours aspects: size, shape/fit, color and fabric, the virtual dressing room showed significant (p = 0.003) better performance on delivering information on the shape/fit than the traditional web shop. While the virtual dressing room did not provide significant different performance over the web shop with respect to delivering information on the fabric, color nor size (p = 0.08), helping choosing the correct size and shape/fit were qualitatively addressed as the main advantages of the virtual dressing room. Wrong size and shape/fit were also found to be the two most important reasons for returning online purchases.

Acknowledgements. The research leading to these results has received funding from The Danish National Advanced Technology Foundation under the research project "Virtual Dressing Room".

References

1. Schaupp, L.C., Belanger, F.: A conjoint analysis of online consumer satisfaction. J. Electron. Commer. Res. **6**(2), 95–111 (2005)
2. Hoffman, D.L., Novak, T.P., Peralta, M.: Building consumer trust online. Commun. ACM **42**(4), 80–85 (1999)
3. Lim, K.: Security and motivational factors of e-shopping web site usage. In: Proceedings of Decision Sciences Institute 2002 Annual Meeting. pp. 611–616 (2002)
4. Limayem, M., Khalifa, M., Frini, A.: What makes consumers buy from internet? A Longitudinal Study of Online Shopping **30**(4), 421–432 (2000)

5. Holte, Michael B.: The Virtual Dressing Room: A Perspective on Recent Developments. In: Shumaker, R. (ed.) VAMR 2013. LNCS, vol. 8022, pp. 241–250. Springer, Heidelberg (2013). https://doi.org/10.1007/978-3-642-39420-1_26
6. LazyLazy.com.http://lazylazy.com/en-DK/content/shoppingfeatures
7. Fitnect Interactive Kft., 2040 Budaörs, Hungary.http://www.fitnect.hu
8. Holte, M.B.: 3D Scanning of clothing using a rgb-d sensor with application in a virtual dressing room. In: Vincent G. Duffy (eds.) Advances in Applied Digital Human Modeling and Simulation: Proceedings of the AHFE 2016 International Conference on Digital Human Modeling and Simulation, Part III. pp. 143–153, Springer, Heidelberg (2016).https://doi.org/10.1007/978-3-319-41627-4_14
9. Marvelous Designer. Product.http://www.marvelousdesigner.com/marvelous/Default.aspx
10. HolteYiGao, Michael B., Petersson Brooks, E.: The Virtual Dressing Room: A Usability and User Experience Study. In: Shumaker, R., Lackey, S. (eds.) Virtual, Augmented and Mixed Reality, vol. 9179, pp. 429–437. Springer, Cham (2015). https://doi.org/10.1007/978-3-319-21067-4_44

A Context-Aware Assistance Framework for Implicit Interaction with an Augmented Human

Eva Lampen[1,2]([✉]) [ID], Jannes Lehwald[1] [ID], and Thies Pfeiffer[3] [ID]

[1] EvoBus GmbH, Neu-Ulm, Germany
eva.lampen@daimler.com, jannes.lehwald@daimler.com
[2] CITEC, Bielefeld University, Bielefeld, Germany
[3] Faculty of Technology, University of Applied Sciences Emden/Leer,
Emden, Germany
thies.pfeiffer@hs-emden-leer.de

Abstract. The automotive industry is currently facing massive challenges. Shorter product life cycles together with mass customization lead to a high complexity for manual assembly tasks. This induces the need for effective manual assembly assistances which guide the worker faultlessly through different assembly steps while simultaneously decrease their completion time and cognitive load. While in the literature a simulation-based assistance visualizing an augmented digital human was proposed, it lacks the ability to incorporate knowledge about the context of an assembly scenario through arbitrary sensor data. Within this paper, a general framework for the modular acquisition, interpretation and management of context is presented. Furthermore, a novel context-aware assistance application in augmented reality is introduced which enhances the previously proposed simulation-based assistance method by several context-aware features. Finally, a preliminary study ($N = 6$) is conducted to give a first insight into the effectiveness of context-awareness for the simulation-based assistance with respect to subjective perception criteria. The results suggest that the user experience is improved by context-awareness in general and the developed context-aware features were overall perceived as useful in terms of error, time and cognitive load reduction as well as motivational increase. However, the developed software architecture offers potential for improvement and future research considering performance parameters is mandatory.

Keywords: Augmented reality · Context-awareness · Human computer interaction · Assistance · Human simulation

1 Introduction

Context-aware assistance applications can be a promising possibility to cope with complexity or novelty of manual tasks. Due to the incorporation of environmental and personal knowledge, individualized instructions are tailored to

© Springer Nature Switzerland AG 2020
J. Y. C. Chen and G. Fragomeni (Eds.): HCII 2020, LNCS 12191, pp. 91–110, 2020.
https://doi.org/10.1007/978-3-030-49698-2_7

the specific needs and goals of the user and environmental requirements. There-fore, such assistance systems for manual tasks are widely investigated, indepen-dent of the specific domain [9,13,16]. With regard to the massive challenges the automotive industry is faced with, context-aware worker assistances gain importance. Shorter product life cycles together with mass customization lead to a high complexity for manual assembly tasks [11]. This induces the need for effective and ergonomic manual assembly assistances and manual assembly train-ings, which guide the worker faultlessly through different assembly steps while simultaneously, decrease their completion time and cognitive load. In particular, the relevance of augmented reality (AR) assistance methods increase, due to the possibility of real time interaction, the combination of the real environment with virtual objects and the spatial correct registration in 3D [2] with the potential for cognitive savings. Most context-aware assistance application methods are goal-[13] or attention-oriented [28] and therefore not presenting information about the way to solve the task, i.e. process-oriented [24]. Furthermore, mostly assis-tances are tailored to specific scenarios and not providing a general system for the development of context-aware assistances in different setups. Therefore, the adaption of those assistance systems and methods is not done in a large scale for the manual assembly, due to technical limitations [35]. While in the literature a simulation-based assistance, visualizing an augmented digital human during manual assembly tasks was proposed [24], it lacks on the one hand the ability to incorporate knowledge about context of the particular scenario through arbitrary sensor data besides spatial information, and on the other hand the extensibility and adaption of the system to other setups. Therefore, in this paper, besides the propose of a general framework for the development of context-aware assistances, the opportunities of the enrichment of context-awareness to a process-oriented human simulation based assembly assistance is subjectively investigated by a preliminary study.

2   Related Work

The developed assistance builds upon a large body of related work. In the follow-ing an overview concerning the related work of the encapsulation of simulation approaches and context-aware assistances during manual tasks is given.

2.1   Exchanging Simulation Approaches

The main idea behind exchangeable simulation approaches is to encapsulate specific behaviour of a complex system into several exchangeable standardized generic units. The general concept is derived from the Functional Mock-up Inter-face (FMI) [6] which is a standard utilized to simulate mechatronical components in a complex system such as vehicles. The proposed concept of encapsulated units was recently adapted to the domain of character animation. Hence, the Motion Model Interface (MMI) with the encapsulated Motion Model Units (MMUs) was presented [14]. By using encapsulated units together with a co-simulation process, various different character animation techniques and algorithms can be incorporated into a common system. For instance, for the simulation of a complex human movement separate MMUs for the modeling of different motion primitives, e.g. walk or grasp, can be combined so that a comprehensive human movement simulation is possible. The output can further be used as input for a human-simulation based assistance. Within this paper, the presented approach of encapsulated units is adapted for the interpretation of sensor data to context. Furthermore, the MMU approach has been utilized to generate the necessary movements of the displayed digital human.

2.2   Context-Aware Assistance

Since context-awareness is utilized to improve applications in different domains [13,16,19], the literature proposes various different definitions for the terms context-awareness and context. Due to the specific character of most definitions and consequently the hard applicability in multifaceted use-cases, the widely accepted context definition proposed by [1] is adopted. Within this definition there is no limitation of context with respect to specific parameters, but rather comprises any knowledge delineated the given status as context. Whereas, in terms of general context-awareness the authors [1] highlighted the importance of the user and the task to be performed, the dimensions of important context for assistances during manual tasks are extended to an environment model [7,10,20] and an interaction model [20,34]. Due to the variety of important context within the specific use-case of assistances during manual tasks, divers context-aware systems are developed and investigated. A wide range of assistances are developed in augmented reality (AR) and categorized as context-aware, due to the fact that AR applications are by definition context-aware, considering the spatial registration of AR content in the real world [15]. However, besides the spatial correct information presentation, there are more complex approaches, integrating algorithms and sensors for the utilization of additional context information and the associated adaption of the presented information. Within different work [5,23] system designs are presented, integrating motion recognition techniques to track body movements and thus, enabling implicit interaction with the systems by utilizing data from camera sensors. Thereby, context information with regard to the current task are concluded and an adaptive information presentation is ensured. Within experiments the developed systems are utilized and the potentials of different goal-oriented assistance methods are investigated [5,22]. Whereas the aforementioned systems are limited to context information derived by the capturing of body movement or object tracking, systems with additional user-centred functionality, e.g. by modeling the cognitive state of the user, are proposed [4,36]. Moreover, Westerfield et al. [36] proposed a modular system architecture to enable the possibility of an adaption to new task sequences, equally to [26,29]. Nevertheless, despite of the encapsulation of decision processes and the final visualization, the extensibility of the systems to integrate and utilize additionally context information is associated with great effort, due to the lack of a general context model. Furthermore, whereas mostly goal and attention-oriented assistance methods are enriched by context-awareness, a process-oriented human simulation-based assistance with the utilization of context information gathered by the Microsoft HoloLens for a step by step assistance was proposed [24]. However, other context-aware systems providing a process-oriented assistance with a digital human are mostly proposed as motor learning techniques in domains such as sport [9,19] and till now not adapted in assembly use-cases.

3   Context-Aware Assistance Framework

With regard to the presented related work, the main objective of this work is to develop a process-oriented context-aware assistance which enables implicit interaction with an augmented human. Therefore, a general encapsulated software architecture for the acquisition and management of context through the interpretation of sensor data is mandatory. Additionally, a base implementation of the framework is useful for the rapid modeling and development of context-aware assistance scenarios.

3.1   Overall Concept

To enable the general development of context-aware assistance systems, a novel concept for the standardized and encapsulated interpretation of sensor data to context, inspired by the presented related work, is proposed. In the following the context categorization of Hong et al. [21] is adopted. Hence, the data gathered by the sensors are further determined as preliminary context, whereas the term of interpreted context is defined as information deduced from preliminary context. Lastly, final context is the context integrated in a model and further sent to context-aware applications.

Context Interpretation Units. The integration of heterogeneous context sources is mandatory for a context-aware assistance. Only with various different sensor types the wide-ranging context of an assembly scenario can be gathered. To reuse developed context information independent of connected sensors within a common system, an encapsulation and standardization of this process is essential. To cope with the complexity of this task, the Context Interpretation Units (CIUs) were developed which have been highly inspired by the architecture and definition of the Motion Model Interface [14]. These units are generic black boxes, which use preliminary context from sensors and produce integrated context based on internal processing routines. By utilizing a suitable middleware technology the implementation of these standardized units are not restricted to one programming language or environment. For example, deep learning models created in Python as well as rule-based systems in C# can be utilized within the system simultaneously. Since these underlying processing mechanisms are not important for the overall framework, an encapsulation of recognition algorithms is consequently possible, if standardized input and output parameters as well as control signals are defined and known within the system (see Fig. 1).

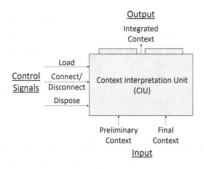

Fig. 1. Abstract illustration of the proposed Context Interpretation Unit (CIU).

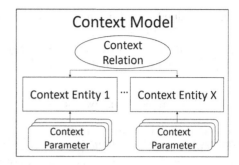

Fig. 2. Abstract illustration of the proposed context model.

Besides mandatory preliminary context by sensors, the input of final context can optionally be stated, since some sensor fusion or the actual recognition might be improved by context-awareness [32]. For example, the recognition of an object inside of a video might be improved, if the last position of it is known beforehand, due to a minimized search area. To control a CIU, independent of the actual implementation within the CIU, several control signals are mandatory. Before a CIU can start its recognition, it first has to load its dependencies and establish connections to the different source and target locations via the connect routine. If a CIU is not needed anymore, their connections can be closed using disconnect and any maintained resources are freed with dispose.

General Context Model. For the opportunity to infer higher-level knowledge, the derived information of the CIUs first has to be integrated into a given context model. To handle the various requirements of different context-aware assistance applications in manual task situations, the idea is to develop a general context model being capable of storing and providing divers context information to registered assistance applications. Therefore, the literature proposes a wide range of different context modeling approaches for a context information management [27]. However, the choice for an adequate approach depends on the specific use-case requirements. Considering the stated requirements of assistance systems for manual tasks an object-oriented approach was developed for the use-case of this work due to its encapsulation, reusability and inheritance functionality [33]. It further allows for complex modeling of relationships which is a huge advantage in the case of assistance systems. The presented approach consists of basic classes, here: context entities, characteristics, here: context parameters, and relations between individuals, here: context relations (see Fig. 2). A typical context entity could be the user itself, a sensor or a component needed for a given task. To further specify and describe a context entity, it can have an arbitrary amount of context parameters attached as attributes. According to the context atoms by [3], it incorporates a name, its value, the source, which detected its current value, and the time of the last detection. To allow the dealing with uncertainty a confidence value [0:1] is further added. In addition to context parameters, pairwise context entities can also be defined by context relations. With the possibility of the definition of context relations, real world relations between entities can be modeled (e.g. relationships between a carried object and the carrying user).

3.2 Technical Framework

The overall technical framework with its data flow, integrating the presented concepts of CIUs and the general context model, is shown in Fig. 3. As it can be seen the developed system consists of three different main parts, namely the context acquisition, the context management and the context-aware assistance application.

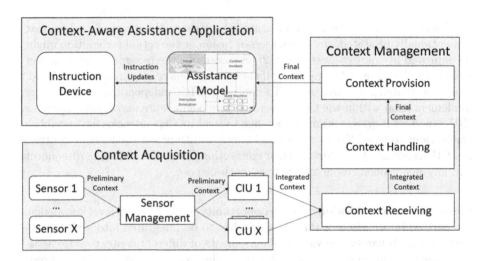

Fig. 3. Proposed software architecture of the context-aware assistance framework.

Context Acquisition. The integration and management of different sensor types, the transmission of preliminary and integrated context and the definition and function of CIUs are part of the overall context acquisition process.

First, the sensor management provides a Message Queue Telemetry Transport (MQTT) [17] broker so that the sensors can connect and deliver their measured preliminary context to it and subscribed clients. Such clients are the CIUs which can listen for distinctive data streams and process their data further; hence, various sensor types can be integrated. Second, the management of the connections is a crucial task of the sensor management. Whenever a sensor connects or disconnects due to failures, the sensor management is utilized to supervise these events and inform dependent processes.

To be able to control these CIUs some meta information about them is necessary for the framework, namely a general description of its behaviour and its input and output parameters. For the input and output parameters, the actual required sensor data and the defined integrated context parameters within the context model have to be known. For the description, a unique ID, the programming language of the unit as well as a dependency list and a confidence item have to be set. With every incoming input a new recognition is performed and the CIU decides whether an update is send. To have a uniform transmission format the updated values are provided by utilizing an integrated MQTT client and a JSON serialized version of the aforementioned context parameter. The incorporated sensors and CIUs in this work are implemented by using Unity 2018.3.2 and .NET Framework 4.6.1.

Context Management. The context management was designed in accordance with the proposed context server architecture by [8]. This enables the access of the modeled and interpreted context data for multiple applications and also moves often needed resource capacity for the context reasoning from the applications to the server. The context management architecture is further divided into three parts, namely the context receiving, context handling and context provision. The context receiving is on the one hand utilized to obtain integrated context of the CIUs by the provision of an MQTT broker endpoint, and on the other hand to manage the CIUs. For that, programming language dependent mediators inspired by the adapters in the MMU framework [14] have been developed which are able to start the CIUs of their language and connect them to their endpoints or disconnect and stop them respectively.

The context handling incorporates the integrated context gathered by the context receiving into a defined context model and processes it further through model related reasoning to higher-level final context. The interfaces for the items of the context model and reasoning were realized in C# (.NET Framework 4.6.1) and the actual base implementations of the classes were implemented within the Unity engine (Unity 2019.1.8) as scripting components. The reasoning interface contains a list of input context parameters and context relations. The base reasoning listens for context parameter changes but does nothing in case of an update. With this basic implementation, the development of sophisticated reasoning approaches based on rules, fuzzy-logic or machine learning should be possible. The usage of a game engine for the modeling and reasoning allows for the development of easy to use designing tools and the usage of GameObjects, their transforms and rendering leads to a better understanding of the overall scene relationships which is helpful especially for the designing of complex models. Relating thereto, since most manual task assistance applications addresses visual sensory modalities, the usage of a game engine has advantages.

After the evaluation of the higher-level context the resulting final context is send to registered assistance applications and CIUs as a serialized version of the updated parameters. The data is transferred by the integration of a MQTT broker of the context provision, likewise to the receiving.

Context-Aware Assistance Application. Similar to sensors, instruction devices have typically only a limited computation power so a client-server architecture via MQTT has been developed analogously to the sensor management. Therefore, the calculations of the process logic within the actual assistance is separated from the output device.

The assistance model receives the updated final context of the context management and includes the model logic of the context-aware assistance application. Respectively, it is responsible for the generation of the context-aware instructions. The assistance model is implemented with Unity 2019.1.8, and incorporates four core components, namely a state machine, scene model, context invokers and instruction generation. Whereas the states and transitions of the state machine are realized as scripting components which references can be set by the developer to certain instruction generation algorithms, the scene model is the actual Unity scene of the assistance. The scene model is updated by the output of the instruction generation algorithms. Hereafter, the resulting changes are send as instruction updates to the subscribed instruction device via MQTT as well as transferred as inputs to the context invokers. With the knowledge out of the updated scene model and the context management, predefined conditions within the context invokers can be evaluated and the state machine can be updated based on the obtained context-awareness. Depending on the assistance application, the instruction updates can be utilized to transfer any serializable object and information to subscribed listeners. Thus, with regard to the instruction updates no limitation considering the addressed stimulus modality of the instruction is given. The only requirements of the device are that it contains one or more MQTT clients which are connected to the broker of the assistance model and that routines are implemented to adapt their information output based on the information delivered by the instruction updates.

4   A Context-Aware Augmented Human Assistance

Besides the proposal of the general concept of an encapsulated architecture for context-aware assistances, the aim of this work is to apply the aforementioned architecture and develop an assistance which enables implicit interaction with an augmented human during the completion of manual tasks. Therefore, based on the underlying related work, we want to enhance the assistance approach presented by [24] due to the incorporation of knowledge derived by various sensors as well as the consideration of social interaction guidelines for the development of additional context-aware features. Therefore, the gap between context-awareness and process-oriented assistances for manual assembly use-cases is addressed.

4.1   Overall Implementation

The stated technical framework with its underlying concepts is utilized for the implementation of the context-aware augmented human assistance. The three main parts of the proposed framework are adapted to the specific requirements.

Context Acquisition. Considering the stated architecture of the context acquisition, two different types of sensors are exemplary connected within the context-aware augmented human assistance, namely the Microsoft Kinect 2 and the Microsoft HoloLens. Therefore, on the one hand, area observations enabled by the depth sensor data of the different Kinects [23] and on the other hand, positional and rotational tracking of the user by the inertial measurement unit data of the HoloLens are available. More precise, the related C# and Unity CIUs supply integrated context of the global position and rotation of the user within the Unity scene of the context model and furthermore, integrated context of changes in specified point of interests (POIs) within the context-model.

Context Management. To integrate the provided context information, the context management comprises the specific context model with its context entities, parameters and relations. Furthermore, adapters have been developed for the currently utilized Unity and C# CIUs. Within the Unity scene a true to scale reflection of the laboratory setup (see Fig. 6) is available. To go into detail, besides the CAD models, a sensor context entity was modeled for each connected sensor. Furthermore, for each POI a context parameter was modeled and added to its corresponding Kinect sensor entity. Similarly, for the position and rotation of the user a context parameter was added to the HoloLens sensor entity, as well as a context parameter of the related view frustum with the frustum quantities of the HoloLens. Moreover, for the matching of the context model to the real world an AR mapping entity was modeled. With the implementation of certain context reasoners higher level context can be utilized. For example, if the parameter of a POI of the rack changes and the user is near the POI a context relation between the user and the part related to the POI is updated.

Context-Aware Assistance Application. With regard to the context-aware assistance application of the technical framework an instruction device as well as the four belonging components of the assistance model are utilized and adapted to the needs of an augmented human assistance application. With regard to the suggestion of a hands-free usage during manual tasks [13], the head-mounted display (HMD) HoloLens is utilized as instruction device. Furthermore, to display an augmented human on the HoloLens an Universal Windows Platform application was created. The scene contains the same digital human and digital component objects as the assistance model. Using initially Vuforia 8.3.8 the position and rotation of an image target, are placed correctly in the real world by updating the AR mapping entity of the context model and therefore, the digital components overlap the real ones. First of all, to be able to assist a user, an assistance sequence has to be modeled utilizing the base implementation of the aforementioned state machine component. For the generation of the instruction, i.e. the movement of the augmented human, the modular MMU framework proposed by [14] is incorporated. Within each state of the state machine the simulation process of the subsequent human simulation data is started or stopped by the control signals passed to the MMU framework. Within the incorporation of the proposed MMU framework, the feasibility of MMUs with pre-captured or pre-simulated motion data, as well as model-driven and data-driven simulation approaches is given. As an output of the states the human simulation data, comprising the updated pose of the avatar and the manipulated digital components, are further incorporated into the scene model and send to the subscribed HoloLens. By utilizing the functionality of context invokers, context-aware features can be realized.

4.2   Context-Aware Features

With regard to social interaction guidelines in AR and by utilizing the stated implementations, implicit invoked context-aware features enhancing the assistance approach of [24] are realized. More precise, four features are integrated in the overall context-aware augmented human assistance, namely the visibility control, progress control, attention control and feedback control.

Visibility Control. A controllable parameter that can enhance the effect of the assistance, is the visibility of the task performed by the augmented human. On the one hand, it is important that the body of the avatar is not obscuring important information and on the other hand, it is important to reduce the discomfort of being inside the avatar's proximity as mentioned by [25]. Due to the updated context information of the user's position, derived by the HoloLens and the updated avatar's position, a predefined condition inside the context invoker can be evaluated at each frame. With consideration of the work on proxemics [18], the implicit visibility control is enabled (see Fig. 4). If the avatar is in the personal space of the user ($\leq$1.20 m), only the avatar's arms are visualized, whereas within the intimate space ($\leq$0.46 m), only the hands are displayed.

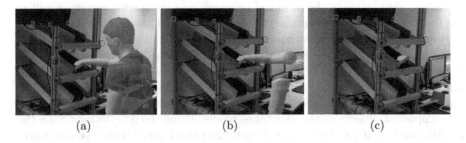

(a)   (b)   (c)

Fig. 4. Exemplary visualization of the proposed implicit visibility control feature that displays (a) the full body, (b) arms and hands and (c) only the hands of the augmented human.

Progress Control. The conformance between the speed of the assistance and the individual character of the user performing a manual task, considering mainly the speed, has an important impact on the assistance's outcome [13]. If the user is spatially or temporally far behind the augmented human, the possibility exists that the user misses important actions. Therefore, the context-aware feature of progress control is implemented, whereby the augmented human waits if the eventuality of information loss exists. A basic chapter functionality is enabled by the evaluation of the distance between the avatar's end position after locomotion tasks and the user's position. For manual tasks with an environment interaction, the provided final context of the observations of the POIs triggers the subsequent movement of the augmented human. Therefore, a more sophisticated chapter functionality besides the basic implementation is integrated.

Attention Control. An attention control feature is added, with regard to the limited field of view (FOV) of the AR device. To minimize searching movements, occurring because the FOV of the HMD might not be superimposed with the POI, pointing movements of the augmented human are implemented. For one thing, the attention guidance is triggered during walking tasks, when the user searches the augmented human and thus looks at a wrong direction, inferred by the final context of the HoloLens sensor entity (see Fig. 5(a)). During manual tasks with an environment interaction, attention guidance is enabled, if a manipulation of the environment at a wrong POI is detected by the Kinects (see Fig. 5(b)). Therefore, if a lack of orientation is recognized based on the aforementioned conditions, the attention control feature is invoked.

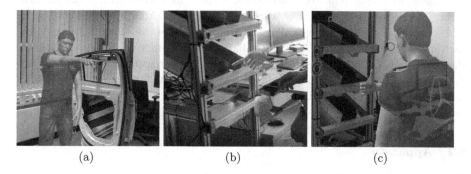

(a)   (b)   (c)

Fig. 5. Exemplary visualization of the proposed implicit (a) attention control during walking tasks, (b) attention control during manual tasks and (c) feedback control features.

Feedback Control. With respect to the guidelines of [13], the motivational state of the user is important regarding the assistance outcome. Thereby, the user's knowledge of the correct completion of the manual tasks with its subdivided chapters is important. As a result of the environment manipulation information derived by Kinects and the knowledge of the predefined task sequence the task completion condition can be evaluated. Via a thumbs-up gesture of the augmented human (see Fig. 5(c)) the user is aware of the completion of particular chapters.

5 Preliminary Study

Regarding the evaluation of the proposed context-aware augmented human assistance with the adaption of the general assistance framework, a preliminary study was conducted. Within the study we investigated the user experience and the subjective perception of the developed context-aware features in terms of time, error and cognitive load reduction, as well as motivational increase.

5.1 Experimental Design

A within-subject study design was utilized with one independent variable with two factor levels, i.e. the different assistance methods. As the baseline method the simple simulation-based assistance by [24] was used and compared against the presented context-aware adaptive simulation-based assistance. With respect to the comparability of the two methods and the definition of context-awareness in AR [15], the basic chapter functionality of the progress control evoked by the distance between the user and the avatar is utilized in all methods as a trigger for the subsequent task. Therefore, the simple simulation and the context-aware adaptive simulation differ respectively by one variable, i.e. context-awareness; whereby insights of the effects can be revealed. Three different manual task sequences, following real-world scenarios, were constructed during the experiment. The sequence of the tasks, each consisting of picking, carrying, plugging and screwing, were the same in all assistances to ensure the same complexity for each method. Furthermore, we counterbalanced the order of the factors across the participants. Besides the measurement of the user experience, obtained by the UEQ-S [31], the participants were asked to rate the four context-aware features in terms of error savings, time savings, cognitive savings and increased motivation.

5.2 Apparatus

For the experiment a laboratory door assembly setup was utilized, covering an environment of $6\,m \times 7\,m$ (see Fig. 6). In the setup, a start zone, picking zone, pre-assembly zone and assembly zone exist. Every zone, except the start zone is equipped with a Kinect. Both sides of the (pre-)assembly zones were used. The rack within the picking zone comprises eleven compartments. With regard to the AR information provision, we utilized a HoloLens as the instruction device for the assistance methods. On the basis of an increase of acceptance due to natural motions, only motion data captured with the XSens Motion Capture system [30], stored in MMUs are presented.

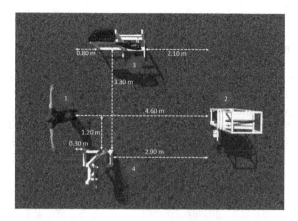

Fig. 6. The visualized constructed work station in Unity containing the start/end zone (1), picking zone (2), pre-assembly zone (3) and assembly zone (4).

5.3   Procedure

First of all, the participants were welcomed by the experimenter. Afterwards they had to sign a declaration of consent as well as complete a demographic questionnaire. Hereinafter, the course of the study was described. It was explained that the participants had to assemble three tasks with their subtasks while they are guided by a worker assistance in AR with the HMD. Moreover, the participants got used to the different questionnaires. To make the participants familiar with the assistance method and the hardware, they had to conduct a short test task. This test task was the same for both assistance methods. During this task all features of the different assistance methods were named and it was ensured, that all features were seen by the participants. After the fulfilment of the test task the participants were asked, whether they would like to repeat this task or start with the actual experiment. It was further clarified that no further questions can be answered during the main experiment. For the start of each of the three tasks the participants were asked to stay at the starting position and to look at the rack. The experimenter started the assistance method remotely as soon as the participants communicated their readiness. Afterwards, the UEQ-S had to be completed and the procedure was repeated with the next assistance method. At the end, the context-aware feature questionnaire was answered by the participants. Overall, the study took approximately 50 min.

5.4   Participants

Overall 6 participants, students and research engineers, took part in the within-subject experiment. The participants (2 female, 4 male) were aged between 24 and 29 ($M = 26.16$ years and $SD = 1.77$ years). Prior knowledge of the assembly tasks were not present for any participant. Furthermore, they did not get any extra rewards for their participation.

5.5   Results

A statistically comparison by considering M and SD of the two assistance methods was conducted for the resulting UEQ-S scores and the Likert scale ratings. Furthermore, for interference statistics the Shapiro-Wilk test as well as the Levene's test proved existences of normal distribution and variance homogeneity. Therefore, a paired sample t-test was utilized to test for significance. Finally the effect size with Pearson's r was quantified with 0.10 for a small, 0.30 for medium and 0.50 for large effects [12].

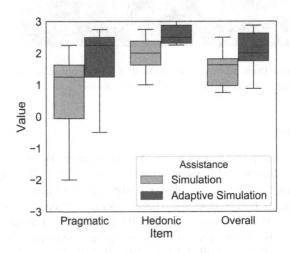

Fig. 7. Box-plot with the resulting pragmatic, hedonic and overall UEQ-S scores for the two assistance methods.

User Experience. For the user experience, the pragmatic and hedonic quality values together with the overall ratings of the methods are shown in Fig. 7. As can be seen, the adaptive simulation was rated to have the greatest pragmatic quality with $M = 1.71$ and $SD = 1.14$, greatest hedonic quality with $M = 2.38$ and $SD = 0.67$ and therefore the greatest overall quality with $M = 2.04$ and $SD = 0.68$. It is followed by the simulation approach which pragmatic quality was rated with $M = 0.67$ and $SD = 1.46$, hedonic quality with $M = 1.96$ and $SD = 0.58$ and overall quality with $M = 1.31$ and $SD = 0.96$. Furthermore, for the overall quality interference tests were conducted. The paired t-test proved that the results are not significant with $p \geq 0.05$ for all three quality values. However, a large effect size $(r_{pragmatic} = 0.98, r_{hedonic} = 0.57, r_{overall} = 0.90)$ can be observed.

Context-Aware Features Ranking. In Fig. 8 the results for the different context-aware features are visualized. As it can be seen, the progress control was perceived as the most useful in terms of error reduction with $M = 4.83$ and

SD = 0.37 (visibility control: 4.33 ± 1.11, attention control: 3.17 ± 1.86, feedback control: 3.17 ± 1.57). In comparison, in terms of time reduction the attention control with M = 4.33 and SD = 0.75 is rated as the most useful function (visibility control: 3.33 ± 1.11, progress control: 3.17 ± 1.07, feedback control: 2.33 ± 1.60). Furthermore, the cognitive load reduction was rated similar to the error reduction with the progress control functionality as the most useful with M = 4.50 and SD = 0.76 (attention control: 4.00 ± 1.41, visibility control: 3.50 ± 1.50, feedback control: 3.33 ± 1.49). On the other hand, the feedback gesture was rated as the most useful means to increase the motivation with M = 4.17 and SD = 0.90 (progress control: 3.67 ± 0.94, attention control: 3.17 ± 1.34, visibility control: 2.33 ± 1.37).

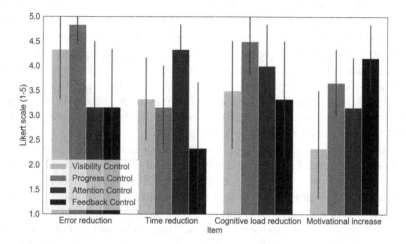

Fig. 8. Barplot with the resulting rankings (5 point Likert scale) of the implemented context-aware features with respect to the four evaluation criteria.

5.6   Discussion and Limitations

Considering the evaluation criteria, the descriptive results demonstrate that the context-aware adaptive simulation improved the user experience in comparison to the baseline method. Whereas both simulation approaches are perceived to have considerable high pragmatic, hedonic and overall quality, the results further suggest that the enrichment with contextual knowledge is an influencing factor with a large effect.

With respect to the underlying industrial use-case of assistance for manual assembly, especially the importance of the pragmatic quality should be taken into consideration. The positive pragmatic quality results could be explained by the perceived cognitive load. The less challenging a task is, due to cognitive load reduction by the assistance, the more practical this system might be with regard to performance parameters such as made errors and needed time. Considering the subjective rating, especially the progress and attention control lead to cognitive savings as well as error and time reduction.

The positive hedonic values for both assistances can be further explained by the participants familiarity with the respective assistance method. It can be assumed that the participants are familiar with situations of motor learning by observation in real-world scenarios, however not in augmented reality. Furthermore, current AR assistance methods mostly utilize small holograms, due to the restrictive FOV of AR devices, whereas the augmented human is normal sized with a body height of 1.75 m. Hence, the ranking of the attention control feature especially reveal positive effects with regard to the needed time and cognitive load savings due to a decrease of searching movements. Therefore, the results suggest, that the context-awareness is especially beneficial with regard to the small FOV of current AR HMDs. Nevertheless, further investigations of the influence of the FOV associated with the context-aware features are crucial.

With regard to the implemented context-aware features, especially the visibility control feature appeared as very helpful during the experiment, due to the fact that for the simple simulation method some participants walked around the avatar instead of stepping inside and therefore missed some information. This effect of the visibility feature can be illustrated by taking the ranking for the error reduction into account. Future research with an objective measured quantity is mandatory to verify the assumption.

Overall the subjective ranking of the features demonstrate in particular the effectiveness with regard to error and cognitive load reduction, whereas the time reduction is only rated above 3.5 for the attention feature. Thereupon, it can be inferred that the presented context-aware assistance with its implemented features take effect especially in learning situations or complex situations, where the need of free attention capacity exists and time saving is less important than faultlessness. However, with the possibility of extensibility and adaptability of the proposed system architecture, other features with the aim of time saving could lead to other results. Summarized, the integration of specific context-aware features depends on the particular requirements of the use-case.

Generally, with respect to the results, the preliminary study indicates that within a laboratory setting an process-oriented simulation-based assistance approach can be enhanced by the enrichment of contextual knowledge with regard to subjective perception. However the results should be verified within a user study with a respective number of participants and the consideration of performance criteria, so that significant results can be revealed. But with the study it was shown, that the overall architecture can be used for context-aware assistance systems in a stable and effective way. During the entire experiment a steady information presentation was given. Furthermore, the proposed overall system architecture was used for both assistance methods, utilizing a different quantity of context information. Altogether, the adjustability of the overall system is given. However, the developed software architecture should be evaluated with the integration of more sensors and more complex context interpretation algorithms. Moreover, the framework offers potential for improvement considering the strong dependencies between the assistance model and the instruction device.

6   Conclusion and Future Work

Based on previous work, the main objectives of this paper was to enhance a simulation-based assistance by incorporating contextual knowledge from sensors. For that, a concept and subsequent implementation of a general context-aware assistance framework was presented. This system facilitates the modular interpretation of sensor data and encapsulates the actual assistance application from the context acquisition and management with the result of a faster development of context-aware assistances, incorporating contextual and virtual scene information. Utilizing the proposed architecture, the previously proposed process-oriented simulation-based assistance was enhanced. The approach is able to adapt its simulation scheme with several context aware features, enabling an implicit control of the visualized augmented human. Therefore, the proposed system in general addresses the open gap between process-oriented assistances and the enrichment of context-awareness.

Within a preliminary study the effect of the developed assistance method with its context-aware features was evaluated subjectively in comparison to the baseline simulation. While no significant results could be measured, probably due to the small amount of participants, the effect size is revealed as large and the results therefore suggest a general validity. Considering the results, it can be seen that the user experience of the adaptive simulation method is rated higher than the baseline simulation. The context-aware features of the adaptive simulation method have an impact especially on the pragmatic value, which is an important factor for assistances and also might have an impact on the perceived cognitive load. Furthermore, the context-aware features were overall perceived as useful in terms of error, time and cognitive load reduction as well as motivational increase. Nonetheless, the proposed approach enhances the baseline simulation-based assistance only subjectively. A user study with more participants and the consideration of performance criteria is mandatory so that the measurable effects of the adaptive simulation can be quantified. Additionally, the proposed concepts, software architecture and implemented assistance have still the potential for improvement. Firstly, the context interpretation units are currently limited to the utilized context information and sensors of this work. By incorporating different sensors and implementing algorithms to interpret their data, other context information could be acquired and consequently additional context-aware features could be created and evaluated for an effective adaptive simulation-based assistance. Secondly, in this work only one context-aware assistance application was running at the same time, due to a close connection as one-to-one relationship between acquired context and utilized assistance application. This connection might be encapsulated by a modular structure for assistance applications through appropriate models and exchangeable data formats. Thus, several other assistances could be easily integrated into the system and started simultaneously, so that a more holistic guiding of a worker is possible.

Acknowledgments. The authors acknowledge the financial support by the Federal Ministry of Education and Research of Germany (MOSIM project, grant no. 01IS18060A-H).

References

1. Abowd, G.D., Dey, A.K., Brown, P.J., Davies, N., Smith, M., Steggles, P.: Towards a better understanding of context and context-awareness. In: Gellersen, H.-W. (ed.) HUC 1999. LNCS, vol. 1707, pp. 304–307. Springer, Heidelberg (1999). https://doi.org/10.1007/3-540-48157-5_29
2. Azuma, R.T.: A survey of augmented reality. Presence Teleoperators Virtual Environ. **6**(4), 355–385 (1997). https://doi.org/10.1162/pres.1997.6.4.355
3. Baldauf, M., Dustdar, S., Rosenberg, F.: A survey on context-aware systems. Int. J. Ad Hoc Ubiquit. Comput. **2**(4), 263–277 (2007). https://doi.org/10.1504/IJAHUC.2007.014070
4. Bannat, A., et al.: Towards optimal worker assistance: a framework for adaptive selection and presentation of assembly instructions. In: 2008 1st International Cotesys Workshop, p. 7 (2008)
5. Bannat, A., Gast, J., Rigoll, G., Wallhoff, F.: Event analysis and interpretation of human activity for augmented reality-based assistant systems. In: 2008 4th International Conference on Intelligent Computer Communication and Processing, pp. 1–8. IEEE, Cluj-Napoca (2008). https://doi.org/10.1109/ICCP.2008.4648347
6. Blochwitz, T., et al.: Functional mockup interface 2.0: the standard for tool independent exchange of simulation models. In: Proceedings of the 9th International MODELICA Conference, pp. 173–184. The Modelica Association (2012)
7. Bubb, H., Müller, H., Schubö, A., Rigoll, G., Wallhoff, F., Zäh, M.F.: CoTeSys progress report 2008: ACIPE - adaptive cognitive interaction in production environments (2008)
8. Chen, H.: An intelligent broker architecture for pervasive context-aware systems. Ph.D. thesis, University of Maryland, Baltimore County (2004)
9. Chen, X., et al.: ImmerTai: immersive motion learning in VR environments. J. Vis. Commun. Image Represent. **58**, 416–427 (2019). https://doi.org/10.1016/j.jvcir.2018.11.039
10. Doerr, K., Arreola-Risa, A.: A worker-based approach for modeling variability in task completion times. IIE Trans. **32**, 625–636 (2000). https://doi.org/10.1023/A:1007659032655
11. ElMaraghy, W., ElMaraghy, H., Tomiyama, T., Monostori, L.: Complexity in engineering design and manufacturing. CIRP Ann. **61**(2), 793–814 (2012). https://doi.org/10.1016/j.cirp.2012.05.001
12. Field, A., Hole, G.: How to Design and Report Experiments, reprint edn. Sage, Los Angeles (2013)
13. Funk, M., Kosch, T., Kettner, R., Korn, O., Schmidt, A.: motionEAP: an overview of 4 years of combining industrial assembly with augmented reality for industry 4.0. In: Proceedings of the 16th International Conference on Knowledge Technologies and Data-Driven Business, pp. 1–4 (2016)
14. Gaisbauer, F., Lampen, E., Agethen, P., Rukzio, E.: Combining heterogeneous digital human simulations: presenting a novel co-simulation approach for incorporating different character animation technologies. Vis. Comput. (2020). https://doi.org/10.1007/s00371-020-01792-x

15. Grubert, J., Langlotz, T., Zollmann, S., Regenbrecht, H.: Towards pervasive augmented reality: context-awareness in augmented reality. IEEE Trans. Vis. Comput. Graph. **23**(6), 1706–1724 (2017). https://doi.org/10.1109/TVCG.2016.2543720

16. Gámez-Romero, J., Serrano, M.A., García, J., Molina, J.M., Rogova, G.: Context-based multi-level information fusion for harbor surveillance. Inf. Fusion **21**, 173–186 (2015). https://doi.org/10.1016/j.inffus.2014.01.011

17. Gündoğran, C., Kietzmann, P., Lenders, M., Petersen, H., Schmidt, T.C., Wählisch, M.: NDN, CoAP, and MQTT: a comparative measurement study in the IoT. In: Proceedings of the 5th ACM Conference on Information-Centric Networking, ICN 2018, pp. 159–171. ACM Press, Boston (2018). https://doi.org/10.1145/3267955.3267967

18. Hall, E.T.: The Hidden Dimension: Man's Use of Space in Public and Private. Bodley Head, London (1969)

19. Han, P.H., Chen, K.W., Hsieh, C.H., Huang, Y.J., Hung, Y.P.: AR-Arm: augmented visualization for guiding arm movement in the first-person perspective. In: Proceedings of the 7th Augmented Human International Conference 2016, AH 2016, pp. 1–4. ACM Press, Geneva (2016). https://doi.org/10.1145/2875194.2875237

20. Hinrichsen, S., Riediger, D., Unrau, A.: Assistance systems in manual assembly. In: Production Engineering and Management, Lemgo (2016)

21. Hong, D., Schmidtke, H.R., Woo, W.: Linking context modelling and contextual reasoning. In: 4th International Workshop on Modeling and Reasoning in Context, pp. 37–48 (2007)

22. Korn, O., Schmidt, A., Hörz, T.: The potentials of in-situ-projection for augmented workplaces in production: a study with impaired persons. In: Proceedings of the Conference on Human Factors in Computing Systems, CHI 2013, p. 6 (2013)

23. Korn, O., Schmidt, A., Hörz, T., Kaupp, D.: Assistive system experiment designer ASED: a toolkit for the quantitative evaluation of enhanced assistive systems for impaired persons in production. In: Proceedings of the 14th International ACM SIGACCESS Conference on Computers and Accessibility, ASSETS 2012, p. 259. ACM Press, Boulder (2012). https://doi.org/10.1145/2384916.2384982

24. Lampen, E., Teuber, J., Gaisbauer, F., Bär, T., Pfeiffer, T., Wachsmuth, S.: Combining simulation and augmented reality methods for enhanced worker assistance in manual assembly. Procedia CIRP **81**, 588–593 (2019). https://doi.org/10.1016/j.procir.2019.03.160

25. Miller, M.R., Jun, H., Herrera, F., Villa, J.Y., Welch, G., Bailenson, J.N.: Social interaction in augmented reality. PLoS ONE **14**(5), e0216290 (2019). https://doi.org/10.1371/journal.pone.0216290

26. Mura, M.D., Dini, G., Failli, F.: An integrated environment based on augmented reality and sensing device for manual assembly workstations. Procedia CIRP **41**, 340–345 (2016). https://doi.org/10.1016/j.procir.2015.12.128

27. Perera, C., Zaslavsky, A., Christen, P., Georgakopoulos, D.: Context aware computing for the Internet of Things: a survey. IEEE Commun. Surv. Tutor. **16**(1), 414–454 (2014). https://doi.org/10.1109/SURV.2013.042313.00197. arXiv: 1305.0982

28. Renner, P., Pfeiffer, T.: Evaluation of attention guiding techniques for augmented reality-based assistance in picking and assembly tasks. In: Proceedings of the 22nd International Conference on Intelligent User Interfaces Companion, IUI 2017 Companion, pp. 89–92. ACM Press, Limassol (2017). https://doi.org/10.1145/3030024.3040987

29. Rodriguez, L., Quint, F., Gorecky, D., Romero, D., Siller, H.R.: Developing a mixed reality assistance system based on projection mapping technology for manual operations at assembly workstations. Procedia Comput. Sci. **75**, 327–333 (2015). https://doi.org/10.1016/j.procs.2015.12.254
30. Schepers, M., Giuberti, M., Bellusci, G.: Xsens MVN: consistent tracking of human motion using inertial sensing (2018). Unpublished. https://doi.org/10.13140/rg.2.2.22099.07205
31. Schrepp, M., Hinderks, A., Thomaschewski, J.: Design and evaluation of a short version of the user experience questionnaire (UEQ-S). Int. J. Interact. Multimed. Artif. Intell. **4**(6), 103 (2017). https://doi.org/10.9781/ijimai.2017.09.001
32. Snidaro, L., García, J., Llinas, J.: Context-based information fusion: a survey and discussion. Inf. Fusion **25**, 16–31 (2015). https://doi.org/10.1016/j.inffus.2015.01.002
33. Strang, T., Linnhoff-Popien, C.: A context modeling survey. In: Workshop Proceedings, Nottingham, UK, pp. 34–41 (2004)
34. Sweller, J., van Merrienboer, J.J.G., Paas, F.G.W.C.: Cognitive architecture and instructional design. Educ. Psychol. Rev. **10**(3), 251–296 (1998). https://doi.org/10.1023/A:1022193728205
35. Syberfeldt, A., Danielsson, O., Holm, M., Wang, L.: Visual assembling guidance using augmented reality. Procedia Manuf. **1**, 98–109 (2015). https://doi.org/10.1016/j.promfg.2015.09.068
36. Westerfeldt, G., Mitrovic, A., Billinghurst, M.: Intelligent augmented reality training for motherboard assembly. Int. J. Artif. Intell. Educ. **25**(1), 157–172 (2014). https://doi.org/10.1007/s40593-014-0032-x

A Literature Review of AR-Based Remote Guidance Tasks with User Studies

Jean-François Lapointe[1]([⊠]) [iD], Heather Molyneaux[1] [iD],
and Mohand Saïd Allili[2]

[1] National Research Council of Canada, Ottawa, Canada
{jean-francois.lapointe,
heather.molyneaux}@nrc-cnrc.gc.ca
[2] University of Quebec in Outaouais, Gatineau, Canada
mohandsaid.allili@uqo.ca

Abstract. The future of work is increasingly mobile and distributed across space and time. Institutions and individuals are phasing out desktops in favor of laptops, tablets and/or smart phones as much work (assessment, technical support, etc.) is done in the field and not at a desk. There will be a need for systems that support remote collaborations such as remote guidance. Augmented reality (AR) is praised for its ability to show the task at hand within an immersive environment, allowing for spatial clarity and greater efficiency, thereby showing great promise for collaborative and remote guidance tasks; however, there are no systematic reviews of AR based remote guidance systems. This paper reviews the literature describing AR-based remote guidance tasks and discusses the task settings, technical requirements and user groups within the literature, followed by a discussion of further areas of interest for the application of this technology combined with artificial intelligence (AI) algorithms to increase the efficiency of applied tasks.

Keywords: Remote guidance · Augmented reality · Artificial intelligence

1 Introduction

The future of work is increasingly mobile and distributed across space and time. Institutions and individuals are phasing out desktops in favor of laptops, tablets, smart phones and/or other mobile digital devices as much work (assessment, technical support etc.) is done in the field and not at a desk. In situations where the assessment, repair or maintenance of a system requires specific expertise, an expert in the field is usually flown in to accomplish the task. This way of doing thing can be costly given the time and money required to travel to the site, thus resulting in reduced productivity.

The advent of mobile augmented reality (AR)-capable digital devices, along with wireless communication networks and artificial intelligence, paves the way to a radical change in work environments. By combining these technologies, we could ask a local novice worker to complete complex tasks under guidance of a remote expert helper who can be located anywhere. This way of doing thing will significantly increase the productivity and/or reduce the cost and response time related to such interventions.

© NRC Canada 2020
J. Y. C. Chen and G. Fragomeni (Eds.): HCII 2020, LNCS 12191, pp. 111–120, 2020.
https://doi.org/10.1007/978-3-030-49698-2_8

This paper reviews the literature describing AR-based remote guidance tasks and discusses the task settings, technical requirements and user groups within the literature, followed by a discussion of further areas of interest for AR researchers. It will also discuss possibilities of integrating AI tools such as deep leaning for enhancing the efficiency and accuracy of AR-based remote guidance. AR is a system whereby the real environment is combined with a virtual environment, created digitally, and is inter-active in real time. Unlike virtual reality where the environment is entirely rendered, AR enhances the real world by adding virtual information and also could include applications that can remove real objects [1].

The immersive qualities of AR show great promise for increased spatial clarity and greater efficiency for remote guidance tasks; however, we found no systematic review of academic literature examining the use of AR for such tasks. This paper provides a literature review of remote guidance tasks with user studies, followed by information on typical scenarios whereby AR for remote guidance could be used, as well as a discussion on future areas of interest for researchers. This paper finally discuss about various possibilities offered by the combination of AR and AI technologies to create some automation in the process in order to increase the effectiveness of current AR-based remote guidance tasks in concrete scenarios such as those faced by first responders [2–5].

1.1 Augmented Reality

The concept of AR has been studied for some time now [6–8] and sits somewhere in the middle of the virtuality continuum [9]. AR is created through the use of physical display devices which can include: fixed devices (tabletop, window); handheld devices (HHD) (phones/tablets) [1]; head-worn devices (HWD) (either optical see through transparent display or video see through opaque display); and projection-based display (PJD) (whereby videos are projected onto objects to be augmented) [10]. Also, other optical devices such as microscopes can benefit from AR [11].

1.2 Remote Guidance

Remote guidance (a.k.a. remote assistance [12], remote coaching [13] or tele-guidance [14]) is a collaboration scenario involving a remote helper guiding in real time a local worker in performing a task on physical objects [15]. Remote guidance can be used by first responders as well as in various fields ranging from medicine, to mining to manufacturing [15]. Remote guidance tasks are typical use cases for AR applications. These tasks can be done via augmented visual instructions with audio either prere-corded [13] or live, coming from a human expert or generated through artificial intelligence [11]. Visual instructions can vary – from directional arrows or lines, shapes, varying colors, virtual hands or other virtual markers for better understanding of the relationship of objects to the environment [13, 15, 16]. The goal is to harness both human and AI capabilities to identify objects and people (for example through object or face recognition) in order to generate virtual content that best fit the real scene and optimize the guidance process.

These types of visual instructions could be applied: to remote guidance for monitoring, assembly [17]; maintenance of equipment in factories [17]; remote guidance for the medical evaluation and intervention on a patient [18]; or remote guidance for disaster damage assessment and fighting for first responders. In the latter case, the technology can be coupled with visual inspection by drones [19] that are remotely guided and extract specific information of interest that can be shared live with the various parties (in-field first responders as well as command and control centers), to maximize the effectiveness and the efficiency of the operations by providing real-time critical information to support the various decision-making processes.

1.3 AR-Based Remote Guidance

Several papers already discussed AR-based remote guidance tasks. Some of the early papers to discuss the topic [20–23] indicate that most of the current systems for remote collaboration (e.g. email as well as audio/video conferencing tools) are designed to support group activities that can be performed without reference to the external spatial environment (e.g. decision making) and that the development of systems to support collaborative physical (a.k.a. spatial workspace collaboration, collaborative physical or remote guidance) tasks has been much slower.

Another indication from Fussell et al. [23] is that information exchanges during collaborative physical tasks generally focus on the identification of target objects, descriptions of actions to be performed on those targets, and confirmation that the actions have been performed successfully. Also, as they speak, collaborators on physical tasks use gestures to clarify or enhance their messages. This paper also describes tools developed to provide remote collaborators the ability to make certain types of gestures by overlaying images, such as a cursor pointer or pen-based drawings, on a live video feed from a workspace. This paper also indicates that collaboration on physical tasks can vary along several dimensions such as the number of participants, temporal dynamics (synchronous vs. asynchronous), type and size of the objects, etc. Like this paper, we will focus here on synchronous collaboration between two remote persons (the local novice worker and the remote expert helper).

For example, Huang and colleagues [15] describe the use of a head-tracked stereoscopic HMD, with sensors and an optical tracker that allows the helper to be immersed in the virtual 3D space of the worker's workspace allowing for two users to see one another's gestures while both working in the field using a hands free system involving a helmet, camera and near-eye display. This user study showed that the use of a 3D immersive interface is helpful for improving user's perception of spatial relation and their sense of co-presence, more particularly for complex tasks.

In another paper [24], Huang and colleagues acknowledge that one of the main issues associated with remote guidance is the loss of common ground. When co-located, collaborators share common ground and are able to constantly use hand gestures to clarify and ground their messages while communicating with each other verbally. However, when collaborators are geographically distributed, such common ground no longer exists, resulting in them not being able to communicate the same way as they do when co-located. As a result, Huang and colleagues focus on the innovation of a shared visual space for gestures in their lab study.

In a separate paper, Fussell and colleagues study a remote guidance task in a case where the remote helper is a mobile robot [23]. In that case, experimental results showed that head movements from the remote robot were effective in the sequential organization of communication. On the other hand, the remote pointing function did not operate ideally within the two reference system of both the instructor and the robot operator.

In [25], Yamashita et al.'s study has remote collaborators using distributed table-tops activities involving real objects with a technique called "remote lag" to alleviate the problems caused by the invisibility of remote gestures. The invisibility being created by occlusion problems on the tabletops or by remote gestures that were missed when a worker concentrated on the work at hand or his/her attention was directed elsewhere or simply by supposition of visibility. The "remote lag" technique consists in an instant playback of the remote gestures which gives a chance to recover from the missed context of coordination. The results of the experiment presented in [25] suggest that this technique greatly reduces the negative effects of the invisibility problems.

Although remote guidance with pointing (with a laser or a mouse) is an important aspect of remote guidance, research results indicates that projecting hands of the helper supports a much richer set of non-verbal communication and is therefore more effective for remote guidance [26].

Finally, Alem et al. [27] suggest that the following requirements for AR remote guidance system in industry:

1) The need for mobility of the worker by using wearables computers and cameras;
2) The need to allow helpers to guide remotely using their hands.

Based on these requirements, a system called HandsOnVideo was built that uses both standard view and panoramic view cameras to provide both a local and a more global view in order to increase the situational awareness of the users. The system has been used by more than twelve participants for three representative tasks, namely: repairing a photocopy machine; removing a card from a computer motherboard and assembling Lego toys. The worker user interface (UI) in this case used a near-eye display and the overall response from the participants' pool is that the system was quite intuitive and easy to use with no discomfort with the near eye display of the worker system.

2 Combining AR and AI

The basic features characterizing AR systems consist of: 1) analyzing 2D/3D scene to detect positions where virtual content is to be added to the real content, 2) accurate 3D registration of virtual and real content and 3) real-time human-machine interaction [28, 29, 33]. The ultimate goal of these systems is to ensure a seamless blending of virtual and real visual content such that an immersed user perceives it a one continuous and natural environment. Apart this requirement, AR-based remote guidance applications pose additional challenges since their aim is also to guide a remote (novice) technician to perform complex tasks, such as repair or maintenance, sometimes subject to space and time constraints [30, 41].

One promising way to build efficient and automatic systems for AR-based remote guidance is to integrate AI technologies. Indeed, AR systems require basic perception of the visual world and its component elements, estimating the position and orientation of 3D objects of interest and accurately aligning virtual content (e.g., object models, annotations) with the real one [31]. Computer vision and machine learning techniques can provide a viable solution to address these challenges, whereby the built AR systems can integrate modules to automatically analyze and parse the visual environment, generate the appropriate virtual content and align it correctly with the real one.

In the past, several methods have used computer vision techniques to enhance the AR basic features for remote guidance systems. Proposed approaches tried mainly to integrate object detection algorithms in remotely guided maintenance or repair applications using AR-based systems. To track objects on interest in the scene, some methods used markers to provide accurate 3D object position in real time [34]. Markers are visual cues which trigger the display of the virtual information. They are normal images or small objects (e.g., rectangles) that are trained beforehand so that they can be easily recognized in the scene. They can indicate what the user is looking at and where the virtual content should be added. However, they are less adaptive to the environment and are sensitive to occlusions.

Other methods use feature points extracted from images to establish object position by matching these points with a preprocessed database of the objects [35]. For example, Gurevich et al. [29] have proposed the TeleAdvisor system to support remote assistance tasks. It is a hands-free transportable device composed of a video camera and a small projector mounted at the end of a tele-operated robotic arm. The system enables a remote expert to view and interact with a technician workspace, while controlling the point of view. To enable accurate AR projections on the scene, the system uses an active tracking procedure estimating the distance between the surface and the device.

In [30], the authors proposed the ARgitu system for AR-based maintenance of robot arms. To deal with the problem of 3D non-Lambertian surfaces, the system integrates computer-aided design (CAD) object models and conics to build an accurate and robust object detection and tracking module. In addition, the system integrates 3D object training based on the CAD geometric features of each object. It uses also a general easy-to-use authoring tool for developing new (virtual) content for remote guidance in advanced manufacturing industry.

Registration is a necessary step in any interactive AR system. It relates to correctly aligning annotations and virtual content with the real view of the environment [1, 31]. Registration accuracy can be affected by relative motion between the camera and objects, changes of object aspects, object occlusions and changes of lighting conditions. To address this issue, past methods have used mainly markers [29] or feature matching [30] to find the best alignment of virtual and real content. Markers are usually easy to detect and track on images and can ensure speed, stability and robustness of the registration, but it does not adapt to the environment relief. Feature matching consists in visually tracking object features such as color, texture, corners, lines or conics [31]. Since features change in appearance with the point of view, these techniques use complex algorithms, which can decrease the robustness of registration. Finally, most of these methods are not fully automatic, since a human is usually needed to extract features in the first image and to match them with the virtual model.

Recently, deep learning (DL) based methods have shown impressive results for object detection and recognition [34–36]. Contrarily to traditional machine learning methods that use hand-designed features, DL methods extract features automatically from large amounts of data. In addition, they have robustness to partial occlusion [36].

In [32], the authors proposed DL for recognizing hand actions captured by static RGBD cameras. The method combines recognition of local interactions and global progress of an activity (e.g., assembly, repair, etc.) to feed the user in real-time with actions and context-sensitive prompts while performing the next step of the operation or recovering from errors. The authors use a DL-based segmentation algorithm [33] to localize hands and recognize their local interactions. They also use a probabilistic model for activity state prediction. Finally, Akgul et al. [40] have used DL for accurate and real-time target tracking and detection in AR systems, which showed very promising results.

Another intrinsic part of AR-based remote guidance systems is the virtual content creation service, known as content authoring. It enables the user to create representations of physical objects such as 3D point cloud models, annotated anchor points, buttons, text, animations and virtual objects, which are then added to the real content of the scene. AR-based systems require suitable authoring tools for the development the virtual content and correctly aligning it with the real one. Most of existing methods usually require the use of complex design tools requiring advanced programming [29–31].

The advent of DL methods can play a key part for virtual content generation. For example, generative neural networks can help in designing realistic 3D and 3D visual content by training on data [37], thus providing a huge potential for AR authoring.

3   Discussion

AR-based remote guidance can be useful in various domains. There are several key components to the use of AR in remote guidance tasks. In general, a good system requires audio communication as well as means for gesture communication (minimally pointing and ideally sketching) and a shared visual space [15, 21, 23, 24, 27]. These requirements place emphasis on the need for environments which have limited background noise, adequate lighting, and a reliable communication link.

Observational studies of physical collaboration suggest that people's speech and action are intricately related to the position and dynamics of objects, other people, and ongoing activities in the environment [23]: therefore, we can already determine that noisy environments are not good candidates for remote guidance unless we can isolate the remote collaborators from that noise.

The same could be said about lighting, i.e. the scene that is to be augmented must be well lit since AR is currently primarily a vision-based technology. Therefore, night or underground operations must provide either appropriate lighting or rely on the use of night-vision systems which themselves rely on image enhancements and/or thermal imaging.

Also, remote guidance requires a communication link between the remote expert helper and the local novice worker. Hence, remote guidance cannot be used in remote areas where no communication link exists or where the latency on the communication link does not allow real-time feedback between both the novice and the expert.

As for the combination of AI and AR, AI technologies such as DL have demonstrated a huge potential to enhance the efficiency and robustness of AR-based remote guidance. Recent advances in DL-based methods including semantic segmentation [33], object detection and recognition [33–36] and image/video annotation [38, 39] offer huge opportunities to build efficient AR-based guidance systems that can enjoy full automation while being adaptive to the environment. These systems can run in real-time while optimizing the guidance process by appropriate augmented content such as sketches, prompts and annotations. Automatic estimation of depth and 3D localization of object boundaries in real-time [33] can also enhance registration accuracy to create immersive experiences of a natural and continuous environment.

Future of AI is very promising where AR systems will have direct benefits from the coming advances. For example, systems can be developed to take into account multiple data modalities (e.g., image, video, sound and text) and spatial and temporal context to optimize the guidance process [41]. Advances in robotics can also enable to help or assist directly novice technicians through a robot arm that performs complex and delicate tasks under the guidance of a remote knowledgeable expert. In addition, systems can employ several cameras to analyze the actions of technician and estimate the progress of a task, while analyzing the object details and state upon which the repair/maintenance task is performed. Semantic segmentation [33] can be used in that regard to identify meaningful regions in an image, such as human hands, buttons or components of an equipment.

Finally, advances of AI can lead to systems enabling self-guidance or remote guidance using robots. Technician workers can often face challenging situations or struggle with equipment malfunctions on sites, while located far from a well-equipped lab and knowledgeable experts. Visual augmentations generated by an onsite or remote computer, which receives input from one or multiple onsite cameras, can be projected to the technician at the physical scene or a see-through device such as smart glasses [42].

4   Conclusion

The literature review on AR-based remote guidance tasks and related user studies indicates that these systems could be used in various fields ranging from medicine to manufacturing to disaster management by first responders. The main usefulness being in the ability for a remote expert helper to guide a local novice worker through the use of the main communications channels (i.e. speech gesture and vision). Within any AR-based remote guidance system, the users must then be provided with a shared visual space (usually a live video feed) and the capability to communicate by speaking, pointing and/or drawing and hand gesturing in order to maximize the usability of the systems. There are specific conditions (good lighting, low acoustic noise, network access) under which using AR for remote guidance would be better suited, according to the work environment as well as the technical requirements needed to establish and maintain a reliable communication link. We also saw that the addition of artificial intelligence (AI) algorithms to these systems can increase the efficiency of applied tasks, and this will likely be an avenue of interest for researchers interested in the use of AR for remote guidance.

References

1. Bonnet, P., Ducher, P., Kubiak, A.: A brief introduction to augmented reality. In: Koelle, M., Linderman, P., Stockinger, T., Kranz, M. (eds.) Human-Computer Interaction with Augmented Reality. Advances in Embedded Interactive Systems Technical Report, vol. 2, no. 4, 30 p. (2014)
2. Aameer, R.W., Sofi, S., Roohie, N.: Augmented reality for fire & emergency services. In: Proceedings of International Conference on Recent Trends in Communications and Computer Networks, pp. 32–41 (2013)
3. Yang, L., Liang, Y., Wu, D., Gault, J.: Train and equip firefighters with cognitive virtual and augmented reality. In: Proceedings of the IEEE 4th International Conference on Collaboration and Internet Computing, pp. 453–459 (2018)
4. Yun, K., Lu, T., Chow, E.: Occluded object reconstruction for first responders with augmented reality glasses using conditional generative adversarial networks. In: Proceedings of SPIE 2018, vol. 10649, 7 p. (2018)
5. Lochhead, I., Hedley, N.: Mixed reality emergency management: bringing virtual evacuation simulations into real-world built environments. Int. J. Digit. Earth **12**(2), 190–208 (2019)
6. Caudell, T.P., Mizell, D.W.: Augmented reality: an application of heads-up display technology to manual manufacturing processes. In: Proceedings of Hawaii International Conference on System Sciences, pp. 659–669 (1992)
7. Azuma, R.T.: A survey of augmented reality. Presence Teleoperators Virtual Environ. **6**(4), 355–385 (1997)
8. Billinghurst, M., Clark, A., Lee, G.: A survey of augmented reality. Found. Trends Hum.-Comput. Interact. **8**(2–3), 73–272 (2014)
9. Milgram, P.: A taxonomy of mixed reality visual displays. IEICE Trans. Inf. Syst. **E77-D**(12), 1321–1329 (1994)
10. Biseria, A., Rao, A.: Human computer interface-augmented reality. Int. J. Eng. Sci. Comput. **6**(8), 2594–2595 (2016)
11. Chen, P.H.C., et al.: An augmented reality microscope with real-time artificial intelligence integration for cancer diagnosis. Nature Med. **25**, 1453–1457 (2019)
12. Schlueter, J.A.: Remote maintenance assistance using real-time augmented reality authoring. Master thesis, Iowa State University, 72 p. (2018)
13. Kim, Y., Hong, S., Kim, G.J.: Augmented reality based remote coaching system. In: Proceedings of the 22nd ACM Conference on Virtual Reality Software and Technology, VRST 2016, Munchen, Germany, pp. 311–312 (2016)
14. Yamamoto, T., Otsuki, M., Kuzuoka, H., Suzuki, Y.: Tele-guidance system to support anticipation during communication. Multimodal Technol. Interact. **2**(3), 55 (2018)
15. Huang, W., Alem, L., Tecchia, F.: HandsIn3D: supporting remote guidance with immersive virtual environments. In: Kotzé, P., Marsden, G., Lindgaard, G., Wesson, J., Winckler, M. (eds.) INTERACT 2013. LNCS, vol. 8117, pp. 70–77. Springer, Heidelberg (2013). https://doi.org/10.1007/978-3-642-40483-2_5
16. Rao, H., Fu, W.-T.: Combining schematic and augmented reality representations in a remote spatial assistance system. In: IEEE ISMAR 2013 Workshop on Collaboration in Merging Realities, 6 p. (2013)

17. Hoover, M.: An evaluation of the Microsoft HoloLens for a manufacturing-guided assembly task. Graduate theses and dissertations, Iowa State University (2018). https://lib.dr.iastate.edu/etd/16378

18. Augestad, K.M., et al.: Educational implications for surgical telemonitoring: a current review with recommendations for future practice, policy, and research. Surg. Endosc. **31**, 3836–3846 (2017). https://doi.org/10.1007/s00464-017-5690-y

19. Jones, B., et al.: Elevating communication, collaboration, and shared experiences in mobile video through drones. In: Proceedings of the 2016 ACM Conference on Designing Interactive Systems (DIS 2016), Brisbane, Australia, pp. 1123–1135 (2016)

20. Kuzuoka, H.: Spatial workspace collaboration: a SharedView video support system for remote collaboration capability. In: Proceedings of the ACM SIGCHI Conference on Human Factors in Computing Systems (CHI 1992), Monterey, California, USA, pp. 533–540 (1992)

21. Ou, J., Fussell, S.R., Chen, X., Setlock, L.D., Yang, J.: Gestural communication over video stream: supporting multimodal interaction for remote collaborative physical tasks. In: Proceedings of the ACM 5th Conference on Multimodal Interfaces (ICMI 2003), Vancouver, British Columbia, Canada, pp. 242–249 (2003)

22. Kuzuoka, H., et al.: Mediating dual ecologies. In: Proceedings of the ACM Conference on Computer Supported Cooperative Work, Chicago, Illinois, USA, pp. 477–486 (2004)

23. Fussell, S.R., Setlock, L.D., Yang, J., Ou, J., Mauer, E., Kramer, A.D.L.: Gestures over video streams to support remote collaboration on physical tasks. Hum.-Comput. Interact. **19**, 273–309 (2004)

24. Huang, W., Alem, L., Tecchia, F., Duh, H.B.-L.: Augmented 3D hands: a gesture-based mixed reality system for distributed collaboration. J. Multimodal User Interfaces **12**(2), 77–89 (2018). https://doi.org/10.1007/s12193-017-0250-2

25. Yamashita, N., Kaji, K., Kuzuoka, H., Hirata, K.: Improving visibility of remote gestures in distributed tabletop collaboration. In: Proceedings of the ACM Conference on Computer Supported Cooperative Work (CSCW 2011), Hangzhou, China, pp. 95–104 (2011)

26. Kirk, S.D., Fraser, D.S.: Comparing remote gesture technologies for supporting collaborative physical tasks. In: Proceedings of the ACM SIGCHI Conference on Human Factors in Computing Systems (CHI 2006). Montréal, Québec, Canada, pp. 1191–1200 (2006)

27. Alem, L., Tecchia, F., Huang, W.: HandsOnVideo: towards a gesture based mobile AR system for remote collaboration. In: Alem, L., Huang, W. (eds.) Recent Trends of Mobile Collaborative Augmented Reality, pp. 135–148. Springer, New York (2011). https://doi.org/10.1007/978-1-4419-9845-3_11

28. Herskovitz, J., Ofek, E., Lasecki, W.S., Fourney, A.: Opportunities for in-home augmented reality guidance. In: Proceedings of the ACM Conference on Human Factors in Computing Systems CHI Extended Abstracts, Glasgow, UK, pp. 1–6 (2019)

29. Gurevich, P., Lanir, J., Cohen, B., Stone, R.: TeleAdvisor: a versatile augmented reality tool for remote assistance. In: Proceedings of the ACM Conference on Human Factors in Computing Systems CHI, Austin, Texas, USA, pp. 619–622 (2012)

30. Zubizarreta, J., Aguinaga, I., Amundarain, A.: A framework for augmented reality guidance in industry. Int. J. Adv. Manuf. Technol. **102**(9–12), 4095–4108 (2019). https://doi.org/10.1007/s00170-019-03527-2

31. Didier, J.-Y., et al.: AMRA: augmented reality assistance for train maintenance tasks. In: Proceedings of the 4th ACM/IEEE International Symposium on Mixed and Augmented Reality (ISMAR 2005): Workshop Industrial Augmented Reality, Vienna, Austria, pp. 1–10 (2005)

32. Schröder, M., Ritter, H.J.: Deep learning for action recognition in augmented reality assistance systems. In: Proceedings of SIGGRAPH, Los Angeles, California, USA, pp. 1–2 (2017)

33. Hu, R., Dollár, P., He, K., Darrell, T., Girshick, R.B.: Learning to segment every thing. In: Proceedings of the IEEE Conference on Computer Vision and Pattern Recognition (CVPR), Salt Lake City, Utah, USA, pp. 4233–4241 (2018)
34. Ren, S., He, K., Girshick, R., Sun, J.: Faster R-CNN: towards real-time object detection with region proposal networks. IEEE Trans. Pattern Anal. Mach. Intell. **39**(6), 1137–1149 (2017)
35. Redmon, J., Divvala, S., Girshick, R., Farhadi, A.: You only look once: unified, real-time object detection. In: Proceedings of the IEEE Conference on Computer Vision and Pattern Recognition, pp. 779–788 (2016)
36. Lin, T.-Y., Goyal, P., Girshick, R.B., He, H., Dollar, P.: Focal loss for dense object detection. In: Proceedings of the IEEE International Conference on Computer Vision (ICCV), Venice, Italy, pp. 2999–3007 (2017)
37. Ro, H., Park, Y.-J., Byun, J., Han, T.-D.: Display methods of projection augmented reality based on deep learning pose estimation. In: Proceedings of the ACM SIGGRAPH 2019 Posters, Los Angeles, California, USA, pp. 1–2 (2019)
38. Laib, L., Allili, M.-S., Ait-Aoudia, S.: A probabilistic topic model for event-based image classification and multi-label annotation. Sig. Process. Image Commun. **76**, 283–294 (2019)
39. Ouyed, O., Allili, M.-S.: Feature weighting for multinomial kernel logistic regression and application to action recognition. Neurocomputing **275**, 1752–1768 (2018)
40. Akgul, O., Penekli, H.I., Genc, Y.: Applying deep learning in augmented reality tracking. In: Proceedings of the 12th International Conference on Signal-Image Technology & Internet-Based Systems (SITIS), Naples, Italy, pp. 47–54 (2016)
41. Zhu, J., Ong, S.K., Nee, A.Y.C.: An authorable context-aware augmented reality system to assist the maintenance technicians. Int. J. Adv. Manuf. Technol. **66**, 1699–1714 (2013). https://doi.org/10.1007/s00170-012-4451-2
42. Essig, K., Strenge, B., Schack, T.: ADAMAAS: towards smart glasses for mobile and personalized action assistance. In: Proceedings of the 9th ACM International Conference on Pervasive Technologies Related to Assistive Environments (PETRA), Corfu, Greece, pp. 1–4 (2016)

Development of an Augmented Reality System Achieving in CNC Machine Operation Simulations in Furniture Trial Teaching Course

Yu-Ting Lin and I-Jui Lee[✉]

Department of Industrial Design, National Taipei University of Technology,
Taipei, Taiwan
tl07588008@ntut.org.tw, ericlee@ntut.edu.tw

Abstract. In schools, due to narrow processing spaces and limited machines, students can only understand the operation and processing procedures of computer numerical control (CNC) machines through the unilateral operation and explanation of technicians or by group operation or observations in turn. Under the existing teaching restrictions, students can only obtain limited operating experience through the partial processing steps of group machine operation. Students are therefore not familiar with the operation of the machines and it is difficult to complete consistent operation procedures, resulting in fear and uncertainty in the operation of the machines. Therefore, this research used augmented reality (AR) technology to simulate the complete operation flow and processing information of CNC processing machines, and combined the practical teaching courses to deepen the students' understanding of CNC machine operation.

In this study, a total of ten participants were recruited to conduct AR system operation experiments. The follow-up verification was conducted through real CNC machine operation and by filling in the System Usability Scale (SUS) to evaluate the experience feedback after using the AR-CNC training system. Finally, the results of this study showed that the AR-CNC training system could not only solve the problem of machining operation interruption caused by students' rotating use of the CNC machine but also solve the hardware limitations of the actual machining space and the machine itself, so that every student could learn how to operate the CNC machine as if they were operating it in person.

Keywords: Augmented reality (AR) · CNC machine · Digital manufacturing · Furniture trial production · Furniture woodworking students · Operation simulation

1 Introduction

1.1 Current Furniture Woodworking Production

Taiwan used to be an important base for global furniture production. It has established a talent training system for woodwork-related vocational schools and departments and has cultivated many outstanding furniture manufacturing talents for industrial

© Springer Nature Switzerland AG 2020
J. Y. C. Chen and G. Fragomeni (Eds.): HCII 2020, LNCS 12191, pp. 121–135, 2020.
https://doi.org/10.1007/978-3-030-49698-2_9

effectiveness. However, with the development of science and technology, the era of digital automation has come. Digital design and digital manufacturing are widely used in various industries. The furniture manufacturing industry has gradually transformed from one based on traditional factories to one based on smart factories. The earlier production model can no longer respond to rapid changes. In a globalized industrial market, furniture manufacturing needs to change the way production lines operate to embrace lower labor costs and higher production efficiency and achieve the most flexible and efficient manufacturing procedures. Therefore, the manufacturing of furniture and the wood industry are undergoing substantial adjustments between the conversion of manpower and automated supply and demand, as well as the building of digital manufacturing capabilities, on the basis of existing production lines. Therefore, Taiwan's furniture and woodworking-related vocational schools are also actively engaged in relevant courses on digital processing and digital manufacturing in talent cultivation, in order to connect with the new era of the employment market.

In addition, under the trend of large-scale overseas furniture factories introducing mechanized production, the vocational training courses for furniture and special woodworking classes have also changed with the change of the times and the employment market. Students are now taught the knowledge and skills of digital manufacturing and CNC machine processing, which have reversed the main course of traditional furniture and woodworking teaching. In the past, furniture woodworking courses mainly focused on strengthening the fine craftsmanship and processing skills of students in furniture woodworking. Today's teaching scene, on the other hand, teaches students about the operation ability of machining and digital manufacturing.

In the course design of furniture woodworking classes, digital manufacturing and CNC processing have become an indispensable part of woodworking teaching, and the application of digital manufacturing and CNC teaching courses more directly echo the importance of using digital manufacturing technology in the furniture production lines of large overseas furniture factories and the necessary conditions for industrial talent demand. Therefore, in the course teaching and talent training of furniture woodworking classes, it is important and necessary to teach students CNC machining and understand the concepts and technology of digital manufacturing in furniture production.

1.2 Current Teaching Situation and Training Focus of the School

Due to the rapid development of science and technology leading to the transformation of the furniture manufacturing industry, in addition to basic woodworking practice skills, the relevant knowledge and operation applications of digital processing and digital manufacturing should be actively included. Quite a number of self-made digital resource platforms can be easily accessed, and they have established the digital manufacturing industry atmosphere from top to bottom. This research was aimed at the entry of CNC for digital production teaching. CNC machine tools can quickly cut and process furniture components designed by software according to computer-aided design (CAD) and computer-aided manufacturing (CAM) to achieve the overall digital design in the digital manufacturing production process. However, this study did not carry out the teaching of CNC machine program writing and the operation ability of

CAD and CAM software; it instead focused on enabling students to incorporate CNC machining concepts into their furniture design and furniture model making courses.

1.3 Current Difficulties in Teaching: A Limited Number of Tools and Insufficient Space

In recent years, Taiwan's woodworking-related schools have taught students the knowledge and skills of digital manufacturing and CNC processing, which have become an indispensable part of the courses. However, due to the limited number of machines and insufficient space in teaching, students can only learn the knowledge and application of CNC machining by rotating operation or by watching the operation of teachers. For students, this learning method cannot effectively allow each student to actually operate and drill the CNC machines for furniture implementation. In addition, a large amount of material is required in the overall processing and application, and the students are unable to go to the CNC machine repeatedly to carry out processing trials. As a result, the types of processed furniture created are quite limited, and there is a lack of spatial correspondence between the processed furniture models and the CNC machine itself. Therefore, the students are unable to conceptually link processed parts with the machining environment of the CNC machines. Even if students can build furniture processing models, it is difficult to understand the correlation between machining methods and CNC machines. Therefore, AR technology can be applied to the simulated operation of CNC machines. Students can use a personal tablet computer to perform a two-stage operation simulation in the factory classroom and the CNC machine. The built-in virtual imaging technology can superimpose virtual 3D machining workpieces on the physical CNC machine, shorten the distance among the machining workpiece, the method, and the machine, and solve the problem of machine space constraints.

Restrictions on the Number and Space of Machines

However, in the teaching of furniture woodworking, because there is no actual large-scale production of the processing machines on the teaching site, it is difficult for teachers to present the production situation of the processing site during teaching. Teachers can only guide students to understand the process of furniture production by means of video or illustrations. In the process of furniture production, because the number of machines is limited and the space is small, the students can only understand the furniture manufacturing and CNC processing methods through the teacher's separate explanation and demonstration of the machining process through rotating operation or observation. Such teaching methods are greatly limited in the actual machine operation. Under this teaching condition, students can only get one-sided and limited operating experience through group operation, which causes fear and uncertainty in operation due to their unfamiliarity and inconsistent execution of machine operation. In addition, from past teaching experience, it can be found that in the case of limited CNC machines, only one student will operate a machine in the classroom, and the rest of the students can only (Fig. 1). In addition, in the process of machine processing, a large amount of processing materials and machine tool wear are required, which results in the students only creating a piece of furniture in a group in order to save materials and reduce the storage space of finished furniture products, and the students cannot conduct multiple processing or diversified furniture production trials. Such teaching conditions in the operation of equipment and space limitations cause a great limitation in teaching.

Fig. 1. The CNC machining space and machine are limited, and students can only observe the operation status

Hardware Limitations in Machining and Machine Operation

Secondly, under the processing limitations of the machine itself, the students' processing objects are also limited to certain types of furniture or the workpieces that can be processed by the school machine, as well as a number of specific processing programs. Limitations of models or functions (for example, the factory of this department only has three-axis processing machines) and processing procedures cannot allow students to deeply turning or surface processing, and because of the time limitations of the course, students can only carry out simple processing methods or create simple furniture parts. During processing, students must wait for the completion of one workpiece before carrying out the next processing procedure; such teaching methods consume a lot of time and limit the students' ability to learn furniture knowledge of different breadths and depths for production methods and projects.

Time Consumption in Operation and Waste of Processing Cost

In addition, since CNC machining requires a considerable amount of workpiece processing time, in the existing implementation courses, subject to the time limit of the course, only one group of students can be provided for CNC machining in one week. The remaining students can only arrange other basic woodworking courses. Due to the limitation of the number of teachers, teachers can only perform CNC machining through group operations (through observation and discussion, it has been found that whether in the design department or the mechanical department, similar situations have occurred in the teaching of CNC machines, indicating that this is already a problem). It also causes a considerable burden on the teachers, who must repeat the demonstration machine operation and drills every week. When the number of machines is insufficient, students can only stand and watch or take turns to perform CNC machine operation drills. The actual time for students to operate and execute the machine is fragmented and intermittent, which is not conducive for students to understand the overall operation of the CNC machine. In addition, the processed furniture also requires considerable storage space. In the case of insufficient space, it also forces the production of teaching furniture to be produced in a small amount or in a group processing form. However, under the application of AR or virtual reality (VR), the machining process and machine operation can be simulated through a virtual CNC machine to simulate the actual machining situation in Fig. 2, which can greatly increase the students' understanding of the contact surface and processing knowledge for the use of the machine when combined with operation on some real machines. This can also reduce the problems of the actual operation and operation interruption in teaching under the conditions of limited personnel and machines.

Fig. 2. The machining process and machine operation can be simulated through a virtual CNC machine

2   Related Work

2.1   Related Cases in AR Technology Assisted Vocational Training and Education

In many related cases, it has been pointed out that AR and VR can be used in vocational training and operational task courses [1]. Because of its high fidelity and strong sense of operational feedback [2], AR and VR can be used as a simulation tool for many machines' equipment operation and teaching training [3]. The simulated operation process can solve many problems, including: 1) the insufficient number of machines and tools and the processing limitations of the machines (for example, only three axes cannot perform five-axis processing, resulting in the limitations of furniture manufacturing); 2) limited space and limited number of people in the teaching field (for example, only one person can operate the machine and the rest can only watch);

3) safety problems in personnel operation (such as the danger of the processing machines [4] or easy damage due to operation [5], in which maintenance is expensive and can only be performed by teachers or technicians); and 4) the 3D machining workpieces created by the processing software do not correspond to the actual machine during processing in space, and students cannot see the operation relationship and correspondence between the processing object and the software or the machine in real time [6]. These problems are excellent entry points for combining vocational training with AR and VR technology. In addition, AR and VR simulation tools can greatly improve learners' interest and motivation in the training content.

Although there are few cases of domestic use of AR and VR in teaching applications on CNC machines, AR and VR have been widely used in other types of vocational training and machines. In terms of operation, they have already achieved quite good training results [3]. For example, there are teaching application cases for students to perform BMW car engine repair through AR technology [7], or the teaching application of assisting welding through VR [8–11]. There are also related teaching cases using AR and VR to let students understand the processing principle and operation of CNC [12, 13]. Some manufacturers have developed virtual reality technology to teach students to operate the surface painting and spray painting of cars and other products (SimSpray - Virtual Reality Paint Training Tool). This teaching method can save up to 50% of the training cost and can greatly reduce the training time and operation cost of vocational training [14–16]. This technology enables students to learn professional knowledge and machine operation from AR and VR and improves students' interest and willingness to learn about the technology. In addition, some related teaching cases have introduced tool machines and factory machines through virtual reality technology, which also reduces the complexity of teaching and increases the students' familiarity with the use of the machines. In addition, AR and VR technologies combined with existing HTC VIVE and operational tasks can effectively integrate the operational perception required by vocational education into the teaching environment. Vocational training emphasizes hands-on implementation and sensory experiences, and it can have an application field in the virtual environment, especially for the combination of AR and VR with physical action, highlighting the limb feedback under the workpiece and machine operating space during furniture manufacturing [17].

2.2 Advantages of AR Technology in Operation Courses

Due to the limitation of the site and the actual consideration of the hardware, AR technology is more suitable to be implemented in the teaching site of CNC furniture production than VR technology, because AR technology can display the superimposed spatial relationship of 3D virtual processing objects and real machines by means of a flat or hand-held device. It is also similar to the operating environment of a real machine (a CNC machine is also operated through a touch screen interface), and it is easy to implement in the actual teaching field, which can save the need for cumbersome VR infrared induction devices. At the same time, compared with the cost of a head mounted display, the cost of a tablet computer is also lower. In the face of 40 students in a woodworking class, AR applications can also be operated by many people at the same time under group operation, thus saving the teaching time and the cost of software and hardware.

Asai pointed out that AR is a new learning tool that can provide learners with a new form of learning [18]. Visual feedback on both spatial perception and operation is of great help to learners [19]. Billinghurst also believed that using AR as a course training strategy can obtain a number of benefits [20]. First, it allows learners to smoothly integrate spatial operations and visual perception feedback in virtual 3D and real environments. AR conducts interactive learning, which can help learners understand the interactive relationship between 3D processing objects and CNC machines. Even if the learners do not have any previous experience with CNC machines, they can quickly understand the concepts. Second, the operation method of AR is simple. Through the guidance of the teacher, students can clearly understand the state of the processing object in a 3D space, and there is no need to imagine. All the processing details include different processes and methods, such as turning over processing, mold hole process-ing, and so on. It is difficult to express and explain concepts in a traditional 2D video image, but AR solves this problem. AR can especially allow students to superimpose 3D objects in the space of the CNC operating machine. Third, in addition, AR enables students to immerse themselves in the learning content, so that learning is no longer merely based on static pictures or text messages; any object form can be presented in 3D in real time, which can make up for the hardware limitations in the processing environment. Any interactive operation can correspond to the processing feedback of the machine with a sense of synchronous operation and space feedback, so as to gain the affection of learning and push the construction of skills. Fourth, AR operation can avoid the unnecessary waste of materials and promote student safety in operation.

Previous studies have directly confirmed that the application of AR technology in teaching is a feasible idea. For example, Shelton and Hedley pointed out that students can use the operation of a 3D interactive model to assist with learning, which could potentially help with the learning of spatial concepts [21]. In addition, 3D animation can help to materialize the concept of space through images, which helps to improve learning cognition and helps students build an understanding of the working methods and processing procedures of 3D processing workpieces. Martín-Gutiérrez also pointed out that AR can assist in vocational training, transform theoretical knowledge into more authentic information presentation, increase the link between knowledge and practical experience [22], adjust course content and design according to the learning content and the students' learning situation, and promote communication and cooperation among students through interactive independent learning content. Besides, AR applications can allow students to learn and understand independently after class. Without the help of teachers, the students can also get better teaching quality and a better learning effect.

2.3   Teaching Methods to Solve the Problems

In this study, the teachers attempted to solve the problems in actual CNC machining teaching through AR application. In addition, they also attempted to solve the three-dimensional space corresponding drop between the operation and the actual machining tools when using commercial processing software (such as NX/PowerMill) in the past, as there is a space cognitive drop between the software operation and actual machining.

The software operation and the actual processing have a spatial cognitive difference, resulting in the software being learned but the students not knowing how to apply it to CNC machining. Students are unfamiliar with the use of machining tools and methods and it is difficult to directly see the relationship between the 2D tool path and the 3D machining workpiece). AR can effectively help learners understand the scale relationship of a 3D machining space, including the relationship between the machining machine and the workpiece (furniture parts). It can let students understand how to turn the surface or process the surface by superposing the virtual 3D processing workpiece onto solid wood or the solid workpiece itself. That is to say, the virtual object constructed by AR provides additional auxiliary information to strengthen the students' cognition of the concept of workpiece turnover and the 3D processing space. Besides, the 3D virtual machining workpieces produced by the modeling software can be superimposed on the plane of the physical CNC machine. This can effectively help students understand the machining relationship between the machining object and the real CNC machine tools and help students quickly construct the concept integration between the machining method and the process. In teaching, through the complete construction of CNC machines and digital processing teaching modules, different machines and processing programs can be practiced through AR, and the field of actual operation is no longer limited to the existing teaching space field. For example, students can experience the operation and processing of workpieces through tablet computers or head mounted monitors in the general classroom space, and they can develop a realistic interface to fuse the operation perception between the workpiece and the machine in a teaching environment. Every student can also possess one machine (the carrier can be a personal tablet computer with low cost) to simulate the processing flow and processing method of the machine operation, which can also reduce the field limitation and processing time of actual processing. It may take a large amount of construction cost and labor investment in the initial stage of system construction, but compared to a large CNC processing machine with millions of movements, this is a worthwhile teaching plan and strategy that is worth investing in. When machines need to be updated year by year or courses need to use larger and more dangerous equipment, under the factors of a limited teaching field and limited funding, and corresponding to the rapidly changing overseas job market, AR and VR teaching systems and high flexibility are urgent and feasible teaching directions.

3   Method

This study This research introduced the complete operation process and simulation steps of furniture woodworking CNC processing machines through AR technology and combined teaching courses in the woodworking field of the school to deepen the students' understanding of CNC machine operation and provide extra training for processing information and production concepts, so that the students could understand the future application trends of smart furniture and woodworking factories as well as the concepts of processing and production in industry 4.0 management.

3.1 Participants

This study recruited ten students with experience in operating CNC to conduct the AR system operation and receive interviews after use to provide questionnaire feedback. The researcher used a furniture manufacturing course to give the participants operation tests and experiments. The participants had previous CNC machine operation experience but were still unfamiliar with CNC machine operation procedures. During the training process, the students were taught and trained separately based on the operating steps, processing knowledge, and industry 4.0 concept mastery, and the subsequent evaluation was carried out through the System Usability Scale (SUS). During the experiment, the students conducted AR machine operation training in groups, presented the AR system in the form of a tablet computer, and used the finished furniture product example of an online open CNC furniture company as the demonstration material for CNC machine learning.

3.2 System Development

Due to the limitation of the school's teaching field, it was impossible for each student to clearly see the instructions of the teacher. In addition, the actual CNC woodworking engraving machine could not allow students to repeat the operation practice. The AR-CNC training system was developed to allow the students to learn independently and allow the operation of the machine and the control console to both be more clearly understood and practiced. The students experienced the operation of the CNC machine and the content of the furniture processing workpiece through the tablet computer in both the general classroom space and the actual factory space, and they integrated the operation perception between the workpiece and the CNC machine in the teaching environment through the virtual interface development.

The AR-CNC training system in Fig. 3 mainly used a tablet computer as a carrier for teaching and operation. The students scanned the graphics card of the processing operation through the video lens of the tablet computer and then superimposed the 3D virtual object onto the real woodworking machine. In the AR-CNC training system, Adobe Illustrator was used to draw 2D identification cards, and software such as C4D/3D MAX was used to make 3D animations. The system was developed through Unity and Vuforia to integrate and define actions. The students then carried out AR operation simulation and learning for each operation procedure and step of the CNC woodworking carving machine.

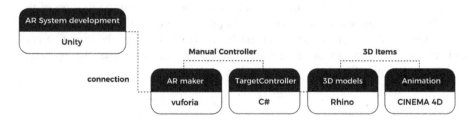

Fig. 3. Integration of AR-CNC training system

3.3   Environment Setting

The AR-CNC training system could display the spatial relationship of the 3D virtual processing object and the real machine by using a tablet or a hand-held device. At the same time, it was similar to the environment in which the real machine operated, and it was in the actual teaching field show in Fig. 4. It was also easier to implement in the teaching course, as it could eliminate the need for a cumbersome VR infrared sensing device. At the same time, the cost of a tablet computer is lower than that of a head-mounted display. It could be operated by more than one person at the same time during group operation, thus saving teaching time and software and hardware costs.

Fig. 4. The AR-CNC training system enabled students to display the spatial relationship of 3D virtual processing objects and real machines by means of a tablet

3.4   Learning Material

This study also defined the operation process of a CNC woodworking engraving machine according to seven major items, including: 1) start-up of the CNC, console, and air compressor; 2) CNC to reset zero return; 3) correction of the X, Y and Z axes of the CNC; 4) selection and replacement of the CNC milling cutter; 5) importation of the target workpiece file into the console; 6) the action of putting stoppers, rubber strips, and processing base plates on the CNC machine table to confirm the fixation of the material; and 7) preview of the screen to start processing on the console. In addition, the students in the interface part of the cutting center also needed the operating procedures corresponding to the processing information and the lathe, the operation process is shown in Fig. 5.

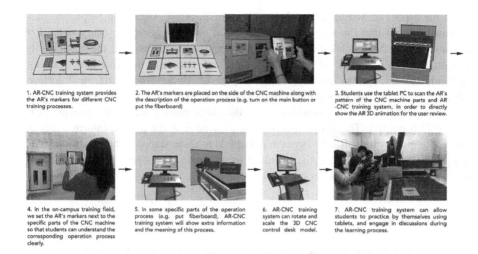

1. AR-CNC training system provides the AR's markers for different CNC training processes.

2. The AR's markers are placed on the side of the CNC machine along with the description of the operation process (e.g. turn on the main button or put the fiberboard)

3. Students use the tablet PC to scan the AR's pattern of the CNC machine parts and AR -CNC training system, in order to directly show the AR 3D animation for the user review.

4. In the on-campus training field, we set the AR's markers next to the specific parts of the CNC machine so that students can understand the corresponding operation process clearly.

5. In some specific parts of the operation process (e.g. put fiberboard), AR-CNC training system will show extra information and the meaning of this process.

6. AR-CNC training system can rotate and scale the 3D CNC control desk model.

7. AR-CNC training system can allow students to practice by themselves using tablets, and engage in discussions during the learning process.

Fig. 5. Training process of the AR-CNC system

3.5 Experiment Processing

Ten participants first operated the CNC woodworking engraving machine using a tablet. The course was mainly divided into the following six unit topics: 1) CNC machine introduction; 2) CNC machining application examples; 3) introduction of the AR teaching machine interface operation and simulation; 4) AR machine simulation processing and CNC machining operation practice; 5) making knock-down furniture (KD) furniture; and 6) finished products and other complete digital manufacturing processes. After training, the ten subjects were given the System Usability Scale (SUS) questionnaire to offer feedback for the analysis of the results and data.

4 Results

System Usability Scale (SUS)

In the questionnaire survey of this study, the researcher scored the system usability scale of AR-CNC system and established five different evaluation dimensions after expert interviews, including "Understanding of Machining Procedures", "Time of Operation", "Accuracy of Operation", "Sequence and Information of the CNC Operation Steps", "Understanding of the Interface Knowledge of the CNC Cutting Machine Center", and other evaluation aspects. Each facet had five sub-questions for a total of twenty questions, and each topic was given a score of 1–7 (in which 1 represented high difficulty and 7 represented low difficulty).

The results showed that in the aspect of Understanding of Machining Procedures, the participants believed that the AR-CNC system could improve their understanding of workpiece processing (4.86 points). In the aspect of Time of Operation, the participants thought that the AR-CNC system could make CNC learning more efficient (4.8 points).

In the aspect of Sequence and Information of the CNC Operation Steps, the participants thought that the AR-CNC system could let them complete every operation step and task (5.52 points). In the aspect of Accuracy of Operation, the participants thought that the AR-CNC system could help them learn and improve their learning motivation (4.98 points). Finally, in the aspect of Understanding of the Interface Knowledge of the CNC Cutting Machine Center, the participants believed that the AR-CNC system could help to understand the functions corresponding to machine processing (5.6 points). The above information showed that the participants provided a high evaluation of the AR-CNC system in regards to understanding the operation steps and processing sequence, and they could also complete each operation step independently through the AR-CNC system.

5 Discussion

The course in this research was a continuous processing course. The teaching started from a simple CNC processing unit before teaching the processing software through the course matching, and then entered into the processing program. Because the processing software could be operated by a PC through the computer classroom, each student could learn to operate the processing software and then take the transferred machine code (G-code) to a CNC machine in the factory for processing. In the past, after learning how to use the software teaching, the students would be faced with an insufficient number of machines and limited space. In the future, students will be able to conduct AR CNC machine simulation in groups in the classroom through AR simulation teaching. Students can directly use a tablet computer and carry out processing drills on the virtual machine in the classroom at the same time. Because CNC machine operation requires familiarity with the process and the workpiece, the operation procedure of the machining interface only accounts for a small part of the whole CNC processing, which means that for students, understanding the furniture form and processing form that the hardware of the machine can process is more important. The CNC machine itself does not have a complicated operation procedure; however, success mainly depends on whether the students can understand the processing limits and method limitations under the processing of the machine. The mastery of the processing object corresponds to the understanding in a 3D space, which represents a gap between the processing machine and software operation, and it is difficult for students to understand why such furniture model files cannot be processed with factory CNC machines. The past teaching field did not allow repeated processing and multiple actual processing simulations. There is also a great teaching gap between processing and multiple actual processing simulations in the operation space and software teaching program, which leads to the fact that the software teaching in the teaching is just a part of it. The processing program must be carried out through another course; therefore it is difficult to obtain real benefits in the connection between the CNC hardware and operating software. However, due to the limitations of the machine and the actual conditions, although the students can understand the use of the processing software, there are no more operation opportunities for them to get the actual processing drill.

Therefore, the design of this course was mainly implemented using the online OpenDesk design resource platform, through which a variety of furniture design drawings were obtained. These furniture drawings were processed and implemented through the CNC machine, and through the integration of the overall course teaching and software and hardware processing, so that the furniture on this platform could be actually processed through the software in the computer classroom of the department and the CNC processing machine of the practice factory. The implementation solution on behalf of the whole could be solved, and AR technology only needed to be added to solve the spatial integration between the processing object and the CNC machine and break the existing framework limitations of the teaching field.

6   Conclusions

The research results showed that the students could understand the relationship between workpieces and methods on the CNC machining through the AR system and could operate virtual machines through AR simulation. In the classroom field and on real CNC machining machines, a virtual 3D image was used to overlap and process the workpiece for operation simulation. After the AR machine operation training, this study confirmed that using the AR system for training had a number of advantages. First, through the AR teaching system, the students could understand the complete processing procedures and steps of woodworking furniture machine operation. It was also easy to assess and remind the students whether each step of the task was actually completed during the operation. Second, using AR for interactive learning allowed the students to smoothly integrate virtual and real concepts between the real processing operation environment and virtual 3D processing objects. Through the visual perception feedback between the physical machine and the virtual processing auxiliary interface of the overlapping woodworking machine, the students could understand the processing state and operation relationship of the 3D processing object on the CNC processing machine. Third, the AR system had a simple operation mode, and the students did not need to be instructed by the teacher. Even if the trainees did not have any previous experience with CNC processing machines, they could quickly understand the operation process and processing concepts. The trainees could learn and operate independently without imagination how to use CNC processing machine. Fourth, the AR system allowed the students to practice repeatedly and avoid unnecessary material waste in actual processing as well as safety concerns in operation. Fifth, the virtual 3D picture of the CNC cutting path could be previewed through AR, and the processing stage and additional production information could be understood. For example, the processing state of a workpiece on the CNC machine table could correspond to the actual part, item number, material item of the furniture production line, and real-time display of the virtual 3D processing progress, which could allow managers to grasp the auxiliary concepts of furniture wood factory management and information in the production link. The students could therefore obtain the application trend of intelligent furniture manufacturing and the concepts of industry 4.0 management.

Acknowledgments. We are grateful to the Executive Yuan and Ministry of Science and Technology for funding under project No. MOST 107-2218-E-027-013-MY2.

References

1. Velev, D., Zlateva, P.: Virtual reality challenges in education and training. Int. J. Learn. Teach. **3**(1), 33–37 (2017)
2. Sherman, W.R., Craig, A.B.: Understanding Virtual Reality: Interface, Application, and Design. Morgan Kaufmann, San Francisco (2018)
3. Seymour, N.E., et al.: Virtual reality training improves operating room performance: results of a randomized, double-blinded study. Ann. Surg. **236**(4), 458 (2002)
4. Le, Q.T., Pedro, A., Park, C.S.: A social virtual reality based construction safety education system for experiential learning. J. Intell. Rob. Syst. **79**(3–4), 487–506 (2015)
5. García, A.A., Bobadilla, I.G., Figueroa, G.A., Ramírez, M.P., Román, J.M.: Virtual reality training system for maintenance and operation of high-voltage overhead power lines. Virtual Reality **20**(1), 27–40 (2016)
6. Cuendet, S., Dehler-Zufferey, J., Arn, C., Bumbacher, E., Dillenbourg, P.: A study of carpenter apprentices' spatial skills. Empirical Res. Vocat. Educ. Train. **6**(1), 1–16 (2014)
7. De Sa, A.G., Zachmann, G.: Virtual reality as a tool for verification of assembly and maintenance processes. Comput. Graph. **23**(3), 389–403 (1999)
8. Zboray, D.A., et al.: U.S. Patent No. 8,747,116. U.S. Patent and Trademark Office, Washington, DC (2014)
9. Wallace, M.W., Zboray, D.A., Aditjandra, A., Webb, A.L., Postlethwaite, D., Lenker, Z.S.: U.S. Patent No. 9,928,755. U.S. Patent and Trademark Office, Washington, DC (2018)
10. Peters, C., Postlethwaite, D., Wallace, M.W.: U.S. Patent No. 9,318,026. U.S. Patent and Trademark Office, Washington, DC (2016)
11. Postlethwaite, D., Zboray, D., Gandee, C., Aditjandra, A., Wallace, M., Lenker, Z.: U.S. Patent No. 9,836,987. U.S. Patent and Trademark Office, Washington, DC (2017)
12. Lin, F., Hon, C.L., Su, C.J.: A virtual reality-based training system for CNC milling machine operations. Ann. J. IIE HK (1996)
13. Kao, Y.C., Lee, C.S., Liu, Z.R., Lin, Y.F.: Case study of virtual reality in CNC machine tool exhibition. In: MATEC Web of Conferences, EDP Sciences, vol. 123, p. 00004 (2017)
14. Yang, U., Lee, G.A., Shin, S., Hwang, S., Son, W.: Virtual reality based paint spray training system. In: 2007 IEEE Virtual Reality Conference, pp. 289–290 (2007)
15. Shilkrot, R., Maes, P., Paradiso, J.A., Zoran, A.: Augmented airbrush for computer aided painting (CAP). ACM Trans. Graph. (TOG) **34**(2), 1–11 (2015)
16. Elsdon, J., Demiris, Y.: Augmented reality for feedback in a shared control spraying task. In: 2018 IEEE International Conference on Robotics and Automation (ICRA), pp. 1939–1946 (2018)
17. Whitmire, E., Benko, H., Holz, C., Ofek, E., Sinclair, M.: Haptic revolver: touch, shear, texture, and shape rendering on a reconfigurable virtual reality controller. In: Proceedings of the 2018 CHI Conference on Human Factors in Computing Systems, pp. 1–12 (2018)
18. Asai, K., Kobayashi, H., Kondo, T.: Augmented instructions-a fusion of augmented reality and printed learning materials. In: Fifth IEEE International Conference on Advanced Learning Technologies (ICALT 2005), pp. 213–215 (2005)
19. Kalkusch, M., Lidy, T., Knapp, N., Reitmayr, G., Kaufmann, H., Schmalstieg, D.: Structured visual markers for indoor pathfinding. In: The First IEEE International Workshop Agumented Reality Toolkit, p. 8 (2002)

20. Billinghurst, M.: Augmented reality in education. New Horiz. Learn. **12**(5), 1–5 (2002)
21. Shelton, B.E., Hedley, N.R.: Using augmented reality for teaching earth-sun relationships to undergraduate geography students. In: The First IEEE International Workshop Agumented Reality Toolkit, p. 8 (2002)
22. Martín-Gutiérrez, J., Fabiani, P., Benesova, W., Meneses, M.D., Mora, C.E.: Augmented reality to promote collaborative and autonomous learning in higher education. Comput. Hum. Behav. **51**, 752–761 (2015)

Virtual Reality (VR) in the Computer Supported Cooperative Work (CSCW) Domain: A Mapping and a Pre-study on Functionality and Immersion

Gitte Pedersen[(✉)] and Konstantinos Koumaditis

Department of Business Development and Technology, School of Business and Social Sciences, Aarhus University, Birk Centerpark, Herning, Denmark
201408187@post.au.dk, kkoumaditis@btech.au.dk

Abstract. This pre-study investigates how Virtual Reality (VR) can be used to support collaborative work in a business setting. Based on a literature review it's explored how immersive technologies like Virtual Reality (VR), Augmented Reality (AR), and Mixed Reality (MR) fit into the Computer Supported Cooperative Work (CSCW) domain. By using the time and space matrix the immersive technologies are classified. Based on the findings, immersive VR supporting synchronous and remote collaboration is chosen for further investigation, where the immersive VR application, MeetinVR, has been tested. Two small-scale experiments have been conducted (n = 3 and n = 10) to test the functionality of the MeetinVR application and the level of immersion when conducting interviews compared to an online communication tool, like Skype. The initial results indicate that an immersive VR application is relatively user-friendly and provide a high level of immersion.

Keywords: Immersive Virtual Reality · Remote collaboration · Computer Supported Cooperative Work · Immersion · Skype

1 Introduction

Digitization has changed the way people work and collaborate by connecting people across time and space [1]. As enterprises are rapidly globalizing employees become more geographically distributed with teams working remotely over the Internet. This brings multiple benefits like mobile, dynamic, and flexible workforces, increase in productivity, and economical benefits by cutting travel expenses and office costs. As business has become global, the idea of an office being a place for locally situated activities, meetings and activities has also changed [2]. This had led to an increasing demand for more flexible and tailorable tools that support effective workforce collaboration and communication in a global environment among geographically distributed teams [1]. With the continuous development of novel collaborative technologies and computer interfaces, a new set of solutions that can support this need

© Springer Nature Switzerland AG 2020
J. Y. C. Chen and G. Fragomeni (Eds.): HCII 2020, LNCS 12191, pp. 136–153, 2020.
https://doi.org/10.1007/978-3-030-49698-2_10

are developed. These novel technologies have been applied in multiple different domains like education training and assistance [3], and business [4] etc. Therefore, new opportunities for augmenting interaction and sharing workspaces to dynamically work, create and share objects across time and space exist [1, 5].

To examine how an immersive technology can benefit global companies with distributed teams working remotely, a research question and three sub-questions are defined to scope this pre-study, as seen below:

RQ: How do Immersive Virtual Reality (VR) applications support collaborative work in a business setting?

- **SQ1:** How do immersive technologies fit into the Computer Supported Cooperative Work (CSCW) domain?
- **SQ2:** How are Immersive Virtual Reality (VR) applications used for collaborative work in modern organizations?
- **SQ3:** What advantages and disadvantages do Immersive Virtual Reality (VR) applications provide compared to traditional online communication tools?

In addition, two hypotheses are formed to supplement SQ3, these are presented in Sect. 3. So, with Sect. 1 presenting the Introduction, the rest of the paper is structured as follow: Sect. 2 depicts the Literature Review, Sect. 3 presents the two small-scale experiments, Sect. 4 analyses the results, Sect. 5 highlights the findings and discusses the results, and the conclusion is presented in Sect. 6.

2 Literature Review

2.1 Computer Supported Cooperative Work (CSCW)

The literature on CSCW is concerned with how the use of computer systems in terms of software tools and technology, often referred to as *groupware*, can support group interaction, sharing goals, tasks, and knowledge among teams, and assist people in their collaboration, communication, and coordination [6].

The CSCW Matrix. Groupware can be categorized by using the time-place matrix in Fig. 1. The first dimension is concerned with *when* the interaction occurs which can take place at the same time (synchronous) or at different times (asynchronous). The second dimension is concerned with the geographical location of the individuals which can be at the same place (co-located) or at different places (remote/distributed). By combining the two dimensions, four categories exist: Co-located & synchronous interaction, Remote & synchronous interaction, Co-located & asynchronous interaction, and Remote & asynchronous interaction [6].

	SAME TIME	DIFFERENT TIMES
SAME PLACE	Face-to-face interaction Ex: electronic meeting system	Asynchronous interaction Ex: shared database
DIFFERENT PLACES	Synchronous distributed interaction Ex: teleconference with shared whiteboard	Asynchronous distributed interaction Ex: email and other messaging systems

Fig. 1. Time and place groupware matrix [5].

Over the years, a paradigm shift in CSCW has become reality as new collaboration technologies have introduced new forms of collaborations [5]. Our focus is to investigate Immersive Technologies (AR/VR/MR).

2.2 Immersive Technologies for Collaboration

Immersive technologies like VR, AR and MR present a new era of collaborative work [7]. These novel technologies in the collaboration field interfaces, create new opportunities for object manipulation, sharing artefacts and knowledge by using a combination of voice, gestures, audio, and graphical information that can be used in the real world, virtual world, or a mix of both, as seen in Fig. 2.

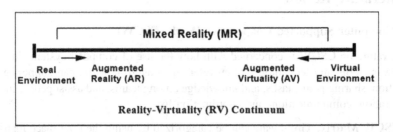

Fig. 2. Reality-Virtuality (RV) Continuum [8].

Virtual Reality (VR) for Collaboration. VR is placed on the right side of Fig. 2, and is a computer-generated pure virtual environment "in which the computer creates a sensory-immersing environment that interactively responds to and is controlled by the behavior of the user" [9]. Today, different VR systems exist providing different levels of immersion, ranging from non-immersive desktop virtual environments (DVE), semi-immersive systems, and fully immersive virtual environments (IVE). DVEs include VR on a desktop screen relying on a keyboard, mouse, joystick, or spaceball and a monitor, and uses exocentric navigation which places the user outside the environment leaving the user with a less immersive experience [10]. Semi immersive VR systems use more sophisticated devices like large screen monitors or screen projector systems that provide detailed graphics, haptic feedback, sounds, etc. Input devices for interaction could be data gloves or joystick balls, providing the user with a medium to high immersive experience [11]. IVEs include egocentric navigation where the user is surrounded by the environment enabling the user to perceive the virtual world as reality [10]. IVEs require a more sophisticated setup like head-mounted displays (HMD), hand held devices, or multiple projections, display walls, tracking devices, spatial- and multidimensional sound, haptic feedback, etc. [11].

In an IVE, the user receives a high-level multi-sensory immersion contributing to a more realistic user-experience, where the user representation is important to create a feeling of presence (FoP). Avatars are often used and can differ from simple 2D visualizations to sophisticated 3D representations. Avatars represent user behavior in the shared virtual environment (SVE) and enable joint actions and rich collaboration via chat, gestures, and object manipulation. The use of self-avatars benefits solving cooperative tasks, increases the trust among users, and contributes to a higher level of co-presence by helping users connect [12].

Co-located and Synchronous Collaboration. A physical environment with immersive projection screens enables people to work together in the same workspace. Such environments surround the user with 2D and 3D information and the user is capable to interact and share visual elements in a face-to-face setting, in which face-to-face communication is supported via speech, gestures, gaze, and non-verbal cues [13]. A well-known example is CAVE, an interactive high-resolution touch display used to engage in co-located multi-user interaction, used within education and product development [14]. Other examples include large stereoscopic projection displays with HMDs which has been used in the automotive industry for task assembly [3].

Research also exist for non-immersive and semi-immersive scenarios where multi-touch wall-sized displays are used for real-time co-sharing of digital content [15], and novel tabletop displays are used for sharing information among users by creating 2D desktop workspaces supporting human-human interaction [16].

Co-located and Asynchronous Collaboration. Asynchronous collaboration is concerned with communicating over multiple periods of time. In the literature, asynchronous co-located VR collaboration mainly focuses on semi-immersive projection screens and tabletop systems where work is supported by shifts, by "handing over", and "taking over" work [17]. Another common example is semi-immersive shared public displays which can be viewed at different times at the same place enabling workers to leave messages, post media elements, and join conversations asynchronously at the same building [18]. Such systems provide the same view for collaborators in the physical workspace in which face-to-face interaction is possible.

Remote and Synchronous Collaboration. This type of VR system supports remote users to work together in a SVE by immersing users into a co-located setting [4], and is often referred to as an IVE. IVEs support remote and real-time multi-user collaboration, easy interaction, information- and data sharing, [19], and are used in many domains like gaming, entertainment, education, therapy, training, [20], healthcare for recovery of lost skills [21], and business for design reviews, decision-making, problem-solving, product development, proposing ideas [20], job interviews [22], and having virtual meetings by enabling shared visualization [4]. Different tools, features and functions are available for directly manipulating objects, navigate, encounter people, and sharing visual artefacts. Also, collaborative Web 2.0 tools and sharing mechanisms like instant messaging, audio, video, teleconferencing, multimedia presentations, etc. can be featured. This enable joint contribution where users can simultaneously work together as data is instantly modified [23].

Remote and Asynchronous Collaboration. Where most VR systems support synchronous activities, asynchronous mode is lacking and not always supported [4, 24]. Although, examples do exist by enabling leaving data and messages for later review, recording the VE or re-playing messages in IVEs [17, 25]. This is especially used within education, where virtual class rooms enable 3D recordings and online discussion boards [24], replaying chemical data [26], or medical training among a teacher and student [27]. For non-immersive educational systems, messaging forums allow asynchronous collaboration. Although, because these features are based on synchronous activities, the VR systems support both synchronous and asynchronous activities [24].

The literature shows that VR is an evolving technology that has been applied in multiple domains and gained recognition for its potential, especially within education, medical use, gaming, and business. With the continuous advancement of VR, it has become more popular and widely available for consumers. With the public release in 2016 of portable and standalone HMDs like the Oculus GO and HTC Vive Focus, Immersive VR technology has become widely available to mainstream consumers. Since then, cheaper devices for smartphones like Google Carboard and the Galaxy Gear VR headset enabled mainstream experiences [28]. With the declining prices of VR devices, the future usage of VR can hugely increase [29].

Augmented Reality (AR) for Collaboration. AR adds a digital layer of computer graphics on top of the physical space enabling users to view and interact in real-time. Therefore, it's placed on the left side of Fig. 2, as collaboration takes place in the physical environment [8]. In general, AR displays can be classified into three categories: 1) See through hand-held displays, 2) HMDs and 3) Projection displays [30].

Co-located and Synchronous Collaboration. See-through HMDs have been used to show graphic objects and allowing real-time interactions. AR has been used within education by adding annotations in real-time [31], or within engineering allowing participants to observe and interact with dynamic visual simulations and CAD models [32]. Local real-time annotations have successfully been used in industrial processes, machinery, and construction for mediating human-to-human interaction [33] and-held devices have also been used for interacting with 3D objects via touch gestures [34].

Co-located and Asynchronous Collaboration. Little research focuses on asynchronous AR collaboration, and multiple challenges exist, like the role time plays, how to capture annotations and different inputs and re-visualize it, and how other forms of communication influence the collaboration. If overcoming this, asynchronous AR can allow multiple users to collaborate back and forth [13, 35]. Via a physical interface, tangible markers can be used for spatial annotations in a work process. When work shifts changes the annotations remains to help and guide workers [35].

Remote and Synchronous Collaboration. Remote AR is used in multiple industries like factory planning, maintenance, product design, and education, where a huge focus has been on assistance, work instructions and training. Remote AR has been used for crime scene investigation among crime scene investigators (local) and experts (remote) [36], within the security domain to exchange context-related information among teams via a video channel and adding spatial annotations, presenting work instructions via camera and 3D hand gestures [37], and within telesurgery for surgical education [38].

Remote and Asynchronous Collaboration. Again, little research focuses on asynchronous AR. Although, a study shows that a mobile application can be used to co-create AR structures by using blocks, where users can build at the *same* time and *different* times. By switching settings, this allows building on top of the other participant's work [39].

Similarly to VR, AR is available over a wide variety of devices and applications, and has been widely used due to the launch of commercial AR applications like Pokémon Go, Snapchat's AR lenses and IKEA Place. AR has therefore achieved mass-market success by bringing mobile AR to the public, and the use of low-cost smartglasses, like Google Glasses, has reached the market for consumer oriented mobile AR, which has showed its potential supporting assembly, maintenance, quality control, etc. Wearable AR has showed the potential of offering immersive experiences in the real environment and can be used for mediating human-to-human interactions [35]. Although, challenges for asynchronous AR still exist [13].

Mixed Reality (MR) for Collaboration. MR brings together the real world and digital objects, meaning that both physical and digital objects co-exist and interact in real-time. MR blends elements from VR and AR as real and virtual worlds are presented together within a single display. MR is therefore placed anywhere between the extrema of the RV Continuum in Fig. 2, as MR is a combination of realities [8].

Co-located and Synchronous Collaboration. MR systems exist where co-located users can view and interact with shared virtual information while viewing the real environment. Examples include see-through HMDs, where users can collaboratively browse the world wide web, wearable computer platforms for virtual annotations [7], and shared physical MR-installations using a position tracking system, large scale projection and mobile VR headsets [40]. Because co-located and asynchronous MR collaboration has not been well studied [17] it has not been able to include.

Remote and Synchronous Collaboration. Examples include wearables like see-through HMDs used within video conferencing in IVEs providing an AR communication space, or by having virtual images of remote participants attached into the real-world environment [7], or used on a MR tabletop to share a MR space among two remote people [41].

Mixed-Presence. MR systems enabling co-located and remote users to collaborate synchronously in a shared visual workspace exist. Collaborative experiences can therefore have a *mixed-presence.* Mixed-presence groupware (MPG) systems fit in between the synchronous co-located- and distributed synchronous category and may also support asynchronous collaboration as well [42]. MPG systems include distributed tabletops, where remote users can synchronously interact. Remote users are represented via video shadows or silhouettes to guide co-located users [43].

Remote and Asynchronous Collaboration. Where no co-located asynchronous MR applications have been found in the literature, some studies focuses on how users in remote asynchronous MR environments can create digital information and re-visit project meetings [44]. Within education, IVEs with both avatars and video of real people augmented with panoramic audio, asynchronous collaboration is supported by discussion forums and 3D recordings [45]. Within design review collaboration, tangible MR systems convert 2D and 3D models into tangible virtual models, where asynchronous activities are supported by redlining errors and saving viewpoints [46]. Annotating systems allow asynchronous annotation activities to be re-visited [47].

Although MR has not matured that fast it has edged toward the mainstream through new and affordable hardware like headsets (HoloLens), smart mobile devices, and display improvement resolution [48].

2.3 Mapping of Collaborative Technologies

Based on the literature the findings of the examined immersive collaborative technologies are mapped in Fig. 3 based on the time and space matrix. Importantly, the mapping seeks to present an answer the first sub-question.

The map shows that different VR, AR, and MR technologies support collaborative work by fitting into one or more of the CSCW quadrants. This shows that different collaboration technologies exist and can be used in many different contexts, and for multiple purposes supporting many different forms of collaboration. Where multiple examples are found on synchronous and asynchronous collaboration for IVEs challenges exist for asynchronous AR, where asynchronous MR has not been well studied. IVEs support remote cooperation by sharing a virtual space in which multiple users can collaborate and share ideas without the physical constraints. VR can be used for global and remote collaboration by using a combination of speech and audio, gestures, text, video, and other collaborative media, and has therefore been chosen for further investigation, as it based on the literature fulfill the needs the most.

Current Immersive Virtual Reality Applications. To be able to test a VR application, it was important to examine available VR solutions. While many VR applications exist like Facebook owned Facebook Spaces, Oculus Rooms and Horizon, or SecondLife, rumii, VR Chat and Google Expeditions, in this study we focus on MeetinVR. MeetinVR is a business focused VR application for collaborative remote meetings.

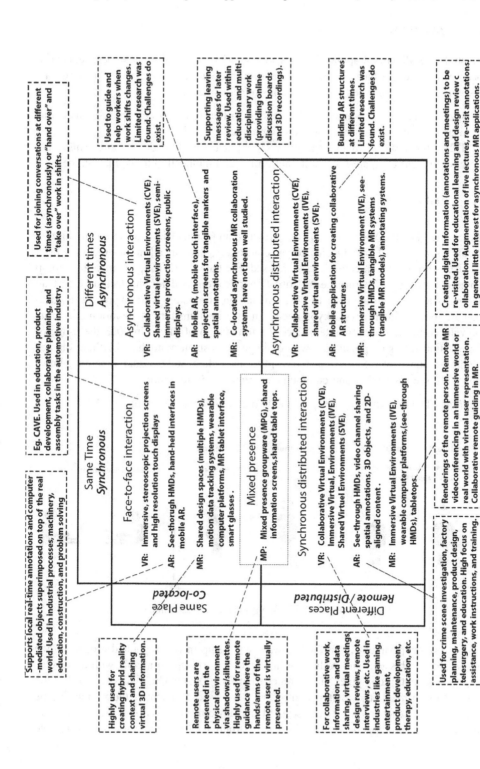

Fig. 3. Mapping collaborative VR, AR, and MR by using the CSCW taxonomy.

3 Experiments

To study the MeetinVR application and answer SQ3, two small-scale experiments have been conducted, for basic tasks (n = 3) and immersion during interviews (n = 10). To test these, two hypotheses have been constructed, such as.

H1: The basic functionality of Immersive Virtual Reality (VR) applications are as user-friendly as traditional online communication tools.

H2: Immersive Virtual Reality (VR) applications provide a more immersive environment compared to traditional online communication tools, like Skype.

3.1 Methods

Hardware. For the VR part of the experiments, an Oculus Rift headset, including two Oculus sensors and two Oculus touch controllers, and an all-in-one Oculus Quest headset with two touch controllers were used. For the Oculus Rift, a compatible laptop computer was used to run the MeetinVR application, and for the Oculus Quest an iPhone was used. In addition to this, two laptop computers with Skype are used to conduct remote interviews. Skype is chosen as a medium for collaboration due to its prevalence in the digital market. Since the foundation of Skype in 2003 the usage of has continued to gain popularity, where Skype users spent more than 3 billion minutes communicating over Skype each day [49]. Its online audio-visual function allows people to see each other and communicate remotely in real-time.

Settings. The experimental setup of the two experiments is seen in Fig. 4.

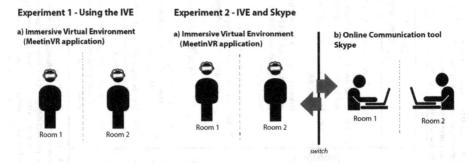

Fig. 4. Experimental setup for the two experiments.

For both experiments, the VR hardware was setup in two separated rooms. In one room, the Oculus Rift and additional hardware was set up on a table with an Oculus compatible laptop computer. In the other room, the Oculus Quest was set up. For the second experiment, two laptop computers were used to conduct the remote Skype interviews. In each room, it was secured that no other sounds or distractions could interrupt the participants. By placing each participant in separate rooms, the remote cooperation was observed. Since the experiments required participants working in pairs, P1 and P2 for experiments 1 executed the experiment in collaboration, where P3 executed the task in collaboration with one of the researchers. The decision to involve the researcher was taken to be able to extract richer observations spectrum out of this pre-study experimentation.

3.2 Immersive Virtual Environment (IVE)

By using the MeetinVR web platform, virtual workspaces were utilized (see Fig. 5a), and PDF files were uploaded. In the IVE, each user is presented via a personalized avatar which enables communication via speech, text, grasp, manipulation of digital information, moving around, sharing objects among teammates. A virtual iPad (seen in Fig. 5b) is provided for each user which serves as a navigation panel on which the user can open uploaded files, write notes, share reactions, take pictures, open screenshots and files, materialize them and place them in the virtual space (seen in Fig. 5c). A 3D pen is also provided for writing and drawing directly in the 3D space or on files, notes, blackboards or walls, depending on the settings of the virtual workspace.

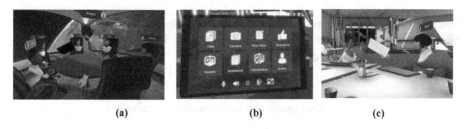

(a)   **(b)**   **(c)**

Fig. 5. Virtual meeting environment with (a) the workspace utilized for the experiments, in (b) the virtual iPad provided in the IVE is seen, where the uploaded files are accessed in the "files" folder. In (c) a file has been materialized and is shared among users in the IVE.

Experiment 1. To test the basic functionality of the MeetinVR application 4 specific tasks were uploaded in the IVE via the web platform and the files appeared in the "Files" folder on the virtual iPad. To guide the participants, similar icons from the virtual iPad (Files folder, camera, etc.), was used in the task descriptions. Before the execution, in-depth instructions based on the tasks were given to each participant in the IVE. While executing the tasks, the interactions of the participants were observed on the VR laptop. After the experiment, the participants were interviewed separately regarding their experience. Then, following similar studies [50] the *NASA Task Load Index (TLX)* was used to measure the overall workload of the participants.

Experiment 2. To test the immersion of the two communication tools, an interview scenario was created. Four interview questions were created fitting into a business context. Before the interview, one of the facilitators gave instructions in the IVE while the participants observed on the VR laptop. To measure the level of *self-efficacy*, each participant was asked separately to rank on a scale from 1–5 how confident they currently felt being capable to execute well in the IVE (find and open the file, and conduct the interview), where 1 means not confident at all and 5 means very confident.

When interviewing in the IVE, the interview questions were uploaded via the web platform and accessed on the virtual iPad. When interviewing over Skype, the same interview questions were printed out on a paper and placed in front of the participants. During both interviews the participants were observed by a facilitator in each room.

Importantly, a randomized approach was utilized to provide a mixed sample of experiments, i.e. some participants started with Skype and then VR, while other pairs the opposite. P1–P4 experienced VR first, where P5–P10 experienced Skype first. After each interview, each participant was handed out a modified version of the Immersive Experience Questionnaire (IEQ) [51] consisting of 24 questions focusing on an interview scenario to measure the subjective experience of immersion after the interview. Last, each participant was again asked to rank their level of *self-efficacy*.

4 Data Analysis

4.1 Experiment 1 – Functionality of the Immersive VR Application

Observations. During the execution of tasks, it was observed that some participants found the execution of tasks more difficult than others. This was furthermore verified when interviewing the participants (Table 1).

Table 1. Observations and interviews from experiment 1.

	P1	P2	P3
Observations	Executed tasks fast, had to wait for P2 Helped P2 by explaining where to click, etc. Closed the tasks instructions, had to memorize	Struggled navigating with the controllers Asked P1 for help when in doubt Closed the tasks instructions, had to memorize Accidentally changed the position of the room (intervention needed)	Executed tasks fast Knew where to click on the virtual iPad Materialized the task instructions and placed it in the IVE Played around with the colors of the 3D pen
Interviews	Effective way of communicating Navigation panel is intuitive. User-friendly interface Natural interaction Felt very present	Effective way of communicating, but training is needed Difficult to use the grapping button and front trigger Felt natural despite being staged Doesn't capture the mimic Felt calm, secure and less nervous	Effective way of communicating Easy due to previous gaming background Resembles real-world interaction Natural interaction. No extreme movements needed Felt very present

NASA TLX. Raw TLX scores of the 6 different TLX dimensions are calculated. To score each dimension, 21 graduations are provided for each dimension ranging from "very low" to "very high". The tick marks range from 0–100 with a 5 point increment between each mark [52]. By finding the marks of the participants the raw scores of each dimension are calculated and seen in Table 2.

Table 2. Raw NASA TLX scores along the 6 dimensions.

	P1	P2	P3
Mental demand	10	80	20
Physical demand	10	20	05
Temporal demand	05	50	15
Performance	85	30	80
Effort	10	35	30
Frustration	30	55	05

The Raw TLX scores show a significant difference in how the participants have experienced the IVE. In general, P1 and P3 have a low overall workload compared to P2, which indicates that they found the IVE intuitive and easy to use. This is especially clear along the *mental demand* dimension, as a lot of mental activity was required for P2. The *physical demand* is scored low, indicating that little physical activity or extreme movements were needed. The *temporal demand* dimensions show that P2 felt more time pressure when executing the tasks, where P1 and P3 scores this low. Also, the *performance* of P2 is scored significantly lower, meaning that the execution of tasks wasn't found to be successfully accomplished. Where the effort level is seen to be lowest for P1, the other participants required a bit more mental and physical work to accomplish the tasks. The Raw TLX scores show that the level of *frustration* is scored the highest for P2 indicating a more insecure execution.

4.2   Experiment 2 – Immersion

Observations. In the IVE, some of the participants struggled with grapping the virtual iPad. It was observed, that when trying to grab it, the participants moved the whole upper body and head, which lead the virtual iPad to move further away from them. Most of the participants struggled to navigate in the IVE and opening the file. To solve this, some of the participants gave each other instructions remotely, although four of the participants asked the facilitator in the room to help them. During the interviews, it was observed that the participants looked at each other in the IVE when speaking and some were using hand-gestures when answering the questions. Over Skype, almost all participants looked around in the physical room at some point when interviewing and seemed highly aware of their physical surroundings.

Immersive Experience Questionnaire (IEQ). The subjective IEQ scores from the participants are analyzed and calculated. To calculate the total immersion scores, each of the 24-items are scored by using a 1–7 Likert scale. Negatively scored items are first inverted (Qs 5, 6, and 7) [51]. Then, all scores are summed up to find the subjective immersion score. Because the questionnaire was handed out twice, two immersion scores for each participant are calculated. Seen Table 3.

Table 3. Immersive Experience Questionnaire (IEQ) scores and differentiation in percentages.

	1. SKYPE	2. VR	Differentiation
P1	80	124	55%
P2	97	117	20,6%
P3	91	111	22%
P4	94	114	21,3%
	1. VR	2. SKYPE	
P5	118	100	18%
P6	110	101	8,9%
P7	127	115	10,4%
P8	111	116	−4,3%
P9	118	89	32,6%
P10	115	106	8,5%

The IEQ scores show that 90% (9/10) of the participants find the interview in the IVE a more immersive experience than Skype, where P8 scores the IVE lower than Skype. To show how many percentages the immersion of the IVE is scored compared to Skype, the difference in percentages is added to the table.

Self-Efficacy. The quantitatively measured self-efficacy scores are seen in Table 4.

Table 4. Measured self-efficacy scores.

	P1	P2	P3	P4	P5	P6	P7	P8	P9	P10
Before using the IVE	4	1	3	4	4	3	4/5	5	4	4
After using the IVE	4	3	4	4	4/5	5	4	4	5	5

The table shows that 8/10 (80%) of the participants rate the self-efficacy the same or higher after using the IVE, meaning that the confidence is the same or has increased. The table also shows that P7 and P8 rate the self-efficacy lower after using the IVE. P7 explained that the level of confidence got lower due to the short instructions and therefore didn't feel secure about using the IVE properly. P8 explained that the many new impressions were overwhelming which made the self-efficacy to decrease.

5   Discussion

To answer the research question of this pre-study, three additional sub-questions have been created. SQ1 seeks to answer how immersive technologies fit into the Computer Supported Cooperative Work (CSCW) domain. To answer this, a literature review on immersive technologies (VR/AR/MR), was conducted. During this research a map of the immersive technologies has been created based on the CSCW taxonomy. Interestingly, the map shows that multiple different technologies and systems exist, fitting into one or more of the CSCW quadrants. For example, asynchronous activities in IVEs are often based on synchronous activities, and therefore seen supporting both aspects. The map illustrates that the immersive technologies support synchronous collaboration well, remotely and co-located. Although, some VR systems are lacking the asynchronous mode, while challenges exist for asynchronous AR, and asynchronous MR has not been well studied. Based on the literature review, it has been seen that VR can aid the need for remote and synchronous collaboration.

SQ2 seeks to answer how Immersive Virtual Reality (VR) applications are used for collaborative work in modern organizations. Both based on the literature review and expert interviews, it was shown that immersive VR is used in companies that have teams distributed in different cities or countries. By using VR, it allows employees to have remote meetings and connect in a co-located setting. A very interesting point is that VR can be used for multiple purposes, like reviewing designs, making decisions, solving problems, develop products, conducting job interviews, and having virtual meetings. VR therefore creates new opportunities for interacting and sharing a workspace to dynamically work, create and share objects.

SQ3 seeks to uncover what advantages and disadvantages Immersive Virtual Reality (VR) applications provide compared to traditional online communication tools. To answer this, two small-scale experiments have been conducted. For the first experiment the initial results indicated that the ability to execute basic tasks in the VR environment differed between subjects, this was also indicated on the observations, interviews, and NASA TLX scores. While the small sample size restricts any validation of the hypothesis it has provided useful insights both from a methodological aspect but also as an initial indicator that is more than likely the VR environment (as it is designed in the current version of the VR application) to have been perceived as user-friendly by most of the participants.

For the second experiment, interviews were conducted over Skype and in the IVE respectively. The initial results indicate that 9/10 of the participants depicted the interviews in the IVE as a more immersive experience than Skype. Interestingly, the results demonstrate a correlation between the IEQ scores and self-efficiency scores as the participant with low IEQ scores for the IVE also show a decrease in the measured self-efficacy, where the opposite is seen for the participants scoring immersion high in the IVE. For the participant seen scoring the IVE more immersive but having a decreasing self-efficacy, a more in-depth and longer introductions to the IVE could influence the self-efficiency score. Thus, the experimental data, confirm the hypothesis constructed, as the immersive VR application provided a more immersive experience compared to Skype.

Based on the expert interviews and the experiments conducted, SQ3 is answered. The experimentation showed that immersive VR applications provide higher levels of immersion compared to Skype. The advantage of VR is therefore the capabilities of immersing users into the virtual environment. A disadvantage based on the experiment was the decreasing self-efficacy scores due to the short instructions and many new impressions in the IVE.

Based on the collected data, this shows that the immersive VR applications intrigued the participants and helped them staying focused during the interview compared to Skype.

6 Conclusion

The purpose of this study is to answer how Immersive Virtual Reality (VR) applications support collaborative work in a business setting. To do so, this study mapped three immersive technologies (AR/VR/MR). The map depicts that VR creates new opportunities for remote and synchronous collaborative work. By providing a high-level multisensory experience, immersive VR applications provide a higher level of immersion compared to traditional online communication tools, and supports collaborative work via object manipulation, sharing artefacts and knowledge by using a combination of voice, gestures, audio, and graphical information. With these capabilities, businesses will be able to benefit from VR, by not only conducting remote virtual meetings, but develop products, review and present designs, brainstorm, train employees, and share information and knowledge in a faster and more efficient way.

References

1. Science, C., Limerick, L.: CSCW: an initial exploration'. Scand. J. Inf. Syst. **5**, 3–24 (1993)
2. Cynthia Pickering, E.W.: An architecture and business process framework for global team collaboration. Intel Technol. J. **09**(02), 373–381 (2005)
3. Salzmann, H., Jacobson, N., Fröhlich, B.: Collaborative interaction in co-located two-user scenarios. In: Proceedings 15th Joint Virtual Reality Eurographics Conference Virtual Environment, pp. 85–92 (2009)
4. Germani, M., Mengoni, M., Peruzzini, M.: An approach to assessing virtual environments for synchronous and remote collaborative design. Adv. Eng. Inform. **26**(4), 793–813 (2012)
5. Hutchison, C.: Computer-supported cooperative work. Research Gate, January 1999 (1999)
6. Ellis, C., Wainer, J.: Groupware and computer supported cooperative work. In: Multiagent System: A Modern Approach to Distributed Artificial Intelligence, pp. 425–457 (1999)
7. Billinghurst, M., Kato, H.: Collaborative mixed reality. In: Proceedings First International Symposium Mixed Reality (ISMR 1999) Mixed Reality – Merging Real Virtual Worlds, pp. 261–284. Springer, Boston (2018)
8. Milgram, P., Takemura, H., Utsumi, A., Kishino, F.: Mixed reality (MR) reality-virtuality (RV) Continuum. Syst. Res. **2351**, 282–292 (1994)
9. Liang, H.N., Lu, F., Shi, Y., Nanjappan, V., Papangelis, K.: Evaluating the effects of collaboration and competition in navigation tasks and spatial knowledge acquisition within virtual reality environments. Futur. Gener. Comput. Syst. **95**, 855–866 (2019)

10. Kozhevnikov, M., Gurlitt, J., Kozhevnikov, M.: Learning relative motion concepts in immersive and non-immersive virtual environments. J. Sci. Educ. Technol. **22**(6), 952–962 (2013)

11. Tucker, C.S.: Investigating the impact of interactive immersive virtual reality environments in enhancing task performance in online engineering design activities, pp. 1–11 (2015)

12. Wright, T., Madey, G.: A survey of collaborative virtual environment technologies. Tech. Rep, pp. 1–16. University Notre Dame-USA (2008)

13. Irlitti, A., Smith, R.T., Von Itzstein, S., Billinghurst, M., Thomas, B.H.: Challenges for asynchronous collaboration in augmented reality. In: Adjunct Proceedings of 2016 IEEE International Symposium Mixed Augment. Reality, ISMAR-Adjunct 2016, pp. 31–35 (2017)

14. Febretti, A., et al.: CAVE2: a hybrid reality environment for immersive simulation and information analysis. In: Engineering Reality of Virtual Reality 2013, vol. 8649, p. 864903 (2013)

15. Liu, C., Chapuis, O., Beaudouin-Lafon, M., Lecolinet, E.: CoReach: cooperative gestures for data manipulation on wall-sized displays. In: Conference on Human Factors in Computing Systems Proceedings, vol. 2017, pp. 6730–6741, May 2017

16. Pan, Y., Steed, A.: The impact of self-avatars on trust and collaboration in shared virtual environments. PLoS ONE **12**(12), 1–20 (2017)

17. Billinghurst, M., Cordeil, M., Bezerianos, A., Margolis, T.: Collaborative immersive analytics. Immersive Analytics. LNCS, vol. 11190, pp. 221–257. Springer, Cham (2018). https://doi.org/10.1007/978-3-030-01388-2_8

18. Carter, S., Mankoff, J., Goddi, P.: Building connections among loosely coupled groups: Hebb's rule at work. Comput. Support. Coop. Work CSCW Int. J. **13**(3–4), 305–327 (2004)

19. Olivier, H., Pinkwart, N.: Collaborative virtual environments-hype or hope for CSCW? Ifl. Tech. Rep. Ser., 13 (2007)

20. Jerald, J.: The VR Book: Human-Centered Design for Virtual Reality, 1st edn. Morgan & Claypool, ACM (2015)

21. Perez-Marcos, D., et al.: A fully immersive set-up for remote interaction and neurorehabilitation based on virtual body ownership. Front. Neurol. **3**, 110 (2012)

22. Beti, R.A., Al-Khatib, F., Cook, D.M.: The efficacy of using virtual reality for job interviews and its effects on mitigating discrimination. In: Unger, H., Sodsee, S., Meesad, P. (eds.) IC2IT 2018. AISC, vol. 769, pp. 43–52. Springer, Cham (2019). https://doi.org/10.1007/978-3-319-93692-5_5

23. Churchill, E.F., Snowdon, D.: Collaborative virtual environments: an introductory review of issues and systems. Virtual Reality **3**, 3–15 (1998). https://doi.org/10.1007/BF01409793

24. Morozov, M., Gerasimov, A., Fominykh, M., Smorkalov, A.: Asynchronous immersive classes in a 3D virtual world: extended description of vacademia. In: Gavrilova, Marina L., Tan, C.J.Kenneth, Kuijper, A. (eds.) Transactions on Computational Science XVIII. LNCS, vol. 7848, pp. 81–100. Springer, Heidelberg (2013). https://doi.org/10.1007/978-3-642-38803-3_5

25. Greenhalgh, C., Flintham, M., Purbrick, J., Benford, S.: Applications of temporal links: recording and replaying virtual environments. In: Proceedings of - Virtual Reality Annual International Symposium, vol. 2002, pp. 101–108 (2002)

26. Lee, J., Quy, P.S., Kim, J.I., Kang, L.W., Seo, A., Kim, H.S.: A collaborative virtual reality environment for molecular biology. In: Proceedings of - 2009 International Symposium Ubiquitous Virtual Reality, ISUVR 2009, pp. 68–71 (2009)

27. García, P., Montalà, O., Pairot, C., Rallo, R., Skarmeta, A.G.: MOVE: component groupware foundations for collaborative virtual environments. In: Proceedings of 4th International Conference Collaborative Virtual Environment, pp. 55–62 (2002)

28. He, D., Westphal, C., Garcia-Luna-Aceves, J.J.: Network support for AR/VR and immersive video application: a survey. In: ICETE 2018 – Proceedings of 15th International Joint Conference E-Business Telecommunication, ICETE, vol. 1, pp. 359–369 (2018)

29. Nararro-Haro, M.V., et al.: The use of virtual reality to facilitate mindfulness skills training in dialectical behavioral therapy for borderline personality disorder: a case study. Front. Psychol. **7**, 1573 (2016)

30. Gurevich, P., Lanir, J., Cohen, B.: Design and implementation of TeleAdvisor: a projection-based augmented reality system for remote collaboration. Comput. Support. Coop. Work **24** (6), 527–562 (2015). https://doi.org/10.1007/s10606-015-9232-7

31. Stephen Carlson, T.S., Ellis, S., Green, A.S.: The studierstube: augmented reality project. Presence Teleoperators Virtual Environ. **1**, 33–54 (2003)

32. Dong, S., Behzadan, A.H., Chen, F., Kamat, V.R.: Collaborative visualization of engineering processes using tabletop augmented reality. Adv. Eng. Softw. **55**, 45–55 (2013)

33. Koumaditis, K., Hussain, T.: Human computer interaction research through the lens of a bibliometric analysis, vol. 10271, pp. 23–37, October 2017

34. Grandi, J.G., Debarba, H.G., Bemdt, I., Nedel, L., Maclel, A.: Design and assessment of a collaborative 3D interaction technique for handheld augmented reality. In: Proceedings of 25th IEEE Conference Virtual Reality 3D User Interfaces, VR 2018, pp. 49–56 (2018)

35. Irlitti, A., Von Itzstein, S., Alem, L., Thomas, B.: Tangible interaction techniques to support asynchronous collaboration. In: 2013 IEEE International Symposium Mixed and Augmented Reality, ISMAR 2013, October 2013, pp. 1–6 (2013)

36. Poelman, R., Akman, O., Lukosch, S., Jonker, P.: As if being there: mediated reality for crime scene investigation. In: Proceedings of ACM Conference Computer Supported Cooperative Work, CSCW, no. February, pp. 1267–1276 (2012)

37. Datcu, D., Cidota, M., Lukosch, H., Lukosch, S.: On the usability of augmented reality for information exchange in teams from the security domain. In: Proceedings of 2014 IEEE Joint Intelligence Security Informatics Conference JISIC 2014, pp. 160–167 (2014)

38. Davis, M.C., Can, D.D., Pindrik, J., Rocque, B.G., Johnston, J.M.: Virtual interactive presence in global surgical education: international collaboration through augmented reality. World Neurosurg. **86**, 103–111 (2016)

39. Guo, A., Canberk, I., Murphy, H., Monroy-Hernández, A., Vaish, R.: Blocks: collaborative and persistent augmented reality experiences, vol. 3, no. 3 (2019)

40. Hagler, J., Lankes, M., Diephuis, J.: Animating participants in co-located playful mixed-reality installations. In: 2018 IEEE 1st Workshop Animation Virtual Augmented Environment, ANIVAE 2018, March 2018

41. Minatani, S., Kitahara, I., Kameda, Y., Ohta, Y.: Face-to-face tabletop remote collaboration in mixed reality. In: 2007 6th IEEE ACM International Symposium, Mixed and Augmented Reality, ISMAR, November 2007

42. Tang, A., Boyle, M., Greenberg, S.: Understanding and mitigating display and presence disparity in mixed presence groupware. J. Res. Pract. Inf. Technol. **37**(2), 193–209 (2005)

43. Robinson, P., Tuddenham, P.: Distributed tabletops: supporting remote and mixed-presence tabletop collaboration. In: Tabletop 2007 - 2nd Annual IEEE International Workshop on Horizontal Interactive Human-Computer Systems, pp. 19–26 (2007)

44. de Belen, R.A.J., Nguyen, H., Filonik, D., Del Favero, D., Bednarz, T.: A systematic review of the current state of collaborative mixed reality technologies: 2013–2018. In: AIMS Electronic and Electrical Engineering 2019, vol. 3, no. Special Issues: Augmented and Virtual Reality for Industry 4.0, pp. 181–223 (2019)

45. Gardner, M.R., Elliott, J.B.: The immersive education laboratory: understanding affordances, structuring experiences, and creating constructivist, collaborative processes, in mixed-reality smart environments. EAI Endorsed Trans. Futur. Intell. Educ. Environ. **1**(1), e6 (2014)

46. Wang, X., Dunston, P.S.: Tangible mixed reality for remote design review: a study understanding user perception and acceptance. Vis. Eng. 1(1), 1–15 (2013)
47. Tseng, P.Y., Haraldsson, H., Belongie, S.: Annotate all ! A perspective preserved asynchronous annotation system for collaborative augmented reality (2019)
48. Noor, A.K.: The HoloLens revolution. Mech. Eng. 138(10), 31–36 (2016)
49. Quartiroli, A., Knight, S.M., Etzel, E.F., Monaghan, M.: Using Skype to facilitate team-based qualitative research, including the process of data analysis. Int. J. Soc. Res. Methodol. 20(6), 659–666 (2017)
50. Koumaditis, K., Chinello, F., Venckute, S.: Design of a virtual reality and haptic setup linking arousals to training scenarios: a preliminary stage. In: 25th IEEE Conference Virtual Reality 3D User Interfaces, VR 2018 - Proceedings, pp. 613–614 (2018)
51. Rigby, J.M., Gould, S.J.J., Brumby, D.P., Cox, A.L.: Development of a questionnaire to measure immersion in video media: the film IEQ. In: TVX 2019 – Proceedings of 2019 ACM International Conference Interaction Experience TV Online Video, pp. 35–46 (2019)
52. NASA Ames Research Center: Task Load Index (TLX). Springer Reference (2012)

Measurement Based AR for Geometric Validation Within Automotive Engineering and Construction Processes

Muhammad Ali Shahid[1]([⊠]), Benjamin-Paul Jesche[2],
Manuel Olbrich[1], Holger Graf[1], Andreas Franek[1], Arjan Kuijper[1],
Ulrich Bockholt[3], and Michael Schmitt[3]

[1] Fraunhofer IGD, Fraunhoferstrasse 5, Darmstadt, Germany
muhammad.ali.shahid@igd.fraunhofer.de
[2] Volkswagen Aktiengesellschaft, 38436 Wolfsburg, Germany
[3] Visometry GmbH, Fraunhoferstrasse 5, Darmstadt, Germany

Abstract. We look at the final stages of the automobile design process, during which the geometric validation process for a design, in particular for the vehicle front end, is examined. A concept is presented showing how this process can be improved using augmented reality. Since the application poses high accuracy requirements the augmented reality also needs to be highly accurate and of measurable quality. We present a Measurement Based AR approach to overlaying 3D information onto images, which extends the existing process and is particularly suited to the application in question. We also discuss how the accuracy of this new approach can be validated using computer vision methods employed under the appropriate conditions. The results of an initial study are presented, where the overlay accuracy is expressed in image pixels as well as millimeters followed by a discussion on how this validation can be improved to meet the requirements posed by the application.

Keywords: Measurement based augmented reality · Measurement arm · Mixed reality · Physical Mock-Up · Constraint analysis · Augmentation accuracy

1 Introduction

Due to the increasing volatility of the markets and a greater demand for customizable products, established automobile manufacturers are faced with high demands with regard to flexibility and quality of production. In order for a manufacturer to be able to assert itself in international competition, existing disadvantages regarding production and manufacturing costs must be countered using innovation. Geometric validation of a vehicle design is a time consuming and costly process, since it involves constructing and inspecting Physical Mock-ups (PMU). Efficiency can be increased when this is done by assessing physical parts with virtual ones using Augmented Reality (AR), thereby creating powerful synergies by combining the physical PMU and virtual DMU (Digital Mock-up) worlds. An AR concept, which is tailor made to meet the requirements of the geometric validation process for a vehicle front end, is discussed after shortly explaining the current process and the problems associated with it.

J. Y. C. Chen and G. Fragomeni (Eds.): HCII 2020, LNCS 12191, pp. 154–165, 2020.
https://doi.org/10.1007/978-3-030-49698-2_11

PMU's are used for geometric validation, especially in vehicle development. Physical models of the front end are built in order to depict engine compartments and undercarriages. These areas are particularly interesting because many components are installed in a small space. Geometrical validation consists of using the PMU's to conduct installation and expansion inspections, clearance inspections and the demonstration of deviations which occur during production and assembly. In addition, future bottlenecks around systems situated between two or more components need to be found. Similarly, possible chafing points on cables, hoses or lines need to be found, because these can rub against other components during vehicle operation. The detection of deviations from design is also part of geometric validation. Flexible components in particular tend to have different installation positions compared to their CAD target positions, which makes them highly susceptible to cause interference for surrounding components.

Small and large groups of participants carry out the inspections, as stakeholders come together to inspect a design from all the different aspects already mentioned and discuss possible solutions, making this a highly collaborative process. In order to aid the process a number of equipment and techniques are used. These can involve using simple rulers to measure distances (for clearance inspection) or simply inspecting the parts visually. Measurement arms, which allow highly accurate coordinate measurements to be made, are also used. These devices are explained in further detailed in later sections, because they are also used in the Measurement Based AR approach we take.

The use of a measurement arm also allows the comparison of the PMU to its DMU counterpart. Using the so-called registration process, which is also explained in more detail in the following sections, the digital coordinate system defined in the vehicle CAD design and the physical coordinate system of the measurement arm are united. In this way, the locations of parts such as bolts can be measured and compared to the design to inspect whether these are in accordance with the design.

Installation spaces with a high component density, such as the vehicle front ends, are modified several times in the early phase of geometric validation as problems are detected and design modifications are made. The components may be unfit for series production or may have dimensional deviations. In this way, components or assemblies are structurally adapted and component positions change in order to meet the complex requirements of vehicle development. The production of the modified components requires time, as well as being costly, and the geometric validation of a modified design is therefore time consuming and costly. The development does not stop while waiting on the production and delivery of a modified part. The development cycle continues during this time but this also increases the complexity of the process, as several versions of interrelated parts begin to exist. Knowing which design version of a certain component is currently installed can become difficult. The mutual inspection of small spaces by a large group of participants is also inherently difficult.

We attempt to overcome some of the existing problems outlined above using augmented reality. For example increasing the speed and efficiency of the geometric validation process by visualizing parts that are not yet physically available in the vehicle front end. This allows the circumventing of delivery times for individual components. Thus, the suitability of the component designs can be examined while waiting on designs to be manufactured and delivered. Different design versions under development can also be projected onto the physical vehicle front carriage and examined for suitability, compatibility or correctness. The PMU's remain to be an essential aspect of the geometric validation and the collective inspection of these PMU's by a large group of stakeholders can be better accommodated by the use of large screens, so that a large number of participants can easily follow the entire process. Since measurements are also an essential aspect of the geometric validation process, measurements between physical and virtual components or the physical components and their own virtual counterparts is also a useful feature of the new system (Fig. 1).

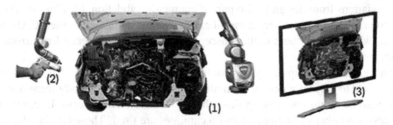

Fig. 1. Augmented Reality in the context of Geometric validation: (1) Physical mock-up with parts missing. (2) Tracking camera pose using a measurement arm. (3) Registration and visualization of virtual components.

The deployment of AR for geometric validation, however, is only feasible if visualization accuracy can be guaranteed. The visualization allows users to hone into and identify potential problem zones, therefore the quality of the superimposition of virtual information onto the camera images must be quantifiable and accurate. In Verification and Results, we discuss an initial study conducted to study this accuracy.

2 Our Concept

Extending the current geometric validation process with AR not only improves the said process, but rather this also provides opportunities to improve AR. Traditional computer vision methods [5–7] can be very robust but still cannot guarantee registration and tracking performance due to their being susceptible to errors caused by visibility conditions, clutter, etc. [4]. We therefore combine the measurement arm[1] already a part of the geometric validation process with a camera in order to achieve Measurement Based AR (see Fig. 2). This is done by attaching the camera to the measurement arm tool-tip and determining the camera-pose relative to the tool center point (TCP) using the hand-eye-calibration (HEC). This means that the camera-pose in the measurement arm coordinate system can be determined at any time using the tool center point pose delivered by the measurement arm and the HEC.

---

[1] FARO 7-Axis 3D measurement unit, https://www.faro.com/, last visited Oct. 2019.

Defining the Object of Interest (OoI) as the object we wish to track in the camera coordinate system, we determine the pose of the OoI in the measurement arm coordinate system using registration. Therefore, using the OoI and the camera poses in the measurement arm coordinate system, the pose of the OoI relative to the camera can be determined at any time. We use the pose of the OoI relative to the camera to overlay the 3D information from the CAD-models onto the camera image using the instant3dHub [10] framework. Since our verification process uses a different approach to perform this step, this is not discussed in further detail here. The measurement arm, registration and HEC, which are combined to achieve measurement based AR, are explained in further detail below.

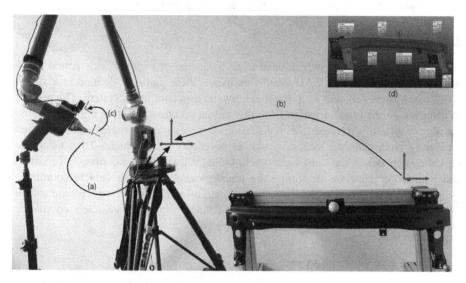

Fig. 2. System setup. (a) Pose of the TCP is provided in the measurement arm coordinate system. (b) The registration providing the transformation from the OoI coordinate system into the measurement arm coordinate system. (c) The HEC, which gives the pose of the camera in the TCP coordinate system. (d) A depiction of the OoI in the design coordinate system along with the locations of the spheres measured by an expert.

It should be noted that though measurement based AR attempts to overcome the shortcomings of certain computer vision techniques, the final augmentation step and the HEC both rely on the camera intrinsic parameters and therefore, these steps involve the use of computer vision. The HEC also uses marker-tracking. Though this reliance on computer vision methods remains, it is still possible to minimize the uncertainty introduced through them, because it is possible to perform the camera intrinsic calibration as well as the HEC under ideal conditions and these are only used as parameters in the actual application. This means that conditions such as changing lighting or reflecting surfaces, which generally affect the performance of computer vision techniques would not be a problem for Measurement Based AR.

2.1   Measurement Arm

The measurement arm is a portable device that can be setup to perform accurate tactile 3D measurements. This means that the pose of the TCP in the measurement arm coordinate system can be determined anytime the measurement arm is operational. It is also possible to determine whether the two buttons on the measurement arm pistol are pressed or released. In this way, when the TCP is at a certain location (for example pressed against a surface) it is possible to determine the TCP pose at this location by pressing a button on the pistol. It should be noted that TCP is the center of a ball-probe attached to the pistol and the system delivers the location of the TCP and not the point on the ball-probe touching a certain surface. This is the probe-compensation problem, which is needs to be accounted for when performing registration.

2.2   Registration

In our approach the OoI's which need to be measured or overlaid with virtual information are defined within CAD files. This means these parts are defined in a virtual coordinate system different from the measurement arm coordinate system. The process of determining the transformation from this virtual coordinate system into our desired coordinate system is referred to as registration. The registration process consists of first measuring predetermined locations such as boreholes on a vehicle. Then using the virtual coordinates of the same locations to build (at least 3) pairs consisting of virtual and real coordinates, we determine the transformation from the vehicle coordinate system to the measurement arm coordinate system using [1]. In this way, we are able to determine the expected position of any part defined within the vehicle's coordinate system accurately within the measurement arm coordinate system.

2.3   Hand Eye Calibration

The hand-eye calibration describes how the camera is located relative to the TCP. This method is named so because it comes from robotics where the robot "hand" is fitted with a camera (the so-called eye) and it is required to combine both these coordinate systems. This problem is defined by two fixed coordinate systems and two mobile objects within each coordinate system, which are fixed relative to each other and the transformation between the coordinate systems, and/or the mobile objects need to be determined. Many approaches to solve this problem exist and this can be formulated in different ways. What is required in all cases however is that the poses of both the objects in each of the coordinate systems are needed in order to solve for the required transformations. Thus, in our case the formulation would be as follows:

$$AX = XB \tag{1}$$

Where A would be the transformation between successive TCP poses in the measurement arm coordinate system and B the transformation between successive camera poses in a reference coordinate system. The camera pose can be determined using an appropriate marker tracking approach.

3   Verification

We quantify the accuracy of our Measurement Based AR approach by simultaneously performing Measurement Based AR explained in the concept section as well as using computer vision techniques on the same data set in order to compare the results of both. In order to overcome the limitations of computer vision methods, we captured data, which was particularly suited for computer vision techniques, while still being typical for the Measurement Based AR. Thus, the pose of an OoI was tracked using the TCP pose from the Measurement Arm, registration and HEC in order to determine the OoI pose in the camera coordinate system, while at the same time detecting the same OoI in the image and computing its pose relative to the camera using computer vision methods. We explain the verification process in the following.

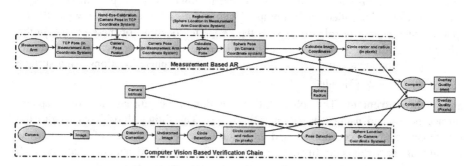

Fig. 3. Measurement based AR and computer vision based verification tool chains

3.1   Measurement Setup

A bumper beam from the car front end (Fig. 2) was chosen to use for the accuracy verification process. This part was selected due to its large size, stability and suitability to use for registration. The carrier was fitted with 4 high precision measurement spheres and was independently measured by an expert using a measurement arm. One of these spheres was chosen to be larger and of a contrasting color to the rest of the environment, because this sphere was used as the OoI. The other spheres were smaller in size and of a darker color, because it was not the intention to detect these in the image. On the computer vision side, the camera intrinsic calibration was the only preparation required to be able to process the captured data with computer vision techniques.

The data collection for the verification process consisted of taking simultaneous TCP pose and camera image measurements. In order to improve the quality of the computer vision processing, the images were taken in such a way that the OoI was located in the middle of the image. In this way the elongation of the sphere image from a circle to an ellipse, caused by the projection of a 3D object onto a 2D surface, was minimized. This made it possible to treat the sphere images as circles instead of ellipses during detection.

Thus a total of 40 data points was captured and processed using the verification concept explained in the following.

3.2 Registration

In order to perform registration for the validation process, a modified approach was taken in order to improve the registration quality. Instead of using boreholes, which are usually used to perform such registration, the measurement spheres were used to perform registration. Measuring these is less prone to error since only well distributed surface measurements on each sphere suffice. Also, special measurement spheres are available, which are manufactured with high accuracy to have known diameters and uniform surfaces. A further advantage was that the OoI, whose pose is normally determined only using registration, could also be measured directly using the measurement arm. In this way the quality of the registration could be inspected. Therefore 3 such spheres were installed on the bumper beam and used for registration, while the 4th sphere which was installed was used as the OoI. The locations of these objects in the reference coordinate system were already known, based on expert measurements performed beforehand. The method for determining the sphere locations using surface measurements as is explained below.

Sphere Measurement. The sphere fitting was done by capturing (at least) 4 sphere surface points and using least-squares fitting [2]. The fitting algorithm provides the sphere center in 3D coordinates and its radius. The center of each of the spheres is available in the virtual coordinate system and, using the sphere centers calculated with the data from the measurement arm, the registration can be performed.

3.3 Hand Eye Calibration (HEC)

The HEC for the verification process was performed using 23 pairs of TCP poses (in the measurement arm coordinate system) and camera poses (in the optical marker coordinate system).

The TCP pose was obtained from the measurement arm and the camera pose using a marker detection approach. The marker detection consisted of using checkerboard detection followed by PnP to solve for the 2D (image) and 3D (checkerboard) correspondences. Thus, the pose of the camera relative to the poster was obtained. Finally using [3] the transformation between the TCP and the camera was calculated, which is the HEC.

3.4 Sphere Projection

In order to find the projection of the sphere as a circle onto the image only 2 parameters need to be calculated; the center and the radius of the circle on the image. Since we already have the pose of the sphere relative to the camera, the center of its circle projection on the image can be found using the camera intrinsic [8]. We do this by simply multiplying the coordinates for the center of the sphere (relative to the camera) with the camera intrinsic to find the ray-representation of the image coordinates.

Dividing the x and the y values of the ray-representation with its z value gives us the image x and y coordinates for the sphere center.

In order to find the radius, we need to consider the focal length of the camera as well as the distance of the sphere from the camera origin and its radius. Furthermore, we use the assumption that the sphere is in the middle of the image, and thus that the line going from the camera origin to the sphere center is perpendicular to the image plane. Thus in order to find the radius of the circle projection of the sphere on the image we used the following relation:

$$\frac{r_i}{f} = \frac{r_w}{\sqrt{z^2 - r_w^2}} \tag{2}$$

The term $\sqrt{z^2 - r_w^2}$ refers to the distance from the camera origin to the visible edge of the sphere, whereas the z refers to the distance of the sphere middle from the camera origin. The r_w and r_i terms refer to the radii of the sphere and its image respectively (Fig. 4).

Fig. 4. The detected sphere (green) and the sphere location projected onto image (red) (Color figure online)

3.5   Circle Detection

The computer vision based approach starts by detecting the OoI sphere in the image. For this, we used Hough circle detection. This method has the advantage that it is available in the OpenCV framework [9] and that it automatically also provides the detected circle middle (in pixels) as well as the radius. We used the calculated radius from the sphere projection step as a parameter for the circle detection. This allowed us to parameterize the circle detection step and did not affect the quality of the results found but helped by detecting only the relevant circle in the image.

3.6 Pose Estimation

The process to detect the location of the sphere in the camera coordinate system was inverse to the process used in Sphere projection. This was calculated by first calculating the distance of the sphere middle from the camera by rearranging Eq. (2) to solve for z. The image x and y coordinates were converted from the ray-representation into the camera coordinate system by dividing them with the image width and height respectively. We multiplied these with obtained z value to get the sphere location in the 3D camera coordinate system.

3.7 Data Assessment

The data assessment consisted of simply comparing the results from both the Measurement Based AR data chain as well as the Computer Vision data chain. Since both data chains produced both the sphere coordinates in the 3D camera coordinate system as well as the image coordinates in 2D pixels, these could both be directly compared to one another. Figure 3 shows how the results from both the data chains are compared at the end of the verification process. In addition, the radii of the circle projections of the spheres on the image were also compared.

4 Results

Comparing the sphere positions determined by both the data chains, the mean error of 19.57 mm, with a minimum error of 5.78 mm, was obtained. The mean error between the circle detected in the image[2] and the circle image coordinates calculated using the MBAR data chain was 10.64 pixels and the best value obtained here was 5.79 pixels. It was interesting to note that a similar comparison of the detected and calculated circle radii yielded a mean error of only 1.02 pixels with a best value of 0.14 pixels.

Since pose estimation based on images can be prone to higher errors in the z-axis, we also looked at the distribution of errors in the different axes. This revealed a particularly high error in the z component of the estimated sphere locations as can be seen in the figure below. We therefore removed 3 outliers from the data in order to recalculate the error means and saw a significant improvement of 3 mm in the sphere location error, while the mean circle location and radius pixel errors only changed marginally to 10.76 and 0.99 pixels respectively. The comparisons of the data with and without outlier removals can be seen in the graphs below (Figs. 5, 6 and 7).

---

[2] The image had a resolution of 1920 × 1080 pixels.

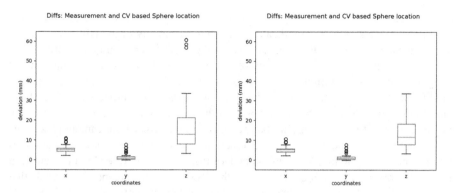

Fig. 5. The x, y and z distributions of the differences between the sphere locations obtained using both data chains. Left: Without outlier removal. Right: With outlier removal.

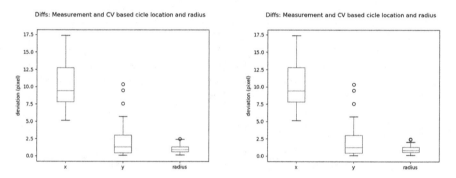

Fig. 6. The x and y as well as the radius distributions for the circle locations and radii obtained using both data chains. Left: Without outlier removal. Right: With outlier removal.

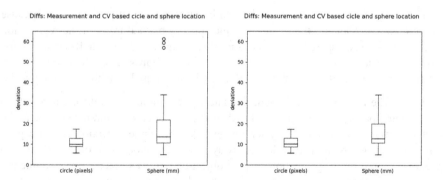

Fig. 7. Distances between the circle and sphere locations in pixels and mm respectively. Left: Without outlier removal. Right: With outlier removal.

Parameters. In order to understand the quality of the parameters we used in both the data chains, we also looked at indicators regarding the quality of the HEC, registration and the camera intrinsic. Of these, we discuss the HEC and registration shortly.

It is difficult to compare the quality of the HEC directly, but since this determined using a (least squares) fitting process. It is possible to inspect how well the resulting HEC fits the input data and how big the residuals of the fitting process are. It is also a characteristic of the HEC, that as opposed to the registration, the error introduced by the HEC does not remain constant, but rather it is a function of the camera pose. This means that looking at an OoI from one direction may show a good superimposition of 3D information, while looking at the same OoI from a different direction or orientation may cause this error to change. Inspecting the HEC from this perspective reveals that HEC needs to be of a better quality, because the translation[3] component of the residuals has a relatively high mean of 3.9 mm, while the rotation component is 0.1°. Both of these can be seen in the distribution shown below (Fig. 8).

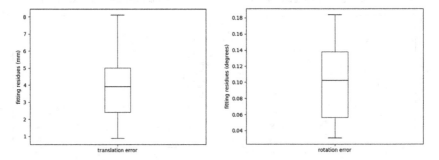

Fig. 8. The distributions of the translation and rotation components of the residuals obtained during the HEC fitting process.

The registration on the other hand could be measured directly in our case, because we were able to compare the location of the sphere obtained through the registration with the location measured using the arm. This comparison revealed that the registration error was 1.08 mm. Though this needs to be improved for the application in question, we see that this parameter is of a good overall quality within our data chain.

Methods. The methods used in both the data chains can also introduce errors, which end up being propagated throughout the data chain to lead to a cumulated error in the results. Particularly on the computer vision side, the circle detection and the pose estimation use assumptions that do not always hold. The elongation of the sphere into an ellipse caused by the projection of a 3D object onto a 2D surface is for example not considered. Furthermore, the pose detection based on circle detection assumes that the center of the sphere lies on the center of the camera image plane. How far these

---

[3] The HEC shows the distance between the TCP and the camera origin to be 100 mm.

assumptions hold, and what the scale of the errors introduced when these are not held, remains to be studied.

5   Conclusions

Looking at the results of both data chains, it is clear that the current approach is not yet of the quality needed to validate the Measurement Based AR approach for geometric validation. This study has been a first step and has allowed the critical components for such a validation approach to be identified.

In particular, the HEC seems to be component, which needs to improve further, as this showed the highest indication of containing errors during the inspection of the residuals from the HEC estimation. More sophisticated methods to relate the pose of the OoI to its 2D projection onto the image also need to be studied, because the distance (z) component of the 3D position errors was found to be particularly error prone during the analysis.

The need for high precision AR, which is immune to the problems that computer vision based approaches suffer from, justifies continued research into this approach. Once the validation approach taken during this exercise reaches the required maturity, the ability to guarantee high quality AR during operational use will be a huge step forward for such applications as the geometric validation process, which require high AR accuracy.

References

1. Kabsch, W.: A discussion of the solution for the best rotation to relate two sets of vectors. Acta Crystallogr. A **34**, 827–828 (1978)
2. Jekel, C.: Obtaining non-linear orthotropic material models for PVC-coated polyester via inverse bubble inflation (2016)
3. Park, F., Martin, B.: Robot sensor calibration: solving AX=XB on the Euclidean group. IEEE Trans. Robot. Autom. **10**, 717–721 (1994)
4. Smeulders, A., Chu, D., Cucchiara, R., Calderara, S., Dehghan, A., Shah, M.: Visual tracking: an experimental survey. IEEE Trans. Pattern Anal. Mach. Intell. **36**, 1442–1468 (2014)
5. Wuest, H., Vial, F., Strieker, D.: Adaptive line tracking with multiple hypotheses for augmented reality. In: Fourth IEEE and ACM International Symposium on Mixed and Augmented Reality (ISMAR 2005) (2005)
6. You, S., Neumann, U., Azuma, R.: Hybrid inertial and vision tracking for augmented reality registration. In: Proceedings IEEE Virtual Reality (Cat. No. 99CB36316) (1999)
7. Dissanayake, M., Newman, P., Clark, S., Durrant-Whyte, H., Csorba, M.: A solution to the simultaneous localization and map building (SLAM) problem. IEEE Trans. Robot. Autom. **17**, 229–241 (2001)
8. Hartley, R., Zisserman, A.: Multiple View Geometry in Computer Vision. Cambridge University Press, Cambridge (2003)
9. OpenCV: Image Processing. https://docs.opencv.org/4.2.0/. Accessed 31 Jan 2020
10. instant3Dhub. https://instant3dhub.org/. Accessed 31 Jan 2020

Augmented Instructions: Analysis of Performance and Efficiency of Assembly Tasks

Eleanor Smith[1]([✉]) [iD], Gordon Semple[2], Dorothy Evans[1],
Kenneth McRae[1], and Paul Blackwell[1] [iD]

[1] Department of Design, Manufacturing and Engineering Management,
University of Strathclyde, Glasgow, UK
eleanor.smith@strath.ac.uk
[2] Booth Welsh, Irvine, UK

Abstract. Augmented Reality (AR) technology makes it possible to present information in the user's line of sight, right at the point of use. This brings the capability to visualise complex information for industrial maintenance applications in an effective manner, which typically rely on paper instructions and tacit knowledge developed over time. Existing research in AR instruction manuals has already shown its potential to reduce the time taken to complete assembly tasks, as well as improving accuracy [1–3]. In this study, the outcomes of several aspects of AR instructions are explored and their effects on the chosen Key Performance Indicators (KPIs) of task completion time, error rate, cognitive effort and usability are assessed. A standardised AR assembly task is also described for performance comparison, and a novel AR experimental tool is presented, which takes advantage of the flexibility of internet connected peripherals, to explore various different aspects of AR app design to isolate their effects. Results of the experiments are given here, providing insight into the most effective way of delivering information and promoting interaction between user and computer, in terms of user performance and acceptance.

Keywords: Augmented Reality · Industry 4.0 · Usability study

1 Introduction

Augmented Reality (AR) uses visual technology to enhance the user's view of the real world with additional digital information, overlaid onto the user's line of sight. In the world of manufacturing, this can have a range of applications; from visualising designed objects in their real-world location to recognising and highlighting key points on production/ control equipment, to displaying live sensor data at the point of use. In this paper, we focus on AR as an alternative to paper instruction manuals in the case of industrial maintenance and assembly tasks. Several research works demonstrate the potential benefits of this approach. Prominent figures in AR research, such as Funk, Erkoyuncu and Sanna have all presented studies claiming the benefits of AR guided assembly including faster task completion and fewer errors [4–6]. On the other hand, research such as that carried out by Zaldívar-Colado et al. suggests Augmented or

© Springer Nature Switzerland AG 2020
J. Y. C. Chen and G. Fragomeni (Eds.): HCII 2020, LNCS 12191, pp. 166–177, 2020.
https://doi.org/10.1007/978-3-030-49698-2_12

Mixed Reality can, in fact, slow down assembly [7], suggesting that AR is not unanimously beneficial to the assembly process. Instead, performance depends very much on the particular design aspects of an AR system. So the question is raised: what makes an effective AR instruction guidance system? And how can we best display information such that operators can easily follow these instructions?

This paper introduces an AR application developed using standard web technologies and AR libraries which can be used to compare user performance when various aspects of app design are changed. A standardised AR assembly task is also proposed, to allow performance comparison between different instruction types. Finally, we present the results of experiments to determine the most effective way of presenting information in AR.

2   Background

AR has many possible uses in industrial maintenance, from view sharing with remote experts [8], to displaying live sensor data [9]. This paper focuses on the most common use – assembly guidance [1]. In this application, AR acts as an alternative to traditional paper-based instruction manuals, delivering task guidance directly in the user's line of sight in the form of text annotations, 2D/3D models, animations or videos [10].

AR can be applied in a number of different forms including:

- Spatial AR systems - which use a series of projectors to highlight relevant locations
- Wearable AR devices - which use optical techniques to combine the user's view of the world with virtual content
- Commercially available smartphones - used alongside video to display virtual content overlaid onto a live camera feed.

In this paper, we focus mainly on the latter option. The two topics of primary importance in this study are user acceptance and user performance when using the AR system.

Funk's use of spatial AR projection in automotive assembly showed a decrease in time taken to complete each assembly, as well as a reduction in errors [4]. Erkoyuncu et al. present the ARAUM (Augmented Reality Authoring for Maintenance) system which demonstrates a reduction in time to perform maintenance tasks [5]. Sanna et al. also demonstrated time and error rate reductions in both skilled and unskilled users following AR instructions to repair laptops [6]. Golanski et al. [11] demonstrated a successful implementation of mobile-based AR applications to support aircraft maintenance technicians. Though some reported the device and interface to be cumbersome, overall it was well received. These results are backed up by Aromaa et al. [12] whose mobile-based AR platform was widely accepted in the global manufacturing company where they were tested, as measured by the QUIS (Questionnaire for User Interaction Satisfaction), SUS (System Usability Scale) and TAM (Technology Acceptance Model).

Conversely, Aschenbrenner et al. [13] found using tablet-based AR applications to repair a switch cabinet did not improve results in terms of time taken or cognitive effort involved. The work of Zaldívar-Colado et al. supports this [7], as they too found Mixed Reality may have a detrimental effect on assembly performance.

The common theme in all these studies is that they present a single system and evaluate it in terms of usability, or performance measures. Sometimes they are compared to a 'control' condition of paper instructions, sometimes no comparison is provided, and in many cases, only a simple comparison of means is used to judge success or failure of a system, rather than a thorough statistical analysis. Each of these systems differs hugely from one another. When we attempt to compare performance between systems, even where consistent measures are available it is impossible to tell whether differences are due to a particular feature of the AR system, the task chosen, or variation in the underlying populations sampled.

Not only is there a need for rigorous, statistically sound comparison between AR and non-AR instructions, there is also a value in attempting to isolate different aspects of AR guidance to identify which have the greatest effect on AR usability and performance ratings.

3   Effect Size Meta-analysis

A meta-analysis of AR usability studies in the field of industrial maintenance tasks was carried out, to identify typical effect sizes in this field of research. Papers were identified from SCOPUS, Engineering Village and IEEE Xplore libraries and screened according to the PICOC Framework [14] criteria outlined in Table 1 below. Any papers using AR to guide humans during industrial maintenance included for analysis, while AR for training purposes, teleoperation of robots or medical uses were out of scope. Technical advances in hardware or software were not considered either, as the focus was on new applications of AR. There also needed to be a measurable indication of performance, and comparison against traditional instructions.

Table 1. PICOC Framework

	Inclusion	Exclusion
Population	Industrial maintenance task	Training applications only
	Human operators	Medical application
	Application	Robotic control/teleoperation
Intervention	Utilisation of AR	Utilisation only of VR
Comparison	Paper/PDF manuals	
Outcomes	Time to complete operation	Hardware/software improvement
	Number of errors	Time to develop an application
	User experience	
Context	Industrial environments	Consumer environment

508 unique records were identified from the search criteria: title or abstract contains ("Augmented Reality" OR "Mixed Reality") AND ("Maintenance" OR "Repair") published since 2013. Once records which were irrelevant, or presented no usable data on user performance were filtered out, 6 remained [6, 7, 15–18]. All 6 presented data on the time to complete the specified operation for both an AR instruction and paper

instruction. Using Cohen's D calculation [19], the effect size was calculated for each study. The results of these calculations are presented in Fig. 1 below, alongside Cohen's standard estimates for small, medium and large effect sizes.

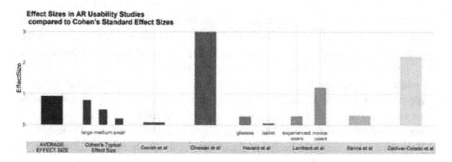

Fig. 1. Effect sizes in AR usability studies

It is clear, that the average effect size in this field (0.871) is closest to Cohen's estimate of large effect size (0.8). This suggests it may be possible to detect statistically significant differences in performance, even in relatively small datasets.

4 Methodology

The aim of this work was to identify the effect of different aspects of the AR application design on user performance. First, definitions are required for "good performance" or "effectiveness" during the assembly process. In the papers reviewed in Sect. 2, the most frequently used measures of performance were Task Completion Time, Error Count, Cognitive Effort (which will be measured using the NASA-TLX scale [20]) and Usability (measured using the System Usability Scale [21]) – these will form the KPIs (Key Performance Indicators) for this work. The 2 independent variables selected for this stage of experimentation are Interaction Method (i.e. how user's control and interact with virtual content) and Display Mode (i.e. what format the instructions are shown in). The levels of each factor are shown in Table 2 below.

Table 2. Independent variables changed in experiments

Interaction method	Native	Users interact with content using the device's native interaction method to navigate instructions i.e. touch screen for mobile
	Voice	Users interact with content using voice commands to navigate instructions
Display mode	CAD	Instructions conveyed to user as 3D models showing where actions should be performed
	Text annotation	Instructions conveyed to the user by concise written instructions, linked to the relevant location by an arrow
	In-situ video	Instructions conveyed to the user by videos of the action to be performed, projected over the relevant location

To explore the effects of these factors, an experiment was designed such that each user performed a short assembly task using Lego bricks, guided by a different version of the AR application (Sect. 4.1). Participants for the experiment were from a convenience sample and consisted mainly (95.8%) of university students, comprising 20 males and 4 females. Performance was then compared across the different versions to identify the factors and levels which produce the best assembly performance. As these two factors are closely related, it is likely that there will be an interaction between them, so it is necessary for a design of experiments to explore every possible combination of factors. Therefore, a fully factorial design is selected.

In addition to performing assembly tasks using Lego bricks, each participant was also asked to complete a similar task using paper instructions, to provide a baseline measurement of their assembly performance. In order to reduce the effect of individual variation on the basis of assembly performance, the results using the AR instructions were then subtracted from the baseline paper results to determine the difference. This will be denoted in the results section by Δ. The order the tasks were performed in was alternated to cancel out possible order effects.

Task time and error rate were recorded through the AR applications, or for paper versions through the investigator recording them. The cognitive effort was measured via questionnaires taken after each assembly, using the NASA-TLX scale [22], a widely recognised measure of cognitive effort. In this case, the raw TLX score was used (i.e. without weightings) as this has been shown to be either more or equally sensitive as the weighted version and much faster for participants to complete [20]. Usability was also determined using a post-experiment questionnaire, based on the System Usability Scale – a fast tool for assessing the ease and enjoyment associated with using IT-based systems [21].

4.1 System Design

The software created for the experiments was written in NodeJS and executed on a Raspberry Pi [23]. This allowed peripheral devices such as smartphones or other internet connected devices to be used for interfacing with the instructions which are controlled on a central webserver. To provide real-time interaction with the assembly instructions, WebSockets [24] were used to update the users display with the appropriate instruction for the task they were required to complete. This architecture was selected as it is not only easily expandable to multiple operators working on a common task, but also for the integration with IoT devices and a wider Industry 4.0 architecture, which could provide additional information.

Three display types were created for investigation:

- CAD Models – a 3D representation of the parts was displayed in the location and orientation of the intended placement.
- Annotations – written instructions were placed in the 3D environment describing the action required whilst indicating the location.
- Video – a pre-recorded video was activated to show the user where to place the parts.

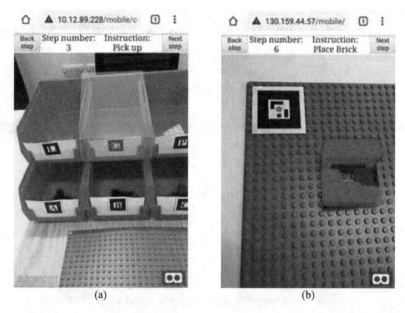

(a)   (b)

Fig. 2. View of instructions showing the location of (a) the selection, and (b) the placement of Lego bricks using virtual CAD models

4.2 Standard Assembly Task

The suggested standard assembly task for these experiments takes inspiration from Funk et al.'s work [4], in which participants were asked to build a section of a wall using Lego bricks. Like Funk's example, the tasks used in the present work use Lego bricks since it is safe, familiar and low-cost. However certain changes have been made. When building Funk's wall, single bricks are added one at a time to an existing partially assembled wall, and there are a limited number of orientations which are possible to place the brick in.

The task presented here instead uses pre-made subassemblies of 1–5 bricks, and the orientation in which they are placed is very important to the next steps. This increased complexity is a better test of AR's capability to display objects in 3D in the existing environment.

The experimental situation was arranged as below in Fig. 3 below, with a different Lego subassembly placed in each tray, and markers to indicate to both the human operator and the AR app, where the bricks should be selected from.

Time and error rate data from the first step of each task was discarded, to discount loading time for the AR web app pages, as this is largely dependent on internet connection rather than the measured factors.

Fig. 3. Experimental set-up

5   Results

5.1   AR vs Paper

First, user performance is compared between the AR application to the use of paper instructions, using a paired samples t-test - a statistical test used to investigate differences between conditions in a repeated measures experiment [25].

Table 3. Comparison of performance using AR and paper instructions

	TLX score		Task time (s)		Error rate (#)		System usability	
	Mean	s.d.	Mean	s.d.	Mean	s.d.	Mean	s.d.
AR	1.845	1.040	157.0	44.90	0.5000	0.8341	39.96	2.694
Paper	1.593	0.8202	52.91	18.78	0.2917	0.6241	36.71	3.114

The results of the paired t-test show that statistically significant differences at the 90% confidence level or higher exist between the two conditions for Cognitive Effort (NASA-TLX Score), Task Time, and Usability. From Fig. 4 below, we can see that while the users perform tasks slower while using the AR mode, they find the system more usable. This is reflected in some of the additional comments recorded from participants, who cited the AR system as being more enjoyable to use.

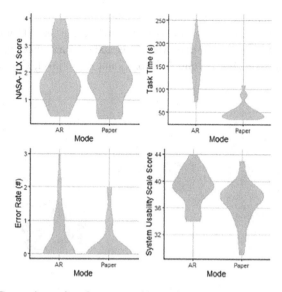

Fig. 4. Comparison of performance with AR instructions to paper instructions

Participants performed more poorly using AR instructions than paper across all but one of the measured variables. This differs from previous studies (described in Sect. 2), and may be due to the length of the task – Funk et al. [4], for example, found that the benefits of AR were greater the more steps each task had. However, the AR condition did still rate more highly on the system usability scale than paper, and enjoyment and ease of use are important factors to consider when implementing new technology.

5.2   AR Treatments

Further investigation into which AR factors lead to the best user performance during the assembly tasks was then undertaken. Table 4 summarises the key statistics generated.

Table 4. Data summary

		Δ TLX score		Δ task time (s)		Δ error rate (#)		Δ system usability	
		Mean	s.d.	Mean	s.d.	Mean	s.d.	Mean	s.d.
Interaction	Native	93.11	58.43	3.472	6.796	0.500	1.382	7.708	10.08
	Voice	115.1	43.81	2.847	10.31	−0.083	0.669	5.000	17.81
Display	CAD	107.3	49.35	2.500	10.33	−0.125	0.641	7.500	8.763
	Text	133.0	45.74	6.979	9.074	0.875	1.356	12.19	10.81
	Video	71.99	46.10	0.000	4.714	−0.125	0.991	−0.625	19.35

As there are multiple independent variables at multiple levels, an ANOVA (Analysis Of Variance) method was chosen to analyse the data. Using the ANOVA test, it was demonstrated that Display Mode has a significant effect on Δ Task Completion Time (95% level, Fig. 5) and Δ Error Count (90% level, Fig. 6).

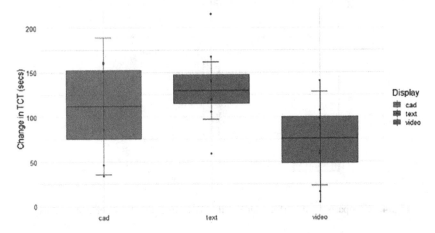

Fig. 5. Effect of display modes on total task completion time

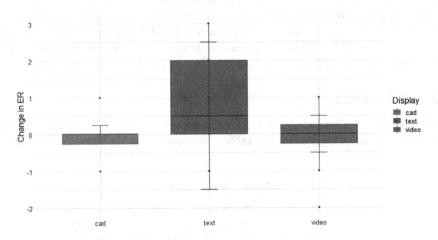

Fig. 6. Effect of display modes on the total error count

Participants using in-situ video-based AR instructions completed the task in an average of 131 s, 26% faster than text-based instructions and 21% faster than those using CAD models superimposed onto the environment.

Using Tukey's Honestly Significant Difference test [26], the greatest performance difference lies between using video to display instructions and text-based annotations. In-situ video was found to produce significantly fewer errors than text-based annotations.

There were too few female participants to draw statistically significant conclusions about the effect of gender on assembly performance using AR instructions. Nevertheless gender-disaggregated data is presented below, in the hope that it may be of use to future researchers performing meta-analyses on the subject.

Table 5. Gender disaggregated performance data (task time)

	Paper		AR	
	Mean	s.d.	Mean	s.d.
Female	95.5 s	59.2 s	167 s	56.7 s
Male	56.3 s	15.0 s	181 s	45.8 s
Overall	**62.8 s**	**31.4 s**	**178 s**	**48.1 s**

6 Conclusions

Although performance when using paper instructions was better than AR for task time, error count and cognitive effort, users reported finding the AR system easier and more enjoyable to use than its paper counterpart, and this is reflected in the system usability scores.

More significantly, it is shown that the way in which users interact with AR content has little effect on any of the performance measures studied. The practical implication of this is that:

a. those implementing AR systems can allow users the option of choosing their preferred interaction method, safe in the knowledge that it will not significantly affect their performance; or
b. this decision is best made on other factors such as background noise levels, and whether or not the user is required to wear gloves or other safety devices which may impair their operation of a touchscreen.

The way in which information is displayed in AR, however, does have a significant effect on performance:

• Using in-situ videos to demonstrate assembly tasks lead to significantly fewer errors than annotated models.
• Video also offered a slight improvement upon CAD models.
• Display mode had a significant effect on-task time - video condition again allows faster task completion than either annotations or CAD models.

This suggests that in-situ videos within an AR environment are a very effective way to display procedural instructions for assembly tasks.

Acknowledgements. This work forms part of a PhD project under the Renewable Engine INTERREG VA programme, which aims to encourage cross-border research and collaboration between the border regions of Scotland, Northern Ireland and the Republic of Ireland. This project, in particular, is a collaboration between the Advanced Forming Research Centre (AFRC) at the University of Strathclyde, and the industrial partner Booth Welsh.

References

1. Palmarini, R., Erkoyuncu, J.A., Roy, R., Torabmostaedi, H.: A systematic review of augmented reality applications in maintenance. Robot. Comput.-Integr. Manuf. Rev. **49**, 215–228 (2018). https://doi.org/10.1016/j.rcim.2017.06.002
2. Funk, M., Kosch, T., Kettner, R., Korn, O., Schmidt, A.: motionEAP: an overview of 4 years of combining industrial assembly with augmented reality for Industry 4.0. In: i-KNOW 2016, Graz (2016)
3. Kosch, T., Abdelrahman, Y., Funk, M., Schmidt, A.: One size does not fit all - challenges of providing interactive worker assistance in industrial settings. In: UbiComp/ISWC 2017 - Adjunct Proceedings of the 2017 ACM International Joint Conference on Pervasive and Ubiquitous Computing and Proceedings of the 2017 ACM International Symposium on Wearable Computers, pp. 1006–1011 (2017). https://doi.org/10.1145/3123024.3124395. https://www.scopus.com/inward/record.uri?eid=2-s2.0-85030868685&doi=10.1145%2f3123024.3124395&partnerID=40&md5=8753b08cb92a1bca7c452d192389664d
4. Funk, M., Kosch, T., Greenwald, S.W., Schmidt, A.: A benchmark for interactive augmented reality instructions for assembly tasks. Presented at the Proceedings of the 14th International Conference on Mobile and Ubiquitous Multimedia, Linz, Austria (2015)
5. Erkoyuncu, J.A., del Amo, I.F., Dalle Mura, M., Roy, R., Dini, G.: Improving efficiency of industrial maintenance with context aware adaptive authoring in augmented reality. CIRP Ann. **66**(1), 465–468 (2017). https://doi.org/10.1016/j.cirp.2017.04.006
6. Sanna, A., Manuri, F., Lamberti, F., Paravati, G., Pezzolla, P.: Using handheld devices to sup port augmented reality-based maintenance and assembly tasks. In: 2015 IEEE International Conference on Consumer Electronics (ICCE), pp. 178–179. IEEE (2015)
7. Zaldivar-Colado, U., Garbaya, S., Tamayo-Serrano, P., Zaldivar-Colado, X., Blazevic, P.: A mixed reality for virtual assembly. IEEE (2017). https://doi.org/10.1109/roman.2017.8172385. https://dx.doi.org/10.1109/ROMAN.2017.8172385
8. Masoni, R., et al.: Supporting remote maintenance in Industry 4.0 through augmented reality. Procedia Manuf. **11**, 1296–1302 (2017). https://doi.org/10.1016/j.promfg.2017.07.257
9. Alam, M.F., Katsikas, S., Beltramello, O., Hadjiefthymiades, S.: Augmented and virtual reality based monitoring and safety system: a prototype IoT platform. J. Netw. Comput. Appl. **89**, 109–119 (2017). https://doi.org/10.1016/j.jnca.2017.03.022
10. del Amo, I.F., Erkoyuncu, J.A., Roy, R., Palmarini, R., Onoufriou, D.: A systematic review of Augmented Reality content-related techniques for knowledge transfer in maintenance applications. Comput. Ind. **103**, 47–71 (2018)
11. Golanski, P., Perz-Osowska, M., Szczekala, M.: A demonstration model of a mobile expert system with augmented reality user interface supporting M-28 aircraft maintenance. KONBiN **31**(1), 23 (2014)
12. Aromaa, S., Väätänen, A., Hakkarainen, M., Kaasinen, E.: User experience and user acceptance of an augmented reality based knowledge-sharing solution in industrial maintenance work. In: Ahram, T., Falcão, C. (eds.) AHFE 2017. AISC, vol. 607, pp. 145–156. Springer, Cham (2018). https://doi.org/10.1007/978-3-319-60492-3_14
13. Aschenbrenner, D., Latoschik, M.E., Schillingz, K.: Industrial maintenance with augmented reality: two case studies. In: 22nd ACM Conference on Virtual Reality Software and Technology, VRST 2016, 2–4 November 2016, Munich, Germany. Association for Computing Machinery (2016). Proceedings of the ACM Symposium on Virtual Reality Software and Technology, VRST, pp. 341–342. https://doi.org/10.1145/2993369.2996305. http://dx.doi.org/10.1145/2993369.2996305

14. Booth, A., Sutton, A., Papaioannou, D.: Systematic Approaches to a Successful Literature Review. Sage, London (2016)
15. Havard, V., Baudry, D., Savatier, X., Jeanne, B., Louis, A., Mazari, B.: Augmented industrial maintenance (AIM): a case study for evaluating and comparing with paper and video media supports. In: De Paolis, L.T., Mongelli, A. (eds.) AVR 2016. LNCS, vol. 9768, pp. 302–320. Springer, Cham (2016). https://doi.org/10.1007/978-3-319-40621-3_22
16. Gheisari, M., Williams, G., Walker, B.N., Irizarry, J.: Locating building components in a facility using augmented reality vs. paper-based methods: a user-centered experimental comparison. In: Computing in Civil and Building Engineering - Proceedings of the 2014 International Conference on Computing in Civil and Building Engineering, pp. 850–857 (2014). https://doi.org/10.1061/9780784413616.106. [https://www.scopus.com/inward/record.uri?eid=2-s2.0-84934286807&doi=10.1061%2f9780784413616.106&partnerID=40&md5=72be0986a0438d7268040a8f6ec9c63e
17. Gavish, N., et al.: Evaluating virtual reality and augmented reality training for industrial maintenance and assembly tasks. Interact. Learn. Environ. 23(6), 778–798 (2015). https://doi.org/10.1080/10494820.2013.815221
18. Lamberti, F., Manuri, F., Sanna, A., Paravati, G., Pezzolla, P., Montuschi, P.: Challenges, opportunities, and future trends of emerging techniques for augmented reality-based maintenance. IEEE Trans. Emerg. Top. Comput. 2(4), 411–421 (2014). https://doi.org/10.1109/TETC.2014.2368833. Art no. 7024955
19. Cohen, J.: Statistical Power Analysis for the Behavioral Sciences. Routledge, Abingdon (2013)
20. Hart, S.G.: Nasa-task load index (NASA-TLX); 20 years later. In: Proceedings of the Human Factors and Ergonomics Society Annual Meeting, vol. 50, no. 9, pp. 904–908 (2006). https://doi.org/10.1177/154193120605000909
21. Brooke, J.: SUS-A quick and dirty usability scale. In: Usability Evaluation in Industry, vol. 189, no. 194, pp. 4–7 (1996)
22. Hart, S.G., Staveland, L.E.: Development of NASA-TLX (Task Load Index): results of empirical and theoretical research (1988)
23. Trifa, V., Guinard, D.: Building the Web of Things: With Examples in Node.js and Raspberry Pi. Manning Publications Co., Greenwich (2016)
24. Pimentel, V., Nickerson, B.G.: Communicating and displaying real-time data with WebSocket. IEEE Internet Comput. 16(4), 45–53 (2012). https://doi.org/10.1109/mic.2012.64
25. Colman, A.M.: Related Scores t Test. Oxford University Press, Oxford (2015)
26. Abdi, H., Williams, L.J.: Tukey's honestly significant difference (HSD) test. In: Encyclopedia of Research Design, pp. 1–5. Sage, Thousand Oaks (2010)

Interactive Mixed Reality Cooking Assistant for Unskilled Operating Scenario

Ke-yu Zhai[1,3]([✉]), Yi-ming Cao[1,2], Wen-jun Hou[1,2],
and Xue-ming Li[1,3]

[1] School of Digital Media and Design Arts,
Beijing University of Posts and Telecommunications, Beijing 100876, China
zkyivy@foxmail.com
[2] Beijing Key Laboratory of Network and Network Culture,
Beijing University of Posts and Telecommunications, Beijing 100876, China
[3] Digital Media and Intelligent Computing Laboratory,
Beijing University of Posts and Telecommunications, Beijing 100876, China

Abstract. As the further development of virtual reality technology, mixed reality (MR) promotes the innovation of human-computer interaction. It can integrate virtual information (objects, pictures, videos, etc.) into the real environment, and directly interact with people. It can greatly improve the efficiency of information reception, reduce the cost of understanding and learning, and improve the fluency and accuracy of operational tasks. In the kitchen scene, when the novices cook according to the recipe, they usually do not perform well in memory and learning, which causes many problems in the cooking process. Therefore, we propose an interactive intelligent cooking system design, which focuses on the five kinds of information that novices need most help in the cooking process, and subverts the traditional recipe with MR presentation. The experiment also shows that the intelligent cooking system can make up for the guidance to novice which is easy to be ignored by traditional recipes, and can effectively improve the user experience of novices.

Keywords: Mixed reality · Cooking assistant · User study

1 Introduction

When completing operational tasks, such as cooking, novices are used to obtaining cooking instructions in the form of pictures and videos from the Internet through mobile phones, tablet computers and other carriers, or browsing recipes directly. However, there is a large conversion cost between the information carrier and the actual application of these courses. Even if the same information, different people often have different degrees of deviation in understanding, which makes the cooking process prone to many problems, and the final cooking effect can also be unsatisfactory.

In this context, it has become a research hotspot to study how to use the new multimedia technology in the system that provides help for users. With the development of VR, AR and MR technology and the popularization of related equipment such as HoloLens and HTC VIVE, the presentation and interaction of information have

© Springer Nature Switzerland AG 2020
J. Y. C. Chen and G. Fragomeni (Eds.): HCII 2020, LNCS 12191, pp. 178–195, 2020.
https://doi.org/10.1007/978-3-030-49698-2_13

made great progress. Such technology creates infinite possibilities for human-computer interaction, can greatly improve the efficiency of information reception, reduce cognitive load, and reduce the entry threshold of operational tasks.

We found that many researches focused on the realization of some technologies, they presented recipes in a novel form, but the disadvantages of traditional recipes themselves failed to improve, and the difficulties that users would encounter in the actual operation process were relatively less considered. This paper focuses on the actual needs and interactive experience of users, and puts forward a design scheme of interactive intelligent cooking system. The scheme is based on MR technology and Hololens, which can provide users with cooking help in the form of natural interaction.

In order to put forward the scheme systematically, we first use Hololens and common display to carry out the contrast experiment of random number table, and further verify the efficiency and naturalness of information receiving in three-dimensional scene. Then we do user study on six proficient and six unskilled people, including cooking process records and questionnaire interviews. From the records and interviews, we conclude a common cooking process and five kinds of information that novices need most help. In addition, we conduct a questionnaire survey for the cooks who are interested in trying new recipes or lack of experience, further analyze the function orientation of the system, and initially put forward the scheme of system design. Then, through the wizard of Oz method to simulate and verify our scheme, the experimental results also show that our ideas make up for the guidance of novices which traditional recipe easy to ignore. Methodically, we put forward the design scheme of interactive intelligent cooking system, which aims to help novices finish cooking easily and with high quality.

2 Related Work

In recent years, researchers have explored the method of using new multimedia technology to assist cooking. In terms of helping memory, Tran et al. [1] designed a capture system. They use visual snapshot records the key steps of cooking, arranges them in the form of comic strips, adds colors and notes to repeat steps and recent steps to remind users. Then they simulate and evaluates the system through Wizard of Oz, hoping to help cookers solve the problem that cooking process is difficult to continue after being interrupted by external information or events, reduce memory loss of cookers.

In terms of recipe guidance, the system proposed by Hamada et al. [2] can extract the cooking process from recipes and guide users to strictly follow the order. Takano et al. [3] follow the same principle, but they use a more intelligent way to visualize cooking scenes in virtual space. Fukuda et al. [4] and Taketoshi Mori et al. [5] take more account of the interaction between the system and the user. Their proposed system can identify the current behavior of the user in a limited space, and then guide the next step. Orsini et al. [6] directly uses augmented reality and image recognition technology on Hololens to detect the user's ingredients and recommend recipes, and then guides the user to cook step by step in the way of linear instructions combined with holographic demonstration.

All of the above researches have explored the recipe guidance separately, but there are some deficiencies in the autonomy of cooking process and the freedom of cooking collocation, and respect for user preferences is a factor that needs to be considered in an interactive cooking system. The system proposed by Fadil et al. [7] can recommend dishes to users from the database according to the season and available ingredients, and combine with collaborative filtering algorithm to collect users' feedback on dishes, and use these feedbacks to better help new users, they call it "Content-Free Recipe Selection". There are two modes in their system, among which "recognition mode" can recognize the objects on the table and the cooking actions of users, and "instruction mode" can provide corresponding operation guidance for users according to the results of recognition mode. At the same time, they use a parallel transformation model to store cooking instructions. The model considers the time sequence of cooking actions in recipes. As long as the model allows, users can freely and flexibly perform cooking actions within a certain range.

On the other hand, there have been many researches on using smart glasses to assist operational tasks. Funk et al. [8] utilized Lego building block standardized task to compare in- situ projection with paper-, HMD- and tablet-based instructions. The research results make them believe that "HMD is not easy to accept", and "The speed of locating a part using in-situ projection and paper instructions is significantly faster, and the speed of locating assembly position using HMD is significantly slower than that using flat and paper instructions, and the assembly is also slower". In addition, compared with the command of HMD, the error rate of using tablet and in situ command is significantly reduced. However, in funk's experiment, HMD was only used to display a static image command in the center of participants' field of view, and it did not play the function of smart glasses very well.

The research of Blattgerste et al. [9] gives full play to the advantages of smart glasses. They used the same standardized task, using Hololens smart glasses to compare with funk et al's three instruction systems. They use AR based in-situ visualization on Hololens, but they implement 3D virtual objects for assembly instructions. This visual effect is also used in smartphones to assess the impact of selected devices. At the same time, they also reevaluated the assistance of HMD instructions and paper instructions. The final results showed that participants completed the task fastest using paper instructions, but hololens had fewer errors than any other system. The experimental results of blattgerste et al. has an important guiding role for our intelligent cooking system, because cooking is a task with low fault tolerance.

In addition, Hasada et al. [10] explored effective display methods of complex tools on smart glasses. They pay attention to three kinds of complex tools in daily life: Avocado knife, bottle opener and can opener, and implement three AR programs to display the instructions of three kinds of tools, they are: image with text, video and 3D animation. Using Hololens, they conducted user study on three display methods, and analyzed how these display methods would affect users' understanding of complex products by measuring the time and degree of task completion and combining with psychological factors investigation. Finally, they found that the most effective way to display tool instructions on smart glasses was 3D animation, which also played a supporting role in our experiment.

In the above research, we found that using smart glasses, such as Hololens, can really play a good auxiliary role in operational tasks. However, in the exploration of the cooking assistant system, researchers mostly consider to help users cook from the recommendation algorithm and step translation (Direct 3D presentation of fixed steps or guidance in smart glasses), while the limitations of the recipe itself have not been improved, the real needs of users for the cooking assistant system have not been studied in depth, and the interaction experience of the virtual interface needs to be improved, this is the focus of this paper.

3   Random Number Table Experiment

As mentioned in the previous description, the researchers found that using Hololens for three-dimensional instruction assistance can make the participants of operational tasks make fewer mistakes. At the same time, for the use of complex tools, three-dimensional visual effect can also play the best auxiliary effect. We believe that this is due to the augmented reality or mixed reality technology provided by Hololens, which makes information reception more efficient. This paper also uses the random number table experiment to verify this, in order to use Hololens as the hardware foundation of intelligent cooking system design.

3.1   Experiment

In this experiment, participants were asked to look for information in a 15 × 15 random number table (see Fig. 1), which was randomly changed in each experiment. We put the random number table in the two-dimensional screen and the three-dimensional virtual scene of Hololens. In both cases, we keep the size of the random number table equal and the sight distance of the tested person equal. The experiment was composed of three sub experiments. There were 15 participants.

03	47	43	73	86	36	96	47	36	61	46	98	63	71	62
97	74	24	67	62	42	81	14	57	20	42	53	32	37	32
16	76	02	27	66	56	50	26	71	07	32	90	79	78	53
12	56	85	99	26	96	96	68	27	31	05	03	72	93	15
55	59	56	35	64	38	54	82	46	22	31	62	43	09	90
16	22	77	94	39	49	54	43	54	82	17	37	93	23	78
84	42	17	53	31	57	24	55	06	88	77	04	74	47	67
63	01	63	78	59	16	95	55	67	19	98	10	50	71	75
33	21	12	34	29	78	64	56	07	82	52	42	07	44	28
57	60	86	32	44	09	47	27	96	54	49	17	46	09	62
18	18	07	92	46	44	17	16	58	09	79	83	86	19	62
26	62	38	97	75	84	16	07	44	99	83	11	46	32	24
23	42	40	54	74	82	97	77	77	81	07	45	32	14	08
62	36	28	19	95	50	92	26	11	97	00	56	76	31	38
37	85	94	35	12	83	39	50	08	30	42	34	07	96	88

Fig. 1. A figure example of random number table

Find Fixed Point Coordinates. Participants looked for the numbers of nine fixed-point coordinates in the random number table in two-dimensional screen and three-dimensional virtual scene, and the fixed-point coordinates were represented by rows and columns. The results showed that the average time of participants in the two-dimensional screen was 32.6 s, and in the three-dimensional scene was 21.4 s. In the 3D virtual scene, the participants get the fixed-point information more quickly, and the subsequent user interviews show that the interaction of the 3D scene will be more natural and real.

Find Consecutive Number. Participants searched for four consecutive numbers in the random number table under the conditions of two-dimensional screen and three-dimensional virtual scene. The results showed that the average time of participants in the two-dimensional screen was 51.2 s, and in the three-dimensional scene was 43.7 s. Under the condition of 3D scene, the participants can get the segmented continuous information more quickly.

Read Consecutive Number. Under the condition of two-dimensional screen and three-dimensional virtual scene, participants read two consecutive lines of numbers at a fast-fixed speed. The results showed that the average time of participants in the two-dimensional screen was 18.7 s, and in the three-dimensional scene was 16.9 s.

3.2 Conclusion and Extension

In the above three experiments, the time difference of experiment three is relatively close, which may be because reading itself has a buffer time, and fast continuous reading cannot fully reflect the real-time nature of information reception. However, these experiments can also show that the performance of 3D scene in obtaining information speed and interaction nature is faster than that of 2D plane carrier.

Based on the experiment of random number table, we extend the concept. Blattgerste et al. [9] mentioned the concept of "in situ ar assistance". Taking Lego building blocks as an example, they used AR technology to fully simulate the building blocks to be assembled at the positions to be assembled. This auxiliary way of "result presentation" can almost save the operator's understanding cost, and make the text or image description better received by the operator. The idea of "in situ assistance" can be better realized by using MR technology on Hololens. Taking cooking scenes as an example, whether it is operation guidance (see Fig. 2) or information presentation (see Fig. 3), the combination of "in situ assistance" and MR technology can give full play to the nature and authenticity of interaction. (see Sect. 6 for more details)

Fig. 2. Cucumber cutting auxiliary line

Fig. 3. Information presentation of dishes

4   Methodology

In this section, we will solve the problem of "what to present" through in-depth user research. The purpose of MRCooking is not to make the novice become a highly skilled chef, but to make the novice more efficient and high-quality when using MRCooking compared with the traditional plane recipes. Therefore, we summarize the cooking mode by collecting the behavior of the proficient in cooking home-made dishes in the family scene, and help the novice get closer to the proficient's cooking mode through the prompt of MR intelligent menu continuity.

4.1 Design

This experiment is an exploratory user study, the purpose is to help novices find hints that are not provided by traditional recipes but are very valuable for optimizing the cooking experience. Participants are divided into skilled cooks and novice cooks. First, the natural cooking status of the skilled cook in daily situations is collected, and a more comprehensive dish is selected from it, following the most common recipes on the Internet. Describe methods for making experimental recipes. Then, let every novice cook finish cooking concerning the experimental recipes, and the whole process is recorded by video. Novices need to conduct in-depth interviews with researchers after cooking. The interviews involved cooking experiences in experiments and cooking experiences in daily life. We will extract the cooking mode of home-cooked dishes from the video records of skilled cooks as a behavioral reference sample. By comparing the behavioral differences between the two in actual operation, we will analyze the general needs of novices to improve. In-depth interviews with novices excavate information that traditional recipes lack, and the novice's personal experience will indicate the importance of this information.

4.2 Participants

A total of 16 participants were recruited to participate in the experiment, including 8 proficient and 8 novices. Proficient people are familiar with the recipe and easy to operate. The cooking frequency of 8 people is more than 3 times a week and the cooking experience is more than 10 years. Among them, 2 are male, 6 are female. The age distribution is between 28–76 years old, the average age is 47 years old. Novices are those who don't cook often and know little about cooking. Eight people have no fixed cooking habits. The number of cooking times is less than once a week, including four women and four men. The average age is 31 years old, ranging from 23 to 55 years old.

4.3 Experimental Environment

The experimental environment is divided into two types: free environment and fixed environment. Collection of the cooking process of the skilled person is performed in their daily cooking environment, ensuring that the subject displays the most natural cooking process in the familiar environment with the placement of items, home seasoning properties, and the condition of the stove. For novices, complete the test in a well-equipped and well-equipped kitchen. Before starting to cook, prepare all the ingredients (unprocessed), seasonings (for quantitative) and kitchen utensils suitable for this recipe for the novice., Tableware, the subjects completed reading and reviewing the experimental recipes on the tablet. The fixed novice environment is convenient for horizontal comparison of the performance of each novice, and the "environmental noise" is eliminated in time, that is, the factors that cause similar inconvenience to the subjects due to environmental defects are eliminated. At the same time, each novice will be equipped with an investigator familiar with the environment when using this fixed environment to assist the novice in becoming familiar with the experimental environment.

4.4   Experimental Process

Skilled Personnel: Operation Records and Field Q & A. After introducing the experimental process to the skilled participants, the experiment started cooking any dish in the scenes of the daily cooking of the skilled person. The researcher suggested that the skilled person trying to choose familiar dishes for cooking. Through the combination of fixed and mobile positions, record the complete operation process of a person who completes a dish, including sight during the entire cooking process, operation methods for pre-processing ingredients, cooking methods, and concurrent operation. Wait, the researcher will ask questions at the right time in the process, including the timing and decision-making method of adding spices, the basis for adjusting the size of the fire, and so on.

After the skilled person completes the complete production process of a dish, record and analyze the behavior in the video and the answers to the questions raised in the process, and summarize the cooking behavior characteristics and cooking patterns of the skilled person.

Novice's Task. To analyze the problems that novices encountered in cooking and the deficiencies of traditional recipes, we let each newbie complete two tasks. For task one, we have selected a highly comprehensive dish from the previously collected cooking video of the pros—oiled spiced egg noodles, so that novices can cook according to the recipe (see Fig. 4). Task 2: After cooking, interview the novices one by one. For interview questions, see Appendix 1. The purpose of these two tasks is to analyze the weak links of novices in cooking and how AR smart recipes should make up for the deficiencies of traditional recipes. We achieve this goal in three ways: First, use the method of controlling variables to compare the gap between the novice and the veteran with the same recipe. Assume that the cooking process of the veteran is used as a reference for the behavior. Compare and analyze where newbies need to improve. Second, let the novices operate with the help of traditional recipes and feel the deficiencies of traditional recipes. Third, conduct user interviews after completing the actual operation, learn about the novice's cooking background, try new dishes, and ask about the real feelings in task one to get the most intuitive user experience. This set of data can also be compared with the performance of novices with the help of smart recipes later to verify whether smart recipes can improve the novice's cooking level from the two dimensions of cooking efficiency and cooking quality.

Experimental Recipe

Ingredients for oil spill noodle with tomato and egg

Tomato		Egg	
	one		2个
Leafy greens		Garlic and garlic sprouts	
	one		4 cloves
Scallion		Red pepper flakes	
	a bit		5–10g
Dried wheat noodles		Light soy sauce	
	5 oz.		1 teaspoon
Salt		Oil	
	a bit		2 1/2 tablespoons

Step1 Prepare the above ingredients.

Step2 Chopped scallion. Cut the tomatoes into pieces. Break up the eggs and add a little salt. Cut up leafy greens.

Step3 Boil the noodles and the leafy greens in the same pot.

Step4 While cooking noodles, heat the oil and stir fry the garlic to produce the flavor.

Step5 Stir fried tomato and egg, a little more salt and more juice than usual.

Step6 Add the cooked noodles and greens to a heatproof bowl, along with the light soy sauce, dark soy sauce, vinegar, crushed red pepper flakes, salt, scallion, cilantro, and minced garlic.

Step7 Meanwhile, heat the oil in a small saucepan until the surface is shimmering then pour the oil over the noodles in the bowls, taking care as the oil will sizzle. Scatter over some coriander then serve immediately.

Step8 Add the tomato and egg and continue to stir. Finish!

Fig. 4. Contents of the experimental recipe

5   Results and Analysis

5.1   Common Behavior

A). When cooking, both hands of the cook are occupied more than 65% of the time, and at least one of the hands is occupied by more than 76% of the time, which is inconvenient to operate, so it is very inconvenient to look at the recipe. For novices, it is necessary to read and recite recipes repeatedly, which causes a great load on cognitive ability.

B). During the cooking process, it is very important to keep the operation table tidy, so electronic products are often placed out of the normal operating field of vision. In the experiment, novices are unfamiliar with recipes, often leave the operation platform and walk to the iPad to read the next operation after completing a small step. When a certain step of cooking, such as scrambled tomato eggs, suddenly remembered that the recipe reminds Usually add more water and lower the cooking shovel. This method of not easily obtaining information will affect the novice operation, making the originally unskilled cooking more confusing. The same is true for the skilled person. When the mobile phone makes a sound, the skilled person will temporarily suspend the operation in his hand.

C). Mastering the time is very important for the cook, and because of the continuity of the time, the cook needs to obtain the time information in time and at any time. In the experiment, we observed that even if some skilled people put the timer on the place where they can see when they are cooking, they are more inclined to ask others for time or timing progress. This is because the memory for time longer than 5 min will bring a certain load to the cook, and the operation of the timer will encounter the problem in a.

D). When cooking, the perspective of the cook is focused on the range of 15° from the center of the eye to the food connection line. During the whole cooking process, the time of lowering the head is more than 80%, and there is almost no idle head up during this period.

The following Table 1 gives Numbers and occurrences of three common problems a, b, and c.

Table 1. Numbers and occurrences of three common problems a, b, and c.

	Inability to operate electronics easily		Leaving the operation table to read a recipe or other information		Leave the cooking bench in search of timing tools	
	The skilled person is inconvenient to answer the phone because of water on hand	The novices are inconvenient to zoom in and out of iPad content because of water on their hands	The skilled person left the table temporarily to read message	The novice left the table temporarily to read the recipe	Skilled person time for a process	Novice watch time
Number of people	5	7	4	8	4	3
Total number of times	5	23	7	33	4	5

5.2   Comparative Analysis of Skilled and Novice Operation

A). About cooking "style"

Partial record of a novice interview.
Q: Which step is more difficult when cooking?
A: Add seasoning. The accuracy of the seasoning directly affects the taste of the dish. Although the recipe says "add 15 g", it is not known how much it is. Some descriptions are "two tablespoons", and I don't know how big the spoon here is.
Q: Are there any things that are not mentioned in the recipe but are more difficult to complete?
A: There are a lot of recipes that you do n't know by default. Novices are unfriendly, such as "stir-fried tomatoes and eggs and take them out." They do n't describe the cooking process in detail. How much fire, but many recipes are described as such.

During the experiment and the usual understanding of novice cooking, the description of "quantity" in the recipe became the most difficult part for the novice to read. Other basic operations will be described in a minimalist way in the recipe, which makes the novice Very confused. And when we observe the skilled cooks, we find that everyone handles the same "basic operation" differently, such as scrambled eggs, heat, oil temperature, when to add salt, how much salt to add, and even woks. And everyone will scramble eggs with their own "style". This "style" is a personal habit formed by long-term cooking. For novices, no personal style has been explored. Therefore, they will rely heavily on the description of the recipe, and demand that the "quantity" and basic operation methods be consistent with the recipe Caused panic.

The skilled person has a personal "style", which essentially has accurate expectations for the results of cooking, and can determine the dosage, heat and time based on feelings; novices do not have a personal "style", and every step taken will cause unknown results. Getting timely feedback will be tangled in a certain operation and reduce efficiency.

B). About operational proficiency

The difference between the proficient and the novice in proficiency is mainly reflected in the following five points:

i. Method and speed of food processing
ii. Familiarity with ingredients
iii. Time planning and process control
iv. Cooking management for multiple pots
v. Ability to handle emergencies

Among the above five points, the advantages of the skilled person are mainly reflected in two aspects: First, the skilled person can keep most of the information in cooking, such as the above-mentioned mastery of food processing methods, ability to deal with sudden problems, and good time The overall planning and process control can take into account the cooking of multiple pots. Second, the accumulated cooking experience makes the proficiency of the skilled person much higher than the novice, so it is significantly better than the novice in terms of familiarity with the properties of the ingredients and the processing speed of the ingredients. Of these two aspects, the second point is not that novices can reach the level of proficiency in a short period of time, and the first point can be made up for by the prompts of auxiliary equipment.

5.3   Cooking Pattern Extraction

After synthesizing the results of novice performance and novice interviews, and referring to the cooking process of skilled persons, we have concluded the cooking mode as shown below (see Fig. 5). To complete a dish, you need to go through the following four main steps: selection and matching of ingredients, pretreatment of ingredients, cooking of ingredients, finishing and serving. Among them, there are two common situations in the selection and matching of ingredients in the first step. One is that the novice completely refers to the required ingredients listed in the recipe, and the other is that the novice looks for new combinations based on the existing ingredients. In the third step of cooking ingredients, many processes need to be serial or parallel, and each process is mainly composed of the cooking method, the quantity of seasoning ingredient, and the cooking time. After analyzing the content of the in-depth interviews, it is concluded that the novices need the most help are the following four aspects: 1) food pretreatment methods 2) cooking methods 3) the quantity of seasoning ingredient 4) mastering the cooking time.

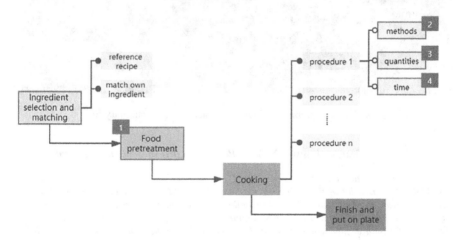

Fig. 5. Cooking Pattern. The numbers in the red boxes in the picture indicate the four problems to be solved (Color figure online)

In addition to these four points, the importance of process control is also reflected in the in-depth interviews with novices, corresponding to the complex relationships of serial and parallel interweaving between different processes in the cooking mode. For each fixed recipe, smart recipes should inform the novice of the entire process structure and progress, so that novices have a rough grasp of the entire process at the beginning of cooking, and get timely feedback during the cooking process, thereby improving cooking efficiency.

6   Recommended Solution

After the above experimental exploration, we finally determined that we need to assist novices from five aspects: food pretreatment, cooking method, ingredients quantities, time, flow. This section introduces the presentation schemes that will be made for these five aspects. And the recommended interface layout.

6.1   Ways of Presenting

Ingredients Pretreatment-Tips for Auxiliary Lines. As mentioned above, MR technology reduces the conversion cost between the information carrier and the actual application compared with the traditional presentation method. When novices do not know how to deal with food ingredients, MR Cooking will attach a "processing auxiliary line" to the ingredients. The position, length, interval, and thickness of the auxiliary line carry a wealth of prompt information. (see Fig. 6)

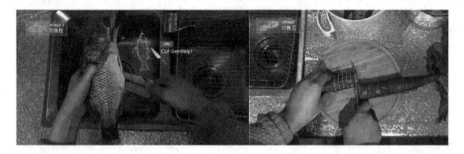

Fig. 6. Novices preprocess ingredients according to auxiliary lines

Cooking Method-Demonstration Video. *Partial record of a novice interview*

Q: When will I try new dishes
A: When there is a lot of time idle at home, it is okay to take a vacation on the weekend. Because I want to eat, I search for recipes online and see food bloggers posting recipes.
Q: Is it a text description or a video presentation?
A: Most of them are video demonstrations. I can intuitively feel the taste of this dish, and then decide whether to try. And watching the video steps will be clearer, but the amount is still unclear.
Q: Why is the video step clearer? What makes you feel better than a description?
A: The amount of information in the video is greater. The continuous action in the video supplements many detailed operations, and the illustrations of the static recipe can only show the situation at a certain moment. And watching the video saves time thinking about intermediate steps, and can better strengthen memory when you are not familiar with recipes.

MR Cooking can easily carry video playback (see Fig. 7). Its characteristics of displaying information in the space allow novices to watch while operating. When novices are confused about the description of the cooking methods described in the recipe, it is undoubtedly a good choice to follow the video operation. In the video, not only can the novices see the example operation methods, but also when the novice does not know whether the operation is correct, correct their operations against the video examples to get feedback.

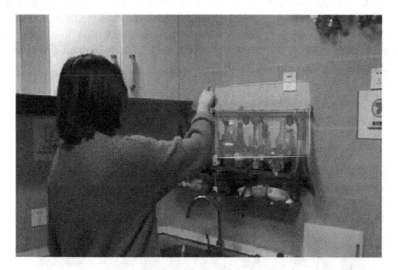

Fig. 7. Users can freely adjust the position and size of the demonstration video in the space

Quantities-Tick Marks. Similar to food pretreatment, MR Cooking can also prompt novices with auxiliary lines (see Fig. 8). Computer vision can estimate the size of any container and suggest tick marks underneath the container. When the novice does not know how much seasoning and how much water to add, MR Cooking can display the

Fig. 8. Display tick marks according to the size of the container

scale mark based on the recipe requirements and the actual container. At this time, the novice just needs to add the seasoning or water to the designated scale line to get a more accurate dosage.

Time-Clock/Timer. Cooking is also the art of the time. The accurate grasp of time is directly related to the quality of cooking. MR Cooking displays the time function in the sight of novices, providing timing, countdown, and clock functions (see Fig. 9). Novices can safely give time calculations to time tools, thereby reducing Memory load, focusing on the operation in the hand.

Fig. 9. Set a timer

Flow-Progress Bar. Skilled people are more skillful in cooking because they have a comprehensive understanding of the processing of each dish and even the preparation of a table, and the recipes are stored in the brain of the skilled person in a three-dimensional form. For novices, it is often only possible to estimate the operation in front of them. Once a problem occurs at a certain step, it is easy to mess around. The role of the progress bar is to establish the overall impression of the process for the novice. You can see on the progress bar which step is taken, how long each step takes, and whether the step is completed will also prompt the novice through the color change. For more complicated processes, the progress bar can also indicate the steps that can be performed simultaneously in a parallel form. For novices, the progress bar is equivalent to "operation map", and the process is clear at a glance.

The extended form of the progress bar is seasoning tips, the purpose of which is to remind novices which seasonings should be added, in what order, and how many seasonings should be added, mainly to let the novices understand the process of cognitive cooking (see Fig. 10).

Fig. 10. The user has completed five of the eight steps and one step has an incorrect operation (orange part) (Color figure online)

6.2   Recommended Layout

We then put forward some suggestions on the general interface content (see Fig. 11). The four parts are shown in the following figure: timeline, timer, demonstration video, seasoning tips can stay in the field of vision, and there are tips for auxiliary lines and tick marks. Freely attach to the target Every part of the interface content should exist in a flexible form and can be added and moved based on the user's habits.

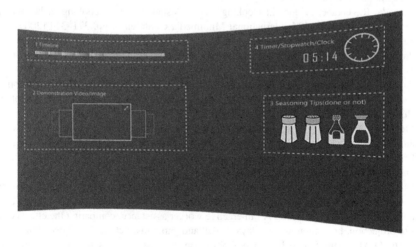

Fig. 11. General interface content suggestions

7 Conclusion

This article proposes an interactive intelligent cooking system MR Cooking design scheme, which combines MR presentation to subvert traditional recipes. In the kitchen scene, when novices are cooking concerning recipes, because they are not skilled, they usually perform poorly in memory and learning, and smart cooking system solutions have a display advantage, enabling people to obtain information efficiently and conveniently. Studies of skilled people and novices have shown that novices need help in five aspects of food preparation, cooking methods, ingredient usage, time control, and process understanding. With these five types of information, novices can reduce the cognitive load and Attention is focused on the preparation of the dishes, making up for the blind spots in traditional recipes.

In the future, we will try to put this system into development and optimize the system by collecting user data. At the same time, some functions in the system require the support of computer vision algorithms, and the performance of the algorithm directly affects the accuracy and effectiveness of suggestions for novices, which will be a new challenge.

References

1. Tran, Q.T., Calcaterra, G., Mynatt, E.D.: COOK'S COLLAGE. In: Sloane, A. (ed.) Home-Oriented Informatics and Telematics. IIFIP, vol. 178, pp. 15–32. Springer, Boston (2005). https://doi.org/10.1007/11402985_2
2. Hamada, R., Okabe, J., Ide, I.: Cooking navi: assistant for daily cooking in kitchen. In: Proceedings of 13th ACM International Multimedia Conference, pp. 371–374 (2005)
3. Takano, T., Ueshima, S.: Cooking studio: cooking simulation from web recipes. In: Proceedings of 2nd International Conference on Creating, Connecting and Collaborating Through Computing, p. 191 (2004)
4. Fukuda, T., Nakauchi, Y., Noguchi, K., Matsubara, T.: Human behavior recognition for cooking support robot. In: Proceedings of IEEE International Workshop on Robot and Human Communication, pp. 359–364 (2005)
5. Mori, T., Kuroiwa, T., Morishita, H., Sato, T.: Assistance with human actions and individuality adaptation by robotic kitchen counter. Proceedings of ASER, pp. 13–20 (2004)
6. Orsini, A., et al.: Augmented reality enhanced cooking with Microsoft HoloLens, Rutgers State University of New Jersey (2017)
7. Fadil, Y., Mega, S., Horie, A., et al.: Mixed reality cooking support system using content-free recipe selection. In: Eighth IEEE International Symposium on Multimedia. IEEE (2006)
8. Funk, M., Kosch, T., Schmidt, A.: Interactive worker assistance: comparing the effects of in-situ projection, head-mounted displays, tablet, and paper instructions. In: Proceedings of the 2016 ACM International Joint Conference on Pervasive and Ubiquitous Computing, pp. 934–939. ACM (2016)

9. Blattgerste, J., Strenge, B., Renner, P., et al.: Comparing conventional and augmented reality instructions for manual assembly tasks. In: Proceedings of the 10th International Conference on Pervasive Technologies Related to Assistive Environments, pp. 75–82 (2017)

10. Hasada, H., Zhang, J., Yamamoto, K., Ryskeldiev, B., Ochiai, Y.: AR Cooking: comparing display methods for the instructions of cookwares on AR Goggles. In: Yamamoto, S., Mori, H. (eds.) HCII 2019. LNCS, vol. 11570, pp. 127–140. Springer, Cham (2019). https://doi.org/10.1007/978-3-030-22649-7_11

Learning, Narrative, Storytelling and Cultural Applications of VAMR

Engaging Place with Mixed Realities: Sharing Multisensory Experiences of Place Through Community-Generated Digital Content and Multimodal Interaction

Oliver Dawkins[1] and Gareth W. Young[2(✉)]

[1] MUSSI, Maynooth University, Co., Kildare, Ireland
Oliver.Dawkins@MU.ie
[2] V-SENSE, Trinity College Dublin, Co., Dublin, Ireland
YoungGa@TCD.ie

Abstract. This paper discusses the motivation and potential methodologies for the use of mixed reality and multimodal interaction technologies to engage communities and members of the public with participation in the active creation and use of urban data. This research has been conducted within the context of a wider research program investigating the use of data dashboard technologies and open data to more effectively communicate information to urban authorities and citizens and enable more evidence-based decision making. These technologies have drawn criticism for promoting objectifying, data-driven approaches to urban governance that have proven insensitive to the specificity of place and the contexts of citizens' daily lives. Within the digital and spatial humanities, there has been growing interest in 'deep mapping' as a means for recovering the sense of place and the nuances of everyday life through the incorporation of spatial narratives and multimedia in their mapping practices. This paper considers the ways in which mixed realities can contribute to these efforts, and in particular the unique affordances of virtual reality for evoking an embodied sense of presence that contributes to the communication of a sense of place via rich multisensory experiences. The paper concludes with the discussion of a pilot study conducted with members of the public. This demonstrates the ways in which virtual environments can be created in ways that maintain contextual and affective links to the places they represent as a result of involvement in 'hands-on' activity of mapping through urban sensing and the capture of place-based media.

Keywords: Mixed reality · Space & place · Deep mapping · Urban sensing · Community engagement

© Springer Nature Switzerland AG 2020
J. Y. C. Chen and G. Fragomeni (Eds.): HCII 2020, LNCS 12191, pp. 199–218, 2020.
https://doi.org/10.1007/978-3-030-49698-2_14

1 Introduction

For more than a decade technology vendors and urban administrations have courted a form of 'smart' urbanism that has sought to leverage technological innovation as a means for monitoring, communicating, and addressing urban concerns. These include the provision and availability of services; the movement, comfort, and safety of people; the management, sustainability, and security of utility and transportation infrastructures; and the impact on and of environmental conditions. The solutions offered by technology providers typically involved the use of advanced information and communications technologies (ICTs) to connect urban sensing infrastructures with cloud-based platforms that facilitate the aggregation, analysis, and visualization of urban data, often at multiple scales and aggregations, and in near real-time. Given the growing range of location-based data available to cities data dashboards, and digital maps, in particular, have become powerful tools for visualizing urban conditions at scale and making spatially informed decisions. In this way, they provide the principal means of enabling 'the spatialised intelligence of the city to represent itself to itself' [37]. Providing local governments with a means for planning, displaying and evaluating the performance of their policy decisions and interventions, they have also become a tool for communicating to other city stakeholders and their wider communities [53].

Despite advances in the technology, effective use of dashboards and online maps requires varying degrees of data literacy and familiarity with the relevant visualization conventions [54]. They also pose problems of context for decision making due to the separation they introduce between the phenomena they represent and the unique spatial and temporal contexts in which those phenomena occur. In the critical discourse on smart cities, these technologies have become symbols for wider trends in the 'datafication' of society; a process by which the ordinary practices of everyday life become quantified as discrete and abstract 'data points' which derive their meaning and value from their position on a map or sequence in a time-series [27]. The concern is that the quantifiable aspects of everyday phenomena take precedence over more nuanced and qualitative understandings of social behavior, otherwise grounded in the unique relational contexts of specific places and practices of everyday life. In the absence of such context non-experts and outsiders can easily reach false conclusions. Moreover, the people and communities those abstractions represent may feel misrepresented in the absence of the daily sights and sounds of their local streets.

Human geographers and researchers working on pervasive and ubiquitous computing in HCI have been particularly vocal in their calls for more citizen-centric, participatory, and place-based approaches to smart urbanism. From the perspective of human geography, it is our sense of place which frames our cultural understanding of human behavior and frames our day-to-day activities in geographic space [47]. In the emerging field of the spatial humanities, new methodologies of 'deep mapping' are being explored to re-inscribe a sense of place back into our maps and spatial representations through the integration of varied place-based media such as written narrative accounts, pictures, and sound recordings:

> "A deep map is simultaneously a platform, a process, and a product. It is an environment embedded with tools to bring data into an explicit and direct relationship with space and time; it is a way to engage evidence within its spatiotemporal context and to trace paths of discovery that lead to a spatial narrative and ultimately a spatial argument; and it is the way we make visual the results of our spatially contingent inquiry and argument." [4, pp. 2–3]

The concept of the deep map has already informed practical research into the construction of online multimedia mapping platforms such as HyperCities [43]. More recent proposals have advanced deep mapping as a means for understanding smart cities through conceptual archaeology and practical excavation, and mapping of their material and media infrastructures [26]. This earlier research provides the point of departure for our own investigation of deep mapping as an activity which can utilize mixed realities, both as a technical means and conceptual framework, to engage communities in a participatory process that leverages new technologies, while accommodating different modes of participation, and different levels of data literacy and technical ability, to viscerally communicate a shared sense of place.

We propose that Mixed Reality (MR) technologies provide an ideal means for undertaking the construction and presentation of deep maps. MR is inherently spatial and affords the potential for experiences of place that incorporate a wide range of data while selectively engaging the entire sensory spectrum. With the aid of MR, physical reality and digital virtuality can be combined to varying degrees. MR represents a continuum of digitally mediated experience which spans the range of unmediated experience of the physical environment at one extreme, to full immersion in entirely synthetic computer-generated environments at the other [28]. Between these extremes, MR can vary the degree and nature of digital content presented to the user, but also the level of interaction between the user, the content presented to them, and the environment in which it is presented. Visual elements can take the form of simple text and image overlays, georeferenced objects and information popups, or even AI characters that respond to the user and the structure of the physical environment. They can also be accompanied by sound and, in some cases, by haptic feedback, engaging multiple senses simultaneously.

Multimodal interactions in MR serve to combine sensory modalities and provide the user with a richer set of interactions [19]. Although multimodality has many different definitions, they can be broadly categorized into three main areas of interest for MR: human-centered, system-centered, and definitions that incorporate human and system-type classifications [51]. As proposed by Moller et al. [31], the latter category of definitions offers the most comprehensive characterization of multimodality for MR, specifically – "systems which enable human-machine interaction through a number [of] media, making use of different sensoric channels" [31]. Furthermore, embodied, multimodal, multimedia interactions have been demonstrated to enhance dynamic, interactive maps in terms of their flexibility, naturalness, and efficiency in use [15,33]. Multimodal MR technologies can, therefore, communicate a wide range of digital content while selectively engaging any or all of the multiple sensory channels available to potential users. This provides opportunities for MR experiences to be more readily tailored to the requirements of particular user groups and offers greater scope for users to engage with the use and generation of data and digital content on their own terms.

Early research into MR indicated that the use of multimodal interaction could help further the understanding of spatial data for non-specialist audiences. Through the combination of immersion, imagination, and interaction [5], multimodal MR platforms presented unique opportunities for urban communities to share rich and nuanced experiences and recollections of place with each other. Our technological horizon has changed since those earlier studies, both through advancements within the fields of augmented reality (AR) and virtual reality (VR), but also in the wider context of mobile telephony, pervasive computing and urban sensing enabled by the Internet of Things (IoT), and the potential of new standards like 5G to provide sufficient bandwidth to support a tactile internet. Within this technological horizon, MR holds great promise as a means for the construction, communication, and sharing of highly engaging, multisensory experiences of place.

Along with the opportunities provided by MR, this research is informed by perspectives on space and place as well as critical studies in geographic information systems (GIS) and complementary approaches formed against the backdrop of pervasive and ubiquitous computing research in HCI. These perspectives inform the development of a hands-on approach to deep mapping with mixed realities through the participatory creation of a three-dimensional immersive virtual environment (IVE). This is intended to demonstrate one of the ways in which digital technologies might be used by communities and their advocates to share and more widely communicate more richly experiential accounts of their own personal and collective sense of place. In this process, it is the activity of mapping through the selective collection of multimedia content that forms the crucial linked, the mixing of realities, between the physical environment, and its virtual counterpart. In pursuing this research we also seek to demonstrate the ways in which these advanced interaction technologies can make data more amenable to non-specialists through the activity of capturing it.

We begin this paper by considering the convergence of concerns from within the fields of human geography, pervasive and ubiquitous computing, and the digital humanities that motivate the practice of deep mapping. We then present an initial case-study outlining some practical approaches to the collective creation of immersive and multisensory experiences of place through engagement with mixed realities.

2   Space, Place, and Critical Geographies

In his seminal study *Topophilia*, geographer Yi Fu Tuan uses this term to frame his study of the 'affective bond between people and place' [48]. Tuan's work developed a phenomenological approach to human geography that focused on embodiment as a guide to understanding the personal, collective and often culturally informed behaviors that express and condition the way we experience space and place:

> *"People of different cultures differ in how they divide up their world, assign values to its parts, and measure them. Ways of dividing up space vary enormously in intricacy and sophistication, as do techniques of judging size and distance. Nonetheless, certain cross-cultural similarities exist, and they rest ultimately on the fact that man is the measure of all things. [...] Man, out of his intimate experience with his body and with other people, organizes space so that it conforms with and caters to his biological needs and social relations."* [47]

For Tuan, our experience of space is initially as an undifferentiated medium through which we move, but one that takes its measure and meaning from the human body and its sensory apparatus. Place refers to those locations in space that solicit our attention and attract us by providing for our comfort and sustenance. On Tuan's account the conditions for the emergence of a sense of place arise through pause in movement, the punctuation of space by the presence of a perceptually remarkable feature or landmark, the naming of the place, the marking of a territory, and ultimately through physical and affective attachments: 'There is no place like home' [47]. Alternative views of place emphasize the role of mobility such as Michelle de Certeau's argument for the constitutive role of movement and dynamics in animate place, understood as a static location he proposes that 'Space is a practiced place' [8, p. 117]. While the different emphasis they each place on mobility and repose leads them to differing conceptions of space and place, they share a fundamental concern for the situated nature of human experience and everyday practices.

In Certeau's The Practice of Everyday Life, the simple act of going for a walk is a form of enunciation, writing in the space of the street in which the pedestrian's body does the writing [8]. Such performative acts of enunciation are contrasted with more 'synoptic' and distantiated forms of readings which he describes by reference to the idea of observing the city streets from the vantage of a tower, in his case the top of the World Trade Center in New York. The logic of this argument juxtaposes two perspectives or subject positions in a way that recalls Roland Barthes' earlier 'mythology' of the Eiffel Tower in which the panoramic 'birds-eye' view simultaneously 'permits us to transcend sensation and to see things in their structure' as a 'concrete abstraction', but to also 'feel oneself cut off from the world and yet the owner of a world' [3]. This theme of the privileging of the visual and its consequences for situated knowledge find emphasis in the work of Donna Haraway:

"Situated knowledges are about communities, not about isolated individuals. The only way to find a larger vision is to be somewhere in particular. The science question in feminism is about objectivity as positioned rationality. Its images are not the products of escape and transcendence of limits (the view from above) but the joining of partial views and halting voices into a collective subject position that promises a vision of the means of ongoing finite embodiment, of living within limits and contradictions–of views from somewhere." [13]

One of the main targets of Haraway's criticism was the 'god trick' performed by new forms of scientific, particularly computer-assisted, visualization which, like Barthes mythology of the Eiffel tower, seemed to enable the possibility of 'seeing everything from nowhere' but also 'to have put the myth into ordinary practice' [13]. What she disputed was the immediate imputation of objectivity to the perspectives of privileged experts who in fact represented partially situated perspectives nonetheless... typically those of white, male knowledge workers. In the 1990s these critical perspectives were embraced by researchers studying the implications of computer-based mapping software or Geographic Information Systems (GIS). John Pickles' edited collection of critical essays Ground truth: The social implications of geographic information systems [36] featured essays that directly cite these thinkers [11,39]. In this context, 'ground truth' refers to measurements and observations made on location in the field as a means of validating the results of analyses based on more remote forms of sensing using satellite imagery, photogrammetry, and light detection and ranging (LiDAR) techniques. The exhortation behind their criticisms was to engage with people and places. The response was a turn to the engagement with places and their communities through participatory mapping, and citizen-science initiatives that emerged in the following decade.

3   The Convergence of Critical GIS and HCI

By the early 2000s, architects and urbanists had already begun speculating on the implications of pervasive and ubiquitous computing for urban design [30] and the emergence of the 'real-time' city as the introduction of mobile ICTs began to change the behavioral dynamics of cities by enabling individual situational decision making [45]. In particular, the introduction of the civilian GPS signal in 2000 fundamentally changed the way many of us navigate urban space beginning with the development of consumer products like the TomTom Sat Nav and Garmin personal GPS. With the introduction of popular online mapping services like Google Maps in 2005 and the subsequent availability of dedicated mobile apps from 2008, the everyday experience of space and place for many of us has become something constructed intermittently and on-the-fly between glances from the physical environment to the abstract arrangement of points, lines, and polygons on our mobile device screens, seamlessly mixing realities. These developments effectively enabled smartphone users to occupy both Barthes' view from above and De Certeau's performance at once by observing their movements updating in real-time over a digital base map on the screens of their devices. In this way aspects of GIS technologies and the view from above had already become a fact of 'ordinary practice' in a way Haraway had conceded it might.

In response to these trends, HCI researchers like Paul Dourish had also adopted phenomenological perspectives reminiscent of Yi Fu Tuan's to better understand embodied interaction [10]. More generally, researchers working in pervasive and ubiquitous computing were engaging expanded notions of what MR might be outside of the context of augmented and virtual reality devices by way of concepts of 'hybrid space' [14] and 'cross-reality' [35] that described environments comprising both physical and virtual elements in varying degrees and configurations. At this time a number of studies in both geography [22] and pervasive computing [12] determined the tone for the critical reception of smart cities in the 2010s.

The smart city movement was typified by the use of technical innovations and data-driven solutions as a means to address urban issues relating to transportation, energy consumption, environmental issues and the everyday challenges of urban navigation through the aggregation and analysis of large volumes of granular and high-frequency data from diverse sources including mobile phone applications, ubiquitous sensing technologies, and other software-enabled infrastructures [21]. Spearheaded by large technology companies like IBM, Siemens, and Cisco it announced itself through largescale developments like Masdar in the United Arab Emirates and Songdo in South Korea, or flagship projects like IBM's Centro De Operacoes in Rio De Janeiro. Alongside important concerns over social justice, much of the criticism focused on the technological aspects of smart cities, particularly its interfaces: the urban control room; and the city data dashboard. By way of synecdoche these provided a focus for criticisms of the tendency for smart cities, thus conceived, to produce and operate exclusively on data-driven abstractions that overlooked the specificities of place-based cultures and their central importance in the everyday lives of urban inhabitants [25,46].

Whether explicitly or implicitly these arguments typically referred back to the earlier arguments derived from Barthes, De Certeau, and Haraway, as transmitted via the perspective of critical GIS. Structurally they juxtaposed the abstract knowledge formed by way of the distantiated 'view from above' or 'god trick', to the more situated knowledge of local people viewed from the ground or street level. However, arguably the terms of the debate had already changed by this time given the fact that countries across the world, not just the West and global north had seen considerable growth in the use of mobile telephony and smartphones. At the same time, the binary framing of these arguments tended to foreclose discussion of the latent opportunities for agency embedded in the affordances of specific digital technologies and interfaces. For example, while urban control rooms and data dashboards may indeed provide abstracted data-driven views of the city, while the former installation has closed doors and requires specialist engineer to maintain it, the latter technology has the potential to be accessible by anyone anywhere, with the further possibility that a sufficiently interested individual might seek the skills to adapt or devise their own [7]. Even perhaps against their proponents' own best intentions, these arguments tended to obscure fundamental material differences in the specific ways these technologies were deployed and used, how, by whom and to what end.

Critical discourse has recognized the ways in which the specific capabilities and limitations of the software used in the representation and design of urban spaces can have a conditioning effect on the outcome [24]. At the same time, researchers have also expressed cautious optimism for the possibilities of emerging technologies such as digitally augmented reality [20], or the use of virtual reality technologies for the creation of multi-sensory maps and environments that might represent and communicate the sense of place and facilitate the sense of agency felt to be missing from other technologies [26]. More recently a number of studies have sought to reengage with the material and situated practices of working with digital information [9], digital maps [52], and data [23]. Against this theoretical backdrop, we engage with Shannon Mattern's proposal for a 'deep mapping' of the smart city as a means of exploring the unique potentials that mixed reality technologies provide for engaging citizens with place by way of digital technologies [7].

4   Deep Mapping

The term 'deep map' was coined by William Least Heat-Moon to describe his exhaustive landscape history of Chase County, Kansas in PrairyErth. What distinguishes the deep map is the evocation of a sense of place through narrative:

> "The deep map offers a way to integrate these multiple voices, views, and memories, allowing them to be seen and examined at various scales. It will create the simultaneous context that we accept as real but unobtainable by words alone. By reducing the distance between the observer and the observed, it promises an alternative view of history and culture through the dynamic representation of memory and place, a view that is visual and experiential, fusing qualitative and quantitative data with real and conceptual space." [4, p. 5]

Through an engagement with the internet, new media, and GIS the concept of the deep map has expanded in by practitioners in the digital and spatial humanities to accommodate the mapping of urban environments and digital media using advances in online maps as platform [43].

In Deep Mapping the Media City Mattern argues that urban experience has always been mediated, whether by digital technologies, maps, images, text, and the written word, or else the human voice [26]. These diverse media continue to support the various functions and purposes typically assigned to the city, whether that of trade, communication, ceremony or human communion. As new technologies and practices have developed to support the flow of people, goods, and services, the urban landscape is formed, in part by, the accretion of their infrastructural support and material residues. This applies to not just the physical stuff of roads, tunnels, telegraph, and fiber-optic cables, whether above or below the surface, but also to the volumes and voids in the city which have been conditioned by the requirements of less tangible or physically persistent forms of acoustical, visual, or wireless transmission:

> *"Knowing the modern media city thus requires that we trace the technologies, architectures, economies, social practices, and so on, that are tangled up in its production. And appreciating the entanglement of these histories will help us to move forward, into the future, in a more critical fashion."* [26, p. 14]

For Mattern, the exploration of urban form and infrastructure, therefore, provides a means for understanding urban practices, past and present. Against a background of academic practices of 'media archeology', associated in particular with the work of Huhtamo and Parrika [18], Mattern proposes a more 'hands-on' approach for engaging with the cultural history of urban environments by utilizing the media available to us in active practices of mapping and media 'excavation': 'a materialist, multisensory approach to exploring the deep material history—that is, a cultural materialist history that acknowledges the physicality, the "stuff" of history and culture—of our media cities' [26, p. XV].

Mattern's point of departure is the kinds of web mapping projects that arise from the curation of volunteered geographic information or from participatory citizen science. Her example is a citizen-made map of the telecom infrastructure in Bangalore. Using the now-defunct metamap platform this enabled community members to map their own paths and points of interest with additional photos, videos, sounds, text, and hyperlinks providing further context: integrating photography, video, and sound recorded submissions, they also encourage the use of 'home-made tools and sensors to explore the visible and invisible electromagnetic city; we make measurements by taking water from street vendors and performing DIY biological analysis (with webcams made into microscopes); [...] we produce expressions of personal subjectivity; we have meetings with experts and witnesses' [6]. The result as acknowledged by its creators is a particularly 'subjective cartography', but one which affords opportunities for learning and the expression of collective agency that might be better attuned to the experiences, requirements and technical capacities of participants. The use of multimedia adds to the richness of such maps but also make their content more accessible to a wider range of audiences.

Within the context of the digital humanities, the deep maps created to date have typically been realized in the form of top-down, two-dimensional web-based maps that provide portals to an archive of georeferenced materials similar to recent commercial offerings of StoryMaps by companies like ESRI. Mattern, however, proposes a new 'multisensory' approach to mapping advances beyond a 'limited politics of engagement' focused on visual spectatorship and engages the aural, graphic, textual, acoustic and haptic registers of subjective and collective experience [26]. By sharing multisensory experiences of place in MR, we can potentially present users with immersive virtual environments via multimodal sensory stimulation – visual, aural, haptic – allowing them to experience a variety of interactive, multimedia encounters. Where traditional perspective-taking exercises rely on imagination, MR allows the viewer to embody another person via first, second, and third-person narratives that are delivered via carefully composed technology-mediated experiences. Empathy is a term that describes the ability to share and understand the emotions of another [16]. Empathy in MR has not only been of interest to multiple disciplines in the past [1,29,38], but it also presents future MR content creators, as artists and filmmakers, with a new platform for storytelling that can be effective in promoting empathy towards specific places and groups of people.

5   Engaging Place with Mixed Reality

Considering the current range of virtual, augmented, and other mixed reality devices on the market, our point of departure is provided by the kinds of interactive, three-dimensional recreations of historic scenes and architectural walkthroughs made possible through 3D modeling and the use of game engine technologies. Advances in web-based 3D graphics are now facilitating the display and curation of such models in the browser through platforms like SketchFab. Along with models created in 3D modeling packages these platforms and collections also include photorealistic representations objects, people, and places made possible by increasingly accessible and automated processes of 'reality capture' which deriving 3D models from photogrammetry and LiDAR.

As has already been noted MR technologies are inherently spatial, and they provide a variety of options for viewing and interacting with 3D content. Mixed Reality describes a continuum of digital mediation in the experience of a user or subjects environment ranging from the direct, unmediated experience of the physical environment they currently occupy through to a fully simulated and synthetic representation of a 'virtual' environment that might be very different to the physical environment they actually occupy at that time. This range is described by Milgram's Reality-Virtuality (RV) continuum [28]. On this account, MR does not describe any one type of experience but a range of possible experiences determined by different degrees of digital mediation that encompasses the increasing mediation of AR on the way to the total immersion promised by pure VR. Despite their sharing of this continuum, AR and VR technologies provide very different affordances for engaging with digital representations of place.

Virtual Reality devices distinguish themselves by design affordances which effect a monopolization of the user's sensory system through a filtering and exclusion of sensory stimulus from their actual surroundings which are substituted by alternative inputs, typically engaging the visual and auditory registers through the head-mounted display (HMD), but also increasingly incorporating the haptic register with improved peripherals like haptic gloves and bodysuits. While the various interaction devices typically associated with AR and VR can be expected to be mixed and matched to provide new affordances within the sphere of MR, virtual reality as a medium provides unique opportunities for evoking an embodied sense of presence and place whether observing sensed representations and recreations of existing environments or when transported to representations of other places and times that may, in fact, be entirely fabricated. In this way, it provides a unique platform for manipulating and relaxing the physical constraints imposed by our physical embodiment. We can, for example, interact with people on the other side of the world while retaining a strong sense of proximity through telepresence supported by social VR platforms. We can also create and immerse ourselves in environments which subtly alter the laws of physics or partake in experiences that place us in the bodies of others. Consumer VR headsets are already becoming less expensive through the introduction of consumer-grade headsets. See-through AR headsets have also been developed for the higher end of the market. Smartphone-based AR that enabled the geolocation of digital content for viewing in-situ had already existed several years before the release of Pokemon Go in 2016. Advances in computer vision and spatial mapping techniques like simultaneous localization and mapping (SLAM) are now enabling greater interaction between computer-generated content, as viewed on devices like Microsoft's HoloLens, and the physical environments they are referenced to. MR provides a means of bridging the divide between physical experience and more abstract data-driven experiences of the environment through the kinds of 'hybrid spaces' and 'cross-realities' discussed in the fields of pervasive computing and HCI.

The impact these kinds of experience will have on their user's sense of embodiment and experience of a place remains to be seen in future research. As with Tuan's account of place, it is the user's sense of embodiment that provides the primary reference for the orchestration of MR experience, even and perhaps most noticeably when those experiences are designed to disrupt the user's sense of scale and embodiment. And just as Certeau's account of enunciative performance in the act of walking, in MR it is typically the user's body that acts as the controller. The main objective for this research is to undertake a practical and formative exploration of the process of deep mapping with mixed realities as an exploration of their potential for leveraging new forms of digital multimedia as a means for conveying multisensory experiences of place that would be meaningful for the communities they represent and engaging for outsiders. To that end, opportunities were sought to develop participatory methods that could be used to directly engage members of the public in the process of deep mapping by assisting in the capture of digital information.

6   Ground Truth in Digital Dublin: Deep Mapping in Virtual Reality

On the 1st June 2019, the first deep mapping workshop was held at the Science Gallery Dublin. Participants were enrolled in advance of the session by way of invitation on the gallery's website [42]. The workshop would involve an exploration of Dublin's Docklands on foot; an area of the city that is now designated

Fig. 1. Alice Vision's Meshroom [49]

as a Special Development Zone (SDZ) – allowing the fast-tracking of planning permissions. Furthermore, this area is currently serving as a testbed for the development of innovative smart city technologies and houses the offices and European headquarters of several large tech companies including Google and Facebook. At the same time, it also borders some of the city's poorer neighborhoods. In preparation for the session, a brief quotation of the late architect and urbanist W.J. Mitchell was distributed which neatly linked our core themes of pervasive sensing, digital mediation, and virtual reality to the site of our study:

> *"Thousands of electronic eyes and ears continuously capture the city's unfolding, interwoven narrative threads, and spin them out into cyberspace. ...In countless spatially and temporally displaced, inherently ambiguous fragments, Dublin electronically doubles itself"* [30]

This reading was suggestive of the many ways in which the contemporary city is digitally sensed and duplicates itself in technologies like the city's own Dublin Dashboard [32]. Our intention was that the workshop participants themselves would act as the roving eyes and ears using their own mobile phones to capture data for a deep map of Dublin City.

After introducing the themes of the workshop through a discussion of the Dublin Dashboard we demonstrated a method for capturing digital images that could be stitched together to create 3D 'reality captures' using free and open-source software like Alice Vision's Meshroom [49] (see Fig. 1). Before leaving the gallery, participants were shown how to effectively capture digital images for the software to process. By using their camera phones to capture multiple overlapping images as they walk around an object, participants create multiple perspectives of the same object which the software can analyze to find points that match between the photographs. Using information about the camera stored in each digital photograph the software can determine the likely position of the

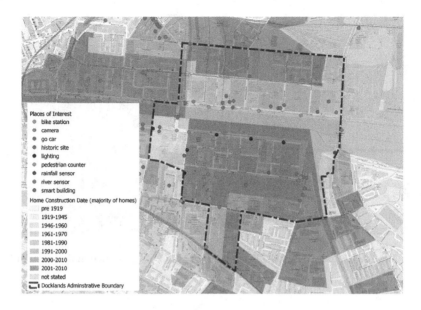

Fig. 2. Docklands map with legend included

camera and distance from each of the matching points in each image. Once many thousands of points have been correlated between each photograph the software is then able to reconstruct a 3D model of the object by linking the matching points together. It is then able to overlay the original images to give the models a photo-realistic texture.

Through this demonstration, we were able to show participants how this method mimics the kinds of remote sensing and photogrammetric processes used by companies like Google in the construction of their online 3D maps. In this way, we also demonstrated how methods that might typically have been associated with Barthes and Certeau's 'view from above' could equally be used from the ground up.

Participants were then invited to spend an hour exploring the nearby Dublin Docklands in small groups, each accompanied by one of our researchers, and to return to the gallery at the end of the session with images of an object that could be processed and added to our deep map. To encourage exploration, participants were each provided with a paper map that would be used as a rough guide for their activity. The maps had differently themed 'points of interest' identifying smart infrastructure and historic sites. We also overlaid a choropleth representation of home construction dates, see (Fig. 2). Crucially, the legend for this map was removed and was later revealed once participants returned to the gallery at the end of the workshop.

Participants were asked to see if they could identify the nature of the collections of points on the map by visiting them in turn to establish their nature and 'ground truth'. While participants explored to find objects to scan and identify

Fig. 3. The open source 3D model provided by Dublin City Council and Smart Dublin [44]

their own points of interest our researchers talked with them and captured other forms of media for the deep map including still images, ambient sound, recordings of our participants' discussions as they went about the activity, and 360-degree videos. Due to time constraints, this activity focused on the area south of the River Liffey and around the Grand Canal Docks. Throughout the session, observational notes were logged by researchers, and participants were encouraged to concurrently vocalize or 'think aloud' as they were performing the specified tasks of the workshop; including what they were looking at, what they were doing, and how they felt towards the objects they interacted with.

After returning to the lab, the map legend was revealed to participants. The aim was not to quiz or test participants but to encourage careful observation. On reflection, participants found that urban infrastructure such as the bike stands for the local bike scheme and the CCTV cameras were much easier to identify than some of the historic sites which were more poorly preserved and more difficult to identify than their designation as specific points of interest might otherwise have suggested. Participants also felt in hindsight that the differences in the age of the buildings on one side of the Dockland's boundary and the other were very apparent when walking along the roads running from the Science Gallery into the Docklands SDZ along its southern border. In this way, we were able to demonstrate the meaning of 'ground truth' and the challenges of representing places through the use of maps in a practical way.

Dublin City Council and Smart Dublin had recently commissioned the creation of a 3D model of the Docklands which they released as open data on the city's open data portal 'Dublinked' in May 2019 [44] (see Fig. 3). The release of the model was intended to supported uses in architectural planning and innovation in mixed realities. The model was, therefore, chosen to provide the base for our mixed reality deep map. Participants were shown the output from

Meshroom and a demonstration of a 3D model of the Dublin Docklands was given in VR (Oculus' Rift) and AR (Microsoft's Hololens). At the end of the session, participants were asked to forward their images for processing and import into our three-dimensional deep map of the Docklands alongside the other media captured on the day.

7 Discussion

The preceding workshop demonstrated one possible approach to the use of methods that engage members of the public in accessible urban sensing that tie the creation of digital media and mixed realities to participatory and enunciative acts in physical space and the creation of a deep map. For those experiencing the deep map via VR or AR after the fact, the deep map offered many of the qualities of an immersive 'reverse field trip' [2]. For those who participated in its construction, through the capture and submission of data, the practical work of deep mapping provided new opportunities for the active development and expression of a sense of place through the acts of selection and curation (see Fig. 4). As a practical activity, the workshop provided opportunities for individuals to explore opportunities for the expression of their own agency, both through their selective exploration of the physical space of Dublin's Docklands, but also through their engagement with the digital techniques we demonstrated, intended to encourage those with sufficient interest and curiosity to go on to try it for themselves [7,55].

Working with MR technologies as a means of experiencing the deep map is not without issues. High-end equipment is still relatively expensive and the experience of wearing HMDs remains overwhelming, and even the best equipment can cause eye strain and discomfort [2, p. 5]. Due to the time constraints of the workshop session, it was not possible to process the participants' digital images on the day to incorporate them in the virtual reality demonstration at the end of the workshop. The limited time we had available also placed constraints on how long participants had to spend practicing the 3D data capture technique we demonstrated and how long they had to explore the area of interest. While we were able to demonstrate the process for one set of photos captured in advance of the session, it would be ideal for participants to have been able to see their own models in the context of the Dublin Dockland's virtual reality experience at the end of the session. While not possible on this occasion, running a day-long workshop with a break, or arranging a follow-up session soon after would be ideal.

When trying the Dockland's model in virtual reality at the end of the session participants noted the lack of people in the simulated environment and felt that it would add to the experience if it depicted realistic human characters within the map. To some extent, this can be taken to corroborate intuitions like Certeau's that place is missing something without being animated by the movement and interactions of others. However, the affinity a user feels towards virtual characters in MR is a complex interplay of their appearance and the sense of their having

(a) Standard images   (b) 3D Model

Fig. 4. Examples of data capture and processing from the workshop

a persona [56]. To convey this sense of human persona it is possible to use live-action capturing technology which can be applied to the environment in the form of stereoscopic 3D film, 360 video capture, and volumetric video [17,34,41]. Again these media are often high bandwidth and require pre-processing of data. An alternative means for users to interact with each other more directly would be through networked telepresence. Based on our discussions with participants it was felt that face to face communication of the kind undertaken during our deep mapping activity would remain a crucial factor in successfully conveying the local knowledge and patterns of activity that contribute to the sense of place. Indeed, significant technical advancements and cultural changes will be required to convince users to abandon face-to-face interactions and first-person experience rather than visiting real-world locations in person [2, p. 180].

In future workshops, we intend to explore the opportunities and challenges posed by telepresence in multiuser environments by integrating elements of our deep mapping in social VR environments such as AltSpaceVR. It is important to recognize that, by their very nature, digital technologies can exclude on the basis of cost and access but also personal interest. Participants in our workshop attended for different reasons and had different interests. In the future, we can seek to engage groups who might not so immediately be inclined toward the technology by providing workshops that explore different means of contributing to and experiencing the deep map.

8   Conclusion

Public participation must not be thought of as a zero-sum game because there are many varying degrees of involvement for sharing ideas and engaging with the public. This research provides an introduction to the possible uses of mixed realities at the intersection of human geographies and HCI to help communities understand and communicate their own sense of place. This work contributes to the development of a wider practice seeking to utilize mixed reality technologies as a means of conducting and communicating place-based studies and community engagement initiatives. The technology poses new opportunities and challenges for community engagement, and the formation of and expression of collective memory through the process of mapping. The use of MR invites new participants seeking to take advantage of the proliferation of new forms of spatial media, but equally, it excludes others who do not have access to the equipment or would be unable to use it effectively. However, despite the great potential for emerging digital media, community research and digital civics initiatives retain too strong an emphasis on analog methods [50]. This is often a highly practical and reasonable response to very real 'digital inequalities' that can be experienced by participants in terms of access, usage, skills, and self-perception [40]. Three-dimensional, multisensory maps presented in MR are not expected to replace their 2D and analog counterparts, these representations will continue to retain their own unique affordances and powers of abstraction. Paradoxically, an account of the deep map's creation may represent the deep map better than the map produced, and ultimately what defines the deep map is the activity of mapping itself.

Acknowledgments. This publication has emanated from research supported in part by the Maynooth University Social Sciences Institute's Early Career Researcher Awards Scheme 2019–2020 and the Science Foundation Ireland (SFI) – under the Investigators' Award Program for the Building City Dashboards Project at Maynooth University (15/IA/3090) and the V-SENSE Project at Trinity College Dublin (15/RP/2776).

References

1. Ahn, S.J., Bostick, J., Ogle, E., Nowak, K.L., McGillicuddy, K.T., Bailenson, J.N.: Experiencing nature: embodying animals in immersive virtual environments increases inclusion of nature in self and involvement with nature. J. Comput.-Mediated Commun. **21**(6), 399–419 (2016)
2. Bailenson, J.: Experience on Demand: What Virtual Reality is, How It Works, and What It Can Do. WW Norton & Company, New York (2018)
3. Barthes, R.: The Eiffel Tower, and Other Mythologies. University of California Press, Berkeley (1997)
4. Bodenhamer, D.J., Corrigan, J., Harris, T.M.: The Spatial Humanities: GIS and the Future of Humanities Scholarship. Indiana University Press, Bloomington (2010)
5. Burdea, G.C., Coiffet, P.: Virtual Reality Technology. Wiley, New York (2003)
6. Chardronnet, E.: Digital dualism versus augmented reality (2011). https://www.ewenchardronnet.com/semaphore/2010/09/bangalore-subjective-cartography-at-european-month-of-photography-2010-2011.html. Accessed 20 Apr 2019
7. Dawkins, O.: Opening urban mirror worlds: possibilities for participation in digital urban dataspaces. In: Whose Right to the Smart City, Plymouth (2017)
8. De Certeau, M., Mayol, P.: The Practice of Everyday Life: Living and Cooking, vol. 2. University of Minnesota Press, Minneapolis (1998)
9. Dourish, D.: The Stuff of Bits: An Essay on the Materialities of Information. MIT Press, Cambridge (2017)
10. Dourish, P.: Where the Action is: The Foundations of Embodied Interaction. MIT Press, Cambridge (2004)

11. Goss, J.: Marketing the new marketing: the strategic discourse of geodemographic information systems. In: Pickles, J. (ed.) Ground Truth: The social implications of geographic information system, pp. 130–170. Guilford Press, New York (1995)
12. Greenfield, A., Shepard, M.: Urban Computing and Its Discontents. Architectural League of New York, New York (2007)
13. Haraway, D.: Situated knowledges: the science question in feminism and the privilege of partial perspective. Feminist Stud. **14**(3), 575–599 (1988)
14. Harrison, S., Dourish, P.: Re-place-ing space: the roles of place and space in collaborative systems. In: ACM Conference on Computer Supported Cooperative Work (1996)
15. Hedicke, V.: Multimodality in human-machine-interfaces. In: Human Machine System Technology: Concepts, Modeling, Design, and Evaluation, pp. 203–230. Symposion Publishing (2014)
16. Hoffman, M.L.: Empathy and Moral Development: Implications for Caring and Justice. Cambridge University Press, Cambridge (2001)
17. Huang, J., Chen, Z., Ceylan, D., Jin, H.: 6-DOF VR videos with a single 360 camera. In: IEEE Virtual Reality (2017)
18. Huhtamo, E., Parikka, J.: Media Archaeology: Approaches, Applications, and Implications. University of California Press, Berkeley (2011)
19. Jerald, J.: The VR Book: Human-Centered Design for Virtual Reality. Morgan & Claypool, New York (2015)
20. Jurgenson, N.: Digital dualism versus augmented reality (2011). http://thesocietypages.org/cyborgology/2011/02/24/digital-dualism-versus-augmented-reality/. Accessed 18 Apr 2019
21. Kitchin, R.: The real-time city? Big data and smart urbanism. GeoJournal **79**(1), 1–14 (2014)
22. Kitchin, R., Dodge, M.: Code/Space: Software and Everyday Life. MIT Press, Cambridge (2011)
23. Loukissash, Y.A.: All Data Are Local: Thinking Critically in a Data-Driven Society. MIT Press, Cambridge (2019)
24. Manovich, L.: Software Takes Command, vol. 5. A&C Black, London (2013)
25. Mattern, S.: Methodolatry and the art of measure. Places J. (2013). https://doi.org/10.22269/131105. Accessed 12 July 2019
26. Mattern, S.: Deep Mapping the Media City. University of Minnesota Press, Minneapolis (2015)
27. Mayer-Schönberger, V., Cukier, K.: Big Data: A Revolution that Will Transform How We Live, Work, and Think. Houghton Mifflin Harcourt, Boston (2013)
28. Milgram, P., Takemura, H., Utsumi, A., Kishino, F.: Augmented reality: a class of displays on the reality-virtuality continuum. Telemanipulator Telepresence Technol. **2351**, 282–292 (1995)
29. Milk, C.: How virtual reality can create the ultimate empathy machine (2015). https://www.ted.com/talks/chris_milk_how_virtual_reality_can_create_the_ultimate_empathy_machine?language=en. Accessed 09 Oct 2019
30. Mitchell, W.J.: Electronic doublin (2002). http://volumeproject.org/electronic-doublin/. Accessed 10 Feb 2020
31. Moller, S., Engelbrecht, K.P., Kuhnel, C., Wechsung, I., Weiss, B.: A taxonomy of quality of service and quality of experience of multimodal human-machine interaction. In: IEEE International Workshop on Quality of Multimedia Experience (2009)
32. National Institute for Regional and Spatial Analysis: The dublin dashboard (2014). http://www.dublindashboard.ie/pages/index. Accessed 12 July 2019

33. Oviatt, S.: Multimodal interfaces for dynamic interactive maps. In: SIGCHI Conference on Human Factors in Computing Systems, New York (1996)
34. Pagés, R., Amplianitis, K., Monaghan, D., Ondřej, J., Smolić, A.: Affordable content creation for free-viewpoint video and VR/AR applications. J. Vis. Commun. Image Represent. **53**, 192–201 (2018)
35. Paradiso, J.A., Landay, J.A.: Guest editors' introduction: cross-reality environments. IEEE Pervasive Comput. **8**(3), 14–15 (2009)
36. Pickles, J.: Ground Truth: The Social Implications of Geographic Information Systems. Guilford Press, New York (1995)
37. Picon, A.: Smart Cities: A Spatialised Intelligence. Wiley, London (2015)
38. Pierce, J.R., Kilduff, G.J., Galinsky, A.D., Sivanathan, N.: From glue to gasoline: how competition turns perspective takers unethical. Psychol. Sci. **24**(10), 1986–1994 (2013)
39. Roberts, S.M., Schein, R.H.: Earth shattering: global imagery and GIS. In: Pickles, J. (ed.) Ground Truth: The Social Implications of Geographic Information System, pp. 171–195. Guilford Press, New York (1995)
40. Robinson, L., et al.: Digital inequalities and why they matter. Inf. Commun. Soc. **18**(5), 569–582 (2015)
41. Schreer, O., et al.: Capture and 3D video processing of volumetric video. In: IEEE International Conference on Image Processing (2019)
42. Science Gallery Dublin: Ground truth in digital Dublin: deep mapping in virtual reality (2019). https://dublin.sciencegallery.com/events/2019/05/ground truthdigitaldublindeepmappingvirtualreality. Accessed 10 Feb 2020
43. Shepard, D., Presner, T.S., Kawano, Y.: Hypercities Thick Mapping in the Digital Humanities. Harvard University Press, Cambridge (2014)
44. Smart Dublin: 3D data model resources for Dublin Docklands SDZ (2019). https://data.smartdublin.ie/dataset/3d-data-hack-dublin-resources/. Accessed 24 Feb 2020
45. Townsend, A.M.: Life in the real-time city: mobile telephones and urban metabolism. J. Urban Technol. **7**(2), 85–104 (2000)
46. Townsend, A.M.: Smart Cities: Big Data, Civic Hackers, and the Quest for a New Utopia. WW Norton & Company, New York (2013)
47. Tuan, Y.F.: Space and Place: The Perspective of Experience. University of Minnesota Press, Minneapolis (1977)
48. Tuan, Y.F.: Topophilia: A Study of Environmental Perceptions, Attitudes, and Values. Columbia University Press, New York (1990)
49. Vision, A.: Meshroom (2019). https://alicevision.org/. Accessed 12 July 2019
50. Wates, N.: The Community Planning Handbook: How People Can Shape Their Cities, Towns, and Villages in Any Part of the World. Routledge, Abingdon (2014)
51. Wechsung, I.: What are multimodal systems? Why do they need evaluation?—Theoretical background. An Evaluation Framework for Multimodal Interaction. TSTS, pp. 7–22. Springer, Cham (2014). https://doi.org/10.1007/978-3-319-03810-0_2
52. Wilson, M.W.: New Lines: Critical GIS and the Trouble of the Map. University of Minnesota Press, Minneapolis (2017)
53. Young, G.W., Kitchin, R.: Creating design guidelines for building city dashboards from a users' perspective. Int. J. Hum.-Comput. Stud. **140**, 102429 (2020)
54. Young, G.W., Kitchin, R., Naji, J.: Building city dashboards for different types of user. J. Urban Technol. (2020)

55. Young, G.W., Naji, J., Charlton, M., Brunsdon, C., Kitchin, R.: Future cities and multimodalities: how multimodal technologies can improve smart-citizen engagement with city dashboards. In: ISU Talks #05: Future Cities (2017)
56. Zibrek, K., Kokkinara, E., McDonnell, R.: The effect of realistic appearance of virtual characters in immersive environments - does the character's personality play a role? IEEE Trans. Visual Comput. Graphics **24**(4), 1681–1690 (2018)

Augmented Reality and Microbit
for Project-Based Learning

Poonsiri Jailungka^(✉) , Siam Charoenseang,
and Chaowwalit Thammatinno

Institute of Field Robotics (FIBO), King Mongkut's University of Technology
Thonburi, Bangmod, Thungkru, Bangkok 10140, Thailand
pu.poonsiri@gmail.com, siam@fibo.kmutt.ac.th,
chaowwalit.thammatinno@gmail.com

Abstract. The research proposes an augmented reality system integrating with the BBC Microbit microcontroller for student's project-based learning. It is a learning tool that helps the students to understand about the augmented reality (AR) and the Microbit technologies. To increase the student's motivation, the final project was conducted as an AR projectile-based shooting game application. The Microbit was also used as an external remote controller. Each player has an AR marker to define the position and the orientation of the player's avatar and the Microbit for shooting the bullets. The learning goal of this proposed system is to help the student to understand about physics simulation related to the projectile, augmented reality, C# programming, the block-based programming with Microbit, basic electronics, hardware communication, computer graphics, painting, and the coordinate system. Furthermore, the proposed system was designed to support for various teaching and learning approaches including the interdisciplinary learning, project-based learning, and STEAM education. This proposed hands-on learning tool assists the learner to understand about the integration of core knowledges in science, engineering, arts, and math. The proposed system was used by 294 participants including Thai high school students, vocational students, and teachers from 3 provinces of Thailand. The experimental results showed that the learning achievement of students received improvement up to 19–36.28% by comparing the average T-scores of pretest and posttest. In addition, the teachers and students showed a good level of satisfaction on using the proposed system in teaching and learning.

Keywords: Augmented reality · Microbit · Project-based learning · Interdisciplinary learning

1 Introduction

Thai government has a policy to implement the Eastern Economic Corridor (EEC) development project [1] in the eastern region, consisting of Chachoengsao, Chonburi, and Rayong by preparing the infrastructure, manpower, and important technology [2]. These areas have been used to support the expansion from the industrial sector and upgrade the development of the area to become the leading economic area in Asia. Especially, the human resources in 10 targeted industry groups or S-curve industries needs to be

© Springer Nature Switzerland AG 2020
J. Y. C. Chen and G. Fragomeni (Eds.): HCII 2020, LNCS 12191, pp. 219–235, 2020.
https://doi.org/10.1007/978-3-030-49698-2_15

developed for both technical knowledge and skills. The targeted industries consist of the next-generation automotive, intelligent electronics, agriculture and biotechnology, food for the future, affluent medical and wellness tourism, robotics, aviation and logistics, biofuels and biochemical, digital, and medical hub. The important targeted groups of development are children, youths, and workers in the EEC areas. They need to have more knowledge and skills about science and technology and life skills in the 21st century with morality and ethics including the ability to adapt to the changes in technology. One of the targeted technologies is an augmented reality (AR), an overlay real-world environment with interactive digital content or context-based digital information [3]. Recently, AR technology has leveraged several high caliber industries such as healthcare, manufacturing, education, automotive, military, retail, gaming, and real estate. [4, 5] In addition, augmented reality application [6] on handheld devices [7, 8] embedded with several sensors can be applied in learning environments in order to turn basic traditional learning into a motivational learning experience and including to enhance visual and cognitive perception [9]. The combination of AR technology [10] with the educational content creates a new type of automated application and enhances the effectiveness and attractiveness of teaching and learning for students in real life. For examples, the augmented reality was introduced in science laboratories [11], in mathematics and geometry class [12] and in technology and engineer like as an applications of augmented reality based natural interactive learning in magnetic field instruction [13], and an experimenting with electromagnetism using augmented reality. Many AR research works in education are applied to a variety of subjects, including the use of technology in science, technology, engineer, arts and mathematics or STEAM education. In addition, an AR game-based learning system could be a key candidate for the next generation of learning environment. In general, game-based learning (GBL) is a learning and training paradigm for engaging learners and stimulating the active learning e.g. problem-solving and learning by doing through a game-like scenario [9]. The AR games are complicated applications and required to combine the principles of game design with instructional contents in order to improve the learning process. Then, the integration of an augmented reality and game-based learning (ARGBL) was the building of structured contents with rules and game elements seem to be natural and effective ways to propose learning experiences [14]. The example of ARGBL was an AR board game, AR card as a book containing game on pages [15] or AR game on handheld computers (Mad City Mystery) [16].

Furthermore, project-based learning (PBL) is a teaching and learning approach which has collaborative learning under the constructive learning theory [17]. Many research studies showed that the project-based learning can help the learners to become active learners who construct their own knowledge by doing their projects [18, 19]. The students who learned with PBL could perfectly perform on their projects with their higher thinking skills under teacher's facilitation.

Hence, this research proposes an augmented reality learning kit for project-based learning that integrates an augmented reality and the Microbit microcontroller. The system is designed to support the students from science and art programs as a supplementary education tool. It utilizes various technologies to support the learning approaches such as interdisciplinary learning, project-based learning, and STEAM education. The proposed learning kit is expected to increase the motivation of the teachers and students for understanding the technologies of augmented reality and microcontroller in project-based learning.

2 Methodology

2.1 System Overview

The proposed AR learning kit consists of two Microbits for two players, one camera, three markers as references of virtual object's positions, and one computer for running the augmented reality application as shown in Fig. 1 and Fig. 2. Microbit is one of the most widely used microcontrollers for teaching and learning [20, 21]. Microbit was designed from the ground up for education with low cost and multiple programming supports. In the proposed system, the Microbit is used as the remote controller that sends the data commands after the player pressed the button. It also displays the feedback information on its LEDs. The camera is used to track the AR marker in the physical environment. The AR markers provides the positions and orientations of any holographic objects in the application. The holographic objects of a player's avatar and a hole are displayed relatively to the AR markers. Then, the avatar of player can shoot a ball after the player pressed the button on the Microbit. In addition, the players can move the AR marker of the avatar to set up and adjust the projectile shooting position and orientation as shown in Fig. 3.

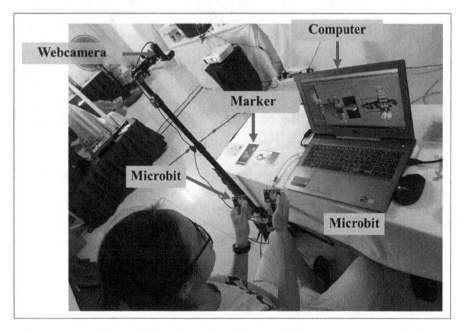

Fig. 1. Components of the proposed system

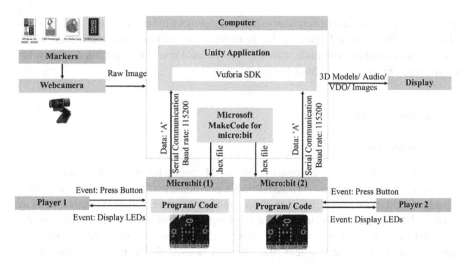

Fig. 2. System dataflow

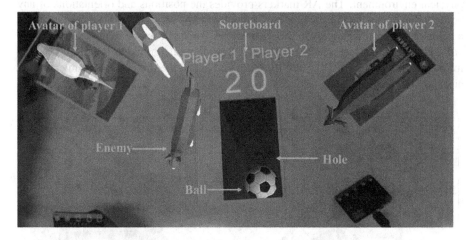

Fig. 3. Virtual graphics in AR shooting game

All software components in the proposed AR learning kit consists of prefabs and script codes. Those components were designed and developed using Unity3D (Version 2017.4.24f1 LTS) [22]. The Unity3D is a software game engine for developing games, movies, virtual graphics, etc. This Unity3D version has a built-in Vuforia AR library. In addition, the 3D models were obtained from the google poly website [23].

Prefab is a copy of the game object or the template [24, 25]. Prefab can store game objects with their properties and components set. Prefab can be reused in many ways. It contains a hierarchy of game objects. In other words, prefab is a container that can be empty or contains any number of game objects. When the students modify the prefab, all its instances will be also updated automatically. The proposed system provides developed 6 prefabs for the template of the game object in Unity3D as shown in Table 1.

Table 1. Developed six prefabs for AR learning kit

Prefabs	Definition
Enemy	Enemy prefab is used as an obstacle in the shooting game such as a cat model and a dog model in Fig. 4. The component of Enemy prefab consists of "MyAI.cs" script. In addition, the 3D model of Enemy can be adjusted to any model
Canvas	Canvas prefab is a text UI. It can display the initial state of game or the result of the game
Scoreboard	Scoreboard prefab is a text UI. It updates and displays the scores of the two players. Scoreboard prefab is configured for the display of the position and orientation relatively with the AR marker of the hole
GameManager	GameManager prefab is an empty game object and has core component script of shooting. The component of GameManager prefab consists of "MyGameManager.cs" script
Hole	Hole prefab is the hole that detects the collision with the ball and updates the score. The component of Hole prefab consists of "MyScoreChecker.cs" script
Throwobject	Throw object is a ball model in Fig. 3. The 3D model of throw object can be adjusted to any 3D model. The component of throw object prefab consists of "MyThrowableObject.cs" script

The student can use prefabs by importing them from the AR learning kit's asset folder. Figure 4 shows how to use prefab in an AR project. First, the student needs to import the developed AR learning kit's source file into the Unity3D assets folder. From inside of the folder, several prepared samples such as audio files, prefabs, C# scripts, 3D models, pictures, serial script and textures are provided. All developed 6 prefabs in Table 1 are also available. When the students want to use an AI prefab, they student need to select my prefab folder and AI folder, and then drag and drop any developed prefab into the scene.

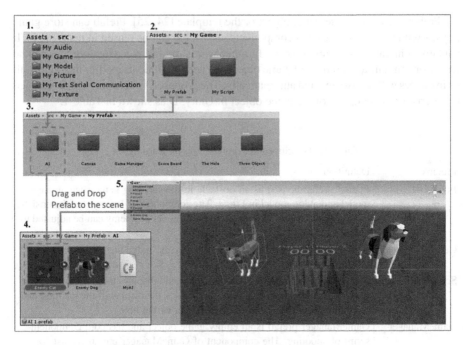

Fig. 4. Using prefabs in AR learning Kit's scene

Game objects in prefab are attached and controlled by the corresponding components. Unity3D allows users to create their own components using scripts. The scripts allow the user to trigger game events, modify component properties over time, and respond to the user input. Thus, the proposed system created and developed the scripts [26, 27] for creating the graphical effects, controlling the physical behaviors of objects, or implementing the customized AI system for characters in the game. The scripts were developed by the C# programming language. In addition, the proposed system provides the implemented scripts for the game as shown in Table 2.

Table 2. C# scripts for AR learning Kit's assets

Scripts	Features	Examples
MyAI.cs	MyAI.cs script is used to randomize the position and orientation of enemy relatively to the AR markers of the hole, player 1, and player 2. Student can adjust the clip_normal parameter as background sound of game and the clip_defense as event triggered sound when the enemies hit the other game objects.	My AI (Script) Script — MyAI CLIP_NORMAL — minions-hellow CLIP_DEFENSE — สนุก ซอมโหดๆถอดๆ short Player Target — None (Game Object)
MyGame Manager.cs	MyGameManager.cs script is used to update the active status of each game object in the scene. The parameters of My Game Manager such as the image target of AR markers, text score, maximum score, and sound effects, can be adjusted.	My Game Manager (Script) Script — MyGameManager Image Target MAP — map Image Target PLAYER1 — Player1 Image Target PLAYER2 — player2 Text Score — Text Score (Text) Text UI — Text UI (Text) Score Player 1 — 0 Score Player 2 — 0 Game Over Score — 10 Audio Game Start — Curious Audio Winner — Kids Cheering - Gaming Sound Audio Game Over — Sound Effect (Background) - S Audio Score Update — coin
MyScor Checker.cs	MyScoreChecker.cs script is used to detect the collision between the balls and the hole, and to update the score.	My Score Checker (Script) Script — MyScoreChecker
MyThrow able Object.cs	MyThrowableObject.cs script is used to detect the collision between the balls and the enemies. The ball of each player is destroyed after it hits the enemy.	Rigidbody Mass — 0.1 Drag — 0.25 Angular Drag — 0 Use Gravity — ✓ Is Kinematic — Interpolate — None Collision Detection — Continuous Dynamic Constraints My Throwable Object (Script) Script — MyThrowableObject
MySeria lPort.cs	MySerialPort.cs script is used for the communication between the Microbit and this application as shown in Fig. 2. Student can set the comport and baud rate of Microbit in this script. The script will check a serial connection and a received character from the serial read. When the Microbit sends a matched values, there will be a command to shoot the ball out and play the sound effect. This script is configured as a child script of the image target of player 1 and player 2.	My Serial Port (Script) Script — MySerialPort COMPORT — COM6 Baud Rate — 115200 Throw Point — p2 (Transform) Throw Object 1 — MyThrowObject 5 Throw Object 2 — None (Game Object) Thrown Sound 1 — player2 (Audio Source) Thrown Sound 2 — None (Audio Source) Shake Sound — None (Audio Source) RENDERER — None (Renderer) Throw Triger —

2.2 Implementation of Augmented Reality and Microbit in Project-Based Learning

The concept of system dataflow in Fig. 2 was used to design and develop for training in a short course. The AR learning kit's assets were the components used to prepare for making an AR application. The final project of student was the AR shooting game. The student developed the AR shooting game in short time by using the proposed system. The learning process of the development of AR application is relevant to the course outline. The major contents follow the five procedures as shown in Table 3.

Table 3. Learning contents of the proposed system in project-based learning

Procedure	Contents	Time (mins)
Preparation	Pretest (AR and Microbit)	15
	Preparation and Creation of Two-Member Groups	10
Learning by doing	Lesson 1: Introduction to Augmented Reality	75
	Lesson 2: Basics Unity3D	75
	Lesson 3: Building Augmented Reality Application	160
	Lesson 4: Introduction to Microbit	90
Project-based learning	Lesson 5: Applying AR Learning Kit in Project-based Learning	180
	AR Shooting Game Challenge with Friends	60
Evaluation	Posttest (AR and Microbit)	15
	Satisfaction Survey	15

Preparation. The students took a pretest for 15 min using either mobile device or computer as shown in Fig. 5. The pretest contained 10 questions about augmented reality and Microbit. The questions were used to test the student's knowledge before learning in a short course and doing a project. After that, students took brain exercises and created a group with two members as shown in Fig. 6.

Fig. 5. AR and Microbit pretest

Fig. 6. Preparation and creation of two-member groups

Learning by Doing. In this procedure, the lecturer conducted the lesson 1 to lesson 4 using the learning by doing approach. Learning by doing means learning from the direct experiences with demonstrations or descriptions of actions rather than taking the normal lectures [28, 29]. In each lesson, the students did several activities with learning of theory, hands-on, taking randomized quiz, and checking their understanding with the trial-and-error exercises. The staff team helped the lecturer to observe and confirm that the students passed the exercise since the knowledge and skills in each lesson were required for the next lessons.

Lesson 1: Introduction to Augmented Reality. This section made the motivation for the learners by introducing them with the augmented reality technology. The activities provided the contents about the current and future augmented reality applications, asked about the idea of AR application in a daily life and career, and showed some AR showcases and the demo of the final project. The activities in this lesson can be shown in Fig. 7.

Fig. 7. Activities in introduction to augmented reality section

Lesson 2: Basics Unity3D. This section guided the student how to use Unity3D for manipulating the 3D model in the virtual environment. The objective of the lesson was to help the students to know how to use the tools and basic components in Unity3D such as scene, game object, components, tools, the 3D coordinate transformation, parent, child, prefab, material, texture, light, physics and rigid body, audio, etc. In each step, the students learned the theory, took hands-on activity, and did the exercises to check their understanding. The example of exercises is shown in Fig. 8. The exercise

1.1 was about how to change the positions and rotations of three cubes in order to block the spheres from hitting the ground after pressing the Play button. The exercise was used to check the knowledge about transformation using the parent and child concept.

In addition, there was a task challenge that students needed to create the chair models in the room and their own scene by applying their own knowledge obtained from the lesson as shown in Fig. 9.

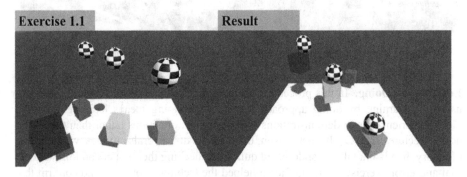

Fig. 8. Example of exercise in lesson 2.

Fig. 9. Task challenge based on knowledge in lesson 2

Lesson 3: Building Augmented Reality Application. This section guided the basic development of AR application using Unity3D and Vuforia SDK. The basic AR application utilizes the AR marker to display the virtual contents relatively with the position and orientation of AR marker. This lesson provided the contents and exercises about using the standard AR marker and customized AR marker with the Vuforia SDK. The objective of the lesson is to teach the students how to create their own AR applications. The activities in this lesson consisted of my first AR with the standard AR marker, using multi standard AR markers, making their own AR markers, and applying the customized AR marker in their own AR applications, respectively. In each step, the students needed to apply the knowledge from the lesson 2 to complete all tasks.

The examples of activities can be shown in Fig. 10, 11 and 12. These activities made the motivation for the students after they can customize both markers and virtual contents in their own AR applications. Furthermore, the student loved to play and take a selfie with friends by using the AR application.

Fig. 10. Development of AR application with standard AR marker

Fig. 11. Sample of customized AR markers

Fig. 12. Development of AR application with customized AR markers

Lesson 4: Introduction to Microbit. This section guided the basic development with Microbit programming. The objective is to help the learner to understand about the Microbit microcontroller, the block-based programming, and the serial communication. The activities provided the contents and exercises about the components of Microbit, the use of input and output of Microbit, and the serial communication between the computer and the external devices as shown in Fig. 13. This lesson defined the exercises that use two Microbits as joysticks. The data from Microbit can be transmitted to Unity3D application for monitoring the obtained values. In the Unity3D application, it applied the AR learning kit by using the MySerialPort prefab.

Fig. 13. Example of activities in introduction to Microbit

Project-Based Learning. Project-based learning (PBL) means an instructional approach designed to give students the opportunity to develop knowledge and skills through engaging projects set around challenges and problems they may face in the real world [17, 30]. In this procedure, the lecturer conducted the implementation of AR learning kit and told the students to do an AR shooting game project. Each team has two members to collaboratively design and build an AR application. This project-based learning activity helps the students to develop a deep content knowledge as well as the skills of critical thinking, collaboration, creativity, and communication.

Lesson 5: Applying AR Learning Kit in Project-Based Learning. This section conducted the implementation of AR learning kit as shown in Fig. 14. The students need to utilize the knowledge from the previous four lessons for creating an AR shooting game for two players. In the process of implementation, the students can customize the game features by self-directed learning. After that, the students were allowed to play and challenge their friends in the AR shooting game.

Fig. 14. Applying AR learning kit in project-based learning

The main concept of lesson is to encourage the students to explore and adjust the parameters of the game's features appropriately by using the knowledge of projectile, basic Unity3D, building of AR application, and Microbit. The examples of activities in this procedure can be shown in Fig. 15.

Fig. 15. Challenge after building an AR shooting game

Evaluation. The task completion was evaluated by the lecture's and staff team's observations to check each step's learning goal indicated in the book manual as shown in Fig. 16. Also, the random selection of students to answer the questions and posttest were conducted.

3 Experimental Results

The sampled population was 229 students who were high school and vocational students. During the training activities, the students involved the learning of theory and the hands-on practice about 50 persons/class. The process of training required 2 days or about 12 h.

Fig. 16. Book manual of AR learning kit

The experimental results show that the learning achievement of students receives improvements by 19%. They were computed based on the comparison of average T-scores of pretest and posttest and the summary of the learning progress can be shown in Table 4.

Table 4. Summary of learning progress of students

Group	Test	N	Min	Max	x̄	S.D.	Avg. T-score	% of Avg. T-Score
Student	Pretest	229	1	10	5.56	1.76	45.66	19.00
	Posttest	229	2	10	7.35	1.95	54.34	

In addition, the teachers took training for coaching the students. The tests compose of 10 questions related to augmented reality, Microbit, applying the learning kit in project-based learning, and STEAM education. The questions are not the same as the student's. The experimental results show that learning achievement of teachers receives the improvements by 36.28% as shown in Table 5.

Table 5. Summary of learning progress of teachers

Group	Test	N	Min	Max	x̄	S.D.	Avg. T-score	% of Avg. T-score
Teacher	Pretest	65	0	10	5.00	1.77	42.32	36.28
	Posttest	65	5	10	8.85	1.42	57.68	

4   Discussion

From the validity evaluation and feedback from the teachers and the experts of Thai office of knowledge management and development public organization (OKMD), it shows that the proposed system can map the lesson plan with the STEAM education using AR learning kit as shown in Table 6.

Table 6. Mapping lesson plan with STEAM education using AR learning Kit

STEAM related subjects	Lesson topics and contents
Science – Physics	1. Know and understand about projectile motion 2. Can apply projectile motion in their own simulation game 3. Can explain why using the simulation is a good tool for studying projectiles 4. Can predict how varying initial conditions affect a projectile path (various objects, angles, initial speed, mass, diameter, initial height, with and without air resistance)
Technology – Augmented Reality (Vuforia) – Marker detection	1. Know and understand about augmented reality technology (AR) 2. Can create art works by utilizing augmented reality contents 3. Understand the relationship of the marker's position and the display of computer graphics 4. Can import 3D models for the computer graphics application 5. Can create marker by themselves and use it in the application development 6. Can apply code and sound file to create interaction between the marker and the computer graphics

(continued)

Table 6. (*continued*)

STEAM related subjects	Lesson topics and contents
Engineer – Basic programming – Basic electronics – Electronics and communication	1. Know the principle of electrical and electronics 2. Know and understand about programming on Microbit microcontroller 3. Know and understand about serial communication 4. Know and understand the communication and transmission of information between the computer and the external devices
Arts – Basic computer graphics – Drawing and painting	1. Can use tools related to computer graphics 2. Can design the scene by placing 3D models 3. Can design their own markers
Mathematics – Coordinate system	1. Know and understand the 3D coordinate system
System integration	1. Can integrate knowledge, augmented reality (AR) technology, and communication between devices

5   Conclusion

The research proposed an augmented reality system integrating with Microbit as a supplementary education tool to help the students to build an AR application in project-based learning. After each lecture was conducted, students needed to take hands-on workshop, answer the quizzes, and do the trial-and-error exercises. The developed system assisted students to understand the concept of physics simulation related to the projectile, augmented reality, C# programming, block-based programming with Microbit, basic electronics, hardware communication, computer graphics, painting, and the coordinate system. After that, students were required to apply the obtained knowledge and skills to build an AR project about a projectile-based shooting game supporting multiplayers. The proposed system reduced the learning time and improved the learning achievement of learners significantly. Furthermore, the teachers and students showed a good level of satisfaction on using the proposed system for teaching and learning.

In the future, several input and output devices should be integrated with the proposed system so that the students can utilize those devices for the real world applications.

References

1. Eastern Economic Corridor (EEC). https://eng.eeco.or.th/en. Accessed 23 Feb 2020
2. Eastern Economic Corridor (EEC): The Prime Gateway to Asia, pp. 1–27. Eastern Economic Corridor Office of Thailand (2019). https://eng.eeco.or.th/en/filedownload/1151/eec-brochure-2nd-english-version
3. Azuma, R.T.: A survey of augmented reality. Presence Teleoper. Virtual Environ. **6**, 355–385 (1997)

4. Light Guide Systems. https://lightguidesys.com/blog/industries-benefitting-from-augmented-reality/. Accessed 23 Feb 2020
5. Silva, R., Oliveira, J., Giraldi, G.: Introduction to Augmented Reality (2003)
6. Sommerauer, P., Müller, O.: Augmented reality for teaching and learning - a literature review on theoretical and empirical foundations (2018)
7. Ruiz, J., Li, Y.: DoubleFlip: a motion gesture delimiter for interaction. In: Adjunct Proceedings of the 23rd Annual ACM Symposium on User Interface Software and Technology, pp. 449–450. Association for Computing Machinery, New York (2010)
8. Lin, P.J., Chen, S.C., Li, Y.H., Wu, M.S., Chen, S.Y.: An implementation of augmented reality and location awareness services in mobile devices. In: Park, J., Adeli, H., Park, N., Woungang, I. (eds.) Mobile, Ubiquitous, and Intelligent Computing. Lecture Notes in Electrical Engineering, vol. 274, pp. 509–514. Springer, Heidelberg (2014). https://doi.org/10.1007/978-3-642-40675-1_76
9. Ştefan, L., Moldoveanu, F.: Game-based learning with augmented reality – from technology's affordances to game design and educational scenarios (2013)
10. Kesim, M., Ozarslan, Y.: Augmented reality in education: current technologies and the potential for education. Procedia Soc. Behav. Sci. **47**, 297–302 (2012)
11. Akçayır, M., Akçayır, G., Pektaş, H.M., Ocak, M.A.: Augmented reality in science laboratories: the effects of augmented reality on university students' laboratory skills and attitudes toward science laboratories. Comput. Hum. Behav. **57**, 334–342 (2016)
12. De Ravé, E.G., Jiménez-Hornero, F.J., Ariza-Villaverde, A.B., Taguas-Ruiz, J.: DiedricAR: a mobile augmented reality system designed for the ubiquitous descriptive geometry learning. Multimedia Tools Appl. **75**, 9641–9663 (2016)
13. Cai, S., Chiang, F.-K., Sun, Y., Lin, C., Lee, J.J.: Applications of augmented reality-based natural interactive learning in magnetic field instruction. Interactive Learn. Environ. **25**, 778–791 (2017)
14. Tobar, H., Baldiris, S., Fabregat, R.: Augmented reality game-based learning: a review of applications and design approaches, pp. 45–66 (2017)
15. Chen, C.H., Ho, C.-H., Lin, J.-B.: The development of an augmented reality game-based learning environment. Procedia Soc. Behav. Sci. **174**, 216–220 (2015)
16. Squire, K.D., Jan, M.: Mad City Mystery: developing scientific argumentation skills with a place-based augmented reality game on handheld computers. J. Sci. Educ. Technol. **16**, 5–29 (2007)
17. PBLWorks. https://www.pblworks.org/what-is-pbl. Accessed 23 Feb 2020
18. Rocha-Hoyos, J., Cedeño, E.A., Peralta, D., Martínez, J., Celi, S.: Project-based learning case of study education in automotive mechanical engineering. Espacios **39**, 1–11 (2018). https://www.revistaespacios.com/a18v39n25/a18v39n25p10.pdf
19. Association of Christian Schools International (ACSI) Blog. https://blog.acsi.org/pbl-one-schools-implementation-and-integration-acsi. Accessed 23 Feb 2020
20. Micro:bit Educational Foundation. Microbit.org. Accessed 23 Feb 2020
21. Halfacree, G.: The Official BBC Micro: Bit User Guide. Wiley (2017)
22. Unity Technologies. Unity User Manual (2017). https://docs.unity3d.com/2017.4/Documentation/Manual/index.html. Accessed 23 Feb 2020
23. Poly.google.com. https://poly.google.com/. Accessed 23 Feb 2020
24. Unity Technologies. Unity - Manual: Prefabs. https://docs.unity3d.com/Manual/Prefabs.html . Accessed 23 Feb 2020
25. The App Guruz Blog. http://www.theappguruz.com/blog/basic-of-prefab-in-unity3d. Accessed 23 Feb 2020
26. Unity Technologies. Unity - Manual: Scripting. https://docs.unity3d.com/2017.4/Documentation/Manual/ScriptingSection.html. Accessed 23 Feb 2020

27. Unity Technologies. Unity - Manual: Creating and Using Scripts. https://docs.unity3d.com/2017.4/Documentation/Manual/CreatingAndUsingScripts.html. Accessed 23 Feb 2020
28. Anzai, Y., Simon, H.A.: The theory of learning by doing. Psychol. Rev. **86**, 124–140 (1979)
29. Reese, H.W.: The learning-by-doing principle. Behav. Dev. Bull. **17**, 1–19 (2011)
30. Schoology.com. Project-Based Learning: Benefits, Examples, and Resources. https://www.schoology.com/blog/project-based-learning-pbl-benefits-examples-and-resources. Accessed 23 Feb 2020

Research on the Perceptual Interaction Model
of Virtual Reality Films

Yunpeng Jia, Ziyue Liu[✉], Chuning Wang, and Lei Xu

Digital Media Creative Laboratory,
Beijing University of Posts and Telecommunications, Beijing, China
877765517@qq.com

Abstract. Virtual reality technology has three basic characteristics: immersion, interaction and imagination. When it combines with film art, it gives a new vitality to the film, allowing the audience to gain immersed audio-visual experience, and let them have more interactive links with the film. However, in the context of film, narrative and interaction are contradictory. How to integrate interaction into film narrative is the focus of this paper. First of all, the paper analyzes the audience's psychological motivation while they are watching films to explore when and how do they want to interact, then proposes a new concept "perceptual interaction" to define the interaction form of VR films, and summarizes the features of "perceptual interaction", including deep immersion and "suitable to film conditions". Though great differences are in the design of interactive forms between different categories of films, "perceptual interaction" has a set of interacting mechanisms at the emotional level, so the interaction mode of "attention - cognition - awaken - interaction - feedback" is proposed, which provides a reference for interaction design of VR films.

Keywords: Virtual reality · Film · Perceptual interaction · Interaction mode

1 Introduction

Virtual reality is a hot technology which has been developing rapidly in recent years. It creates a virtual world by simulating environment and perception. With interactive devices, people can freely shuttle between reality and illusion. At present, VR technology has been initially applied in various industries. Under the momentum of its rapid development, the traditional film and TV industry has also begun to explore a new creative expression of VR and video, which has given birth to a new form of film art – VR film.

As a new combination of computer technology and film art, VR movies have unique advantages in creating immersion and interaction of film narrative. It not only subverts the audio-visual experience of traditional films, but also builds a bridge between audience and content in the interactive relationship. It constructs a panoramic and three-dimensional illusory space, provides the audience with a sense of "happening" time, and gives them great freedom to participate in the story process as a real role. Through the enhancement and extension of their body sensory system, the audience can interact with the virtual space to explore and enjoy immersive experience.

J. Y. C. Chen and G. Fragomeni (Eds.): HCII 2020, LNCS 12191, pp. 236–248, 2020.
https://doi.org/10.1007/978-3-030-49698-2_16

It cannot be ignored that the immersion and interactivity of VR technology, while enriching the form of film experience, has become the biggest contradiction affecting film narrative. On the one hand, in order to create a real sense of immersion, VR films give viewers the right to watch 360 degrees freely in the virtual world. However, the consequence of the right opening is that directors can no longer restrict audiences' focus through fixed frames, which will be a challenge to the narrative content and narrative form of VR films. On the other hand, the technical characteristics of VR films enable audiences to participate in the construction of virtual world system as participants. By setting interaction points, audiences' participation consciousness is strengthened to meet their psychological demands of participating in and influencing the story process. The dominant value of audience in virtual system is emphasized. However, due to the limitation of technology development at this stage, the interactive form of VR films is relatively limited. Most of the interactive forms of VR films are selected through the digital interface of virtual space. This mode of choice often causes narrative pause, which makes the original smooth story stop abruptly. Only after the audience makes a decision, the story can develop smoothly. This "forced-interaction" affects the fluency of film narrative, and also weakens the audience's immersion experience.

Nowadays, more and more scholars have expressed their thoughts on the interactive mode of virtual reality films. Lanjun Qin believes that "in order to create a better immersion experience, VR needs to hide the interactive interface, so that users can interact with the virtual world in the same way of interacting with the real world" [1]. Garcia O.D.R. of Keio University put forward a seamless multi-threaded film model, which captures the audience's interest points and triggers a new plot while audiences don't know this [2]. In my view, to explore the interactive mode of VR films, we should first clarify a deeper problem, that is, why do audiences have the desire to interact in the process of watching movies, and what kind of psychological appeals do they have? On the basis of a full understanding of this, the exploration of interaction mode can only be followed and has more practical significance.

2 Psychological Motivation of Audiences to Watch Movies

The film is an entertainment product that generates new demands after the improvement of the living standard. It relies on modern technology and uses visual images and sound effects as expressions to shape the image and reflect social life. The art form of film is mainly divided into two forms in shaping the world. One is to "restore" the real world, and the other is to "create" a virtual world. Regardless of the content form, the ultimate goal is the same: to touch the emotions in the audience's subconscious layer by constructing the story world, and make the audience get short-term emotional release, experience the changeable and colorful life in the film. As early as the beginning of 20th century, the German psychologist Hugo Minsterberg put forward the view that "the film does not exist in film, or even on the screen, but only in the thought of realizing it [3]." The semiotic aesthetician Susan Langer called the film "Dream Works" [4], which embodied a concept: film is the extension of reality. It is a holy place to provide emotional satisfaction. Therefore, the audience's psychological motivation is mainly reflected in the following two kinds:

2.1   Entertainment Motivation–Physiological Satisfaction

Movies have been in the form of leisure and entertainment products since its birth. The primary purpose of the audience is to satisfy their own physiological needs, that is, the pleasure of the senses. As a species with seven passions and six desires, there are many kinds of primitive desires need to be satisfied. However, due to the limitation of the real conditions, the audiences are in a state of self-repression but can not be released in the real world. The appearance of the film just reconciled this contradiction, allowing the audience to enjoy the pleasant sensation of desire-releasing and obtain physiological satisfaction in the process of watching movies.

The direct contact point of this physiological satisfaction is the construction and presentation of the film audio-visual language system. No matter what kinds of films, the director tells a story centered on "others" through the combination of sound and picture. The audience pours their curiosity into the story to satisfy their voyeuristic desire, and at the same time, they also feel the feelings of the voyeurs in the story and get superimposed audiovisual pleasure. Traditional movies create a suitable peeping environment by letting the audience sit in the house and turn off the lights, leaving only a bright screen. VR movies greatly enhance sensory stimulation by constructing a panoramic virtual space to let audiences enter it and peep at the "lives of others" at close range.

The satisfaction of entertainment motivation is the basic emotional satisfaction in the movie watching behavior. Regardless of traditional movies or VR movies, the audience only needs to perform the "look" action to get the sensory experience, but different movie themes, when the audience is watching, will present different psychological tendencies. For example, when watching a comedy film, the audience gets a sense of relaxation or even a laugh. When watching an action film, it is a thrilling and decompressing violent pleasure.

2.2   Catharsis Motivation–Spiritual Satisfaction

In addition to satisfying entertainment motivation, emotional catharsis is also a major appeal of viewers. As a dream factory, movies are similar to dreams in some aspects. Freud said in his book The Analysis of Dreams that "Dream is the satisfaction of desire" [5]. When people dream, they intend to reconstruct their consciousness in order to pursue positive stimulation, which will lead to the search of external consciousness and related memory. The so-called "substitution" is a reflection. In order to form a complete cognition, they need to feel the experience of others and generate the potential consciousness of treating themselves as others. The film satisfies the audience's imaginative construction of the inner desire. When the audience substitutes their own consciousness into the movie character, they will unconsciously construct the story development according to their own thinking. When the behavior of a movie character deviates from the psychological expectations of the audience, it will produce the idea of "If it is me, what will I do", "If it is me, I will definitely not be", and even want to make some key decisions instead of movie characters.

This process of role transformation is the audience's psychological transfer through empathy, it's also a self-recognition. At this stage, the audience's subjective consciousness of watching movies is gradually strengthened, and self-consciousness is constantly injected into the film characters, so they can vent their psychological feelings while watching movies and obtain life experiences which can not be experienced in real life. As Roman Danylak said, "Expression and self-reflection through interactive film, then, offers new ways of being and a subsequent shift in the existing cultural definition of 'self.'" [6] In traditional films audiences can only participate in imaginative stories in their self-consciousness, while VR films give audiences the ability to interact with stories in a real way, satisfying their demands for participation in stories through interaction, and allowing them to experience different life roles.

3 The Characteristic of Perceptual Interaction in VR Films

As we all know, film is an art that pays attention to emotional communication. The scriptwriter's construction of plot structure and the director's sculpture of lens pictures are to convey the spiritual core of the film to the audience, and to have a dialogue with the audience's inner heart. Nowadays, with the support of virtual reality technology, film has expanded from plane dynamic art to space interactive art. The audiences get the opportunity to interact with the plot while watching movies. The interaction should be driven by emotion in the context of virtual reality movies. Movie narrative triggers audience's emotion, and audience's emotion acts on narrative process in reverse. The means of action is to intervene in the film through interactive behavior to achieve a close integration between the audience and the narrative space.

VR films combine virtual reality technology with film art, its interactive mode should also adapt to the artistic form of film, that is, turn from cold technical operation to warm emotional expression. The elements we call "interaction" in VR films can refer to the interaction and connection between stories, scenes and audiences in a broad sense [7], and this kind of interaction that based on emotion we call it perceptual interaction.

As an emotion-driven natural interaction, perceptual interaction has the following characteristics in VR movies:

3.1 Deep Immersion

The purpose of space creation is to give the audience a deep immersive experience. Therefore, in the process of film narrative and interactive design, the narrative breakpoint should be minimized to ensure the complete and smooth presentation of the story. The principle of perceptual interaction is to fully mobilize the audience's sensory resonance in the film narrative space, set up interaction nodes according to the audience's emotional fluctuations, hide the interaction interface in the space environment, and integrate the form of interaction into the development of the plot perfectly, allowing the audience to interact naturally with the figurative characters (people or objects) in the story to achieve a deep immersion. The so-called naturalization is "non-deliberate". All the actions of the audience in the process of watching movies are the manifestation of their inner emotions. The design of interactive interface should emphasize the fidelity as much as possible, so that the audience can rely more on real life experience and habits to interact. For example, in the plot, if the protagonist faces the choice of drinking coffee or drinking cola, we should not use the digital interface to let him select "coffee" or "cola", but should induce viewers to choose according to real-world rules. For example, in a beverage store scene, the audience and the clerk make a choice through voice interaction (Fig. 1); when using a vending machine, it can be designed as a digital interface click mode, but its interface needs to be attached to the main body of the machine (Fig. 2).

Although perceptual interaction is driven by internal emotion, it should be perceptible, that is, the audience can realize that their behavior has an impact on the film. That can strengthen the subjective position of the audience in the virtual space, and enhance the audience's role in the virtual environment through the necessary feedback.

Fig. 1. Voice interaction with virtual shop assistants

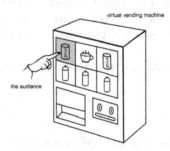

Fig. 2. Selection of touch points for virtual vending machines

3.2 "Suitable to Film Conditions"

We know that films have a very wide range of categories, different types of films with different themes often have far different narrative styles and effects. Similarly, the interactive forms of VR films can not be generalized. There is no universal interaction that can be applied to all types of movies, especially emotion-oriented narrative films. Copying other movies mechanically often makes them look different. Therefore, in the design of interactive forms, we need to comprehensively consider the characteristics of the context of the films, the psychological state of the viewers when watching such films and the degree of desire for interactive behaviors, so as to make the interaction "tailored to the film" and maximize the value of interaction in VR films.

At present, common movie types include comedy, romance, action movies, science fiction films, suspense films, horror movies, etc. The sensory experience of different movies varies greatly to audiences. For example, the romance film can make the audience deeply feel the beautiful emotions of human beings; the comedy film can give the audience a relaxed and pleasant experience; the science fiction film brings more rich audio-visual stimulation, and the suspense film gives the audience the pleasure of exploration through solving the puzzle. The initial psychological appeal of audiences is also different when watching these films. For movies with realistic storytelling and focus on the relationship between the characters in the play, what the audience longs for is pure emotional experience. So "watching" is the key behavior of this kind of film, in this case, the interaction form should be designed more "light", it can even be just an eye contact, all we can do is to reduce the burden of audiences while watching movies. But for the films whose dramatic conflicts are detached from reality and are dedicated to the ups and downs of the plot development, the audiences are eager for a sense of participation. Such films are suitable for setting some heavy interaction points (interactive nodes that affect the progress of the story) to satisfy the audience's desire for watching movies.

In the design of specific interactive forms of different types of films, we should pay attention to the visual invisibility and psychological invisibility of interaction. Visual invisibility means that "interaction is a part of narrative" and we should make the interaction interface absorbed into story environment. Psychological invisibility means that "the timing and content of interaction meet the expectations of the audience" and creates the psychological identity of "this should be so" in the audiences' deep heart. [8] Therefore, when writing a play, it is necessary to imagine how stories can bring immersion and creative interactive experience to the audience. For VR films, infinite space, diversified plots, visual music, content creativity, image language and sound and even the use of tactile and olfactory elements are the keys to dialogue with the audience [9].

4   Exploration of Perceptual Interaction Model

Although there are great differences in the design of interactive forms between different categories of films, perceptual interaction, as a means of information exchange between audience and virtual image world, has a set of interacting mechanisms at the emotional level. As the receiver of interactive node information, the audience has the right to choose information actively. The selection process basically follows the five stages of "attention-cognition-awaken-interaction-feedback" (Fig. 3).

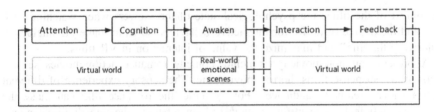

Fig. 3. Five stages of perceptual interaction

4.1 Attention

For the audience, no matter how the form of the film changes, the first step to generate the desire for interaction is always to attract attention. Virtual reality movies break through the limitations of traditional picture frames. In a 360-degree space, the audience's attention is greatly dispersed, and most of the information in the space can not get the attention of the audience. Therefore, it is an important consideration for designing the virtual space interaction point to deeply analyze the audience's psychology, tap the psychological demands of the audience when they watching movies, and improve the attractiveness of interactive elements.

Potential guidance in VR space plays an important role in improving audience's attention. Physical features such as color, sound and environment in image space can all be resorted to sensory experience. What we need to do is to guide audiences to pay attention to the interaction interface through rational settings and let them carry out the next step as we expected. It should be pointed out that the attention guidance of VR images is not limited to "visual Attention", more accurately is "Perceptual Attention" which includes visual, auditory, tactile and other senses. [10] In the specific implementation strategy, we can make the following attempts: (1) creating visual contrast to emphasize interactive objects: giving interactive objects different attributes from other objects through the design of color, shape and other dimensions to enhance the audience's attention while they explore the virtual space (Fig. 4); (2) recalling the audience's attention through sound: sound in space can help viewing. When the audience loses focus in space, it can be recalled by sound guidance (Fig. 5).

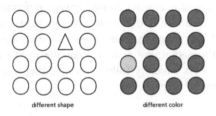

Fig. 4. Creating visual contrast

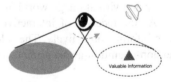

Fig. 5. Voice recall attention

Bakker, S. et al. have pointed out that interaction design needs to consider people's attention at different levels in their research. According to the attention level, interaction are divided into three types: focused interaction, peripheral interaction and implicit interaction [11]. When precise control is needed, the attention of the audience should be focused on one point; when inaccurate control is needed, the interface can be set within the scope of attention; and when no independent control of the audience is needed, the interactive interface can even be set outside the viewer's attention field (Fig. 6).

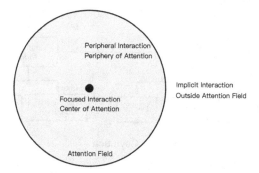

Fig. 6. Interaction types and attention levels

4.2   Cognition

Cognition is the process of the brain processing and understanding the information which it pays attention to. On the basis of paying full attention to spatial information, audiences will be able to participate in the interactive process only after they have awareness of the objects which they have focused on. In VR movies, the audience's cognition is actually the understanding of the specific object in the film environment and the relationship between the object and the environment. The interactive interface is an important narrative element of VR movies, to construct the link between the audience and the virtual space is to let the audience form the correct cognition in the brain primarily.

In terms of cognitive attributes, the human brain mainly reflects the spatial characteristics of the interface, including shape, size, orientation and depth features. These features can help the audience to select important information from the rich environmental elements, while the rest of the information is regarded as cognitive background. From the psychological point of view, this reflects the selectivity of audience perception. At the same time, perception also has integrity, that is, the individual will recognize things as a unified whole. Even the same elements may have different meanings in different narrative contexts. Audiences recognize the interaction interface based on spatial features, but their judgment and decision-making on the interaction behavior actually originates from the subjective information organization of the whole narrative environment.

In terms of cognitive form, it can be divided into two categories: model cognition and exploratory cognition. Model cognition means that audiences already have relevant experience in the real world. In the past experience, the relationship model between things has been established. When dealing with similar objects in the virtual environment, the existing modes can be matched and reused. Exploratory cognition is relatively complex, and its content may be beyond real life, requiring audiences to spend a certain amount of energy to obtain information, identify information and form understanding, exploratory information can better meet the needs of active participation of the audience, we can use innovative ideas or exquisite audio-visual to cater to the audience's psychology (Fig. 7).

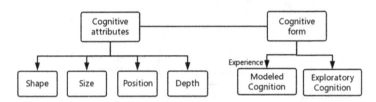

Fig. 7. Cognition

4.3   Awaken

Noticing information and forming inner cognition in virtual space, the next step is to awaken the audience's emotional experience. Generally speaking, audiences who have experienced the same or similar situations in real life will have a deeper emotional resonance with what they see and hear in the virtual world, and try to use the experience of the real world to deal with what they meet in the virtual world.

The awakening stage is actually the transfer process of audience's thinking from the virtual world to the real world. When the audience is immersed in the virtual space, they will receive the sensory stimulation from the virtual environment. The film creator's arrangement of design in the narrative system and content presentation will give the audience continuous emotional stimuli, and the audience's aesthetic feelings will gradually improve in the plot perception. Until the psychological immersion state of viewing is reached, the boundary between the virtual and the real in the audience's consciousness will be blurred, the emotions of the audience in the real world are awakened, then the desire of the audience to interact with virtual environment is further stimulated.

The psychological stimuli of the environmental factors on the audience make their emotions reach a state of excitement from calm, and they may be expressed as pleasure, sadness, surprise, fear, anger, etc. We can divide the degree of awakening into three levels: primary awakening, intermediate awakening, advanced awakening, and the degree of emotional arousal directly affects the intensity of the audience's behavioral activities. In the primary awakening stage, the audience can experience the emotions conveyed by the film, but have no desire to participate in; in the intermediate awakening stage, the audience has a clear personal emotional inclination, eager to participate and seek identity; in the advanced awakening stage, the audience has a strong and clear emotional appeal, the audience has strong and clear emotional appeals, eager to participate in the film interaction, and gain control in the process, constructing a self-subjective image (Fig. 8).

Fig. 8. Emotional arousal level

4.4 Interaction

After the audience is fully awakened and mobilized, they will have a desire to interact with the virtual world. The interaction in virtual reality movies mainly occurs between the audience, the characters, objects and the development of plots. The specific form varies according to the type and content of the film, but it can be generally divided into two types: experiential interaction and decision-making interaction.

Experiential interaction focuses on enhancing the audience's viewing experience and creating an immersive virtual environment. The audience can interact lightly with the people or things in the play to show their sense of existence, but the overall trend of the plot is still in the hands of the director, and the audience plays more of a "by-stander" role. Experiential interaction is a weakly engaged interaction of VR movies. Simple, interesting and natural forms of interaction are preferred for this model. While meeting the basic needs of the audience, the light interaction can provide more exciting satisfaction. For example, when the story develops to an important moment, design the character in the drama turn to the viewer and even communicate with the audience; in a birthday party, let the audience blow candles and then extinguish the flames, these all can enhance the audience's experience of representation.

Decision-making interaction is more focused on the process of audience participation in the film narrative. In some important plot propulsion points, multiple branches are set up to allow the audience to make choices. Therefore, the audience also needs to take more responsibility for the results. Decision-making interaction in the mode of perceptual interaction is not simply to choose through the pop-up window, but to design nodes when the audience's emotions are fully mobilized, and hide the interface in the characters or objects of the plot, so that the audience can interact in a near-real way driven by the original emotions. In this case, the director's control over the audience is greatly weakened. If the story is to be developed according to the presupposition, the audience should be given various hints in the previous narrative, so that they can choose the answer we prepared for them in the interactive decision-making." (Fig. 9).

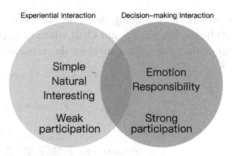

Fig. 9. Interaction form

4.5 Feedback

A complete interaction process should be the interaction between the audience and the virtual space. The audience interacts with the virtual space after emotional excitement. The virtual space should also give corresponding feedback after receiving instructions, so as to make the audience realize that their behavior really has an impact on the movie space and confirm their sense of existence in the virtual world. As mentioned above, some scholars believe that interactive movies should capture the audience's interest points in the unconscious situation, which can satisfy the audience's curiosity, but then the audience may not realize that the development of the plot is out of their "subconscious choice", and the sense of participation and interaction with the plot will be greatly weakened.

Clear feedback for the audience in the virtual environment is actually an encouragement to their behavior, allowing the audience to enjoy the pleasure of watching film and enjoy the sense of existence in the virtual space and the sense of accomplishment of manipulating the story. The specific form of feedback and the type of interaction echo each other:

Experiential feedback is mainly aimed at experiential interactive operation, which is realized by body feedback touch. The development direction of virtual reality technology is to simulate the body perception system of human visual, auditory, tactile, olfactory and motion perception, which makes the virtual world infinitely close to reality. When a viewer watches a VR movie and tries to correlate with any element in the film, ideally, the viewer should get feedback through body perception. For example, when the viewer holds up a cup of hot water in the virtual environment, he will feel the temperature and weight of the cup; when the viewer enters the dark room and presses the light switch, he will have tactile feedback of touching the switch, auditory feedback of pressing the switch and visual feedback of turning on the light instantly.

In addition to the above-mentioned body perception feedback, decision-making feedback is also a form of feedback. This kind of feedback acts more on the psychological level of the audience. Whether the development of the plot meets the psychological expectations of the audience and whether it can further mobilize the emotions of the audience are all the feedback manifestations of VR films on the behavior of the audience (Fig. 10).

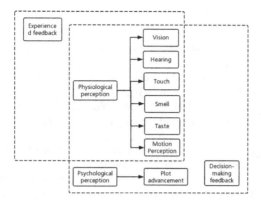

Fig. 10. Feedback types

5 Conclusion

As a new art form combining traditional movies with virtual reality technology, virtual reality film has injected new energy into the art of film and also brought a new way of watching movies to the audience. We hope that the audience can not only immerse themselves in the narrative space of the film to experience the story, but also hope that the audience can have more autonomy and freedom to control the story. Immersion and interaction, these two inevitably exist contradictions. How to balance interaction and film narration are new propositions of film creation under the background of new technology.

No matter how the technology changes, the essence of the film is always to convey emotion through the content. All technical means are only external aids to help the film express emotions more deeply and thoroughly. By exploring the entertainment and catharsis motivation of the audience, this paper proposes an emotional interaction model for VR films based on the audience's emotions, and introduces in detail each link of the emotional interaction "attention-cognition-awaken-interaction-feedback". Perceptual interaction is meant to make the interaction fit the narrative of the film more closely and serve the content experience of the film. It is also a means of "adapting to the circumstances of the film", which requires the creator to choose the appropriate interactive content, interactive time and interactive form according to the content of the film.

VR film is still a new art nowadays. There is no fixed mode of creation, and its interactive form is limited by the technical constraints. With the progress of technology and the explosion of creativity, VR film will certainly emerge more abundant forms of interaction in the future.

Acknowledgement. This study is a stage achievement of the National Social Science Fund Art Project of China "Research on Film Creation Based on Virtual Reality Technology" (Approval No. 17BC051).

References

1. Qin Lanjun, F.: Interaction and story: VR's narrative ecology. Lit. Art Stud. **12**, 101–111 (2016)
2. Garcia, O.D.R.F., Tag, B.S., Ohta, N.T., et al.: Seamless multithread films in virtual reality. In: Proceedings of the Eleventh International Conference on Tangible, Embedded, and Embodied Interaction, pp. 641–646. ACM, New York (2017)
3. Hugo Munsterberg, F.: Hugo Munsterberg on Film: The Photoplay: A Psychological Study and Other Writings. Routledge, New York (2002)
4. Susanne, K., Langer, F.: Feeling and Form: A Theory of Art Developed from Philosophy in a New Key. Macmillan Pub Co, New York (1953)
5. Sigmund Freud, F.: The Interpretation of Dreams. Macmillan Pub Co, New York (1913)
6. Danylak, R.F., Edmonds, E.S.: Interactive film and the multiplied self. ACM Comput. Entertain. (2008)
7. When talking about VR interactive movies, what are we talking about? http://www.87870.com/news/1711/29861.html
8. Jia Yunpeng, F., Li Xin, S.: Film interaction and audience psychology. Film Rev. (15), 66–70 (2018)
9. Similarities and Differences between VR Film Making and Traditional Film Making. http://www.dooland.com/magazine/article_860642.html
10. Shi Chang, F.: Narrative aesthetics of VR image: perspective, guidance and body interface. J. Beijing Film Acad. (2017)
11. Bakker, S.F., Niemantsverdriet, K.S.: The interaction-attention continuum: considering various levels of human attention in interaction design. Int. J. Des. **10**(2), 1–14 (2016)
12. Cho, J.F., Lee, T.H.S., Ogden, J.T., et al.: Imago: presence and emotion in virtual reality. In: Proceedings of SIGGRAPH 2016 ACM SIGGRAPH 2016 VR Village, Article No. 6. ACM, New York (2016)
13. Vallgarda, A.F., Winther, M.S., Mørch, N.T., et al.: Temporal form in interaction design. Int. J. Des. **9**(3), 1–15 (2015)
14. Sun Lue, F.: VR, AR and film. J. Beijing Film Acad. **03**, 13–21 (2016)
15. Yin Chao, F., He Renke, S.: Applications of semiotics in interaction design of VR gesture. Packag. Eng. **34**(22), 13–15 (2013)
16. Sun Wei, F.: Interactive Media Narrative Research. Nanjing Institute of Art (2011)
17. Li Jinhui, F.: Discussions on VR visual image creation hidden in reality. J. Beijing Film Acad. **03**, 22–27 (2016)
18. Zhang Tingting, F., Tian Feng, S., Lu Wei, T., et al.: Survey of VR applications in interactive films and games. J. Shanghai University (Nat. Sci.) **23**(03), 342–352 (2017)
19. Ding Zhong, F., Tian Yigui, S.: Confrontation and integration: re-discussing the audience consciousness and other context of VR narration—starting from the 74th Venice international film Festiva. Film Lit. **08**, 4–6 (2018)

Interactive Narrative in Augmented Reality: An Extended Reality of the Holocaust

Yunshui Jin[1,2] , Minhua Ma[2] , and Yun Liu[1(✉)]

[1] Tongji University, Shanghai 201804, China
{jinyunshui,liu.yun}@tongji.edu.cn
[2] Staffordshire University, Stoke-on-Trent ST4 2DE, UK
yunshui.jin@research.staffs.ac.uk, m.ma@staffs.ac.uk

Abstract. In this research, the author described new narrative media known as Immersive Augmented Reality Environment (IARE) with HoloLens. Aarseth's narrative model [17] and all available input design in IARE were reviewed and summarised. Based on these findings, *The AR Journey*, a HoloLens app aiming at interactive narrative for moral education purpose, was developed and assessed. Qualitative methods of interview and observation were used and the results were analysed. In general, narrative in IARE were proved to be valid for moral education purpose, and findings including valid narrative structure, input model, design guidelines were revealed.

Keywords: Interactive narrative · Augmented reality · Mixed reality · Holocaust · Moral education · Microsoft Hololens

1 Introduction

Stories can be told in various media such as books, drama, films, video games and Virtual Reality (VR). Video games are powerful as they provide an active, exploratory, multi-sensory process for participants, while VR is also noticeable for its immersive experience of presence and sensory vividness [1]. With the invention of HoloLens, a Head Mounted Display (HMD) for Augmented Reality (AR), a new form and media for narratives has emerged. This new AR device differs from the previous hand-held devices (e.g. mobile phone) or VR because it overwhelms participants sense by filling the space with virtual holograms and spatial sound through the HMD, but still keeping them connected with the real world. HoloLens can be considered as a new media which creates the unique Immersive Augmented Reality Environment (IARE) where virtually holographic characters and objects can be mixed into real-world space seamlessly while participants observe, walk and interact with things in the real-world environment. IARE enables people to navigate and interact with a physical space freely while watching a performance of holographic characters. Unfortunately, existing researches mainly focused on practical usage of AR with HoloLens, such as architectures and automobile design, medical training, touring guide, etc. [2, 3]. There is limited research on how to use IARE for storytelling. Though a research from George Tech University suggested that mixing character into real-world environment had no improvement for narrative [4], the technology they used didn't create an authentic IARE, because they

© Springer Nature Switzerland AG 2020
J. Y. C. Chen and G. Fragomeni (Eds.): HCII 2020, LNCS 12191, pp. 249–269, 2020.
https://doi.org/10.1007/978-3-030-49698-2_17

just overlaid a flat 2D character instead of mixing a holographic 3D character in a physical space. Hence the authors plan to investigate the potentials of narrative in IARE based on HoloLens and assess the effectiveness of this narrative.

2 Literature Review

2.1 Challenges of Narrative in Museums for Moral Education

Narratives are proved to be a powerful method for empathy such as perspective taking and emotional engagement [5]. Many researchers claim positive association between empathy and prosocial behaviors [6, 7]. Jin et al. [8] summarised empirical evidences that prosocial video games are beneficial for youth's moral development. All these findings suggest narrative is valid and powerful for moral education.

The National Holocaust Centre and Museum (NHCM) is one of the few museums employing the narrative technique to unveil the history and enable young generations to carefully examine, commemorate and learn from the tragedy of the Holocaust. *The Journey*, one of its permanent exhibitions, tells the story using environment storytelling technique through the eyes of a fictional Jewish boy Leo who survived the Holocaust and came to the UK via the *Kindertransport*[1]. Six rooms are restored to show how Jewish's life look like including Leo's family living room, Leo's classroom in his school, the street after Night of Broken Glass, the tailor's shop of Leo's family, a train carriage for *Kindertransport* and refuge in the UK. In each room, audience can watch a short video of Leo giving a monologue of what he saw, heard, experienced and felt at that time. The visitors can experience the complete story gradually by going through each room, interacting with objects and watching videos. *The Journey* is a text free and tactile exhibition, designed mainly for young audience. However, most visitors experienced *the Journey* as part of their visit.

The major challenges of *the Journey* exhibition are identified according to the NHCM website [8], literature [9] and the authors' observation on site:

- Inclusiveness: *The Journey* is originally designed as a group visit experience for young audience with a tour guide, thus storytelling may be plain and shallow for individual adult visitors.
- Accessibility: the NHCM is far from the downtown area of a small city with limited public transportation. It is difficult to make the learning experience accessible in the widest range of places and formats, to continually reach new audiences and provoke attitudinal change across all communities.
- Attractiveness: as younger generations prefer modern interactive methods derived from their evolving personal technologies [10], storytelling via interactive digital technologies such as video games, VR and AR would be more effective and appealing.

---

[1] Kindertransport was the title for historical events that British government made efforts to bring Jewish children out of Nazi Germany, occupied Austria and Czechoslovakia before the outbreak of World War II. During a nine-month period, 10,000 Jewish children aged between 1 and 17 were transported to the UK.

2.2   Recent Advance of AR/MR HMD

Hololens 1 was released at the end of 2016 offering a solution for fully-immersive experience mixing virtuality and reality. Hololens is an HMD, featuring a 35° viewing angle see-through holographic lenses (waveguides), spatial understanding by real-time 3D scanning, gaze tracking, hand gestures input, voice recognition and built-in speakers for spatial sound [11]. Hololens 1 can partly understand and recognise real world information such as walls, floors, ceilings, chairs and put a stable hologram into the real-world space, e.g. audience can watch a holographic virtual character "seating" on a real-world sofa talking to them.

In July 2018, a similar AR-HMD device named Magic Leap One was launched in the market. It is equipped with a LCOS screen with a higher definition of 1280 × 960, offering a wider viewing angle of 50°, larger RAM of 8 GB and better CPU [12]. It also has the several functions similar to HoloLens 1 and the additional eye tracking function. However, reviewers discovered that Magic Leap One achieved higher Field-of-View (FOV) by sacrificing image resolution and brightness, which made text cloudy and the virtual image darker.

In February 2019, HoloLens 2 was released as the most advanced AR/MR device on the market. The HoloLens 2 catches up in terms of FOV with a 52° viewing angle and screen resolution of 2K per eye [13]. Moreover, HoloLens 2 stands out with a much improved hand-tracking technology, eye tracking, voice recognition and better ergonomic design. Users can directly manipulate virtual hologram by hand (without any symbolic hand gestures) and perform dictation recognition offline. HoloLens 2 outperforms Magic Leap One on almost every aspect except it is heavier.

In addition, Microsoft also released specific software development kit known as Mixed Reality Toolkit (MRTK) [14] while other companies like HP Inc. released their own immersive AR headset with the motion controllers in the past two years.

In summary, the hardware and software development kit are keeping improving during the past five years. Though there are still limitations which affect audience's immersive experience, such as narrow FOV, limited CPU computing power, great enhancement has achieved in terms of display quality, input methods, software development modules, which makes narrative in IARE using real-time 3D characters possible. Currently, HoloLens 2 is not available yet in the consumer market. Hololens 1 is still the best available choice for research and study purpose considering better development environment of MRTK and future migration to HoloLens 2.

2.3   Related Research on Narrative in AR

There are two distinct properties of HMD AR as well as HMD VR compared with other medias. *Presence* is one of them, which refers to a subjective user experience of being into the virtual or mixed-reality environment rather than the actual physical locale [15]. Different from the flat screen, HMD is a binocular device which can not only help user perceive the accurate size of an object, but also cover the large part of user's vision to generate an overwhelming sensory feeling.

The other feature is *agency*, which refers to the ability to "do something" in the experience—to interact or react rather than simply perceive. Agency is the core of

VR/AR experience because virtual environment (VE) within headset gives the audience the native agency of looking [16]. In other words, IARE has the built-in nature of interaction as audience would like to have more ability to interact with the environment rather than looking.

Regarding the feature of presence and agency, one important feature of narrative in IARE is *real time*. Real time here doesn't indicate the same concept of video games, which means to update the content 60 times per second. Real time in this case addresses that the time within the story is contingent, e.g. the enactment of an actor should be in accordance with the real world so that it can speed up or slow down. Real time is in fact incompatible with certain narrative forms such as literature or film. Because in film, the performance of an actor can easily accelerate or decelerate via editing and montage. R. Aylett and S. Louchart claimed real time as an important feature in VR in their research [17]. Though they had a different interpretation of real time as *"From an authorial point of view, it would imply the author writing, telling and displaying the story at the same time as the reader is reading or viewing it."*, they had an insight for the influence of real time in narrative:

- It could bring certain constraints on the dramatic intensity of any narrative.
- The theatre's typical episodic structure and the concept of 'off-stage' activity can be used to produce some sense of temporal and spatial richness.
- A narrative in real time must be either multiple, interactive or exceptionally rich in dramatic features.
- Participative forms of narrative such as video games, Interactive and Improvisational theatre (IT/IMPROV), can enlighten the potential approach and methods for storytelling in VR.

Due to the lack of theory and barrier of the technical issues, there are few attempts made for narrative based on HoloLens. Fortunately, *Fragments*, a suspense & adventure narrative experience of HoloLens developed by Asobo Studio, is a good exploration and many people reported positive feedback about it. The success of Fragments further revealed potential for narratives in IARE.

Besides, IARE is probably effective for narratives of serious purpose rather than suspense or adventure types if the above three issues of narrative in museum (in Sect. 2.1) are taken into consideration. IARE can involve hologram of virtual characters that enable the richness and more possibilities of a profound storytelling suitable for adults. Further, IARE can also adapt easily to a new real-world space and projects the virtual characters, furniture and object into the new one. Lastly, the experience of narrative in IARE aligns with the experience of video games and immersive theatre, which is affable and approachable for young adults. However, the valid narrative structure and input design for the narrative in IARE aiming at moral education remains unclear.

2.4   Research Questions

As Sect. 2.2 summrises that the computing power of AR device is limited for now, the vividness of hologram can't be guaranteed. Section 2.3 makes a hypothesis that narrative in IARE could be valid for moral education purpose and further points out the narrative structure needs to be investigated as well as the input design. Therefore, the author proposes the following Research Questions (RQ):

RQ1: How much dose the vividness of character in IARE affect audience's perception?
RQ2: What's the valid narrative structure for narrative in IARE in terms of moral education?
RQ3: What's the valid input design for narrative in IARE?
RQ4: Are narratives in IARE engaging for audience?
RQ5: What are the design guidelines for narrative in IARE to achieve moral education goals?

In order to answer the above questions, an interactive narrative application on HoloLens named *The AR Journey* was scheduled to be developed by the author for the NHCM. It aimed at Holocaust education by telling the story of Jewish boy Leo through an augmented reality experience.

3   Design of *The AR Journey*

The design process started with a series of observations (Stage 1) to investigate the behavioural traits of users wearing HoloLens for a storytelling experience. This process revealed users' common behavior and feedback in IARE with HoloLens. Based on these information, the second stage explored Aarseth's narrative model for games and proposed a modified "quest game" structure for narrative in IARE. The third stage concluded current input types and input models for IARE and selected two input models among them. Visual content design and programming were then completed and the alpha version was published (Stage 4). In the final stage, *The AR Journey* was tested in NHCM and later evaluated (Stage 5) by a small group of experts, and the app was revised according to their feedbacks to be ready for final experiment.

3.1   Stage 1: Preliminary Study

User observation: The observational analysis revealed the general behavioural patterns of the user who were invited to experience the HoloLens suspense & adventure game, *Fragments*.

- Pattern 1: most users felt uncomfortable physically when wearing HoloLens 1st headset over 20 min.
- Pattern 2: many users had difficulty learning and implementing the air tap gesture, the HoloLens input gesture.
- Pattern 3: most users tended to stand still when watching the enactment of characters.
- Pattern 4: most users reported the narrow FOV issue was a distraction.

These behavioural patterns form the initial guideline of *The AR Journey*.

3.2 Stage 2: *The AR Journey* Narrative Structure

Following the suggestion of examining narrative model for games (Sect. 2.3), Aarseth's model [18], which is grounded on Chatman's concept of *kernels* and *satellites*[2] [19], is interesting. As Table 1 showed, he clarified the difference between linear story, nonlinear story, linear game, quest game and "pure" game. As the purpose of *The AR Journey* is moral education and the story of a Leo's family involved in Kindertransport should be conveyed clearly, audience aren't allowed to have the full influence on the kernel of the story, which means the "Pure" game type is excluded. On the other hand, in order to improve the inclusiveness of the experience, audience should have some limited influence on the story and some constitutive events can then contribute to the diversity and depth of the narrative experience. Therefore, quest game type is the idea choice for *The AR Journey*, which allows alternative branch of the kernel and possible supplementary events (satellites).

Table 1. Classification of narratives based on audience's influence on kernels and satellites

Kernel influence	Satellite influence	
	Not possible	Possible
No influence	A linear story (War & Peace)	A linear game (half-Life 2)
Choose alternatives	A nonlinear story (hyperfiction)	Quest game (**The AR Journey**)
Full influence	N/A	"Pure" game (Chess, Minecraft)

Coincidentally, IARE has the built-in nature that allows the user walk within a real world space and touch, interact with real world props and objects where satellites can be embed. Additional stories and information can be revealed and unfolded when users explore the room. By this way, audience can keep moving instead of standing still all the time (Pattern 1 in preliminary study).

In summary, as Fig. 1 shows, the narrative structure of *The AR Journey* consists of a kernel, which employs a branched narrative structure, and several satellites. Storytelling of the kernel part or satellites part are triggered by props in Leo's living room. The diary is the key prop that can activate the kernel part while other props such as radio, gramophone, suitcase, newspaper, etc. can launch the satellites part. Audience are able to perceive the story by exploring different props and make different choice leading to different branch of the story. As a result, using this narrative structure, different audience can have their own path to experience the story to get their own understanding and reflection.

---

[2] Chartman claimed a *kernel* is the key event that makes people recognise the story and *satellites* refer to the constitutive and supplementary events; take away the kernel and the story is no longer the same while satellites are what can be replaced or removed while still keeping the story recognizable.

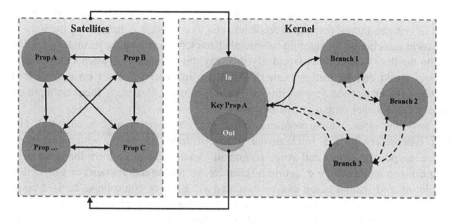

Fig. 1. Narrative structure of The AR Journey

3.3   Stage 3: *The AR Journey* Interaction Design

As described in the last section, all storytelling is triggered by audience through interaction and audience need to choose branches of the story via an input interface. Thus, interaction design is important not only for natural experience of the story, but also for *suspension of disbelief*[3] (Fig. 2). Presence in IARE, which shares the similar concept of suspension of disbelief, refers to experiencing the mixture of the virtual environment and real world, even rather than the actual physical locale. Witmer [15] found that responsive and controllable interaction is critical to produce presence in a virtual environment. As a result, simple interactions with straightforward feedback like turning on/off a virtual light, opening/closing a virtual drawer, pulling/closing a curtain, can suspend audience's disbelief. It is not necessary to trigger an event or introduce a story piece after every interaction. Meanwhile, interactions with complex feedback, such as determining the story branch, triggering a voice record, reading a diary, can help audience understand the narrative when they put together all the story fragments.

Secondly, it is essential to design secondary interactions that can generate (unlock) new input targets to trigger subsequent interactions (Fig. 2), e.g. one opens a drawer and then find a diary in the drawer; after the audience opens the diary, a postcard slips on the floor; the audience picks up the postcard to read words on it. In this case, picking up the postcard is the secondary interaction of opening the diary, which is also the secondary interaction of pulling the drawer. Significantly, secondary interaction in IARE can make audience feel the environment more convincible as it is exactly the same way in the real world, this is different from many user interaction design concepts which tend to feedback the information as direct as possible.

Thirdly, audience communicate within IARE through input on input targets and output. It is important to recongise that input targets in IARE could be real world

---

[3] A film terminology refers to the temporary acceptance as believable of events or characters that would ordinarily be seen as incredible. This is usually to allow an audience to appreciate works of literature or drama that are exploring unusual ideas.

targets as well as virtual world targets, and so are the output. Besides, input on virtual input targets can output real world feedback, and vice versa, e.g. turning off the light in real world can change the lighting on virtual characters, throwing the virtual switch can turn on the floor lamp in real world. By this way, the boundary between virtual world and real world can be further blurred. However, in order to center on the research questions and ensure the accessibility of The AR Journey, this study focus on input on virtual targets to get output in virtual world.

Lastly, the input, which consists of input type and input model, is analysed. The input type refers to the fundamental genre of input in IARE which are gaze, manipulate/point/commit, and voice command. Audience can perform the same type using different apparatus, e.g. action of gaze can be performed via head or eye, action of pointing and manipulation can be executed via hand or controllers. Table 2 compares the merit and limitation of different apparatus aiming at same input type. In summary, it reveals that eye gaze and head gaze are different. Eye gaze is more implicit, inaccurate, faster, easier, and usually used as an alternative input channel while head gaze is more accurate, reliable but slower and discomfort. For manipulation/point/commit, there are several possible apparatus including direct manipulation by hand, symbolic hand gestures, and different controllers (the *motion controllers*[4], the *HoloLens clicker*[5], the Xbox controller, etc.) Direct manipulation by hand, which is only supported for HoloLens 2, is the ideal choice as it is nature, institutive to use and consistent with the real world manipulation [20]. The motion controllers are more precise and stable with tactical feedback but draw a clear line between virtuality and reality [21]. Hand gestures are not recommended in most cases as they are inconvenient to learn and remember, and fatigue users easily [22]. Voice command has great potential as it is hand-free, natural and low effort but unreliable at present, especially in non-English or noisy environment [23].

It is important to understand that different input types can be combined or used alone with their own conventions to form an input model, which are listed as followings [25]:

- *Direct manipulation* is an input model that involves touching holograms/real world objects directly with one's hands or controllers. (Hololens 2 only)
- *Point and commit* is a 'far' input model that enables users to target, select and manipulate 2D content and 3D objects that are out of reach using hand gestures or controllers.
- *Gaze and commit* is a far input model using eye/head gaze and commit action via hand gesture, controllers or voice command.

---

[4] The motion controllers are hardware accessories developed by Microsoft that extend the user's physical capabilities by providing precise 6DoF tracking, several buttons and tactile feedback while using one or both hands. They are compatible with all mixed reality headset with Bluetooth.

[5] The HoloLens Clicker (clicker for short) is the peripheral device built specifically for HoloLens 1 & 2. It is a miniature controller that lets the user click on whatever he or she is looking at and there is a motion sensor inside to check the clicker's up, down, left, and right.

Table 2. Comparison of different input types and their apparatus

Input type	Apparatus	Merit & limitation
Gaze	Eye gaze [24]	Merit: - High speed pointing - Low effort - Implicitness - (can always be) Alternative input channel
		Limitation: - eye-gaze is "always on" - Leave before click issue - Difficulty in small targets - Ragged eye-gaze movements - Tracking unreliability
	Head gaze	Merit: - Accurate and explicit - Reliable
		Limitation: - Slower pointing - Possible discomfort (e.g., neck strain)
Manipulate/Point/Commit	Hand (Direct Manipulation, hand gesture, hand pointer)	Merit: - Institutive for direct manipulation - Fast learning curve - Consistent with real world manipulation - No need to hold a controller all the time
		Limitation: - Hand gestures and pointer are not natural and not easy to learn - Hand gestures tend to fatigue users - More effort - Direct manipulation only supported by HoloLens2 - False triggering issue for direct manipulation

(*continued*)

Table 2. (*continued*)

Input type	Apparatus	Merit & limitation
	Controller (Motion controller, clicker, Xbox controller)	Merit: - Precise and allowing for fine grained interaction - Stable tracking - Low effort for commit - Consistent with current VR standard manipulation - Some tactile feedback - Good compatibility (with Bluetooth)
		Limitation: - A visible and tangible interface/barrier between the user and the world - Hands are always occupied - Some, e.g. clicker, can only track simple and limited movement - Takes time to learn for complex controller
Voice command	Voice	Merit: - It's routine and natural way - Totally hands-free - Low effort, especially good at traversing complex interfaces
		Limitation: - Unreliability issue (of input detection) - Bad performance with non-English input - Take time to learn - Interference in shared spaces & privacy issue - Challenge for dictation recognition - Weak in continuous input control

- *Gaze and dwell* is a hand free input model. The user keeps gazing (with their head or eyes) at the target and lingers there for a moment to activate it.
- *Voice input* is a hand free input model by using one's voice to command and control an interface, e.g. the user can read a button's name out to activate it.

As HoloLens 2 is still not available in the consumer market and the motion controllers are too large to eliminate the gap between virtual world and real world, input models of direct manipulation and point and commit are filtered out. Eye gaze is also filtered out

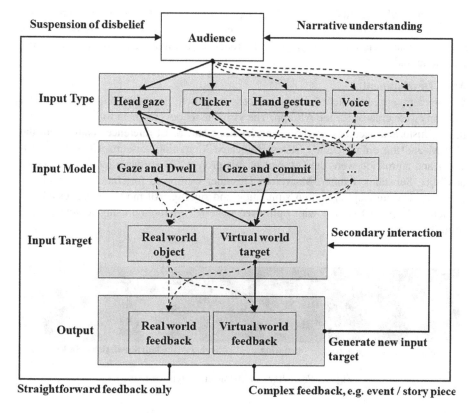

Fig. 2. Interaction design in IARE (Solid line is the path adopted by *The AR Journey*)

because it is only supported by HoloLens 2. Voice input is rejected as the Chinese voice input is poorly supported and hand gestures have proved problematic in our preliminary study. In summary, there are two path of interaction design left for the *AR Journey*, which are head gaze and commit with the clicker and head gaze and dwell (Fig. 2). Both interactions aim at virtual targets and lead to output in virtual world. To make the environment more convincible subjectively, some secondary interactions and interactions only with straightforward feedback are supposed to be included.

3.4   Stage 4: *The AR Journey* Development Process

Script Development
The script and dialogue were rewritten based on an existing script from a parallel project of the virtual journey app [26] in collaboration with experts from the NHCM to ensure historical accuracy. The dialogues and plots are designed based on survivors' testimonies and facts of the past. In light of the above narrative structure and interaction design, the story focused on a debate between Leo's parents happened in the living room. The main story employed a branched structure which raised three questions to

the audience who can make choices for the protagonist Leo. The story can be triggered by opening Leo's diary, while some fragments, such as isolation in school, dad's favorite music, were hidden in props in the room including a gramophone, newspaper, telephone, radio, etc.

Asset Development

4 characters, approximate 15 min' character animation, 11 props, and around 20 UI elements were created for the AR app. The visual asset development followed the same rule of historical accuracy as the script development. Most references came from the NHCM and the online United States Holocaust Memorial Museum. Character modelling and animation were the key part of this project. 3D software including Zbrush, 3ds Max, Substance Painter, Marvelous Designer were used for character modelling, texturing, UV unwrapping, cloth simulation and rigging. All models were tested and refined in Unity 3D engine with optimised material for mobile using texture baking (Fig. 3).

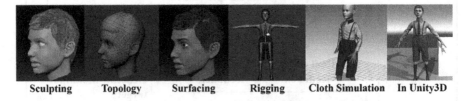

Sculpting   Topology   Surfacing   Rigging   Cloth Simulation   In Unity3D

Fig. 3. Procedures of character design for Leo

Software Development

The programing was developed in Unity 3D game engine. The main challenge for programming was the character's natural and autonomous behaviour and the HoloLens' input module. To enable the audience to communicate with Leo using gaze, gesture and voice, Leo needs natural eye contact, face to face conversation, and some social intelligence, e.g. to respond, look at and walk towards the user. In order to achieve the autonomous response, characters were based on program-controlled motion clips with Inverse Kinematics (IK). There are also many pre-defined keyframe animations. Thus, how to make seamless blending between the above two animation systems was the key. The main technique here is to use the *Playable* module of Unity 3D for seamless blending of character animations. Each pre-defined keyframe animation and program-controlled motion clip is a playable note and could be connected via a mixer note. The strength of each channel of the mixer could be adjusted dynamically in real time. There are two timeline playables in this design in order to ensure a smooth blend between different pre-defined animations. A special Animation Layer Mixer is used here to have a separate control of upper body and expression known as an avatar mask.

Moreover, a *gaze and dwell* module was developed, since it is not built-in for HoloLens 1. Gaze and commit with a clicker is a built-in module. Consequently, the audience can interact with virtual characters and objects either by *gaze and dwell* or *gaze and click*.

3.5   Stage 5: Quick Assessment and Iteration

When the development was done, it was tested in the NHCM (Fig. 4), and different input models were assessed and bugs were identified. 5 users including students and teachers from the game or design department were invited as testers. The main findings according to the common feedbacks from the testers are as followings:

- Input model of gaze and dwell was difficult to use in this case, as there is an issue of "Observation vs. commit". Because the FOV is narrow in HoloLens, Audience tend to put the choice in the middle of the view to read, which would accidently also trigger the choice while still reading the it.
- The low framerate caused discomfort.
- Ambient sound was too noisy to hear the character's dialog.
- Leo's voice sounded too old for a boy.
- Expression was stiff.
- Leo's skin was too oily.

Later, input model of gaze and dwell was abandoned, and the voice acting, material of skin, ambient sound and expression were modified. Framerate was improved above 50 fps in accordance with official guidelines [27] and suggestions from the developer community [28].

Fig. 4. Screen captures of *The AR Journey* in NHCM

4 Experiment

Participants
31 university students were recruited to participate in the experiment, and 29 of them (14 females, 15 males, Tongji University, Shanghai, China) has completed the experiment while 2 of them quitted due to the hardware failure. Participants aged from 17 to 26 years old (M = 21.97, SD = 2.15) came from all kinds of majors like film, engineering, journalism, animation, etc. There was no grading associated with the exercise but 10 dollars' voucher as compensation for completing the experiment and the interview.

Procedure and Materials
The materials used in the study included an interactive HoloLens app named *The AR Journey*, a semi-structured interview regarding perception of mixed reality, narrative, and user experience. In order to ensure the reliability of the experiment, the voice acting and subtitles were reproduced in the participants' own language: Chinese.

As Fig. 5 showed, the room, a lab in Tongji University, was selected for this experiment, which was decorated with cherry wood floor and some European-style furniture to be consistent with Leo's living room of the exhibition in NHCM. AR headset HoloLens 1st was used featuring a 35° viewing angle see-through holographic lenses (waveguides) with HD definition screen (720p), Intel Atom x5-Z8100 CPU (1.04 GHz), 2 GB RAM, built-in speakers capable of spatial sound, and a HoloLens clicker (its peripheral).

Participants entered the room and took part in the experiment one by one. Firstly, they had 2 min to go through a short paragraph about Holocaust to get the idea of the general background of the story. Then participants were guided to get familiar with the HoloLens headset and the operation of Hololens clicker less than 1 min. When the tutorial was finished, participant could then explore the room, find the story behind the items, and interact with the story. The process of exploration lasted from 12 min to 16 min depending on the number of items the participants explored. Lastly, the participants were asked to take off the headset and had an 8-min interviewed with author.

Fig. 5. Participant is taking part in the experiment in China (left); the hologram mixed into the real-world space participants can see with HoloLens (right)

Measures

Qualitative methods including interview and observation were used for assessment and evaluation. The semi-structured interview was designed based on questions from Narrative Engagement Scale [5], Presence Questionnaire (PQ) [15], IBM's Computer System Usability Questionnaire (CSUQ) [29], and The Intrinsic Motivation Inventory (IMI) [30]. The interview questions focused on aspect of narrative understanding, perceived presence, user experience of input, engagement, enjoyment and suggestions. The process of the experiment was video recorded for further behavior analysis.

5   Results and Discussion

5.1   Interview Results

In this section, a brief descriptive analysis of the interview results is shown before being brought into the context of the discussion in the next section.

Interview questions are as follow:

- Q1: Do you feel the characters or environment are unnatural? If so, what aspect is unnatural?
- Q2: Do you feel the above unnatural characters or environment intervened your overall experience? If so, to what extent?
- Q3: Do you feel the interaction are uncomfortable? If so, what aspect is uncomfortable?
- Q4: Do you remember any impressive plot? please describe it.
- Q5: What do you think of Leo's story? please describe it.
- Q6: How do you like the experience? Please describe it and give some examples.
- Q7: How do you dislike the experience? Please describe it and give details.
- Q8: Would you recommend this experience to your friends? If so, why?

To analyze the results, a two-cycle, simultaneous coding procedure was applied. The first cycle established an initial, in vivo coding. The second cycle used a holistic pattern coding method in order to provide both a summary of the content and a point of reference for the discussion of specific quotes [31]. The second cycle codes and results are shown in Fig. 6.

In Q1 and Q2, the participants were asked to assess general experience for holograms and holographic character. 26 subjects (89.6%) thought the experience was acceptable (Code 1), and 22 subjects (75.9%) spotted the flaws of the holograms or character but claimed this flaw cause little interference on them (Code 2). The reasons were interesting. Some statements were:

"...I noticed the motion of character was unnatural, but I felt my attention was mainly focused on the story, therefore, I quickly ignored these flaws..."

"...I thought it was because my sense was overwhelmed by these holograms. Consequently, I became more tolerant to the 3D characters' unnatural expression ..."

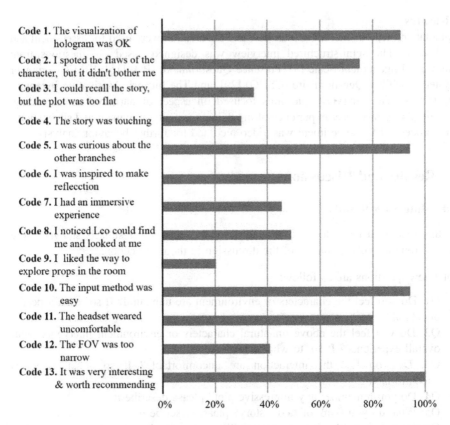

Fig. 6. Coded answers to interview questions (Horizontal axis shows percentage of participants who mentioned these in their responses)

In Q3, the participants were asked to assess the input method. 27 subjects (93%) thought the input method was easy to learn and appropriate for this interactive narrative (Code 10). However, 2 subjects disagreed with this input, their statements were:

"...I felt more like directly using my hand to touch, press or grab the virtual hologram instead of using this clicker, maybe hand gestures could be better than the clicker..."

"...I wanted to use the clicker just like a laser pointer instead of using head gaze to control the 'mouse cursor'..."

In Q4 and Q5, the participants were asked to assess the narrative with HoloLens. 27 subjects (93%) were interested in this choice-based storytelling (Code 5). 13 subjects (45%) were inspired to reflect about meaningful issues (Code 6). 10 subjects (34.5%) thought the story itself was flat with few dramatic conflicts (Code 3). 9 subjects (31%) mentioned that the story affected them emotionally (Code 4). Some statements were:

"...I was struggling to make decision to support mom or dad. Their statement both sounded reasonable. I chose to support mom in the end, but I was also curious about what if I chose to support dad ..."

"...I wanted to know more about Hitler Youth, so I made the first choice. Actually, I was still curious about the second choice..."

"...I had a deep impression on the choice for issue of equality. It made me think our own society..."

"...The dialogue were too much and too flat, I felt I was distracted..."

"...The story was a little bit boring. I would like to see a Nazi officer breaking into the house. That can be breath-taking..."

"...It also reminded me a movie about Holocaust I just watched, I felt so sorry about Leo..."

"I felt so connected with Leo. When he walked towards me, I also stepped towards him..."

In Q6, the participants were asked to describe the positive experience during the narrative. 14 subjects (48%) thought it was empathetic and interesting that Leo could detect, look at and walk towards them (Code 8). 13 subjects (45%) reported to perceive immersion or presence (Code 7). 6 subjects (20.1%) preferred the way to explore props within a real-world space (Code 9). Some statements were:

"...I felt I was talking to Leo, because he was looking at me when he talked..."

"...I noticed Leo was gazing at me, but sometimes I would feel a little uncomfortable under the gaze of his eyes..."

"...I had the illusion that Leo was really there, especially when he walked towards me..."

"...I didn't pay too much attention on what's the virtual stuff and what's the real stuff, I mean I was immersed into this experience..."

"...I felt like I was transferred to Leo's room. I thought more furniture's like carpet on the floor, window curtains could let you feel more real..."

"...The dialogue were too long, I liked to explore stuffs in the room, more explorative props could be even better..."

"...I liked to explore different clues to get the whole piece of the story. I thought the idea of investigating props in the room was great. On the other hand, a branched storytelling was not interesting as the choices were predefined and limited..."

In Q7 the participants were asked to describe the negative experience during the narrative. 23 subjects (79.3%) thought HoloLens was bad for ergonomic design (Code 11). and 12 subjects (41.3%) pointed out the narrow FOV issue (Code 12). Some comments were:

"...The headset was too loose. I used my hand to hold it all the time and my arm ached now..."

"...The headset was too tight to squeeze my head, especially in the later part I was distracted badly..."

"...I felt good at the beginning. The headset became heavier and heavier after a while..."

"...It was odd that I could only see the hologram in front of my head. I saw nothing out of the corner of my eye. That was weird ..."

Lastly, all participants (100%) described this activity as an interesting experience and would like to recommend it to their friends (Code 13). Though the reasons were different. Some statements were:

"...because the experience was very fresh and fancy..."

"...I thought the story was also good and invoking, I would like to share with my friend ..."

"...because it was more engaging than a flat-screen film ..."

"...because I wanted to know the other branch of the story ..."

5.2   Discussion

Several interesting findings were revealed based on the above data analysis. The main issues for narrative in IARE are problems with hardware including the ergonomics and narrow FOV. Though most participants (79.3%) complained about the comfort of HoloLens and many of them (41.3%) recognised the disruptive influence of the low FOV, majority of participants still (89.6%) thought the IARE with current device (HoloLens 1st) was acceptable, and all of them (100%) gave positive comment in terms of enjoyment and was willing to recommend the experience to others. As described in Sect. 2.2, HoloLens 2 has improved the viewing angle and ergonomic design, it is believed that IARE can be further enhanced with HoloLens 2 and has a positive future as the hardware is keeping advancing in recent years.

The computing power of HoloLens is still limited because of the headset-embed CPU, which can only afford the artificial 3D characters and environment. However, most participants (75.9%) seemed to have high tolerance of these artefacts. Attention attracted on narrative, low expectation of AR content and novelty of HoloLens were mentioned most as the underlying reasons. The criticism focused on the body movement and facial expression of the 3D character. This provides guidance for developers that less effort can be placed on asset development, especially on realistic texturing and material. It is also important to note that the weak computing power issue can be possibly solved in the near future as the rapid development of 5G technology.

The modified "quest game" structure employed in this study was proved to be effective. Almost all the participants (93%) hold the positive attitude towards the selectable branched story design while a small number of them (20%) was keen on exploring props and searching details of the story. Meanwhile, there were arguments about the organisation of the props which were supposed to have more inter-connection to achieve a more consistent storytelling. Moreover, almost half of the participant (45%) were inspired to make a reflection of equality and discrimination. Briefly speaking, the narrative was valid in this study for moral education purpose. Interestingly, there were the contradictory attitude on story itself: one third of participants (34.5%) thought the story was flat due to the tedious dialogue and lack of dramatic conflicts while another one third (31%) described the story as touching. One possible reason was that students had different background knowledge of moral issues. Students who were interested in moral issues inclined towards the story.

Almost all the participants (93%) thought the input design is feasible in this study as they felt it was very easy to learn and to use. In addition, natural and autonomous response of virtual characters was vital for interaction as half of the participants (48%) experienced empathy or connectedness with Leo because they either noticed the eye contact or Leo could turn around and find them to talk. Besides, HoloLens 2 is close to be released into the market, manipulation directly by hand is possibly the best input choice and more versatile for narrative in IARE.

6 Conclusion and Future Work

This research introduced a new narrative media known as IARE with HoloLens. *The AR Journey*, a HoloLens app aiming at interactive narrative, was developed for the NHCM and evaluated through qualitative methods.

To conclude, modified "quest game" type is proved to be a valid narrative structure in IARE, and the input model of "gaze and commit with clicker" is valid for a click-through experiences. The design guidelines were discussed and summarised according to the analysis of collected data,

This research hopes to serve as an initial attempt to release the potential of a new form of narrative using AR technologies, and further explorations in this direction, e.g. to expand understanding or to develop design guidelines, to further investigate the interaction with real world objects, to evaluate the new input models in HoloLens 2, are bound to be fruitful and exciting in the future.

Acknowledgement. This work was jointly funded by the National Key Research and Development Program of China (2018 YFB1004903) and Staffordshire University in the UK. We would also like to acknowledge the support from Jake Lynch for script development and the support from Elinor Rosa Williams, Zhang Nan, Zhang Zian, Yu Guodong for motion capture.

References

1. Ryan, M.-L.: Narrative Across Media: The Languages of Storytelling. U of Nebraska Press (2004)
2. Hammady, R., Ma, M., Strathern, C., Mohamad, M.: Design and development of a spatial mixed reality touring guide to the Egyptian Museum. Multimedia Tools Appl., 1–30 (2019)
3. Hanna, M.G., Ahmed, I., Nine, J., Prajapati, S., Pantanowitz, L.: Augmented reality technology using microsoft HoloLens in anatomic pathology. Arch. Pathol. Lab. Med. **142**(5), 638–644 (2017)

4. Dow, S., Mehta, M., Macintyre, B., Mateas, M.: AR façade: an augmented reality interactive drama. In: Proceedings of the 2007 ACM Symposium on Virtual Reality Software and Technology, pp. 215–216 (2007)
5. Busselle, R., Bilandzic, H.: Measuring narrative engagement. Media Psychol. 12(4), 321–347 (2009)
6. Hoffman, M.L.: Interaction of affect and cognition in empathy. Emot. Cogn. Behav., 103–131 (1984)
7. Saarni, C., Crowley, M.: The development of emotion regulation: effects on emotional state and expression. In: Emotions and the Family: for Better or for Worse, pp. 53–73(1990)
8. Obama, B., Biden, J.: Remarks by the president and the vice president on gun violence. In: The White House Office of the Press Secretary, 16 January 2013
9. Nikonanou, N., Bounia, A.: Digital applications in museums: an analysis from a museum education perspective. In: Karagiannidis, C., Politis, P., Karasavvidis, I. (eds.) Research on e-Learning and ICT in Education, pp. 179–194. Springer, New York (2014). https://doi.org/10.1007/978-1-4614-6501-0_13
10. Best, K.: Making museum tours better: understanding what a guided tour really is and what a tour guide really does. Mus. Manag. Curatorship 27(1), 35–52 (2012)
11. Hololens 1 Hardware Specification page. https://docs.microsoft.com/en-us/hololens/hololens1-hardware. Accessed 31 Jan 2020
12. Magic Leap One Homepage. https://www.magicleap.com/magic-leap-1. Accessed 31 Jan 2020
13. Hololens 2 Hardware Specification. https://docs.microsoft.com/en-us/hololens/hololens1-hardware. Accessed 31 Jan 2020
14. Microsoft's Documentation of The Mixed Reality Toolkit (MRTK). https://microsoft.github.io/MixedRealityToolkit-Unity/README.html. Accessed 3 Jan 2020
15. Witmer, B.G., Singer, M.J.: Measuring presence in virtual environments: a presence questionnaire. Presence 7(3), 225–240 (1998)
16. Newton, K., Soukup, K.: The Storyteller's Guide to the Virtual Reality Audience. The Stanford D School (2016)
17. Aylett, R., Louchart, S.: Towards a narrative theory of virtual reality. Virtual Reality 7(1), 2–9 (2003)
18. Aarseth, E.: A narrative theory of games. In: Proceedings of the International Conference on the Foundations of Digital Games, pp. 129–133. ACM (2012)
19. Austin, T.R., Chatman, S.: Story and Discourse: Narrative Structure in Fiction and Film. Cornell University Press, New York (1980)
20. Microsoft's Documentation of Direct Manipulation with Hands. https://docs.microsoft.com/en-us/windows/mixed-reality/direct-manipulation. Accessed 31 Jan 2020
21. Microsoft's Documentation of Motion Controllers. https://docs.microsoft.com/en-us/windows/mixed-reality/motion-controllers. Accessed 31 Jan 2020
22. Microsoft's Documentation of Hand Gestures. https://docs.microsoft.com/en-us/windows/mixed-reality/gaze-and-commit#composite-gestures. Accessed 31 Jan 2020
23. Microsoft's Documentation of Voice Input. https://docs.microsoft.com/en-us/windows/mixed-reality/voice-input. Accessed 31 Jan 2020
24. Microsoft's Documentation of Eye-gaze-based Interaction. https://docs.microsoft.com/en-us/windows/mixed-reality/eye-gaze-interaction. Accessed 31 Jan 2020
25. Mixed Reality Interaction Models Documentation from Microsoft. https://docs.microsoft.com/en-us/windows/mixed-reality/interaction-fundamentals. Accessed 31 Jan 2020
26. O'Brien, D., Lawless, K.A., Schrader, P.: A taxonomy of educational games. In: Gaming for Classroom-Based Learning: Digital Role Playing as a Motivator of Study, pp. 1–23 (2010)

27. Ferguson, C.J.: Violent video games and the Supreme Court: lessons for the scientific community in the wake of brown v. entertainment merchants association. Am. Psychol. **68**(2), 57 (2013)
28. Lemola, S., Brand, S., Vogler, N., Perkinson-Gloor, N., Allemand, M., Grob, A.: Habitual computer game playing at night is related to depressive symptoms. Pers. Individ. Differ. **51**(2), 117–122 (2011)
29. Lewis, J.R.: IBM computer usability satisfaction questionnaires: psychometric evaluation and instructions for use. Int. J. Hum. Comput. Interact. **7**(1), 57–78 (1995)
30. McAuley, E., Duncan, T., Tammen, V.V.: Psychometric properties of the intrinsic motivation inventory in a competitive sport setting: a confirmatory factor analysis. Res. Q. Exerc. Sport **60**(1), 48–58 (1989)
31. Saldaña, J.: The Coding Manual for Qualitative Researchers. Sage, Thousand Oaks (2015)

Learning in Virtual Reality: Investigating the Effects of Immersive Tendencies and Sense of Presence

Aliane Loureiro Krassmann[1]([⊠]), Miguel Melo[2], Bruno Peixoto[3], Darque Pinto[3], Maximino Bessa[2,3], and Magda Bercht[1]

[1] Universidade Federal do Rio Grande do Sul, Porto Alegre, Brazil
alkrassmann@gmail.com
[2] INESC TEC, Porto, Portugal
[3] Universidade de Trás-os-Montes e Alto Douro, Vila Real, Portugal

Abstract. The goal of this study is to examine the effects of the sense of presence and immersive tendencies on learning outcomes while comparing different media formats (Interactive VR, Non-interactive VR and Video). An experiment was conducted with 36 students that watched a Biology lesson about the human cells. Contrary to expected, the results demonstrate that the Non-interactive VR was the most successful format. Sense of presence and immersive tendencies did not have an effect on learning gain, and the latter was not a critical factor to experience the sense of presence. The findings provide empirical evidence to help understand the influence of these variables on learning in VR.

Keywords: Virtual Reality · Video · Sense of presence · Immersive tendencies

1 Introduction

The technology of Virtual Reality (VR) allows the creation of vivid and highly realistic 3D Virtual Environments (VE). In this sense, it can be a useful tool for education, especially in disciplines where it is important to visualise learning materials (e.g. Chemistry and Biology) [1], allowing students to develop a better understanding of the relationship among components by engaging with information from multiple roles and perspectives. Students also have the opportunity to experience subject matter that would be difficult if not impossible with conventional methods, in a more stimulating and motivating setting, where learning can be both challenging and fun [2].

One of the keys aspects involved with the VR experience is the sense of presence. According to Heeter [3], "the sense of being there" is the best definition of presence in this context, where the users feel like they are part of that virtual world such as the real world. Consequently, it is the degree of how much the user feels present in that VE. Literature suggests that this is a crucial aspect for learning in VR, as it is connected to many constructs influencing its process, as attention and focus [4, 5]. Studies have already demonstrated a positive relationship between sense of presence and performance, as Schrader & Bastiaens [6] and Lee, Wong & Fung [7].

© Springer Nature Switzerland AG 2020
J. Y. C. Chen and G. Fragomeni (Eds.): HCII 2020, LNCS 12191, pp. 270–286, 2020.
https://doi.org/10.1007/978-3-030-49698-2_18

Several physiological reasons collaborate to explain the association between sense of presence and learning. According to Riva, Waterworth & Murray [8, p. 10], "presence is a core neuropsychological phenomenon whose goal is to produce a sense of agency and control: I am present in real or virtual space if I manage to put my intentions into action". Tjon et al. [9], discovered that the feeling of presence during a VR experience was associated with a decrease in electroencephalography (EEG) frontal alpha power, which in Neuroscience indicates a stronger engagement.

Another important factor of a VR experience is the immersion, which differs from the sense of presence as it refers to an objective description of the used technology, including the stimulus-driven variables vividness and interactivity [10]. For example, the use of Head-Mounted Displays (HMD) allows more immersion than just use a screen (desktop-based VR). Immersion is considered one of the main factors influencing the sense of presence, in that a higher level of immersion can predict a higher presence [5, 11, 12].

Despite that, each individual has its own immersive tendencies, which is the propensity to experience immersion [11]. It refers to an individuals' tendency to become involved in situations and maintain focus on current activities [12]. People with high immersive tendencies can more easily ignore external distractions and focus on their experiences, becoming unaware of the immediate environment and the passage of time. Studies have shown that its relation with the sense of presence is also positive, in that high immersive tendencies lead to higher levels of presence [13].

Nevertheless, which role do these variables really play when the goal is to use VR for learning? Schrader & Bastiaens [6] hypothesise that immersive tendencies function as a moderator on the relationship between the sense of presence and performance. In spite of that, although they found that the immersive tendencies were a predictor of the sense of presence, it did not significantly influence learning outcomes.

Aiming to contribute with this discussion, we investigate the effects of immersive tendencies and sense of presence in the learning gain while performing a comparison across three different media formats: a control Video one, and two experimental of immersive VR, Interactive and Non-interactive. Following the work of Makransky, Borre-Gude & Mayer [14], learning is defined as the demonstration of declarative knowledge, including basic facts and terminology related to the subject, assessed by means of objective retention tests.

2   Related Work

Few studies have added both the immersive tendencies and the sense of presence on the investigation of learning outcomes when VR is used as a media format. Notwithstanding, when the measuring of the variables does not obey a scientific rigour to enable a fair comparison, the results can be hindered, reducing the enthusiasm of teachers and researchers to invest in the costly job of developing instruction in VR. Parong & Mayer [15], for example, concluded that a slideshow group scored significantly better than a VR group on the overall performance. However, the following "a" and "b" variables were not properly controlled in their experiment.

a) *Format of instruction.* In the study of Parong & Mayer [15] the VR animation was automatically-paced and the slideshow presentation was self-paced, as the users determined the rhythm of access. Thus, participants were not in the same passive posture in both conditions. Also, although they ensured that both lessons contained the same words, one version had spoken and the other had printed format; and one version had dynamic graphics and the other graphics in static form.

b) *Measure of learning outcomes.* Instead of an objective pretest-posttest approach, Parong & Mayer [15] opted for a self-reported background knowledge questionnaire as a pretest, justifying they did not want to create a "testing effect", in which the pretest primes learners to construct answers before the instruction. Their posttest consisted of 20 questions based on the lesson, including 16 factual questions in multiple-choice format and four conceptual questions in short-answer format.

Lee, Wong & Fung [7], by their turn, although used a desktop-based VR setting, provide empirical evidence on the causality relationship between the sense of presence and learning outcomes, with students participating in a frog dissection simulator. Despite including the sense of presence and other personal aspects such as an individual's motivation and learning style, they did not investigate the immersive tendencies. Also, students did not participate in different conditions of media format.

Bulu [16], also using desktop-based VR, developed a virtual campus to examine the relationship among three types of sense of presence (social, place and co-presence), satisfaction and immersive tendencies, counting with the participation of preservice teachers. It was identified that the immersive tendencies were related to the sense of presence, which, in turn, was a predictor of satisfaction. Besides not comparing different conditions of media, learning outcomes were also not evaluated.

Schrader & Bastiaens [6] investigated if the sense of presence and learning were related to immersive tendencies in the outcomes from an educational computer game (desktop-based VR) in the area of Physics. Participants were students from highschool, and as a result, the immersive tendencies were positively related to the sense of presence and both trivial and nontrivial learning outcomes. However, the authors also did not test different conditions of media format.

Differently from these three studies and similar to Parong & Mayer [15], the work of Murray, Fox & Pettifer [17] did occur in an immersive VR setting. Participants used an HMD to navigate a virtual city. Among the variables measured, the immersive tendencies and the sense of presence, which, as a result, were not correlated. Thus, the authors suggest that other psychological factors such as dissociation might provide a better indication of the likelihood that the sense of presence will be experienced. Learning was not evaluated and a comparison of different media was not performed.

Allcoat & Mühlenen [1], on the other hand, did compare media formats: interactive immersive VR, passive video watching and traditional textbook. The learning materials were the same text and 3D model of a plant cell for all three conditions. They concluded that the VR condition showed better learning results, suggesting that the "active learning" model plays an important role. Although the emotional response was evaluated, immersive tendencies and sense of presence were not.

Olmos-Raya et al. [18] also compared different media formats, that varied in levels of immersion: high, with HMD device, and low, with tablet and no additional device. Participants received animated contents about History and were evaluated regarding knowledge retention. As a result, better learning outcomes were obtained in the high immersive condition. The authors also evaluated the student's emotional response and motivation, but the immersive tendencies and sense of presence were not considered.

Khashe et al. [13], conversely, found no significant difference in participants' sense of presence and performance while interacting with two different platforms that varied levels of immersion. Although there was a strong positive relationship between immersive tendencies and presence, the same was not found for immersive tendencies and performance. The VE focused on pro-environmental behaviours and performance was measured by means of office-related tasks (time spent on reading passages and reading comprehension). That is, they did not investigate learning as the demonstration of declarative knowledge, assessed through objective retention tests [14].

Finally, in the study of Makransky, BorreGude & Mayer [14], the consequences of learning the same instructional content (safety training) through different instructional media (text, desktop-based VR and immersive VR) were examined. Similar to the previous studies, they confirmed the idea that learning in VR was more motivating than conventional media (text), and the more immersive setting obtained better learning outcomes. Sense of presence and immersive tendencies were also out of their scope.

Table 1 summarises the different aspects investigated in each of the related studies, highlighting a research gap when considering all five aspects/variables that are scoped by this paper.

Table 1. Comparison of the related work

	Immersive VR setting	Sense of presence	Immersive tendencies	Learning outcomes	Media comparison
Lee, Wong & Fung [7]	No	Yes	No	Yes	No
Bulu [16]	No	Yes	Yes	No	No
Schrader & Bastiaens [6]	No	Yes	Yes	Yes	No
Murray, Fox & Pettifer [17]	Yes	Yes	Yes	No	No
Parong & Mayer [15]	Yes	No	No	Yes	Yes
Allcoat & Mühlenen [1]	Yes	No	No	Yes	Yes
Olmos-Raya et al. [18]	Yes	No	No	Yes	Yes
Khashe et al. [13]	Yes	Yes	Yes	No	Yes
Makransky, Borre-Gude & Mayer [14]	Yes	No	No	Yes	Yes
Present study	**Yes**	**Yes**	**Yes**	**Yes**	**Yes**

In addition to including both the immersive tendencies and the sense of presence in the investigation of learning outcomes, the difference of this study lies in seeking for a fairer analysis, by means of:

a) comparing a Non-interactive VR animation to a Video format, delivering the content in an automatic continuous equal pace, ensuring both passive modes of instruction, adding a third Interactive VR condition, as the literature suggests benefits from promoting more active learning [1];
b) performing an objective assessment of learning, by means of equal pre and posttests, allowing to infer learning indexes that can be directly associated with the intervention.

According to Stanney, Mourant & Kennedy [19], it is essential to control for such factors so that it is not erroneously concluded that performance is enhanced by immersion (or other factors) when the improvement might be directly related to the fact that subjects received more or different training time or training trials, for example.

3   Materials and Method

This study has an experimental between-subjects design, in which the independent variable is the media format (Interactive VR (IVR), Non-interactive VR (NVR) and Video (V)), and the dependent variables are the learning gain and the sense of presence. The immersive tendencies are collected for studying a possible correlation with the sense of presence and the learning gain. Participants were equally and randomly assigned to one of three conditions of media format.

In this sense, the following hypotheses are tested, divided into three main axes.

Media and Learning Outcomes (MLO)
MLO1. The learning gain is higher in Interactive VR than in Non-interactive VR.
MLO2. The learning gain is higher in Non-interactive VR than in Video.
MLO3. The learning gain is higher in Interactive VR than in Video.
Sense of Presence (SP)
SP1. The sense of presence is higher in Interactive VR than in Non-interactive VR.
SP2. The sense of presence is higher in Non-interactive VR than in Video.
SP3. The sense of presence is higher in Interactive VR than in Video.
SP4. The sense of presence is positively correlated with the learning gain.
Immersive Tendencies (IT)
IT1. The immersive tendencies are positively correlated with the sense of presence.
IT2. The immersive tendencies are positively correlated with the learning gain.

3.1   Participants

Participants were 36 students (20 male, 12 female) from Universidade de Trás-os-Montes e Alto Douro, located in Portugal. Their ages ranged between 16 and 49 years old (M = 23.86, SD = 6.85), with a distribution very proximal on each of the three experimental groups (M = 23.67, M = 22.83, M = 25.08). They were enrolled in a graduate (n = 14, ~39%) and undergraduate courses (n = 18, 50%) in knowledge areas distinct from Natural Sciences, which is the area of the instruction used in the study (e.g. Multimedia and Engineering). Some participants (n = 4, ~11%) were from the secondary school of the same University.

Participants were asked to rate their experience with computers. Approximately 47% (n = 12) affirmed having an intermediate experience. The remaining were divided into specialists (n = 11, ~31%) and individuals with basic experience (n = 8, ~22%). Regarding knowledge on VR, they were divided in basic (n = 13, ~36%), intermediate (n = 11, ~30%), specialist (n = 7, ~20%), and a small parcel indicated having no knowledge on VR (n = 5, ~14%). However, the majority affirmed having previous experience with immersive VR, meaning they have tried HMD before (n = 29, ~80%).

3.2   Materials

For the purpose of this study, a 12-min Biology lesson in VR was selected: "The Body VR, a Journey Inside the Cell", freely available on the Steam repository [20]. In this animation, the user has a full 360-degree view and is "shrunk" to travel through the bloodstream, while a narrator explains the purpose and structure of cells within it (Fig. 1). The narration was translated from English to Portuguese and recorded in a new track, as the native language of the participants is Portuguese. The original background ambient sounds were maintained.

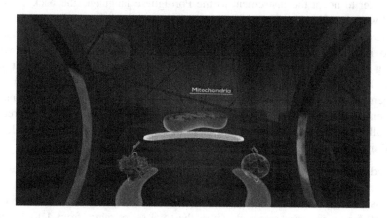

Fig. 1. Screenshot of "The Body VR, a Journey Inside the Cell".

Participants in the VR conditions received the visual stimulus using HTC Vive. This HMD features a 110° viewing angle and a resolution of 1080 × 1200 pixels per eye and allows the real-time tracking of the head position. As for the Interactive VR (IVR) condition, it was added the possibility of interacting with some of the 3D objects presented in the screen using the hand controllers (touching, moving, rotating and changing size).

In the Video (V) condition, it was used a 2D recording of the central view of the VR animation, which was displayed in a conventional computer screen. In all conditions, participants were not allowed to navigate the animation (play, pause, fast forward or rewind), ensuring that all three groups had the same pace of information and visuals to learn with, with the only difference being the media format. Thus, all formats had the same duration (12 min).

The laptop configuration, in short, consists of Intel Core i7-7700HQ processor, NVIDIA GeForce 1070 graphics card, 16 GB of RAM, with a 17″ Full HD (1920 × 1080) IPS screen and Windows 10 operating system. The headphones were Bose QuietComfort 25 with noise-cancelling. The same laptop and headphones were used in all three experimental conditions.

3.3   Instruments

Three instruments were used for data collection, all presented to participants in paper-based printed format: Immersive Tendencies Questionnaire (ITQ), knowledge test and ITC Sense of Presence Inventory (ITC-SOPI).

ITQ. Immersive tendencies were measured using the questionnaire from Witmer & Singer [11]. It contains 18 items with 7-point Likert scale response options (e.g. 1 = never, 4 = sometimes, 7 = very often). The sum of the points corresponds to an individual's immersive tendency. Thus, the range of possible scores is 18–126, and the samples' mean score was 76.66 in the original study.

In order to adapt the instrument to the Portuguese language, the back-translation method was used [21, 22]. First, it was translated from English into Portuguese by two of the researchers together. Then, the Portuguese version was individually translated back to English by two Computer Science doctorates specialising in VR, without knowing the original version. They were all Portuguese natives and fluent in the English language. Subsequently, each researcher demonstrated their agreement or disagreement with the back translation of each item, by calculating the percentage of agreement in a 10-point scale, where 1 = not agree and 10 = extremely agree. The results allowed the inclusion of all the items, as the calculated values were all above 80% of agreement.

Knowledge Test. According to the content presented in "The Body VR, a Journey Inside the Cell" [20], the researchers elaborated a test consisting of 10 multiple-choice questions. Each question had five answer options, with 1 point given for each correct answer (0 for an incorrect answer). Thus, the total score range from 1 to 10. It was initially constructed in English and then translated to Portuguese.

The test was designed to examine participants' knowledge of basic Biology concepts and procedural information involved in the animation, and it was validated by a Natural Sciences professor (Portuguese native, English fluent), who analysed the correspondence and adequateness of each question in both languages.

The same test was applied before and after the intervention (pretest and posttest); the only difference was the order the questions appeared to avoid bias. In the pretest, the questions followed the logic of events described in the animation, and in the posttest, it did not. Improvement from pretest to posttest was used as a measure of learning gain.

ITC-SOPI. In order to assess participant's sense of presence, a validated 44 item 5-point Likert scale (ranging from 1 to 5) questionnaire originated from Lessiter et al. [5] was selected, due to its cross-media comparison capabilities. The instrument is divided into four factors, described as follows, with one item not inserted in none of them (item B6).

a) Spatial Presence (SP) (19 items): the ability to physically control and manipulate aspects of the displayed environment (even using unsophisticated control devices);
b) Engagement (E) (13 items): a measure of a user's involvement, interest in the content of the displayed environment, and their general enjoyment of the experience;
c) Ecological Validity/Naturalness (EVN) (5 items): related to the believability, realism of the content, naturalness and solidity of the environment;
d) Negative Effects (NE) (6 items): headache, eye strain, tiredness, and other negative effects that may be associated with the media format.

We used a reduced validated 35-item Portuguese version from Vasconcelos-Raposo et al. [23], which maintains these four factors.

3.4 Procedure

Upon arrival, participants were welcomed at the facilities of the MASSIVE (acronym for Multimodal Acknowledgeable multiSenSory Immersive Virtual Environments) laboratory and were randomly assigned to one of the three experimental conditions. They were briefly explained the general educational purpose of the study, and started by filling the consent form with demographic questions. Then, the ITQ and the knowledge pretest were filled in the sequence.

The intervention was conducted individually, in a dim and controlled room, where participants were isolated from external variables. They remained seated in the centre of the room, which corresponds to the centre of the animation. In the VR conditions, the researchers helped the participants equipping the HMD, ensuring that it was properly fitted and that they were comfortable with it.

Immediately after the experience, participants filled the knowledge posttest. Then, the ITC-SOPI and, finally, were thanked and dismissed.

3.5 Analysis

Descriptive and inferential statistics were measured using SPSS 18 software, with a confidence level of 95% and Bonferroni adjustment within each simple main effect. Wilcoxon Signed-Rank Test was used in paired-samples tests and the correlation tests were performed using the Spearman's test. To assess the normal distribution of the data, a Shapiro Wilk's test was applied.

When a normal distribution was verified, the homogeneity of variances was analysed using the Levene's test and, if it was not violated, an One-way ANOVA test was performed for three groups and an independent samples t-test was run for two groups. When a normal distribution was not verified or the assumptions of the One-way ANOVA were not met, a Kruskal-Wallis H test was performed for three groups and a Mann-Whitney's U test was run for two groups.

4 Results

Results for the normality tests indicated the use of non-parametric tests in most cases ($p < 0.05$), except with the scores of the ITQ ($p = 0.876$) and the factors Spatial Presence and Ecological Validity/Naturalness of the ITC-SOPI, which have a normal distribution ($p = 0.722$, $p = 0.117$).

In the following section, we perform a sample characterisation to evaluate if there was bias introduced by the participant's immersive tendencies or previous knowledge.

4.1 Sample Characterization

Regarding immersive tendencies, the One-way ANOVA test has revealed no statistical significances between the three groups for $p < 0.05$ ($F(2,36) = 2.275$, $p = 0.119$, 0.429, O.P $= 0.429$), as presented in Table 2. Due to the moderate-to-large effect ($\eta p^2 < 0.119$) and considerable O.P. (<0.40), post hoc tests were applied to verify the possible occurrence of a Type II error, which was not confirmed. Thus, the sample can be considered homogeneous in relation to immersive tendencies.

Table 2. One-way ANOVA of the Immersive Tendencies Questionnaire

ITQ Score	Groups						p-value	η_p^2	Observed power
	IVR		NVR		V				
	M	SD	M	SD	M	SD			
	79.67	14.32	89.83	10.92	90.33	14.19	0.119	0.121	0.429

Regarding the pretests, the Kruskal-Wallis' test maintained the null hypothesis of equality between groups ($\chi^2(2) = 0.796$, $p = 0.672$, $\eta^2 = 0.036$) (see Table 3).

In this sense, it can be verified that the sample is homogeneous: all participants start on an equal footing regarding previous knowledge and immersive tendencies, allowing to assume that these factors will have no influence on the results presented in the following sections.

4.2 Media and Learning Outcomes

Table 3 allows observing that all the groups performed better on the posttest, with a positive learning gain. When comparing all the pretest and posttest scores via a

Wilcoxon Signed-Rank Test (z = 2.18, p = 0.29), it can be verified that the learning gain was statistically significant after the intervention.

Concerning the analysis by group, participants in the NVR condition obtained the highest mean score on the posttest (M = 6.83, SD = 2.52), followed by the V (M = 6.33, SD = 2.67) and the IVR group (M = 6.17, SD = 2.17), respectively. This is a preliminary indication that learning performance might be better in the Non-interactive VR condition, with an average knowledge increase of 1.25 points, leaving behind the Interactive VR (1.17) and the Video (0.42) conditions.

Table 3. Results for the knowledge tests and learning gain

Knowledge	Groups					
	IVR		NVR		V	
	M	SD	M	SD	M	SD
Pretest	5.00	2.86	5.58	2.31	5.92	2.39
Posttest	6.17	2.17	6.83	2.52	6.33	2.67
Learning gain	1.17	2.76	1.25	2.01	0.42	1.83

In the sequence, the MLO hypothesis tests are presented.

MLO1. The learning gain is higher in Interactive VR than in Non-interactive VR
The results show that the IVR group did not outperform the NVR group (1.17 of learning gain in comparison to 1.25). Also, the Mann-Whitney's U test did not reject the null hypothesis of equality between groups, considering the values of learning gain (U = 63.00, z = −0.531, p = 0.595). Thus, we cannot confirm the MLO1 hypothesis.

MLO2. The learning gain is higher in Non-interactive VR than in Video
Although the results show that the NVR group did outperform the V group (1.25 of learning gain in comparison to 0.42), the Mann-Whitney's U test did not reject the null hypothesis of equality between groups, considering the values of learning gain (U = 52, z = −1.178, p = 0.239). In this sense, we cannot confirm the MLO2 hypothesis.

MLO3. The learning gain is higher in Interactive VR than in Video
Although the results show that the IVR group did outperform the V group (1.17 of learning gain in comparison to 0.42), the Mann-Whitney's U test did not reject the null hypothesis of equality between groups, considering the values of learning gain (U = 61.500, z = −0.620, p = 0.535). In this sense, we cannot confirm the MLO3 hypothesis.

4.3   Sense of Presence

According to the authors of the ITC-SOPI [5], the scores for each factor cannot be combined into one overall sense of presence; it must be analyzed individually. They also clarify that the item referring to characters being aware of the user's presence

(B23 from the original version, B20 from the Portuguese version) has to be ignored when the evaluated VE does not contain characters, which was the case of the tested animation.

Considering these assumptions, Table 4 presents the results of the ITC-SOPI factors for each research group. It allows observing that the mean scores for the IVR group were the highest for all factors, followed by the NVR and the V groups, respectively. This result indicates that participants in the Interactive VR condition achieved a higher sense of presence than the other two groups. Also, participants in the Non-interactive VR achieved a higher sense of presence than in the Video condition, which was the less stimulating in this regard.

Table 4. Results for the ITC-Sense of Presence Inventory

ITC-SOPI factors	Groups					
	IVR		NVR		V	
	M	SD	M	SD	M	SD
Spatial presence	3.62	0.50	2.67	0.60	2.24	0.62
Engagement	3.52	0.54	3.33	0.47	3.02	0.81
Ecological validity/naturalness	3.80	0.62	3.40	0.68	3.13	0.78
Negative effects	1.57	0.96	1.47	0.67	1.36	0.33

On the other hand, the score for the Negative Effects factor was also higher in the IVR group (M = 1.57, SD = 0.96), which means that participants in this condition experienced more uncomfortable feelings like headache, eyestrain, dizziness and nausea. Following the same logic, the NVR group was the second-highest (M = 1.47, SD = 0.67), and the V group had the lowest mean score for Negative Effects (M = 1.36, SD = 0.33). However, the overall scores were low in all conditions, indicating that this factor did not have a significant impact on participants' sense of presence. In the following, the SP hypothesis tests are presented.

SP1. The sense of presence is higher in Interactive VR than in Non-interactive VR
The results show that the ITC-SOPI score was higher in the IVR group than in the NVR group for all factors, and the independent samples t-test also rejected the null hypothesis for Spatial Presence (t(22) = 4.006, p = 0.001). However, the Mann-Whitney's U test and the t-test, respectively, maintained the null hypothesis for Engagement (U = 60.000, z = −0.703, p = 0.482) and Ecological Validity/Naturalness (t(22) = 1.442, p = 0.163). The Mann-Whitney's U test also maintained the null hypothesis for Negative Effects (U = 63.500, z = −0.207, p = 0.612). Thus, we can partially confirm the SP1 hypothesis, that the sense of presence is higher in the IVR than in the NVR condition, in what concerns spatial presence.

SP2. The sense of presence is higher in Non-interactive VR than in Video
Although the results show that the ITC-SOPI score was higher in the NVR group than in the V group for all factors, the independent samples t-test and the Mann-Whitney's U test, respectively, did not reject the null hypothesis for Spatial Presence (t(22) = 0.855, p = 0.113) and Engagement (U = 60.500, z = −.670, p = 0.503). For the factors Ecological Validity/Naturalness and Negative Effects, the independent samples t-test and the Mann-Whitney's U test, respectively, also maintained the null hypothesis (t(22) = 1.653, p = 0.402, U = 65.000, z = −0.412, p = 0.680). In this sense, we cannot confirm the SP2 hypothesis.

SP3. The sense of presence is higher in Interactive VR than in Video
The results show that the ITC-SOPI score was higher in the IVR group than in the V group for all factors, and the independent samples t-test did reject the null hypothesis for Spatial Presence (t(22) = 5.732, p < 0.001). However, for Engagement, the Mann Whitney's U test maintained the null hypothesis (U = 51.000, z = −1.232, p = 0.218). The independent samples t-test also rejected the null hypothesis for Ecological Validity/Naturalness (t(22) = 2.231, p = 0.036), but the Mann-Whitney's U test maintained the null hypothesis for Negative Effects (U = 60.500, z = −0.681, p = 0.496).

Therefore, we can partially confirm the SP3 hypothesis, that the sense of presence is higher in the IVR than in the V condition, in what concerns spatial presence and ecological validity/naturalness.

SP4. The sense of presence is positively correlated with the learning gain
Considering the values of learning gain and the scores of the ITC-SOPI factors from the three research groups, the Spearman's test maintained the null hypothesis for the factors Spatial Presence (rs = 0.177, p = 0.301), Engagement (rs = 0.080, p = 0.641), Ecological Validity/Naturalness (rs = 0.163, p = 0.341) and Negative Effects (rs = −0.135, p = 0.433). Thus, we cannot confirm the SP4 hypothesis.

4.4   Correlation of Immersive Tendencies with the Sense of Presence and Learning

In the sequence, the IT hypothesis tests are presented.

IT1. The immersive tendencies are positively correlated with the sense of presence
Considering the ITQ and the ITC-SOPI scores, the Spearman's test maintained the null hypothesis for all factors: Spatial Presence (rs = −.081, p = 0.639), Engagement (rs = 0.181, p = 0.290), Ecological Validity/Naturalness (rs = 0.171, p = 0.319) and Negative Effects (rs = 0.024, p = 0.890). Therefore, we cannot confirm the IT1 hypothesis.

IT2. The immersive tendencies are positively correlated with the learning gain
Considering the values of learning gain and the scores of the ITQ from the three research groups, the Spearman's test maintained the null hypothesis of correlation (rs = −.079, p = 0.648). In this sense, we cannot confirm the IT2 hypothesis.

5 Discussion

The discussion of results is organized by the three hypotheses axes that were tested.

5.1 Media and Learning Outcomes

The results show that all three research groups performed better on the posttest, achieving a statistically significant positive learning gain. This finding suggests that all conditions have actually contributed to knowledge retention, allowing to agree with the study of Allcoat & Mühlenen [1], when concluding that VR can be a compelling alternative to traditional didactic approaches, with similar performance levels and improved engagement.

However, the supposition that learning outcomes would be higher in the Interactive VR condition was rejected. Contrary to expected, participants in the Non-interactive VR condition obtained a higher knowledge increase, meaning it was the most successful format, although not statistically proven. It means that when comparing both passive modes of instruction delivered in an automatic continuous equal pace (Non-interactive VR animation to Video), the VR was more prominent.

This fact suggests that learning is not a result of graphics or visuals, as these were the same in both conditions. Instead, it appears to be attributable to immersion [1]. Students in the immersive conditions (VR) could see around just naturally moving their heads, giving them a 180° of vision that Video condition students didn't have. The possibility to visually examine their surroundings more naturally in the VE allowed them to better acquire the information they needed to understand concepts. In this sense, we can extend the findings of Olmos-Raya et al. [18], in which better learning outcomes were obtained in the VR condition as compared to a tablet, and of Makransky, Borre-Gude & Mayer [14], in which the same occurred while comparing VR to a textbook.

On the other hand, we cannot corroborate with Allcoat & Mühlenen [1] when they associate VR to the pedagogic model of active learning, suggesting that it plays an important role. That is, at least the way our more active condition was modelled (Interactive VR), with the use of hand controllers. Additional explanations for this result can be linked to the instructional design theories of Cognitive Load [24] and Multimedia Learning [25]. Studies that endorse this finding are discussed as follows.

Cognitive Load. The extrinsic cognitive load associated with the use of a highly visual and interactive technology may have caused a "seductive detail" [26]. Makransky, Terkildsen & Mayer [27] identified that students learned less in the more immersive condition insofar as realism was a distraction not relevant to the instructional goal. According to Whitelock et al. [2], although "being there" is very motivating, it can take up too much of the users' attention and produce a cognitive overload when it comes to understanding conceptual notions. In the study of Schrader & Bastiaens [28], the high-immersion condition was more demanding in the working memory, and the consequent extrinsic cognitive load made learning more difficult.

Multimedia Learning. Parong & Mayer [15], while using the same lesson of this study [20], found that the slideshow format was more effective for learning than the immersive VR. They suppose that this could have been due to the coherence principle, which calls for eliminating extraneous material. As students were "placed" in the blood-stream, with various cells constantly moving past, being able to look in any direction to see these movements, their attention was diverted from the important material. In our case, the use of hand controllers might have contributed to exacerbating the coherence principle of multimedia learning, distracting students from the learning content.

In a similar perspective, there is also the novelty factor [26]. Although most participants affirmed having previous experience with VR, this technology is not part of the students' daily life. That is, they were probably more dazzled by the novelty of the technology that didn't pay so much attention to the lesson. And the use of hand controllers may have aggravated this perspective.

5.2   Sense of Presence

Results for the sense of presence dimension followed the expected logic: highest in the Interactive VR group, followed by the Non-interactive VR and the Video groups, respectively. However, the hypotheses tests to statistically prove these differences were partially accepted, concerning only two factors: a) spatial presence was higher in the Interactive VR than in the other two conditions; and b) ecological validity/naturalness was higher in the Interactive VR than in the Video condition.

According to Tjon et al. [9], spatial presence is the most studied aspect of presence and is most directly related to the presence experience itself. Its importance is also highlighted by Riva, Waterworth & Murray [8], who suggest that it may be key to persuasion as it promotes a more natural interaction with the user's surroundings. Persuasion, by its turn, is a communication strategy to induce someone to accept an idea, an attitude, or to perform an action; a fundamental key to learning. Conversely, the authors state that a low spatial presence may degrade the user experience, consequently hindering the expected outcomes.

Together with the significant difference in ecological validity/naturalness, this finding shows that the possibility of interacting with 3D objects in the VR animation, by means of hand controllers, added realism to the experience. It allows corroborating that the naturalness of the interactions and how closely it mimics real-world experiences affect how much presence is reported [11], and that this factor can be linked to the ability of individuals to adopt behavioral patterns similar to that observed in everyday life, and therefore to respond to it in a more realistic way [29].

However, the hypothesis that the sense of presence would be positively correlated with the learning gain was refuted. Thus, we cannot agree with the studies of Schrader & Bastiaens [6] and Lee, Wong & Fung [7], which showed that an increased sense of presence did lead to better learning outcomes. However, they did not compare different media formats. In our study, the fact that the Interactive VR condition was the highest at the sense of presence might have influenced this result. Linked to the previous section, the reasons for this result can be grounded in the theories of Cognitive Load [24] and Multimedia Learning [25].

5.3   Immersive Tendencies

Although participants in the Interactive VR condition had the lowest score for immersive tendencies, meaning they would be less inclined to feel the sense of presence, their scores were the highest in all ITC-SOPI factors. This result indicates that, contrary to the original study of Witmer & Singer [12], immersive tendencies were not a critical factor for the subjects to experience the sense of presence.

Therefore, the first hypothesis, that immersive tendencies would be positively correlated with the sense of presence, was rejected, allowing us to agree with the work of Murray, Fox & Pettifer [17], in which these variables were also not correlated. However, we cannot corroborate with studies of Schrader & Bastiaens [6], Khashe et al. [13] and Bulu [16], in which a positive relationship between immersive tendencies and sense of presence was identified.

The second hypothesis, that immersive tendencies would be positively correlated with the learning gain, was also refuted. In this sense, we can extend the results of Khashe et al. [13], which also did not find a positive association between immersive tendencies and performance. On the other hand, we cannot endorse the study of Schrader & Bastiaens [6], in which the immersive tendencies were positively related to both trivial and nontrivial learning outcomes.

It must be highlighted that our study has some differences from the ones mentioned in this discussion, as pointed out in the related work section. At the same time that it demonstrates the unprecedented character of the research, it also indicates that the results must be taken accordingly.

6   Conclusion

Creating educational applications for VR can be a laborious and costly endeavour [1]. In this sense, it is essential to investigate whether and in which ways these applications are useful for learning or not.

In order to contribute to understanding the potential of VR technology to support learning, this study analysed the sense of presence and the immersive tendencies of individuals across three different media formats of the same lesson, seeking for fair comparisons. We provide empirical evidence that immersion can really contribute to enhance learning, leading to better scores than a similar passive mode of instruction (Video). However, the supposition that adding interactivity to VR would result in better outcomes was rejected, and the findings were grounded on instructional design principles of Cognitive Load [24] and Multimedia Learning [25]. The sense of presence and the immersive tendencies appeared to be not critical factors in this equation.

As limitations of the study, it must be pointed out the small sample size, which did not allow the extraction of statistically significant differences in some cases, and the fact that it was a laboratory-controlled study. Field studies must be conducted to extend the findings in contexts of formal and non-formal educational.

Also, the use of knowledge retention tests as the only instrument to infer learning outcomes can be considered a limitation. Makransky, Borre-Gude & Mayer [14], for instance, added realistic measures of transfer, aimed to assess deep understanding and performance. The authors suggest that the evidence would not be found that if they had conducted only a retention test. Furthermore, a more in-depth study controlling the principles of the mentioned instructional design theories is needed, including the variables analysed in this study.

References

1. Allcoat, D., Mühlenen, A.V.: Learning in virtual reality: effects on performance, emotion, and engagement. Res. Learn. Technol. **26**, 10–25304 (2018)
2. Whitelock, D., Romano, D., Jelfs, A., Brna, P.: Perfect presence: what does this mean for the design of virtual learning environments? Educ. Inf. Technol. **5**(4), 277–289 (2000)
3. Heeter, C.: Being there: the subjective experience of presence. Presence Teleop. Virt. Environ. **1**(2), 262–271 (1992)
4. Dengel, A., Mägdefrau, J.: Presence is the key to understanding immersive learning. In: Beck, D., et al. (eds.) iLRN 2019. CCIS, vol. 1044, pp. 185–198. Springer, Cham (2019). https://doi.org/10.1007/978-3-030-23089-0_14
5. Lessiter, J., Freeman, J., Keogh, E., Davidoff, J.: A cross-media presence questionnaire: the ITC-sense of presence inventory. Presence Teleop. Virt. Environ. **10**(3), 282–297 (2001)
6. Schrader, C., Bastiaens, T.: Relations between the tendency to invest in virtual presence, actual virtual presence, and learning outcomes in educational computer games. Int. J. Hum.-Comput. Interact. **28**(12), 775–783 (2012)
7. Lee, E.A.L., Wong, K.W., Fung, C.C.: How does desktop virtual reality enhance learning outcomes? A structural equation modeling approach. Comput. Educ. **55**(4), 1424–1442 (2010)
8. Riva, G., Waterworth, J., Murray, D.: Extending the self through the tools and the others: a general framework for presence and social presence in mediated interactions. In: Interacting with Presence, pp. 9–31. Sciendo Migration (2014)
9. Tjon, D.M., Tinga, A.M., Alimardani, M., Louwerse, M.M.: Brain activity reflects sense of presence in 360° video for virtual reality. In: 28th International Conference on Information Systems Development (ISD 2019), August 2019
10. Slater, M., Wilbur, S.: A framework for immersive virtual environments (FIVE): speculations on the role of presence in virtual environments. Presence Teleop. Virt. Environ. **6**(6), 603–616 (1997)
11. Witmer, B.G., Singer, M.J.: Measuring presence in virtual environments: a presence questionnaire. Presence **7**(3), 225–240 (1998)
12. Banerjee, P., Bochenek, G.M., Ragusa, J.M.: Analyzing the relationship of presence and immersive tendencies on the conceptual design review process. J. Comput. Inf. Sci. Eng. **2**(1), 59–64 (2002)
13. Khashe, S., Becerik-Gerber, B., Lucas, G., Gratch, J.: Persuasive effects of immersion in virtual environments for measuring pro-environmental behaviors. In: ISARC Proceedings of the International Symposium on Automation and Robotics in Construction, vol. 35, pp. 1–7. IAARC Publications (2018)
14. Makransky, G., Borre-Gude, S., Mayer, R.E.: Motivational and cognitive benefits of training in immersive virtual reality based on multiple assessments. J. Comput. Assist. Learn. **35**, 691–707 (2019)
15. Parong, J., Mayer, R.E.: Learning science in immersive virtual reality. J. Educ. Psychol. **110**(6), 785 (2018)

16. Bulu, S.T.: Place presence, social presence, co-presence, and satisfaction in virtual worlds. Comput. Educ. **58**(1), 154–161 (2012)
17. Murray, C.D., Fox, J., Pettifer, S.: Absorption, dissociation, locus of control and presence in virtual reality. Comput. Hum. Behav. **23**(3), 1347–1354 (2007)
18. Olmos-Raya, E., Ferreira-Cavalcanti, J., Contero, M., Castellanos-Baena, M.C., Chicci-Giglioli, I.A., Alcañiz, M.: Mobile virtual reality as an educational platform: A pilot study on the impact of immersion and positive emotion induction in the learning process. Eurasia J. Math. Sci. Technol. Educ. **14**(6), 2045–2057 (2018)
19. Stanney, K.M., Mourant, R.R., Kennedy, R.S.: Human factors issues in virtual environments: a review of the literature. Presence-Teleop. Virt. Environ. **7**(4), 327–351 (1998)
20. The Body VR, Journey Inside the Cell (2016). Steam Repository. http://www.thebodyvr.com/journey-inside-a-cell. Accessed 31 Oct 2019
21. Brislin, R.W.: Back-translation for cross-cultural research. J. Cross Cult. Psychol. **1**(3), 185–216 (1970)
22. Hambleton, R.K., Zenisky, A.L.: Translating and adapting tests for cross-cultural assessments (2011)
23. Vasconcelos-Raposo, J., Melo, M., Teixeira, C., Cabral, L., Bessa, M.: Adaptation and validation of the ITC-sense of presence inventory for the Portuguese language. Int. J. Hum. Comput. Stud. **125**, 1–6 (2019)
24. Sweller, J.: Cognitive load theory, learning difficulty, and instructional design. Learn. Instr. **4**(4), 295–312 (1994)
25. Mayer, R.E.: Multimedia learning. In: Psychology of Learning and Motivation, vol. 41, pp. 85–139. Academic Press (2002)
26. Moreno, R., Mayer, R.E., Spires, H.A., Lester, J.C.: The case for social agency in computer-based teaching: do students learn more deeply when they interact with animated pedagogical agents? Cogn. Instr. **19**(2), 177–213 (2001)
27. Makransky, G., Terkildsen, T.S., Mayer, R.E.: Adding immersive virtual reality to a science lab simulation causes more presence but less learning. Learn. Instr. **60**, 225–236 (2017)
28. Schrader, C., Bastiaens, T.J.: The influence of virtual presence: effects on experienced cognitive load and learning outcomes in educational computer games. Comput. Hum. Behav. **28**(2), 648–658 (2012)
29. Slater, M., Lotto, B., Arnold, M.M., Sanchez-Vives, M.V.: How we experience immersive virtual environments: the concept of presence and its measurement. Anuario de Psicologia, **40**(2), 193–210 (2009). Meeting 37(1), 612–616

Empeiría*: Powering Future Education Training Systems with Device Agnostic Web-VR Apps

Matthew E. Miller[2] , Yuxin Yang[1] , Karl Kosko[1] ,
Richard Ferdig[1] , Cheng Chang Lu[1] , and Qiang Guan[1(✉)]

[1] Kent State University, Kent, OH 44240, USA
{yyang45, kkosko, rferdig, cclu, qguan}@kent.edu
[2] Case Western Reserve University, Cleveland, OH 44106, USA
mem311@case.edu

Abstract. This paper presents *Empeiría*, which uses cutting-edge technologies and novel virtual reality systems to enhance future in-class education training. *Empeiría* incorporates JavaScript, WebGL, WebVR, and powerful web graphics engines like Babylon.js to create immersive training experiences. It demonstrates a useful application of computer science concepts and increases the dissemination of edge technologies across academic disciplines. Most importantly, *Empeiría* improves education technology and professional training through the creation of two major software products; an immersive experience editing system (*Empeiría-E*) and an immersive experience viewing system (*Empeiría-V*). We show how these virtual reality systems can lead to more effective training and improve our understanding of trainees.

Keywords: Virtual reality · Babylon.js · Education technology · Computing methodologies · Virtual reality · Human-centered computing

1 Introduction

Videos of classroom instruction and students' learning are commonplace among tools used to train future and practicing teachers, and similar patterns of video use are found among other professions [1]. The use of such videos has demonstrated positive effects on teachers' professional knowledge. Despite the demonstrably positive effects and usefulness of videos for professional practice, there is a need to improve how well such videos represent the context of teaching. Recently, this desire has led to the introduction of 360-videos in teacher training [2–4]. Whereas what is viewable in a standard video is pre-selected by the videographer, 360-video format better reflects the teaching context by recording a spherical view of the classroom scenario and allowing viewers to adjust the field-of-view. In [2], authors found that this differentiation increases the perceptual capacity of a video, or what is perceivable in a recording. Put another way,

---

* *Empeiría* – Greek for "Experience".

© Springer Nature Switzerland AG 2020
J. Y. C. Chen and G. Fragomeni (Eds.): HCII 2020, LNCS 12191, pp. 287–300, 2020.
https://doi.org/10.1007/978-3-030-49698-2_19

teacher- trainees who view 360-videos are able to notice more professionally relevant events and describe these events in more detail than their counterparts who watch a standard video of the same lesson. By increasing the perceptual capacity of a video, 360-videos increase trainees' perceived immersion in the experience, thus better approximating a trainee's sense of observing the classroom in-person.

Prior studies of 360-videos describe recording from a single camera perspective [3, 4]. However, this doesn't accurately approximate reality as teachers seldomly stand in one place for an entire lesson, but instead move about the room. Thus, we sought to develop a multi-perspective, 360-video editing, viewing and sharing platform to further improve teacher training and more broadly, professional development; while also overcoming barriers to entry like technical expertise or coding experience.

Empeiría allows for members of a profession, that lacks technical expertise or coding experience to create immersive, 360-video training experiences. Its mission is to enable educators to improve their professional knowledge by immersive training simulations. To that end, *Empeiría* allows educators to easily create immersive training sessions, edit and augment them with annotations, distribute them to trainees, and collect data about the trainees' interaction and performance.

This paper will explore *Empeiría*'s creation and the creation of novel, virtual reality, systems from a computer scientist's perspective. It will show how WebVR, WebGL, JavaScript, and powerful graphics engines like Babylon.js (BJS) [5]. can be integrated to create convincing, immersive experiences and training simulations. It will make a case for device-agnostic web apps, modern web technology, and the utility of highly accessible products. *Empeiría* is an open framework for creating virtual reality, immersive professional development simulations, viewing those immersive sessions, and analyzing trainee's performance. *Empeiría* is device agnostic and works with most commodity head mounted displays (HMDs). The only requirement being a compatible web browser. This is made possible through our approach of leveraging web technology, WebVR and BJS to provide highly accessible service.

Empeiría has two major components; a simulation editor and a simulation viewer. The editor, *Empeiría-E*, allows educators to produce training simulations for distribution. The viewer, *Empeiría-V*, allows trainees to experience a production simulation and records quantitative data about their experience like which annotations they interact with, the camera perspectives they choose to use, their device's orientation over time, and their gaze vector. To better understand how these components work, it's important to conceptualize the educator's workflow.

The educator's workflow begins with the deployment of multiple 360-video-cameras throughout various locations in a classroom. Next, the educator begins recording the in-class session, from multiple perspectives. Once finished recording, the educator uploads the session's recordings to *Empeiría* and begins the editing/ production process. During the editing process educators augment the scene and enhance the session with virtual annotations that guide trainees involvement and professional noticing. After editing and augmentation, the simulation is distributed to trainees for consumption and improvement of their professional knowledge. Once distributed, the trainees enter the immersive experience from within *Empeiría-V*, the viewing system. As trainees experience the simulations, annotations they interact with, camera perspectives they choose to use, device's orientation overtime, and gaze vector are recorded (among other things) in a remote database-system for post-hoc analysis. This post-hoc analysis reveals trends, behaviors, and other insights that help educators, trainers, and researchers answer key questions.

Beyond the technical features, there exists several additional functional requirements such as the product needs to be widely accessible (device agnostic, cross platform), low cost to entry (open source), and easy to use (good design). The software product needs to be responsive, have good performance, and high quality of experience (QoE). It needs a simple user interface and a simple immersive experience. We expect that educators have limited exposure to novel technologies and limited technical expertise, as well as restricted device offerings and potential budget concerns.

Empeiría's significance is its demonstration of a novel application of WebVR and device agnostic web applications to the education technology space. It defines an open framework for editing 360-videos, adding annotations, creating immersive learning experiences, and distributing those experiences to users. It demonstrates how existing works can be pulled together and synthesizes to create a powerful software product which gives post-hoc insights to educators and researchers. Additionally, its supports the creation of better educators and, in turn, more prepared students. The implication being that more prepared students results in a better and more capable American community. Furthermore, it promotes the use of BJS and WebVR which will likely power the future of virtual reality on the web, cross platform functionality, and overcome major hurdles in the dissemination and popularization of virtual reality.

2   Related Work

As a multifaceted and cross-discipline project, that includes human-computer-interaction (HCI), this work relates many works. *Human-Computer Interaction* when describing its comprehensive account of the multidisciplinary field HCI: "it balances the technical and cognitive issues re-quired for understanding the subtle interplay between people and computers, particularly in emerging fields like multimedia and virtual environments." and a subtle interplay it is, there's so much going on it's hard to reconcile everything and for brevity, we won't attempt to [6]. The remaining portion of this section will describe the most critically relevant aspects of HCI as it overlaps with VR, web technology, and eye tracking.

In regards to the computer science literature: it touches upon HCI, virtual reality, 360-videos, eye tracking and the broad disciplines of web technology. In this case, web technologies are modern JavaScript and specifications like WebVR, and BJS. In regards to educational aspects like training and education technology; it touches upon teaching, practice, reflection, recall, cognitive load, physiological response, and the potential of immersive experiences to increase professional noticing and improve training.

In any case, there is an abundance of related work on these topics. However, there's limited work on building open and comprehensive frameworks (like ours). There's even less work that synthesizes many technologies to meet specific concerns in education technology. Note that, there's even less work (likely none) on building these comprehensive frameworks as device agnostic web apps powered by libraries like BJS, utilizing WebGL, and supporting WebVR. Attributes which we believe are important to the accessibility, dissemination, and support of virtual reality on the web. This is likely what our contribution to the science is, formulating an open framework and demonstrating a novel use of WebVR. The remainder of this section will be split into sub-sections that explore relevant work as major topics.

2.1 Virtual Reality

There's general research about virtual reality in the classroom [7]. There is work on combining virtual reality with mobile eye tracking to create experimental environments [8]. And, actually this process is so well established that we mention it here as a major consideration of our project, although it hasn't been fully integrated into our framework. In the case of [3], the objective is to study and experiment with shoppers as they move through and visually investigate a virtual store, but this is similar to what we are doing with education trainees as we study their navigation of the immersive classroom experience. There's work on real time gaze mapping in virtual environments, which is an interest of ours, and there's research on people getting sick from simulations, but findings that they are less prone to sickness when actively engaging with the scene/content, which is something we experienced [9, 10].

Cinematic Virtual Experience. In this case, the user is not experiencing a featured film, but instead a professional development/training media. The approaches and work are still applicable to our interest. There's research on increasing recall within these cinematic virtual experiences via gaze direction and flickering [11]. The primary candidate of these methodologies being publishers of educational or corporate training content (very similar to our stakeholders) [11]. There's work on guiding the users attention in 360-videos using videography and filmography techniques [12]. There's work on the effect of camera height, actor behavior, and viewer position on the user's experience of 360-videos [13]. All of these are considerations as we interact with our open framework and the creation of training simulations.

2.2 Web Technology

Device Agnostic Web Apps. There's work on WebVR, BJS, and the device agnostic possibilities of VR [14]. There's research on leveraging HTML5 and WebGL for simulation based Training in the U.S. Military to improve experience accessibility and dissemination, which again, is very similar to our interests [15]. There's a case study on a WebVR device agnostic web application for immersive museum exhibitions [16]. There's work on immersive 360-degree social experiences which is similar to our product, in that it uses modern web technologies [17]. There's research on making device agnostic products with web5VR framework, which is again similar to our approach [18]. However, none of these works provide an open framework for immersive experience augmentation, creation, dissemination, and trainee analysis. We consider them, but they aren't adequate to meet our needs.

BabylonJS. We chose to use BJS for our framework for reasons which are omitted here, but further explained in the System Design section. There's some relevant support for BJS as a performant and superior WebGL framework which is something we agree with and we used to make our selection [19]. Here's another example of BJS powering a WebVR application that is device agnostic, cross platform, only requires a browser [20]. However, again it doesn't suit our specific purpose.

WebVR. This article makes a good case for furthering the adoption of virtual reality with WebVR content, cross platform approaches, and HMDs, focusing on accessibility and compatibility with a broad-band of devices [21]. We consider some WebVR specific dev approaches, like an agile development approach to WebVR applications called "Roll & Raid". It attempts to improve the development of WebVR applications through lower cost, higher efficiency, stronger adaptiveness, and easier team management [22]. Here we find the most applicable case for WebVR, a product called AmbeintVR; it has a great description of why WebVR is so useful for device agnosticism, cross platformality. It is one of the most relevant papers to our work as it makes a similar case for WebVR [23]. Web-based GIS application for real-time interaction of underground infrastructure through virtual reality (uses BJS) [24]. Building a WebVR 360 viewer for the experiment, similar to what we are doing, but again lacks the full open framework aspect and immersive professional training [25]. These works set a precedence, but each lack what's required of *Empeiría*.

3 Research Significance

This section describes, in clear terms, why we our research is significant. It reiterates some of the previous points which we alluded to and further down the research significance into several major perspectives.

3.1 Computer Scientist's Perspective

It demonstrates a novel WebVR application that is device agnostic and highly accessible. It defines an open framework for editing 360-videos, adding annotations, creating immersive professional training experiences, and distributing them to users. To the best of our knowledge, no other works introduce a comprehensive open framework that fulfills these specific immersive training, education technology, requirements. Note that, our open framework might be used for any other type of training simulation [15]. Furthermore it demonstrates how existing technology can be synthesized to create new capabilities, and a rich and capable software product that provides stakeholders with a broad array of insights.

3.2 Educator's Perspective

For the educator, our work is significant because it improves the immersive training experience, trainees' detail recognition, and the perceptual capacity of 360-videos. While making these improvements, it reduces barriers to entry like technical expertise and cost. Furthermore, it leads to the creation of better educators, and in turn more prepared students.

3.3   Researcher's Perspective

It builds upon existing research works and demonstrates how valuable data can be collected from virtual reality experiences. It speaks to how that data might be visualized and interpreted. Unlike previous works, it uses a novel logging schema that suits our specific education technology stakeholder. Ultimately, It defines how edge technologies can help us better understand the user's experience and our training simulations. Where previous works falter, we bring the benefits of a comprehensive open framework.

4   System Design

There are several approaches to building virtual reality experiences: native-platform-dependent, native-cross-platform, or non-native platform-independent web app. However, these approaches require users to download, install and update dedicated applications. This complicates the user's life, but also further complicates developers' lives. Developers must go through and comply with app stores, appease publishers, and overcome learning curves associated with shifting between development platforms.

With the capabilities of modern web browsers, features that previously attracted developers to native applications are becoming dually available for web apps. Furthermore, with the creation of Progress Web Applications (PWAs) and accelerated WebGL rendering, web apps gain the offline-capabilities and performant features that made native development appealing. Considering this and the increasing capabilities of web browsers, building VR applications using HTML5, WebGL and JavaScript has become a seriously appealing development alternative.

Instead of going through restrictive app stores, these immersive experiences can be deploy directly to users, from the web. In this way, adoption-friction is reduced and users can explore immersive apps with nothing more than a web browser. Moreover, application updates and changes are adopted immediately and pushed to users independent of store-publishers. For these reasons, virtual reality on the web has great promise, long legs, and is our chosen approach to the ed-tech problem.

The ability to access rich VR experiences without a download or install is naturally appealing. For a developer to be able to create VR content for the masses using simple, affordable tools is obviously fantastic. Best of all, powerful and versatile libraries like BJS are fueling innovation and creating regularity in the development-process. For example, BJS' video-dome and VR-experience-helper allowed us to rapidly produce our immersive framework which can be distributed to phones, laptops, and HMDs. However, amidst the potential are limitations which provide challenges for us and other new WebVR techniques.

To tackle our project's mandates we create an open and extensible framework for immersive training experiences, that utilizes the modern web approach. We create a WebVR, WebGL, 360-video, and JavaScript framework which enables users to create annotated video immersive experiences and disseminate those immersive sessions for other users to consume. We primarily utilize BJS to interface with WebGL and create WebVR experiences. In addition, our app aims to report and profile trainees' behavior as they interact with the immersive scene. The result is a highly accessible, modular, and low-cost platform for educators. *Empeiría* is able to discover information about trainees' behavior, experience, and expertise. It can integrate with any data visualization and insight pipeline that quantifies performance metrics and makes complex information easily digestible. Figure 1 shows a high-level system architecture of *Empeiría*.

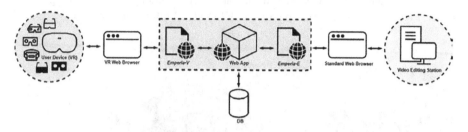

Fig. 1. The system architecture of *Empeiría*.

4.1 Immersive Canvas Architecture

Foundational to *Empeiría* are its immersive canvases. The immersive canvases are where viewing sessions happen and editing sessions take place. The major architectural components of an immersive experience canvas are shown in Fig. 2. *Empeiría-E* has six canvases which allow multi-perspective simulation editing and creation. *Empeiría-V* has one canvas which allows a viewer to experience an immersive session. The canvases utilize BJS Video Domes and HTML-Canvas to render 360-videos on *Empeiría-V* and *Empeiría-E*. Other functionality like VR experience helper and annotation manager are also built upon BJS. Whenever a WebVR experience takes place, there is an immersive canvas involved.

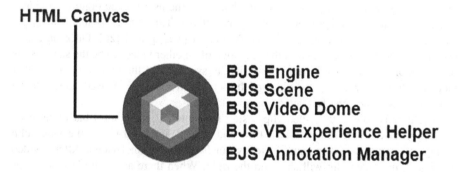

Fig. 2. The immersive canvas architecture

The engine drives the virtual scene's rendering. The scene is an object which contains a camera, lighting, video dome, vr-helper, and annotation management panel. In general, most components belong to the scene. A constant loop renders it in conjunction with a BJS engine.

4.2   Empeiría-E: The Editor

The first module of *Empeiría* is *Empeiría-E*, a multi perspective tool. It allows educators to view and edit six camera perspectives simultaneously. They can edit the videos independently or as a collection. The editor provides the user with the capability of controlling and editing videos, and the capability of adding and controlling annotations. Figure 3 shows an example of the 360-Video Editor (*Empeiría-E*).

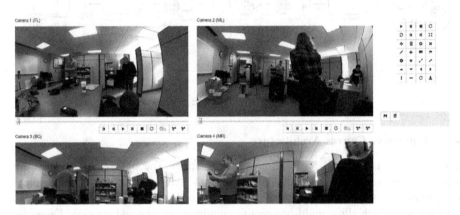

Fig. 3. Screenshot of *Empeiría-E*

Video. Each canvas (video feed) has a control bar and a slide bar which allows the session editor to skip backwards, skip forwards, play, pause, stop, restart the video, show the current time of the video, or cut video clips. There is also a more powerful master-toolbar on the right side of the page which has universal video controls like play-all, pause-all, jump-all, sync-all, etc. that allow the user to reconfigure the videos and create consistency between camera perspectives. This master-toolbar allows the user to select an active canvas via a DOM-tree inspecting tool [26]. Once an active canvas is selected, the user can set the play time of all other videos to be the same as the play time of the video of the active canvas, i.e. synchronize the play time of all other videos with the play time of the video of the active canvas. Also the user can toggle the active canvas to become full screen or normal size.

The user is able to cut video clips using the button in the control bar under each canvas. After the user selects a start time and an end time of a video, the video clip during selected time will be automatically cut from the original video. After a video clip is cut, the video clip will show on the right. When there are multiple video clips and the user wants to adjust the play order of those video clips, the user can drag any video clip and drop the video clip to a proper position as the user's wish. If the user thinks any video clip is redundant, the user can delete that video clip. After having video cut completed, the user can save the video clips sequence and create a final training experience narrative.

Camera 1 (FL)

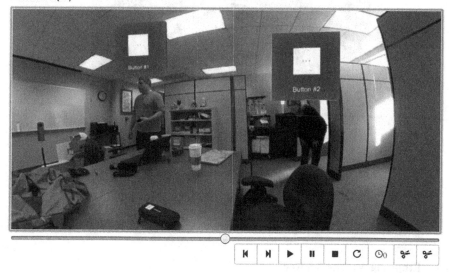

Fig. 4. Screenshot of video annotations.

Annotation. Whenever there is an active canvas, the user can add annotations of different types like text, button, comment, flag, exclamation, star and so on, to that canvas. After annotations are added, the user can control any annotation the user wants. The user has to first select an active annotation by clicking any annotation the user wants to control. There are several buttons under the master-toolbar providing the user with the ability to control annotations. The user can change the text on annotations, move the position of annotations, rotate annotations, adjust the size of annotations, and delete annotations as the user wishes. After adjusting one annotation, the user can deselect the active annotation in case of misoperating the annotation or the user can select another annotation, letting the new annotation to become active and deactivating the previous one. An example of video annotations is demonstrated in Fig. 4.

Working Principle of the Editor. The editor works by manipulating virtual scenes that belong to multiple HTML5 canvases. For each canvas, there is a BJS Engine which handles the scene's rendering. BJS and the associated JavaScript allow us to create and manage the virtual scene, camera positioning, lighting, enabled controllers, etc. Primarily this is done by the use of a BJS Video Dome which is a convenient class allowing us to play and manipulate 360-videos. It does this by essentially projecting the video on an inverted sphere. So, we can conceptualize the editing framework as a collection of six spheres which are edited, viewed, manipulated independently of each other. Although it isn't obvious from the camera's perspective that you're inside a sphere, it becomes obvious if you scroll out (Fig. 5).

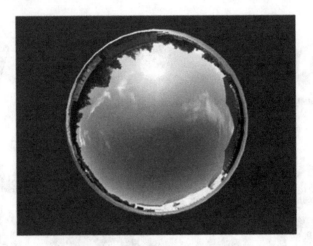

Fig. 5. Video dome at a distance

4.3   Empeiría-V: The Viewer

As shown in Fig. 6, the VR-Viewer (*Empeiría-V*) has all the standard capabilities available in a modern web browsing experience. There is also a session interaction reporting component in the background which is the most important aspect of the viewer. The session interaction reporting reports data about user's headset orientation over time, gaze vector, etc. This session reporting is the primary data which drives the insights and analysis of the Extended Reality team and their education technology objectives.

Fig. 6. Screenshot *Empeiría-V*

Figure 7 portrays an immersive experience which is occurring on a conventional laptop, not an HMD. This is made possible because the framework is device agnostic and works with any compatible browser. Note that, it additionally works on an Oculus Go.

Fig. 7. Inside a VR session

4.4 Data Model

We have designed the following data models in our framework. Figure 8 presents entities in our data models and their relationships. "User" entity records information of each user. "Video" entity records information of each video. "Annotation" entity records information of each annotation. "VideoClip" entity records information of each sequence of video clips. "ViewerSession" entity records information of user's behavior when using the viewer. The relationship between two entities are represented by an arrow. All relationships between entities in our data models are one-to-many relationships, i.e. the entity pointed by the arrow has multiple entities that is on the other side of the arrow. One "User" entity has many "VideoClip" entities, "Video" entities, and "ViewerSession" entities. And one "Video" entity has many "Annotation" entities.

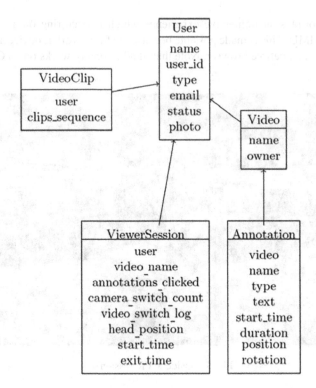

Fig. 8. Data model and relationships

5 Conclusion and Future Work

Immersive training experiences with high perceptual capacity 360-videos are improving professional development and training effectiveness. Trainees that are involved with immersive experiences can recall more details than their counterparts which experience standard videos. However, educators lack a convincing framework for creating immersive experiences, distributing them to trainees, and analyzing performance. *Empeiría* introduces that solution and helps extend the possibilities of professional development tools.

Furthermore, *Empeiría*, does so in a way that is open, highly accessible, device agnostic, platform independent, and novel. It takes advantage of cutting-edge technologies like Babylon.js, WebVR, and commodity HMDs. It offers a platform for mass-distributed WebVR, immersive experiences and attempts to overcome the software engineering challenges of working with developing specifications. The result is a powerful product and open framework for immersive training experiences, performance reporting, and simulation editing that requires only a browser. Ultimately, it provides a specialized and novel product for education technologists and enables developers to easily extend the framework with conventional web technologies.

This paper presented an introduction and overview of the open *Empeiría* framework, it proposed an existing education technology problem and provided a novel application of computer science to solve it. It explored the established literature on HCI, virtual reality, WebVR, and building immersive experiences for the web. Finally, it demonstrated concrete examples of the framework's components and its underlying architecture.

Future work will focus on developing and extending upon this early prototype of *Empeiría*. As part of this development, we will investigate video streaming and network optimization techniques, novel data visualization techniques, and other promising product improvements. Eventually, eye tracking functionality will be added to augment commodity HMDs and improve post-hoc trainee analysis. Beyond that, new techniques in artificial intelligence, machine learning, and computer vision are being investigated to extend our analysis capabilities and make judgements about the content of immersive experiences, student and trainee behavior, and performance trends.

Project progress can be found at https://xr.kent.edu/.

Acknowledgement. This project is funded by National Science Foundation, Grant #1908159. Any opinions, findings, and conclusions or recommendations expressed in this paper are those of the author(s) and do not necessarily reflect the views of the National Science Foundation. David Catuhe (@Deltakosh) and his team at Microsoft for creating BJS, the backbone of our project, and for his trouble-shooting responsiveness on BJS-forum.

References

1. Grossman, P., Compton, C., Igra, D., Ronfeldt, M., Shahan, E., Williamson, P.: Teaching practice: a cross-professional perspective. Teachers Coll. Rec. **111**(9), 2055–2100 (2009)
2. Kosko, K., Ferdig, R., Zolfaghari, M.: Preservice teachers' noticing in the context of 360 video (2019)
3. Roche, L., Gal-Petitfaux, N.: Using 360° video in physical education teacher education (2017)
4. Walshe, N., Driver, P.: Developing reflective trainee teacher practice with 360-degree video. Teach. Teach. Educ. **78**, 97–105 (2019). https://doi.org/10.1016/j.tate.2018.11.009
5. "Babylon.js: Powerful, Beautiful, Simple, Open - Web-Based 3D At Its Best," *Babylon.js*. https://www.babylonjs.com. Accessed 31 Jan 2020
6. Preece, J., Rogers, Y., Sharp, H., Benyon, D., Holland, S., Carey, T.: Human-Computer Interaction. Addison-Wesley Longman Ltd., Boston (1994)
7. Pantelidis, V.S.: Virtual reality in the classroom. Educ. Technol. **33**(4), 23–27 (1993)
8. Meißner, M., Pfeiffer, J., Pfeiffer, T., Oppewal, H.: Combining virtual reality and mobile eye tracking to provide a naturalistic experimental environment for shopper research. J. Bus. Res. **100**, 445–458 (2019). https://doi.org/10.1016/j.jbusres.2017.09.028
9. Kraus, M., Kilian, T., Fuchs, J.: Real-time gaze mapping in virtual environments. In: Presented at the EUROVIS 2019 : 21st EG/VGTC Conference on Visualization (2019). https://doi.org/10.2312/eurp.20191135
10. Sharples, S., Cobb, S., Moody, A., Wilson, J.R.: Virtual reality induced symptoms and effects (VRISE): comparison of head mounted display (HMD), desktop and projection display systems. Displays **29**(2), 58–69 (2008). https://doi.org/10.1016/j.displa.2007.09.005

11. Rothe, S., Althammer, F., Khamis, M.: GazeRecall: using gaze direction to increase recall of details in cinematic virtual reality. In: Proceedings of the 17th International Conference on Mobile and Ubiquitous Multimedia, Cairo, Egypt, pp. 115–119 (2018). https://doi.org/10.1145/3282894.3282903

12. Sheikh, A., Brown, A., Watson, Z., Evans, M.: Directing attention in 360-degree video, 29-9 (2016). https://doi.org/10.1049/ibc.2016.0029

13. Keskinen, T., et al.: The effect of camera height, actor behavior, and viewer position on the user experience of 360° videos (2019). https://doi.org/10.1109/vr.2019.8797843

14. Jovanovi, A.: Review of modern virtual reality HMD devices and development tools, p. 5 (2017)

15. Maxwell, D., Heilmann, M.: Leveraging HTML5 and WebGL to address information assurance barriers for simulation based training in the U.S. military leveraging HTML5 and WebGL to address information assurance barriers for simulation based training in the U.S. Military (2017)

16. Oliver, A., del Molino, J., Cañellas, M., Clar, A., Bibiloni, A.: VR macintosh museum: case study of a WebVR application. In: Rocha, Á., Adeli, H., Reis, L.P., Costanzo, S. (eds.) WorldCIST'19 2019. AISC, vol. 931, pp. 275–284. Springer, Cham (2019). https://doi.org/10.1007/978-3-030-16184-2_27

17. Gunkel, S., Prins, M., Stokking, H., Niamut, O.: WebVR meets WebRTC: towards 360-degree social VR experiences. In: 2017 IEEE Virtual Reality (VR), pp. 457–458 (2017). https://doi.org/10.1109/vr.2017.7892377

18. Serpi, M., Carcangiu, A., Murru, A., Spano, L.D.: Web5VR: a flexible framework for integrating virtual reality input and output devices on the web. In: Proceedings ACM Hum.-Computer Interacting, vol. 2, no. EICS, pp. 4:1–4:19 (2018). https://doi.org/10.1145/3179429

19. Nordin, M.: An optimal solution for implementing a specific 3D web application (2016)

20. JPEG White paper: Towards a Standardized Framework for Media Blockchain and Distributed Ledger Technologies (2019)

21. Dibbern, C., Uhr, M., Krupke, D., Steinicke, F.: Can WebVR further the adoption of Virtual Reality? (2018). https://doi.org/10.18420/muc2018-up-0249

22. Shen, Z., Jia, J.: Agile development of WebVR applications. Int. J. Virtual Real. 9(3), 47–52 (2010). https://doi.org/10.20870/IJVR.2010.9.3.2778

23. Verma, S., Carlson, D.: AmbientVR : blending IoT interaction capabilities with web-based virtual reality (2017)

24. Jurado, J.M., Graciano, A., Ortega, L., Feito, F.R.: Web-based GIS application for real-time interaction of underground infrastructure through virtual reality. In: Proceedings of the 25th ACM SIGSPATIAL International Conference on Advances in Geographic Information Systems, Redondo Beach, CA, USA, pp. 1–4 (2017). https://doi.org/10.1145/3139958.3140004

25. Pakkanen, T., et al.: Interaction with WebVR 360° video player: comparing three interaction paradigms. In: 2017 IEEE Virtual Reality (VR), pp. 279–280 (2017). https://doi.org/10.1109/vr.2017.7892285

26. 骆也, luoye-fe/dom-inspector (2019)

Did You Say *Buttonless?* Exploring Alternative Modes of Sensory Engagement for Augmented Reality Storytelling Experiences

Richard Olaniyan, Travis Harvey, Heather Hendrixson,
and Jennifer Palilonis$^{(\boxtimes)}$

Ball State University, Muncie, IN 47304, USA
{arolaniyan, tcharvey, hahendrixson, jageorge2}@bsu.edu

Abstract. Augmented Reality designers and content creators continue to explore ways to engage audiences. However, studies have yet to focus on how different modes of interaction affect understanding and immersion in AR environments. To address this, a simulation and focus group was conducted to elicit feedback about five different modes of interaction: sound, touch, haptic feedback, presence, and gesture. Results identified four themes, with gesture interaction garnering more appeal and immersion than alternatives. Accessibility and self-consciousness in public settings were illuminated during the simulation, which highlighted barriers related to some modes of interaction.

Keywords: Augmented Reality · Immersive technology · User experience

1 Introduction

Worldwide use of Augmented Reality (AR) is on track to surpass one billion by 2020, and the demographics of AR users are also evolving. Although most AR users are young adults, older adults are adopting AR at a steady rate. For example, older generations are achieving health improvement goals through AR apps like Pokemon Go, with their increasingly tech-savvy grandchildren [1]. Likewise, an increasing number of gaming experiences center on augmented reality, and AR is used in educational contexts, to enhance shopping experiences, to facilitate home improvement activities, and more. AR's pervasiveness has even prompted designers to propose new design principles for this space. For example, AR research has found that regardless of the audience demographics, design clutter limits user engagement and length of use. Mindful UX implores designers to "keep it simple," recognizing that each additional screen or click may cause AR interfaces to be cumbersome and confusing. The more inputs required by AR interface design, the higher the likelihood that users will abandon the flow.

As AR continues to expand, successful experiences must satisfy specific user experience needs for a broader demographic of users. However, little explores AR user experiences that center on alternative modes of engagement, such as gesture, sound, haptics, and presence. Gesture refers to instances in which users physically enact specific movements to interact. For example, if a game on a mobile device requires a participant to

© Springer Nature Switzerland AG 2020
J. Y. C. Chen and G. Fragomeni (Eds.): HCII 2020, LNCS 12191, pp. 301–313, 2020.
https://doi.org/10.1007/978-3-030-49698-2_20

unlock a new level, a player might be prompted to make a physical hand movement that mimics the unlocking of a door. Sound refers to instances in which user attention and interaction is driven by audio, like a voice guiding drivers while using mobile GPS apps. Haptic feedback refers to instances in which a device emits a vibration to convey information. For example, a video game controller might rumble as the player veers from a racetrack onto a rough road. Finally, presence refers to instances in which a device's GPS capabilities are used to sense and react to a user's location. For example, haptic feedback is engaged with a *Pokemon Go* player approaches a Pokestop.

Certainly, different modes of feedback are more or less appropriate, depending upon the context of use and type of experience. However, user preferences are also relevant. Thus, a team of researchers at a mid-sized Midwestern university developed a series of prototypes for a location-based AR experience intended for use in concept testing of user engagement preferences. Prototypes were specifically and individually designed to test five discrete modes of sensory engagement and interaction: touch, gesture, sound, haptic feedback, and presence in a physical space. For this experiment, AR content included storytelling about campus history in a location-based AR experience.

Concept testing research was conducted to conceptualize a storytelling experience and to determine user requirements for this location-based augmented reality deployment. To implement concept testing, researchers adapted elements of the Triptech method [2] for evaluating early design concepts. This approach uncovers critical user requirements for a location-based AR experience and informs future developments. With this in mind, the project presented here was designed to discover the levels of engagement that alternative forms of interaction contribute to the user experience and whether they may be more engaging than the traditional button-centered paradigm used by a wide variety of apps and interactive products. This paper chronicles the process of testing five modes of sensory engagement using focus groups, simulations, and surveys based on the Triptech Method. With a focus on engagement and understanding, the satisfaction levels of the five modes are compared, evaluated and discussed.

2   Review of Literature

Advancement in smart device technologies and the popularity of smartphones have created a competitive AR mobile app market. From 2017 to 2025, the estimated market size is projected to increase from three billion to 198 billion dollars [3]. This relatively new technology is also highly accessible. While large corporations may hire professional developers to create AR apps, there are numerous inexpensive AR software options available allowing novice designers to create an experience adding to a competitive market. Insights and innovative solutions are needed to stand apart in the AR crowd. This section is an overview of recent research regarding AR user experience strategies and how the touch, sound, haptic, gesture and presence modes of engagement have been used to heighten user engagement.

2.1   AR User Experience

One strategy a Scandinavian dairy company called Arla used to build an AR audience was to appeal to emotions. Researchers conducted a study designed to test participant's emotional responses while interacting with an Arla milk package. When the container's AR code was scanned, an animated kitten jumped from the container and explored the surrounding environment, inviting users to play and interact. By swiping the screen, users could pet the cat and trigger him to do tricks. Participants overwhelmingly reported positive emotions, such as inspiration, encouragement, and excitement. Through the mode of touch, participants were able to mimic the experience of playing with an actual cat, which generated positive emotions. The authors recommend fostering opportunities to interact with AR content through "multiple natural methods, such as speech, touch, and gestures," to promote realism [4]. To attract and retain users, app designers must also consider how to choose interaction modes thoughtfully. Although touch and sound are familiar and require little instruction, there are potential downsides to keeping interactions routine. A study conducted to determine the effect of AR on retail customer experience, satisfaction, and willingness to buy, found that customers require stimulation, self-expression, and novelty to remain interested and engaged [5].

2.2   Touch

Touch may be a universal standard for mobile devices, but accuracy within the small screen remains difficult for many users. Experimental methods to solve this challenge, such as the TouchTap technique, have been developed, but the awkwardness of the technique often detracts from the experience, resulting in no significant change in user satisfaction [6]. Another downside touch interaction is the tendency for users to accidentally trigger an unwanted interaction. According to one study, 1,536 of 4,188 touch event data samples were unintended actions by users, with the vast majority made on the outer edges of the screen [7].

2.3   Sound

Sound is another mode of interaction familiar among mobile device users. In a study conducted to discover HCI guidelines when designing spoken command interactions, researchers found that although sound led to cognitive recall, frustration exists when sound moves at a pace that leaves users "feeling rushed or missing parts of the interaction" [8]. Notifications are one-way app designers employ to keep users engaged. Although sound alerts can be efficient at gaining user attention, they are also perceived as annoying and distracting, which leads many users to disengage. This challenge has led developers to create deep learning technologies that send notifications at more acceptable times for users [9].

2.4 Haptics

Haptic feedback is well-known, but not as widely used as touch and sound. Recently, however, there has been more discussion about the connection between haptics and emotional responses. The EmoJacket is a wearable jacket designed to enhance emotional immersion and is constructed with vibrotactile actuators throughout the arms, chest and neck. Research found by stimulating certain areas of the body through vibration, an associated emotional reaction occurs, which enhances specific feelings. When participants wore the EmoJacket while viewing a film clip focused on love, haptic feedback was used to heighten feelings of love. Participants reported an average 35% increase in both immersiveness and heightened emotional experiences while watching the clips and wearing the jacket than when without it [10].

2.5 Presence

Presence refers to tracking technology that senses users' locations and reacts to movement. Markerless Augmented Reality accurately detects and maps real-world environments, making it possible to place virtual objects in a real context and anchor them in place without a QR code. Successful use of this technology can be found at public cultural sites and inside museums. The MuseumEye project invited participants to explore a structured AR walkthrough Leeds museum in which objects appeared when approached. The app sensed a user's location and responded accordingly without requiring the user to stop and scan an object or QR code. This gives participants a seamless tour through the museum with very little distraction or interruption. Seventy-seven percent of participants reported that using the AR technology made the experience more enjoyable and more immersive [11].

2.6 Gesture

Gesture is a lesser-known mode of interaction, but the use of it as a UX design dimension is on the rise. This technology centers on accelerometer-based or gyrometer/magnetometer behaviors in smartphones. Hand Shaking Authentication was developed as a novel protection mechanism for smartphone security. However, because human movements can vary slightly during each attempt, successful authentications can require several attempts [12]. A study to gauge participant satisfaction when asked to create their own workable gestures found that despite some frustration about the need for repeated attempts; however, participants overwhelmingly enjoyed the gesture engagement [13].

3 Methodology

Triptech method [2] is used "evaluate UX in the early process of product development." This method includes use of a survey and then focus group. The survey is used to "assess the relative frequency and perceived importance of user needs independently from how we plan to address them" [2]. Focus groups then allow participants to give feedback about design solutions created to address needs identified in the survey.

Coupled with focus groups, storyboards can also be used to demonstrate a particular technology scenario and then assess perceived user needs independently from how a particular product intends to address them. For this study, focus groups elicited feedback about participants' familiarity with and opinions of different modes of interactivity. This method is well suited for the early phases of user experience design when user feedback can effectively guide a better understanding of preferred modes of engagement.

After asking a set of questions to determine user preferences, participants were presented with storyboards and low-fidelity prototypes to illustrate a scenario for each of the five sensory modes outlined above. To enrich results, the User Engagement Scale Short-Form (UES) [14] was administered. The UES is a 12-item survey ideally suited for early feedback about human-computer experiences.

3.1 Part One: Simulation

Simulation sessions were conducted with 28 participants, who visited five stations, each focused on a different mode of interaction. At each station participants were given instructions before engaging with a prototype designed for a specific interaction type. The UES survey was then administered to measure perceived levels of immersion. Four sets of three questions related to perceptions of immersion, frustration, appeals, and personal positives with each mode of interaction. Personal positives refer to users' perceptions that an interaction type is worthwhile, rewarding, or otherwise interesting. Upon completion of the survey at one station, each participant moved on to the next station until all five were complete.

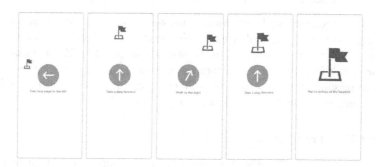

Fig. 1. Screen display of the presence simulation. The visuals served as on-screen instructions that participants followed to direct them to a desired location.

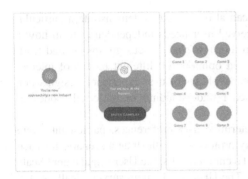

Fig. 2. The first screen for the touch simulation appeared when participants began to walk. The second screen appeared when they arrived at a certain location. Screen three loaded when "enter gameplay" was tapped.

Presence. For the presence mode of interaction, participants were handed a mobile device and told to follow the on-screen instructions that directed them to a location. Figure 1 shows the screens associated with the presence mode of interaction.

Sound. For the sound mode of interaction, participants were asked to mill around the testing room carrying a mobile phone that gave audio instructions. The first pre-recorded message explained, "when you hear this sound [bell ding] you have reached the hotspot." Participants then continued to walk until they heard the pre-recorded audio sound of the bell and a voice confirming they had arrived at the hotspot.

Haptic. For the haptic mode of interaction, participants were again asked to mill around the room with a mobile device in search of a hotspot. Once the hotspot was reached, the mobile device generated a unique haptic pattern confirming their arrival.

Touch. For the touch mode of interaction (Fig. 2), participants were instructed to walk around the room guided by on-screen instructions. They were then required to touch the buttons on the mobile device screen to indicate they had arrived at the hotspot. Participants concluded the test by touching the "enter gameplay" button.

Gesture. In the gesture simulation, participants were given a mobile phone and asked to play a gesture-based dice roll game. This game had a single, six-sided die that responded to the physical movement of the phone in a spatial XYZ axis measured by the phone's built-in gyrometer/magnetometer sensors. To allow enough time for participants to reasonably interact with the rolling feature, they were asked to continue rolling the dice by moving the phone until they rolled a six.

3.2   Part Two: Focus Group

Thirty-two people participated in three separate focus groups. Each interaction mode was presented separately in 10 storyboards, two for each mode. The first storyboard highlighted a scenario meant to elicit feedback about features that facilitate *understanding,* and a second storyboard illustrated scenarios meant to elicit feedback about *immersive features*. Figures 3 provide one example of how each set of storyboards was designed. Participants were provided with a cursory definition of each mode to ensure they had a baseline understanding of each storyboard. They were then asked: *Does the application effectively help you understand where you are?*

Fig. 3. These illustrations represent storyboards for the gesture mode of interaction. Similar storyboards were developed for the other four modes of interaction.

After participants were shown the second storyboard, they were asked questions designed to elicit feedback about their perceived levels of immersion and understanding. Participants were also allowed to discuss any additional thoughts about each mode of interaction. Focus group sessions were audio-recorded and transcribed.

4   Results

These methods resulted in two types of data. Results from the UES survey provided quantitative feedback about participants' perceptions of immersion, frustration, appeals, and personal positives for each interaction mode. Focus groups resulted in qualitative feedback about levels of immersion and understanding of the different modes.

4.1   Part One: Simulation

UES survey questions are grouped into four thematic areas: Immersion [items 1, 2, 3], Frustration [items 4, 5, 6], Appeal [items 7, 8, 9], and Personal Rewards/Positives [items 10, 11, 12]. Participant responses were grouped according to each thematic area (Figs. 4, 5, 6 and 7).

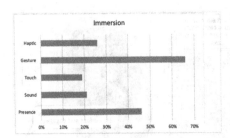

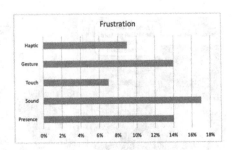

Fig. 4. Items 1–3 combine to indicate users' overall sense of immersion.

Fig. 5. Items 4–6 combine to indicate users' overall sense of frustration.

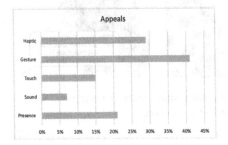

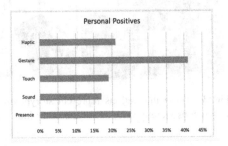

Fig. 6. Items 7–9 combine to indicate users' overall sense of appeal.

Fig. 7. Items 10–12 combine to indicate personal positives expressed by users.

Participants reported they were most immersed in the gesture mode of engagement. Similar trends are evident in the responses to two other questions in this thematic area. However, participants reported the least level of immersion when using the touch mode of interaction. Participants also reported that they were most frustrated by the sound mode of engagement. The touch mode, however, provided the least frustration.

Participants reported the highest level of appeal with gesture interaction. The touch mode of interaction, however, garnered the least appeal across all three questions. Participants also reported gesture was the most worthwhile, rewarding, and/or interesting, with sound interaction scoring the lowest in those same categories.

4.2   Part Two: Focus Group

Focus group recordings were transcribed and analyzed for thematic patterns. Key remarks and moments when the overwhelming majority of participants agreed were chronicled. The content was organized by mode of interactivity and key findings relevant to the majority of participants were highlighted for each mode (Table 1).

Table 1. N = number of participants who shared similar statements during the focus group.

Mode	Key finding	Representative quote	N
Sound	Sound can be overwhelming or distracting, so participants often keep their phones on silent	"I have my phone on silent all the time. If I have any sort of ringtone it is a haptic vibrate."	30
Haptic	Adds a dynamic quality to user experience	"I enjoy having the vibration on, ... in Skyrim if you are shooting an arrow with a bow it will give you a different sensation than if you are going sword to sword ... I like how the vibration will give you the sense that you are not moving some random object but that you are engaged."	29
Gesture	Self-conscious about acting out physical gestures in public	"But I can see, like by yourself, or if you are walking around just trying to catch something or do whatever. It was just kind of awkward and feel people watching you."	22
Presence	It provides a reliable sense of understanding of one's location	"For me, it's very reassuring to know that something is keeping track, I also live alone, so for some documentation to know about my whereabouts."	28
Touch	Touch is expected. It is vital and taken as standard	"And think nowadays how many screens do you come across that are not even touch screens? I mean like TVs and stuff like that, I mean most computers all phones are almost touch screen."	30

Sound. Participants reported that while in public, sound is not appealing. Subsequently, nearly every participant indicated a preference to have their phones on silent at all times. All participants noted that the only time sound is truly necessary for comprehension is when watching videos on platforms like You Tube and Netflix. However, many participants reported that sound adds to a sense of immersion, specifically when playing video games on home consoles, and several participants said they refrain from using sound on handheld devices. One participant indicated that sound was a key to his ability to successfully feel immersed during gameplay on his Xbox at home. Furthermore, another participant distinguished the need for sound during gameplay on their console as opposed to playing games on the mobile device. The participant explained that they never focus solely on gameplay while using their mobile device, instead, they are "usually doing two things at the same time." The participant noted: "I am putting all of my attention into [playing the game at home]."

Haptic. Many participants said haptic feedback clearly offered a second layer of engagement in a variety of gameplay examples. A few participants agreed with this statement: "...with the video games. If your controllers die, ... I notice it. And I am sitting there and it's not vibrating. You miss it." Haptic feedback was viewed as a significant mode for providing notifications and more in-depth immersion. A few concerns were raised regarding the pairing of vibration and the physical affordances portrayed with action. If haptic feedback fails to match an action, then participants reported it is annoying. Participants claimed that haptic feedback is most effective when precisely paired with real-life occurrences, such as explosions or firing a gun. As one participant explained, "Some video games, if you are running it's vibrating, I don't want that. I want something actually happening. I don't like vibrations happening the whole time."

Gesture. Participants most frequently voiced concerns about feeling self-conscious about completing gestures in public spaces. To offset the discomfort, participants agreed that subtle movements with a group of friends made gameplay less awkward. One participant shared, that when "interacting with my phone in public, I try to make it as discreet as possible, so that I am not too present in the world. I don't want to be super eccentric with my body. If the gestures were to happen, if they were like subtle gestures." Despite this aversion, the second most frequently voiced theme related to how gesture added to the immersion. "I think that because you are actually making the gesture that you want to do in the game, it makes it feel like you are literally in the game." Participants widely accepted that gesture was a novel form of interactivity.

Presence. Participants felt positive about the mode of presence, claiming it provided understanding and clarity in regard to their actions. Experiences shared mostly related to situations in which presence helped users while they traveled to new locations or felt lost. Many participants shared scenarios in which presence can aid in security and safety. One participant shared a story about a recent Uber ride: "when they've made a wrong turn, and before I noticed there was a wrong turn, I got a notification from the app … letting me know that your driver is off course. My options were an emergency call or I feel safe. And then I felt safe."

Touch. The mode of touch resulted in the fewest number of focus group insights. Participants widely claimed that touch interactivity is beneficial when making simple and direct actions. Participants claimed that touch is better suited to affirming their decisions, as it makes them feel confident that the device was registering their requests. Participants shared an overall familiarity with touch and on-screen buttons, but this mode failed to elicit any interest or attraction. It was agreed upon that the touch mode is reliable but generates little to no sense of immersion in general.

5   Discussion

Collectively, the simulation experiments and focus groups resulted in the identification of three key themes, which are outlined in the sections that follow.

Presence and Gesture are Regarded as More Immersive by Users. Across the five engagement modes tested, presence and gesture clearly received the most positive feedback, while sound and touch had the lowest positive feedback. One possible reason for this could be novelty. Engaging with a mobile device with touch and sound is likely not remarkable to users because it is routine. As with driving a car after years of experience, little thought or confusion arises during the ride in regard to the driving process itself. Instead, one may commonly dissociate or go to *autopilot,* and awareness of efficiency arises. The same is true when a man takes out his mobile device to check email, for example. After taking this action numerous times, little thought or reflection occurs.

Conversely, new experiences are by nature immersive because they are fresh and require more attention than more familiar situations. This is also known as the novelty effect. "The novelty effect is an increased motivation to use something, or an increase in the perceived usability of something, on account of its newness. When novelty eventually fades, usage patterns and/or perceived usability changes" [15]. As presence and gesture are less commonly used modes of engagement with often highly special- ized uses, participants were less familiar, and by the data results, more immersed and satisfied with their experiences. While both modes remain engaging, it would be predictable that satisfaction may decline after the novelty effect has passed.

Users are Concerned About How They will be Perceived When Engaging Some Modes in Public Spaces. The majority of participants showed a preference for modes that would reduce their public portrayal and "awkwardness." In both the simulation and focus groups, the haptic and gesture modes of interaction received positive remarks and rated highest for clarity and certainty. However, nearly all participants voiced an aversion regarding the public disturbance sound causes, preferring haptics as a less disruptive prompt. Participants also mentioned they are apprehensive about engaging in noticeable physical motions in public due to possible embarrassment. Despite the highly positive feedback the gesture mode received, too much physicality in the public may dissuade users from the experience. Participants shared concerns that moving about while using a gesture motivated app alone in public would make them feel uneasy. Participants also noted that the demands of a gesture-based app are far more acceptable when used with a small group of friends and everyone is exercising the gestures together. Sound, gesture, and even presence each raised concerns about unwanted public attention and had the potential to cause distress among participants. Haptic feedback was more appealing to the users as a way to skirt this concern, however, some participants said vibrations could be invasive.

Haptic Feedback may also Provide a Necessary Alternative Option for Users with Disabilities. A blind participant shared significant approval for sound and haptic feedback and voiced concerns about the other modes. This participant also advocated for combining modes of interaction. When partnered with sound, the haptic mode can be best suited for those who are blind or have issues with sight. Likewise, users who are deaf or hard of hearing may also find that this mode preferable. Haptic feedback has been used in even more rare cases of "deafblindness." Deafblindness – defined by the Nordic Welfare Center as "a combined vision and hearing impairment of such severity that it is hard for the impaired senses to compensate for each other" – is a circumstance that uniquely demands the use of haptics. With different forms of stimulation patterns and the application of this mode in wearables and "smart" textiles, scientists and doctors hope to improve perception, communication, and quality of life for people with deafblindness [16]. Some participants shared concerns about the frequency of haptic feedback, noting that over time, it may become a nuisance to have haptics for a wide range of prompts. Yet, results from the haptic feedback simulation show an overwhelming enthusiasm for this type of interactivity.

5.1 Limitations and Future Work

Some limitations exist related to this study. First, the age group of participants ranged from approximately 18–40 and all were affiliated (students, faculty, or staff) with a mid-sized Midwestern university, which may have limited demographic diversity. Second, the environment was controlled and did not represent a natural use setting. To test these modes in the wild, with a fully functional mid to high-fidelity app, could provide new insights.

Future work could investigate user engagement when combining various modes. For example, the gesture mode of interaction could be supported by sound for greater immersion. If the user was asked to complete an unlocking gesture to advance to a new level in a game, the accompanying sound of a lock opening would likely enhance the experience while offering confirmation the required action is complete. Studying mode combinations in the wild with a fully developed app is recommended. Additionally, the current findings are presented for designers of mobile augmented reality apps. However, the mode responses identified above are potentially transferable to other interfaces such as tablets and tabletops. Future work could investigate the applicability of the mode engagement using other technologies.

References

1. Althoff, T., White, R.W., Horvitz, E.: Influence of Pokémon go on physical activity: study and implications. J. Med. Internet Res. **18**(12), e315 (2016). https://doi.org/10.2196/jmir. 6759
2. Séguin, J.A., Scharff, A., Pedersen, K.: Triptech: a method for evaluating early design concepts (2019). https://doi.org/10.1145/3290607.3299061
3. Liu, S.: Global Augmented Reality Market Size 2025 | Statista, 19 December 2019. Statista website. https://www.statista.com/statistics/897587/world-augmented-reality-market-value/. Accessed 28 Feb 2020
4. Dirin, A., Laine, T.: User experience in mobile augmented reality: emotions, challenges, opportunities and best practices. Computers **7**(2), 33 (n.d.). https://doi.org/10.3390/computers7020033
5. Poushneh, A., Vasquez-Parraga, A.Z.: Discernible impact of augmented reality on retail customer's experience, satisfaction and willingness to buy. J. Retail. Consum. Serv. **34**, 229–234 (2017). https://doi.org/10.1016/j.jretconser.2016.10.005
6. Fuccella, V., Martin, B.: TouchTap (2017). https://doi.org/10.1145/3125571.3125579
7. Matero, J., Colley, A.: Identifying unintentional touches on handheld touch screen devices (2012). https://doi.org/10.1145/2317956.2318031
8. Murad, C., Munteanu, C., Cowan, B.R., Clark, L.: Revolution or evolution? Speech interaction and HCI design guidelines. IEEE Pervasive Comput. **18**(2), 33–45 (2019). https://doi.org/10.1109/mprv.2019.2906991

9. Huang, T.H.-D., Kao, H.-Y.: C-3PO: Click-sequence-aware deeP neural network (DNN)-based Pop-uPs recOmmendation. Soft. Comput. **23**(22), 11793–11799 (2018). https://doi.org/10.1007/s00500-018-03730-5

10. Arafsha, F., Alam, K.M., Saddik, A.E.: EmoJacket: consumer centric wearable affective jacket to enhance emotional immersion (2012). https://doi.org/10.1109/innovations.2012.6207766

11. Hammady, R., Ma, M., Powell, A.: User experience of markerless augmented reality applications in cultural heritage museums: 'MuseumEye' as a case study. In: De Paolis, L.T., Bourdot, P. (eds.) AVR 2018. LNCS, vol. 10851, pp. 349–369. Springer, Cham (2018). https://doi.org/10.1007/978-3-319-95282-6_26

12. Yan, J., Qi, Y., Rao, Q., Qi, S.: Towards a user-friendly and secure hand shaking authentication for smartphones (2018). https://doi.org/10.1109/trustcom/bigdatase.2018.00162

13. Ashbrook, D., Starner, T.: MAGIC (2010). https://doi.org/10.1145/1753326.1753653

14. O'Brien, H.L., Cairns, P., Hall, M.: User engagement scale–short form (2018). https://doi.org/10.1037/t67720-000

15. Koch, M., Von Luck, K., Schwarzer, J., Draheim, S.: The Novelty Effect in Large Display Deployments – Experiences and Lessons-Learned for Evaluating Prototypes, 8 June 2018. from EUSSET Digital Library website: https://dl.eusset.eu/bitstream/20.500.12015/3115/1/ecscw2018-exploratory-paper-3.pdf. Accessed 1 Mar 2020

16. Korn, O., Holt, R., Kontopoulos, E., Kappers, A.M.L., Persson, N.-K., Olson, N.: Empowering persons with deafblindness (2018). https://doi.org/10.1145/3197768.3201541

Using Laser Scans and 'Life History' to Remember Heritage in Virtual Environments

Lori C. Walters[(✉)], Robert A. Michlowitz, and Michelle J. Adams

University of Central Florida, Orlando, FL 32826, USA
{lcwalter, rmichlow}@ist.ucf.edu,
michelle.adams@ucf.edu

Abstract. When building is demolished or at risk, it is important to capture more than just a visual of the brick and mortar we need to preserve the structure's community ties its "life history" - the human element; the stories of design, construction, community activity, and events are lost with the passing of each individual associated with it. One tool that can be utilized is the terrestrial laser scanner, which can capture an authoritative record of a structure or object at a moment in time. Comprehensively, scans are useful documentation to assist site restoration in the event of a natural disaster, fire, war, or deterioration due to weather. This value has been demonstrated with both the 2019 fire at Notre Dame and the UNESCO/CyArk conservation efforts at the Ananda Ok Kyaung temple that was impacted by an earthquake in 2016. Working in conjunction with local communities, researchers are able to solicit private collections of memorabilia, photographs, and documentation that cannot be found in archives and libraries. The life history approach combines the detailed laser scans with this rich multi-disciplinary documentation to capture the structure's place in the community broadening its utility to enhance VR and AR experiences.

Keywords: Life history · Terrestrial laser scanning · Heritage · History · Culture · Community heritage · Virtual reality · Augmented reality · 3D model

1 Introduction

The 2019 Notre Dame fire was a crystallizing moment that focused public attention on how an iconic structure serves as a touchstone of a community. The cathedral's dark stone masonry walls, flying buttresses, giant stained-glass Rose windows, and soaring nineteenth-century spire exclaimed to all they were in Paris. There are many such structures - Great Britain's Palace of Westminster, Machu Picchu, Rome's Colosseum, or the Tokyo Imperial Palace - that serve as both local and global touchstones that unequivocally deserve expansive documentation efforts. Such heritage sites are but a single brushstroke, as for every Los Angeles International Airport Theme Building, there are countless iconic local structures like the "Glass Bank" in Cocoa Beach, Florida, whose documentation assists in creating a nation's well-hued portrait. It is imperative that efforts are made to digitally capture these local sites in a moment in

© Springer Nature Switzerland AG 2020
J. Y. C. Chen and G. Fragomeni (Eds.): HCII 2020, LNCS 12191, pp. 314–326, 2020.
https://doi.org/10.1007/978-3-030-49698-2_21

time while it is still possible to document compelling oral histories, illustrative photos, and memorabilia to develop a comprehensive "life history."

While in the United States, the National Trust for Historic Preservation is at the forefront of "making sure that the icons of the past remain with us in the future," this is an effort that is unattainable all too frequently [1]. For instance, a mid-century treasure, the former Founders National Bank in Oklahoma City, was demolished in 2018 to make way for new development [2, 3]. Structures of all eras face demolition, but mid-20th-century commercial & institutional buildings often elicit a deep sense of apathy by the public, as many also feel the structures are not old enough to be considered "historic" and therefore possess little value beyond uses/taxes/rents [4–6]. Additionally, there are concerns about the energy efficiency of buildings designed prior to the 1973 oil crisis and a failure to comply with current accessibility standards [7]. Increasing land values in urban areas and the desire to maximize profit, combined with changing needs of communities, places many of these mid-century structures at risk for demolition or significant alteration. The Sunbelt is an area in the United States stretching from California to Florida, where this is more frequently seen as it developed rapidly after World War II during the ascendancy of mid-century modern architecture.

2   What Is Life History?

Documenting a structure's 'life history' addresses its conception by the architect and engineer, birth by the construction workers, its maturation by those who occupy it, and death by the demolition crew. A method of accomplishing this is by conducting 3D terrestrial laser scans, structured light scans for fine detail, and gathering other forms of digital data onsite while contextualizing it through contemporaneous photographs, documents, structural prints, ephemera, and oral histories of individuals associated with the building. Such a holistic approach of capturing of a structure's place within a community emphasizes those ties - the human element; said stories of design, construction, community activity, and events within their walls are lost with the passing of each individual associated with a building. Collectively, this documentation can be used to create proportionally, accurate, and detailed recreations of a structure that can be explored in a virtual environment.

The concept of life history of a building that serves as the basis for the development of an encompassing record evolved from several earlier projects by the School of Modeling, Simulation, and Training (SMST) researchers. In 2005, the State of Florida Bureau of Historic Preservation funded *Shadows of Canaveral* to virtually recreate several significant launch complexes at Cape Canaveral Air Force Station as they appeared in the 1950s and 1960s, similar to how the *Rome Reborn* project (v1) presented Rome in 320 A.D. [8]. Because the original launch gantries, such as those at Launch Complex 14 where John Glenn's Atlas rocket lifted-off from in 1962, were dismantled in the 1970s, the project's 3D models were developed by digital artists in the *Autodesk Maya* 3D modeling and rendering software from blueprints and thousands of photographic images and displayed to Web users as pre-rendered scenes in *Adobe Flash*. Space worker oral histories that were conducted earlier in conjunction with the *US Space Walk of Fame Foundation* provided the impetus to reach out again to local community members who worked at Cape Canaveral. These individuals who had worked at the Cape during the 1950s/1960s were critical in validating the accuracy of the launch complex models and provided guidance on finer details that could not be determined by period images. While the project was initially envisioned as purely architecture-centric, it became clear that the former space workers should be integrated into the environment as guides to add a level of humanity to what was initially a sterile virtual world. Additionally, since "Cape Canaveral" culture was not confined to the military installation, it was necessary to incorporate aspects of the nearby community of Cocoa Beach, Florida, into *Shadows of Canaveral*. This was achieved by enabling users to virtually visit the Starlite Motel in Cocoa Beach and interact with period-appropriate artifacts to demonstrate how the Space Race permeated the era's culture [9] (Fig. 1).

Fig. 1. Render of Launch Complex 14 Blockhouse from Shadows of Canaveral

ChronoLeap: *The Great World's Adventure*, supported by the National Endowment for the Humanities (Grant No. HD5020707) and the National Science Foundation (Grant No. DRL-0840297), was the next step in the evolution of the SMST life history methodology. Utilizing a virtual recreation of 1964/65 New York World's Fair (NYWF) as a backdrop for exploration, *ChronoLeap* provided a multi-disciplinary environment designed for children and adolescents between ages 9 and 13 addressing the evolution of science and technology from the mid-1960s to when the project was launched in 2013. Highly accurate and detailed models of the NYWF pavilions and Fairgrounds were incorporated with educational games to facilitate the science, technology, engineering, and mathematics (STEM) learning. Where *Shadows* utilized *Adobe Flash* over the Web, *ChronoLeap* was a downloadable experience developed using the open-source, object-oriented graphics rendering engine (OGRE), and allowed users to explore the virtual world freely. By design, World's Fairs are short-lived events that provide an excellent opportunity to study a specific period in time, but because of its temporary nature, the majority of the pavilions constructed were demolished or removed at a Fair's closing - this resulted in unique challenges for developing 3D models. While blueprints of significant pavilions, such as the Ford and New York State, were available, 3D model development of many of the smaller pavilions, such as the Underground Home, had to rely on historic images [10].

While photographs were critical for both the development of *Shadows of Canaveral* and *ChronoLeap* - where the two differ significantly is the source of the images. With *Shadows*, there was an abundance of official government and aerospace contractor 8″ × 10″ images. *ChronoLeap* relied heavily on print photographs and slides taken by World's Fair visitors and were critical in supplementing pavilion publicity images found in traditional archives. These images provided glimpses into hidden less glamorous areas of the Fair such as loading docks, food vendors and souvenir stands. The *ChronoLeap* project sought-out visitors to the Fair and cultivated the larger 1964/65 New York World's Fair collector community to secure visitor images, documents, and ephemera to develop over 100 structures to create the experience and provide cultural details to linking the Fair to the mid-1960s [9]. Since the lifespan of a pavilion was five years or less from conception to demolition, this led to the development of 'micro' life histories of the structures. These micro life histories addressed design, construction, and demolition when possible, focusing heavily on operation during the Fair and visitor experiences. As the overwhelming majority of the pavilions were demolished in 1966/67, there was little opportunity for laser scanning or other forms of digital preservation (Fig. 2).

Fig. 2. Render of New York State Pavilion from ChronoLeap

The School of Modeling, Simulation, and Training acquired its first terrestrial laser scanner, *FARO Focus3D S120*, in 2013 and elected to laser scan one of the few remaining structures from the 1964/65 NYWF. Designed by noted 20th Century architect Philip Johnson and Richard Foster, the New York State Pavilion (NYSP) was a calling card to the future as envisioned in the 1960s. At 220 feet, its Astro-View observation towers provided an expansive view of the Fairgrounds while the colorful Tent of Tomorrow provided an overall sense of futuristic whimsy. After the Fair's closing, the Pavilion quickly fell into disrepair during New York City's economic crisis of the 1970s. SMST researchers decided laser scanning could assist in the documentation of the once storied pavilion's structural issues and serve as a new tool in the life history concept's toolbox.

3 The Value of Terrestrial Laser Scanning

Terrestrial laser scanning is a process that captures highly detailed digital measurements of structures, which can be recorded prior to their demolition, impending modification, or simply document a moment in time. Laser scanners capture the Cartesian coordinates of billions of points within 3D space by reflecting a laser off any surface it encounters, thus creating an accurate 3D point cloud that can also contain color or structural material information. These devices are used extensively in engineering, architecture, archaeology, historic site preservation, crime scene investigation, and other fields. The scans are useful documentation to assist site restoration in the event of a natural disaster, fire, or war. Recently, the value of this has been demonstrated with both the 2019 Notre Dame fire or in the destruction of World Heritage treasures in Iraq and Syria [11]. Structures that a nation considers to be a national treasure can benefit from periodic laser scanning which can record deterioration due to weather and pollution over time.

Buildings are a deep expression of our life and experiences connecting us, providing the physical environment of our communities and life experiences. Fundamentally, people encounter them as 3D physical spaces, yet as Professor Erik Champion notes, the majority of historical experiences tend to be 2D and text-driven [12]. Architectural drawings inform us of the intentions of designers for the use of a built space, but in the context of life history, the goal is to "humanize" the building and evoke its social history. Three-dimensional capture of a structure enables the understanding of a building as employees and the public saw it. Additionally, some cities, towns and architectural firms have purged older drawings; thus, laser scanning is an effective tool to capture dimensions and details rapidly.

4 The New York State Pavilion - from ChronoLeap to Laser Scanning

Laser scanning the New York State Pavilion afforded SMST researchers the opportunity to transition from developing artist-generated 3D models in *Autodesk Maya* from 2D resources such as architectural drawings and images to incorporating digital tools that enable an accurate 3D capture of a structure. In the first major project after acquiring the *FARO* laser scanner, SMST partnered with CyArk, a non-profit organization chartered to "digitally record, archive and share the world's most significant cultural heritage" sites [13]. Permission to scan the pavilion in Flushing Meadows-Corona Park was provided by the New York City Department of Parks & Recreation, who allowed access to areas normally closed to the public, including the Tent of Tomorrow interior. Scanning the NYSP utilized three laser scanners, *FARO Focus3D S120*, *FARO Focus3D X330*, and *Leica ScanStation C10*, to capture 105 scans of the pavilion over a three day period. The research team shot many digital images to document the state of the structure in 2014 and to serve as texture images to further enhance the existing 3D model. Additionally, the laser scan data was able to confirm small modifications that had been made to the structure following the close of the Fair (Fig. 3).

Fig. 3. Render of New York State Pavilion laser scan – intensity mode (Source: CyArk)

5   Cocoa Beach Glass Bank - Modeling from a Laser Scan

Shadows of Canaveral reflected the influence that the activities of nearby Cape Canaveral had on the culture and architecture of the communities surrounding the launch facility. Many businesses sported Space-Age names such as the Astrocraft, Polaris, Satellite, and Moon Hut, but perhaps the most impressive manifestation of this influence was the Cocoa Beach (FL) Glass Bank (First Federal Savings & Loan Association of Cocoa - Cocoa Beach branch). The bank was designed by Reginald Knight, a Sarasota School architect, as a calling card to the future. Upon opening in 1962, the structure quickly garnered the nickname of the "Glass Bank" as its exterior glass curvilinear walls suggested it was a forerunner for envisioned 21st Century lunar bases. Unfortunately, as with many architects' cutting-edge designs, this building had many led to numerous issues, including leaking, echoes, and heating and cooling, ultimately facing significant modification in the early 1980s. By 2014, because of hurricane damage, the building was condemned and faced demolition. The City of

Cocoa Beach permitted access to laser scan the structure just prior to the demolition, and this was conducted in November/December 2014 with the *FARO Focus3D S120* terrestrial laser scanner [14, 15]. The Glass Bank's demolition in January 2015 prevented any additional onsite information gathering - including laser scans and photography.

The Glass Bank provided an ideal opportunity to utilize the point cloud data from a laser scan to assist in virtually recreating the structure as it appeared in 1963. This version of the building represented the architect's original vision before significant modifications in 1965 and 1980/81. Unlike the previous *Shadows of Canaveral* and *ChronoLeap* projects, the availability of Glass Bank images, from the 1960s to assist in the digital reconstruction, were limited as the structure was not as photographed to the extent of launch complexes or World's Fair pavilions. Additionally, the original blueprints were no longer held by the City of Cocoa Beach nor the families of the building's architect, engineer, and construction company researchers contacted. The point cloud acted as a template to the modeler, enabling him to depict the building's unique facade and arches accurately. Exterior and interior details were augmented with historical images, ephemera, and oral histories [14, 15] (Fig. 4).

Fig. 4. Render of the "Glass Bank" laser scan – color mode

Sharing an early version of the Glass Bank model with those familiar with the structure in the 1960s reinforced the value of oral histories and interviews in developing realistically detailed models that capture not only a place, not only a place in time. This simultaneously feeds the life history as an archive of community information and a virtual environment that can be shared by all. Observing how the preliminary 3D model elicited the recollections of several individuals, it was decided to place the model in the *Unity* game engine to allow the people to "walk" around the virtual Glass Bank.

This brought back the memories of their time working there and/or events associated with the structure were brought to the forefront, thus furthering enhancing the structure's life history. An additional datastream that we were unable to capture in this case was the environmental sound. While evaluating this and other projects, the researchers determined that the capture of a building's character does not end with imagery. When creating virtual environments from actual structures, the environmental sound is equally important. The echo of voices, a floor's creak, or the rush of traffic are not merely sounds, they are the breath of a building, and environmental sound capture further enhances the structure's larger life history (Fig. 5).

Fig. 5. Virtual Cocoa Beach "Glass Bank" from 1963 in Unity

6 Beyond a Single Building

To further expand upon the life history concept, researchers laser scanned structures across the Cocoa Beach community in addition to the Glass Bank, including City Hall and a contemporaneously constructed church. This documentation cluster is innately synergistic in capturing information from simultaneous events within the community and the larger era's influence, enabling a deeper overall understanding of the evolution of the community. Constructed in 1962, the Cocoa Beach Municipal Building embodied the influence of the nearby Cape and beckoned to the future President John F. Kennedy's lunar pledge had set in motion in May 1961. The First United Methodist Church of Cocoa Beach is an excellent example of Space-Age religious architecture, with its high roofline that soared above most of the 1962 Cocoa Beach skyline when construction began. A cross that resembles a rocket launching into the heavens is prominently featured outside. Together the life histories of these structures provide an opportunity to examine the community from three unique perspectives enabling a deeper understanding of how it evolved. This method of simultaneous life history capture is ideal in small communities such as Cocoa Beach, population 11,737, where there is a high probability of oral history interviewees having valuable reflections of numerous structures and their communal importance as well as personal photographs and ephemera [16].

To further enhance the community-oriented life history, SMST researchers elected to digitize the Mayor Robert P. Murkshe collection held by the Florida Historical Society. Murkshe served as Mayor of Cocoa Beach from 1963 to 1972, which was a decade of exceptional expansion of the small city. The collection included personal documents, photographs, and ephemera that added period-specific details. Extending the research to include such significant figures of a locale's history assists weaving together the collective life histories (Fig. 6).

Fig. 6. Render of interior of First United Methodist Church of Cocoa Beach - laser scan

7   St. Augustine Lighthouse

Standing at 165 ft., the St. Augustine Lighthouse is exemplar of the tall lighthouses that populate Florida's flat coastal terrain [17]. The current lighthouse was completed in 1874 and is comprised of brick and possesses a first-order Fresnel lens light capable of reaching 24 nautical miles [18]. The St. Augustine Lighthouse and Maritime Museum is a primary area tourist destination and provides educational tours for students of all ages, and is dedicated to locating and preserving artifacts from shipwrecks off the coast. Wrecks were not a rarity as there were many dating to 16th and 17th century Spanish fleets that sank on their journey returning the riches of the 'New World' to Spain. Currently, the museum holds over 19,000 artifacts pertaining to the St. Augustine Lighthouse and maritime wrecks [19].

The St. Augustine Lighthouse and Maritime Museum provided researchers access to laser scan the lighthouse facilities in January 2020. Due to the height of the lighthouse, the *Leica ScanStation P40* was used in conjunction with the *Leica RTC360* to capture the exterior of the structure. A *FARO Focus3D S120* was used to scan the interior of the lighthouse keeper's cottage in the lighthouse compound. This project differed in several respects to previous ones conducted by the researchers and offered a new avenue for the life history methodology, due to its age, there is no possibility of speaking with individuals associated with its design, construction, and early operation. Therefore, the living first-hand personal historical accounts, but rather the focus on the preservation efforts and the transformation of the lighthouse from an active United States Coast Guard facility to that of a private museum. Because of this situation, the search for pre Second World War heritage is being conducted through traditional archival research and public outreach (Fig. 7).

Fig. 7. Render of St. Augustine Lighthouse point cloud in intensity mode.

The St. Augustine Lighthouse Archaeological Maritime Program provides an excellent alternative opportunity to extend the life history concept with a greater emphasis on the smaller artifacts preserved at the site. Museum personnel indicated a desire to enable visitors the opportunity to have a level of physical interaction with artifacts, and this was especially true with the school-age children who visited the facility. Several smaller artifacts were scanned with detail capturing hand-held structured light scanner, and then 3D printed. Structured light scanners, unlike laser scanners, project light patterns onto an object and then record how the light has changed, thus determining the shape of the object [20]. These scanners, such as the *Artec Spider* which was utilized by the researchers, are frequently used to capture intricate building details such as carvings in addition to small artifacts. Among the objects scanned was the original key to the lighthouse, which was then 3D printed using a *Stratasys J750* (Fig. 8).

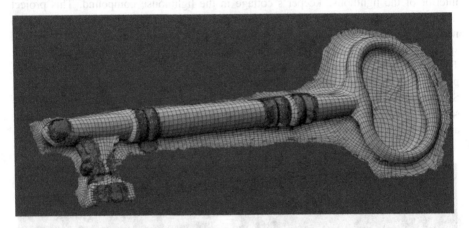

Fig. 8. Unretouched mesh of St. Augustine Lighthouse key.

8 Building Virtual Environments

By creating a life history for a structure or object, the potential for more encompassing virtual environments is possible. The most basic use of a life history is as a "check" of accuracy and historic ambiance. The creation of a baseline of "correctness" for virtual environments is key to them being useful in sharing information. Another way life histories can be used is in the creation of more accurate 3D models by utilizing captured point clouds. A series of scans are required to produce a 3D point cloud representation of a structure and environment, and by combining them, researchers, engineers, and the public can begin to understand the context. Point clouds from terrestrial laser scanning can inform the 3D model in two significant ways:

1. Using measurements to directly or indirectly guide the shape and dimensions of a structure or object.
2. Meshing (i.e., using software to create a polygonal object mesh) a decimated point cloud of an object or structure.

This would result, after properly texturing the resulting 3D model and integrating into a virtual or augmented environment, a useful tool for teaching or training. Depending on a project's goals, mesh conversion is not essential for HMD exploration as 3D point clouds can also be viewed directly in HMD devices such as *HTC Vive*, *Oculus*, *Magic Leap One* or *Microsoft HoloLens*. While not providing the cinematic qualities of a textured mesh environment, it enables rapid 3D exploration of a scanned area and has limited interface capabilities including measurement and notations. Creating realistic virtual training environments for first responders and others would be beneficial since they could encounter a wider variety of realistic scenarios. Another use would be accurate historical worlds and buildings that no longer exist, as many people who lament the 1963 demolition of a bygone treasure like New York's Pennsylvania Station would surely enjoy sharing it with those too young to know its splendor [21, 22]. Finally, the preservation of life history information and use to create virtual environments allow current and future world builders to imagine newly created spaces that never existed. This spark of creativity is important to building virtual environments for entertainment in addition to training.

9   Conclusions

The life history methodology not only informs the creation of a virtual recreation, but it also results in an enduring archive of a structure and the community it is located in. It can inform the accurate recreation of virtual environments and provide tools to gather more details while they are still available from first-hand participants. Capturing a full breadth of details are critical when creating authentic historical or history-based virtual worlds. As VR (and AR) take an increasingly important place in how we teach and learn about human history and culture, the life history methodology will allow for more accurate environments. While we are using this method for Post World War II topics, this can still be used for a wide variety of subjects from the past where no people are alive by harvesting details from diaries and using specific subject matter experts. The archival significance of each life history project is greater than its potential use by future academics and virtual world builders; it is the ability to provide members of the community a greater understanding of their collective heritage. The information gathered is akin to a perishable food that is rotting away, so it is critical to provide future historians, sociologists, and virtual world builders the rich archive of information to understand periods of time from bygone eras. In the end, it is better to gather too much detail than not enough; future researchers can sift through the mass of information provided by a building's life history and use the most relevant and important pieces to tell their specific stories.

Acknowledgments. The authors would like to thank the following for their assistance and contributions National Science Foundation, National Endowment for the Humanities, State of Florida - Bureau of Historic Preservation, Florida Historical Society, Langan Engineering, CyArk, Leica Geosystems AG, FARO Technologies, Inc., The City of Cocoa Beach (FL), New York City Department of Parks & Recreation, First United Methodist Church of Cocoa Beach (FL), St. Augustine Lighthouse and Maritime Museum (FL), PD3D Lab and Mr. Justin Barton, Ms. Alice Kramer, Ms. Vivian Lindauer, Mr. Joseph Romano, Dr. Randall Shumaker, Mr. Jack Stubbs, and Mr. Alex Zelenin.

References

1. National Trust for Historic Preservation Discover America's 11 Most Endangered Historic Places for 2019. National Trust for Historic Preservation. https://savingplaces.org/stories/11-most-endangered-historic-places-2019. Accessed 9 June 2019

2. Franklin, S.: A major mid-century modern bank in Oklahoma City gets leveled. Archit, Newsp (2018)

3. Rostochil, L.: Another one bites the dust: founders national bank. In: OkieModSquad (2019). https://okcmod.com/2018/10/another-one-bites-the-dust-founders-national-bank/. Accessed 20 Feb 2020

4. Morgan, J.: Mid-century buildings the 'ugly ducklings' of historic preservation? In: Medium (2018). https://medium.com/iowa-history/mid-century-buildings-the-ugly-ducklings-of-historic-preservation-afff7215aa65. Accessed 4 June 2019

5. Prudon, T.H.M.: Preservation of Modern Architecture. Wiley, Hoboken (2008)

6. French, C.M.: Introduction. Forum. J. **24**, 5–8 (2010)

7. Bock, G.: Making sense of mid-century modern. In: Tradit Build (2017). https://www.traditionalbuilding.com/features/making-sense-mid-century-modern. Accessed 9 June 2019

8. Walters, L.C., Hughes, C.E., Smith, E.: Shadows of canaveral: the application of VR to a post world war II subject. In: Computer Applications to Archaeology 2009, Williamsburg, VA, USA (2009)

9. Walters, L.C., Michlowitz, R.: A retrospective perspective of the digital recreation of mid-century subjects. Vis Ethnogr 5 (2016). https://doi.org/10.12835/ve2016.2-0066

10. Walters, L.C., Hughes, D.E., Gértrudix Barrio, M., Hughes, C.E.: ChronoLeap: the great world's fair adventure. In: Shumaker, R. (ed.) VAMR 2013. LNCS, vol. 8022, pp. 426–435. Springer, Heidelberg (2013). https://doi.org/10.1007/978-3-642-39420-1_45

11. Farrell, S.: Using Lasers to Preserve Antiquities Threatened by ISIS. N.Y. Times (2015)

12. Champion, E.M.: Digital humanities is text heavy, visualization light, and simulation poor. Digit. Scholarsh. Humanit. (2016). https://doi.org/10.1093/llc/fqw053

13. CyArk About CyArk. In: CyArk. https://cyark.org/about. Accessed 19 Feb 2020

14. Walters, L.C., Michlowitz, R.A.: A retrospective perspective on the digital recreation of mid-century subjects. Vis Ethnogr (2016)

15. Walters, L., Michlowitz, R., Adams, M.: Closing the loops: using iteration to document a structure's life history and create realistic virtual recreations (2017)

16. U.S. Census Bureau QuickFacts: Cocoa Beach city, Florida. In: U.S. Census Bur. https://www.census.gov/quickfacts/fact/table/cocoabeachcityflorida/POP060210. Accessed 19 Feb 2020

17. St. Augustine Lighthouse. In: U.S. Coast Guard. https://www.history.uscg.mil/Browse-by-Topic/Assets/Article/1991134/st-augustine-lighthouse/. Accessed 19 Feb 2020

18. Light List Volume 3 2020. US Coast Guard, Department of Homeland Security, Washington, DC (2020)

19. St-Augustine-Lighthouse History - St. Augustine Lighthouse. In: St Augustine Light House. https://www.staugustinelighthouse.org/get-involved/about-mission-uvp/history/. Accessed 19 Feb 2020

20. Georgopoulos, A., Ioannidis, C., Valanis, A.: Assessing the performance of a structured light scanner. In: International Archives of Photogrammetry, Remote Sensing and Spatial Information Sciences, Vol. XXXVIII, Part 5, p. 6. Newcastle upon Tyne, UK (2010)

21. Chhaya, P.: The rise and fall of penn station: preservation's origin story now on PBS. In: National Trust History Preservation (2014). https://savingplaces.org/stories/rise-and-fall-penn-station-preservations-origin-story-now-pbs. Accessed 19 Feb 2020

22. Allison, E.: Historic preservation in a development-dominated city: the passage of New York City's landmark preservation legislation. J. Urban Hist. **22**, 350–376 (1996). https://doi.org/10.1177/009614429602200304

Study on Learning Effectiveness of Virtual Reality Technology in Retail Store Design Course

Chu-Jun Yang[✉] and Chih-Fu Wu

The Graduate Institute of Design Science, Tatung University,
40, Sec.3 Zhongshan N. Rd, Taipei 10452, Taiwan
563499854@qq.com

Abstract. Information and communication technology is regarded as a crucial tool in the field of education. The Retail Store Design course in Shunde Polytechnic includes industry–education integration and a project-oriented teaching approach. Various types of retail store design projects are introduced through different channels, and project-based teaching is implemented in accordance with a market-oriented design studio workflow. The interactive nature of virtual reality technology can transform conventional teaching from passive into active learning, thus improving teacher–student communication and information transmission in the classroom. This study adopted virtual reality technology as a tool to facilitate teaching and learning.

A 720° virtual reality training system was developed using Photoshop and the 720yun application to provide students with a virtual survey experience for the retail store construction site before remodeling. The Retail Store Design course of Shunde Polytechnic was used as an example to evaluate the system according to three aspects: onsite survey accuracy, onsite survey speed, and learning enjoyment.

Participants were recruited from students enrolled in the Retail Store Design course at Shunde Polytechnic; a set of objective and subjective questionnaire measurements were designed and distributed to the aforementioned students.

The results demonstrated that virtual reality yielded more satisfactory learning achievements compared with conventional teaching methods. Using virtual reality technology for the virtual survey of construction sites in the Retail Store Design course was extremely valuable and effective for students.

Keywords: Design education · Retail store design · Virtual reality technology

1 Introduction

The development of information and communication technology plays a very important role in many areas of transformation and optimization. At present, information and communication technology is regarded as one of the important tools to optimize learning process in the field of education (Cho 2011). Retail store design refers to the environment created by retail companies to improve sales of goods, including the external storefront design, store interior design, and product display. Retail store

© Springer Nature Switzerland AG 2020
J. Y. C. Chen and G. Fragomeni (Eds.): HCII 2020, LNCS 12191, pp. 327–337, 2020.
https://doi.org/10.1007/978-3-030-49698-2_22

designers implement store-specific designs based on the type, content, positioning, and level of a brand. The design of a store directly reflects the service image of the brand, which results in the customer's impression. A detailed and appropriate store design is conducive to building the atmosphere of a retail store, thus encouraging customers to purchase products and increasing the operating revenue of the store.

Market changes have resulted in considerable challenges to the design industry. Therefore, to cultivate more retail store designers with both practical and professional expertise, the demand for project design training has increased. The ability of a retail store designer to survey and analyze a construction site affects their subsequent formulation of design plans and has a critical impact on the final implementation of the project. Accordingly, more satisfactory training methods are required to improve the onsite analysis capabilities of retail store designers.

Numerous Chinese universities are currently engaged in deep collaboration with enterprises to introduce actual design projects as the curriculum tasks for store design courses. Through such projects, students integrate their vocational capability training, vocational quality cultivation, and professional expertise transfer. As described by Edward T. White the site design process is divided into the eight chronological steps in the design process.:

The first step is defining the problem and its definition.

The next step involves programming the site as well as site and user analysis, which is focused on in-depth below.

The third step deals with schematic design of a site plan as well as a preliminary cost estimate for the site.

Step four involves more developed designs and a detailed cost estimate.

Step five is the construction documents or the plan.

Bidding and contracting for the project follows as step six.

Construction then will take place as step seven. (White 1983)

The present study focused on the second stage of the project design process (onsite survey); virtual reality technology was applied as an instrument in the curriculum to provide a new teaching method for retail store design. In addition, this study evaluated whether this method improved students' learning effectiveness. The aims of the study were as follows:

Compare the accuracy of students' onsite surveys when using virtual reality technology and conventional teaching methods.

Compare the speed at which students conducted onsite surveys when using virtual reality technology and conventional teaching methods.

Compare the students' learning enjoyment when using virtual reality technology and conventional teaching methods.

Three hypotheses were proposed on the basis of these study aims:

Hypothesis 1: Compared with conventional teaching methods, virtual reality technology yields a deeper understanding of onsite conditions, thereby improving the accuracy of onsite surveys.

Hypothesis 2: Compared with conventional teaching methods, using virtual reality technology in a retail store design course yields a deeper understanding of onsite conditions, thereby increasing the speed of onsite surveys.

Hypothesis 3: Compared with conventional teaching methods, using virtual reality technology in a retail store design course yields a deeper understanding of onsite conditions, thereby enabling students to enjoy their learning more.

To evaluate these hypotheses, a 720° virtual reality training system was developed using Photoshop and the 720yun application to provide students with a immersive virtual exploration experience. The system was applied to the Retail Store Design course of Shunde Polytechnic, which served as a case study.

2 Related Theoretical Foundations

2.1 Design Education

Design is about problem solving. Design education is learning how to apply practical methods, prior knowledge, and natural talent to solve new problems. Design education is the teaching of theory and application in the design of products, services and environments. It encompasses various disciplines of design, such as concept design, architecture, landscape architecture, graphic design, user interface design, web design, packaging design, industrial design, fashion design, information design, interior design, sustainable design, transgenerational design, and universal design. The values and attitudes which underlie modern design schools differ among the different design schools (Casakin and Gabriela 1999).

2.2 Project-Based Learning

Project-based learning (PBL) is a student-centered pedagogy that involves a dynamic classroom approach in which it is believed that students acquire a deeper knowledge through active exploration of real-world challenges and problems (Edutopia 2016). A project-based curriculum is a curriculum model that is oriented toward specific work processes. This approach uses the typical projects of an enterprise or professional activity as an educational vehicle; the focus of the curriculum is skill project training, and completion of the project is the main learning mode. This alternative project-driven curriculum teaching model is intended to develop students' knowledge and capability and train students to meet the requirements of economic and social development. Industry–education integrated project-based learning has various key features. First, the conventional disciplinary curriculum teaching model is dismissed in favor of cultivating vocational expertise and highlighting students' subjectivity. Second, preparation for employment is included throughout the teaching process, and the learning content comprises typical professional tasks. Finally, the learning environment includes actual work locations; thus, professional awareness and professional considerations, such as energy conservation, environmental protection, product quality, and work safety, can be effectively cultivated (Yin 2019).

2.3   Project-Based Learning of Display Design

Skolnick, Lorenc, and Berger categorized retail store design as a type of exhibition design and proposed that its purpose is to display the products of a company or enterprise (Skolnick et al. 2008). Retail store design requires considerable flexibility, because all interior items, including exhibition stands, display tables, and shelves are likely to be repositioned or replaced according to seasonal and trend changes. Therefore, designers must incorporate a company's annual marketing strategy into retail stores to develop display spaces with high visibility.

Vocational education in China is currently following the display economy trend. Project-based teaching has been implemented in display design training courses to improve teaching quality and cultivate marketable display design talent (Liu 2010). Project-based teaching programs for display design have adopted industry–education integration and project-oriented teaching methods to instruct students by incorporating display design projects into the course.

The Retail Store Design course at Shunde Polytechnic introduces various retail store design projects through different channels and implements project-based learning in accordance with the market-oriented design studio workflow. The aim of the course is for students to acquire the following vocational capabilities: (1) Students should be able to conduct a retail store project and perform onsite surveys according to the requirements of the design tasks, and they should be able to extract the key elements and produce an investigation report. (2) Students should be able to propose response strategies according to their investigation results and implement an appropriate holistic plan based on these strategies. (3) Students should be able to conceive design plans through brainstorming; draw sketches proficiently; develop their design plans according to the functional requirements, quality requirements, design specifications, and industry standards of retail store projects; and publish their designs using computers and models. (4) Students should be able to draw a ground plan, elevation view, section view, and node detail illustration for commercial display projects. (5) Students should be able to estimate project budgets, formulate construction plans, and communicate with the employer, and they must be able to properly evaluate their own work.

The accuracy of a construction site survey and analysis of the retail store design affect the formulation of subsequent design plans and have a critical impact on the final outcome. In the existing curriculum, onsite surveying is taught through the following conventional teaching methods: (1) if the project location is close to the school and conditions permit, teachers lead students to the project site to perform onsite survey; (2) if the project location is far from the school or students are unable to visit it, teachers use single-angle images of the construction site, together with the original architectural drawings for analysis. Although the second method is the most common approach, this teaching method prevents students from conducting a holistic observation of the site and limits their understanding of space. This makes the course boring and inefficient, especially for students with weak foundations and those who are not interested in the course.

2.4   Virtual Reality for Education

With the evolution of information and communication technology, change and improvement become very essential in many sectors. Education sector considers information and communication technology as one of the most important tools to develop learning process (Sampaio et al. 2010). However, virtual reality technology has been widely used to optimize the teaching process, thereby improving students' learning effectiveness. Virtual learning environment integrates the traditional way of education by bringing the real world into the classroom (Koskela et al. 2005). Whyte divided Virtual reality systems into two main categories: Immersive Virtual and Non immersive (Whyte 2002). Immersive virtual reality systems is replaced with head mounted display unit (Bouchlaghem et al. 1996). In this system, the viewers supposedly are not totally immersed using more generic hardware. It is as window-on-a-world systems in which the virtual reality can be seen through display screen (Cruz-Neira et al. 1993).

In this study, a new teaching method based on Non immersive virtual reality technology was proposed. A 720° view of the project site was used as the teaching instrument, and the passive learning obtained from conventional teaching was transformed into active learning through this interactive technology, thus facilitating favorable teacher–student communication and information transmission in classroom teaching.

3   Methodology

A 720° virtual reality training system was developed using Photoshop and the 720yun application to provide students with a nonimmersive experience for a virtual survey of a retail store construction site before remodeling. Students enrolled in the Retail Store Design course at Shunde Polytechnic were recruited for this study. The research process progressed according to the following seven main steps:

Step 1: A retail store design project suitable for experimentation was chosen.
Step 2: The project site was visited to capture single-angle photographs and produce 720° virtual reality scenes of the project site.
Step 3: The objective and subjective measurement questionnaires were designed.
Step 4: Participants were recruited from the Retail Store Design course.
Step 5: Participants completed the measurement questionnaires based on the images or the 720° virtual scenes.
Step 6: Questionnaire results were collected.
Step 7: Results were analyzed and discussed (Fig. 1).

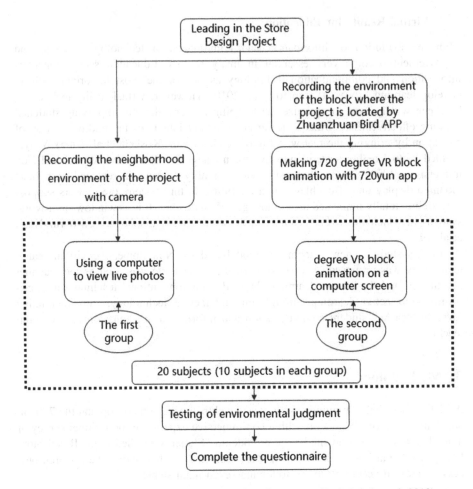

Fig. 1. Production process for 720° virtual reality scenes (Bashabsheh et al. 2019)

3.1   Production Process for 720° Virtual Reality Scenes

The 720° virtual reality scenes used in this study were produced through the following three steps.

1. The store design for the ZENboo clothing brand was selected from among the retail store design projects for industry–education integrated display design studios at Shunde Polytechnic.
2. The environmental conditions of the street and interior space at the project site were recorded using the Zhuan Zhuan Niao application (see Fig. 2).
3. Images of the environment were imported into the 720yun application to generate a 720° virtual reality scene.

Fig. 2. The environmental conditions of the street and interior space at the project site were recorded using the Zhuan Zhuan Niao application.

3.2 Participants

In this study, 20 students from the Retail Store Design course at Shunde Polytechnic were randomly recruited. Their average age was 20 ± 2 years, and they all had a foundation in art design.

3.3 Performance Measures

To assess significant differences in learning effectiveness for the two teaching methods, both objective and subjective measurement methods were adopted. An objective measurement was applied to measure fixed elements, semifixed elements, and nonfixed elements in the site interior. Students' accuracy in understanding the project site environment and their speed of completion were assessed. Conversely, a subjective measurement questionnaire used a five-point Likert scale to assess six items indicating students' satisfaction with the teaching method.

3.4 Experiment Procedures

Figure 1 illustrates the experimental steps adopted in this study. The participants were randomly divided into two groups, each comprising ten participants.

In the first group, 14 single-angle images (six for the outdoor environment and eight for the indoor environment) were employed to provide the participants with an understanding of the onsite environment.

In the second group, four 720° virtual reality scenes (two for the outdoor environment and two for the indoor environment) were employed to provide an understanding of the environment. By clicking the link on the course webpage, the participants could access a window containing the 720° virtual reality scene of the project site. The participant could adjust the angle and zoom in the scene by clicking and scrolling the mouse, respectively (see Fig. 3).

Fig. 3. 720° virtual reality scenes

Before answering the questionnaire, the participants first completed personal information, including previous experience with virtual reality technology. Subsequently, the participants completed the objective measurements and subjective questionnaire in the same environment. The time taken by the participants to complete the objective measurements was recorded (see Fig. 4).

Fig. 4. The participants completed the objective measurements and subjective questionnaire in the same environment.

4 Experiment Results

4.1 Site Survey Accuracy

The result of the independent samples t-test in Table 1 demonstrates a significant difference between the site analysis accuracy results of the two groups, $t(18) = -2.39$, $p = 0.028$, $d = 1.079$. The accuracy results of the image group ($M = 8.90$, $SD = 1.19$) were inferior to those of the virtual reality group ($M = 10.20$, $SD = 1.22$). This revealed that virtual reality technology can improve understanding of the onsite conditions for onsite surveying in the Retail Store Design course, thereby improving the students' accuracy. Thus, Hypothesis 1 was supported.

Table 1. Results of testing hypothesis of onsite survey accuracy

	Mean (standard deviation)		Degrees of freedom	t	p	Effect size (d)
	Images ($N = 10$)	VR ($N = 10$)				
Results	8.90(1.19)	10.20(1.22)	18		−2.39	.028	1.079

4.2 Site Survey Speed

The result of the independent samples t-test analysis in Table 2 demonstrates a significant difference between onsite survey speed for the two groups, $t(18) = −3.06$, $p = 0.007$, $d = −1.371$. The speed of the image group (M = 8.70, SD = 4.45) was significantly slower than that of the virtual reality group (M = 3.80, SD = 2.40). This revealed that virtual reality technology can improve understanding of the onsite conditions for onsite surveying in the Retail Store Design course, thereby enhancing students' onsite survey speed. Thus, Hypothesis 2 was supported.

Table 2. Results of testing hypothesis of survey speed

	Mean (standard deviation)		Degrees of freedom	t	p	Effect size (d)
	Image ($N = 10$)	VR ($N = 10$)				
Time	8.70(4.45)	3.80(2.40)	18	3.06	.007	−1.371

4.3 Enjoyment in the Learning Process

The results of the independent samples t-tests in Table 3 revealed significant differences in preference level, discomfort in use, and assistance provided between the two groups. The preference level of the virtual reality group (M = 4.60, SD = 0.69) was higher than that of the image group (M = 3.80, SD = 0.78), $t(18) = −2.49$, $p = 0.02$, $d = 1.086$. The discomfort in use of the virtual reality group (M = 1.80, SD = 0.78) was lower than that of the image group (M = 3.10, SD = 0.99), $t(18) = 3.23$, $p = 0.00$, $d = −1.459$. Finally, assistance provided by the method for the virtual reality group (M = 4.60, SD = 0.69) was higher than that for the image group (M = 3.90, SD = 0.87), $t(18) = −5.65$, $p = 0.00$, $d = 2.554$.

Table 3. Results of testing hypothesis of enjoyment in the learning process

	Mean (standard deviation)		Degrees of freedom	t	p	Effect size (d)
	Image ($N = 10$)	VR ($N = 10$)				
Preference level	3.80(0.78)	4.60(0.69)	18	−2.40	.02	1.086
Successful opening	4.30(1.25)	4.90(0.31)	18	−1.47	.15	0.659
Successful operation	3.90(1.28)	4.80(0.42)	18	−2.10	.05	0.945
Scene clarity	4.00(1.15)	4.30(0.67)	18	−.70	.48	0.319
Discomfort in use	3.10(0.99)	1.80(0.78)	18	3.23	.00	−1.459
Help provided	3.90(0.87)	4.60(0.69)	18	−5.65	.00	2.554

These results also revealed no significant differences in successful opening, successful operation, and scene clarity between the two groups. For successful opening, the difference between the virtual reality group (M = 4.90, SD = 0.31) and the image group (M = 4.30, SD = 1.25) was not significant, t(18) = −1.47, p = 0.15, d = 0.659. For successful operation, the difference between the virtual reality group (M = 4.80, SD = 0.42) and the image group (M = 3.90, SD = 1.28) was not significant, t(18) = −2.10, p = 0.05, d = 0.945. Similarly, for scene clarity, the difference between the virtual reality group (M = 4.30, SD = 0.67) and the image group (M = 4.00, SD = 1.15) was not significant, t(18) = −0.70, p = 0.48, d = 0.319.

The t-test results for preference level, discomfort in use, and assistance provided indicated that using virtual reality technology enabled students enjoy their learning process more than those using the conventional method. Moreover, no significant differences were observed between the methods in terms of successful opening, successful operation, and scene clarity. Hence, the resolution and operation difficulty of the 720° virtual reality scene were appropriate to avoid operation difficulties. Therefore, Hypothesis 3 was supported.

5 Conclusions

In this study, virtual reality technology as a teaching tool for a Retail Store Design course was presented and compared with conventional teaching methods. The results revealed the following findings:

Virtual reality technology has clear advantages over conventional teaching in terms of the accuracy and speed of onsite investigation.

Virtual reality technology can improve the students' learning interest and enhance the effectiveness of classroom teaching.

Despite improving learning effectiveness and efficiency, virtual reality technology did not increase the students' operation difficulty, and the clarity of the scene was maintained.

Acknowledgements. The author would like to extent the sincerest gratitude to the Graduate Institute of Design Science, Tatung University, and Shunde Polytechnic for providing their assistance with this study. In particular, the author would like to thank the teachers and students of the Graduate Institute of Design Science, Tatung University, for their valuable comments regarding this study.

References

Cho, N.K.: Service Details: A Total of 115 Cases Were Displayed, 1st edn. Oriental Publishing House, Japan (2011)

White, E.T.: Site Analysis: Diagramming Information for Architectural Design. America, Architectural Media Ltd. (1983)

Casakin, H., Gabriela, G.: Expertise and the use of visual analogy: implications for design education. Des. Stud. **20**(2), 153–175 (1999)

Project-Based Learning. http://www.springer.com/lncs. Accessed 15 Mar 2016

Crane, B.: Using Web 2.0 Tools in the K-12 Classroom, p. 7. Neal-Schuman Publishers, New York (2009)

Bashabsheh, A.K., Alzoubi, H.H., Ali, M.Z.: The application of virtual reality technology in architectural pedagogy for building constructions. Alexandria Eng. J. **58**(2), 713–723 (2019)

Yin, Y.: The reform and practice of project-based course teaching based on the integration of industry and education——take the business presentation design course as an example. Art Educ. Res. **2019**(03), 108–111 (2019)

Liu, Z.: The attempt of project curriculum reform for the display design major in higher vocational colleges. Vocat. Educ. Res. **2010**(04), 29–31 (2010)

Skolnick, L., Lorenc, J., Berger, C.: What Is Exhibition Design?. China Youth Publishing House, Beijing (2008)

Sampaio, A.Z., Ferreira, M.M., Rosário, D.P., Martins, O.P.: 3D and VR models in civil engineering education: construction. Autom. Constr. **19**(7), 819–828 (2010)

Koskela, M., Kiltti, P., Vilpola, I., Tervonen, J.: Suitability of a virtual learning environment for higher education. Electron. J. e-Learn. **3**(1), 23–32 (2005)

Whyte, J.: Virtual Reality and the Built Environment, 1st edn. Built Environment, London (2002)

Bouchlaghem N., Thorpe A., Liyanage, I.G.: Virtual reality applications in the UK's construction industry, CIB Report, pp. 89–94 (1996)

Cruz-Neira, C., Sandin, D.J., DeFanti, T.A.: Surround-screen projection-based virtual reality: the design and implementation of the CAVE. In: Proceedings of the 20th Annual Conference on Computer Graphics and Interactive Techniques, pp. 135–142. ACM (1993)

VAMR for Health, Well-being and Medicine

Development and Human Factors Considerations for Extended Reality Applications in Medicine: The Enhanced ELectrophysiology Visualization and Interaction System (ĒLVIS)

Jennifer N. Avari Silva[1,2,3](✉) ⓘ, Mary Beth Privitera[4] ⓘ,
Michael K. Southworth[3] ⓘ, and Jonathan R. Silva[2,3](✉) ⓘ

[1] Department of Pediatrics, Cardiology, Washington University in St. Louis
School of Medicine, St. Louis, MO, USA
jennifersilva@wustl.edu
[2] Department of Biomedical Engineering, Washington University in St. Louis,
McKelvey School of Engineering, St. Louis, MO, USA
jonsilva@wustl.edu
[3] SentiAR, Inc., St. Louis, MO, USA
[4] HS Design, Gladstone, NJ, USA

Abstract. With the rapid expansion of hardware options in the extended realities (XRs), there has been widespread development of applications throughout many fields, including engineering, entertainment and medicine. Development of medical applications for the XRs have a unique set of considerations during development and human factors testing. Additionally, understanding the constraints of the user and the use case allow for iterative improvement. In this manuscript, the authors discuss the considerations when developing and performing human factors testing for XR applications, using the Enhanced ELectrophysiology Visualization and Interaction System (ĒLVIS) as an example. Additionally, usability and critical interpersonal interaction data from first-in-human testing of ĒLVIS are presented.

Keywords: Extended reality · Mixed reality · Medical applications · Cardiac electrophysiology · Ablation accuracy

1 Introduction

The rapid expansion and development of extended reality (XR) hardware (including virtual, augmented and mixed realities) has resulted in a corresponding expansion in medical applications and clinical studies utilizing XR, ranging from medical education and patient rehabilitation to surgical guidance [2]. Each of these XR technologies has specific usability benefits and challenges that will drive usability, acceptance, and adoption. Development of novel solutions, matching the technologies to the clinical needs and unique context are central to successful solutions.

© Springer Nature Switzerland AG 2020
J. Y. C. Chen and G. Fragomeni (Eds.): HCII 2020, LNCS 12191, pp. 341–356, 2020.
https://doi.org/10.1007/978-3-030-49698-2_23

The authors have developed a mixed reality (MxR) solution to empower physicians who perform minimally invasive cardiac procedures. The Enhanced ELectrophysiology Visualization and Interaction System (ĒLVIS) has been developed to address the unmet needs in the cardiac electrophysiology (EP) laboratory. In this manuscript, we will discuss the development and human factors testing of ĒLVIS as an example of matching an appropriate technology with an unmet clinical need, practical design considerations in development and human factors testing and usability data from first-in-human testing.

2 Extended Reality Spectrum

The XRs encompasses the continuum from fully immersive virtual realities, through mixed realities and minimally intrusive augmented realities. While the XRs represent a spectrum, there are discrete technological advantages and limitations that constrain appropriate use cases (See Table 1).

Table 1. Descriptions of the extended realities are illustrated as a progression from virtual to mixed reality, along with an example of a head mounted display (HMD), and technologic advantages and disadvantages.

	Virtual Reality (VR)	Augmented Reality (AR)	Mixed Reality (MxR)	Yet to Come...
Description & Images	Digital Replaces Physical	Digital Separated from Physical	Digital Integrates with Physical	?
Example of Head Mounted Display				
Advantages	Price Graphics Immersive environment Several hardware options	Ability to see and interact with natural environment	Ability to see and interact with natural and digital environments	
Disadvantages		Price Limited hardware options	Price Limited hardware options	

2.1 Virtual Reality

Virtual Reality (VR) offers the user an immersive experience where the user can have meaningful interactions in a completely digital, virtual environment but is no longer able to interact with their native, or natural, environment. The level of immersion of VR experiences is dependent on the class of system used. Most frequently, VR hardware utilizes head mounted displays (HMDs) which can be sub-classified as mobile, tethered or stand-alone.

Phone-based, mobile VR displays, such as Google Daydream View and Samsung Gear VR, require a phone to be inserted into the HMD. This class of display only enables the user to experience their environment from a single position at a time, and therefore tends to provide the user with a less immersive experience. The advantage of mobile VR HMDs is that by being more affordable and portable, the applications based on mobile VR offer increased accessibility to a wider number of users, including those with limited mobility. There has not been significant development of medical applications using mobile VR headsets.

Standalone VR HMDs, such as the Oculus Quest and Go, provide some of the accessibility of mobile VR but with some of the technical capabilities of tethered VR to bridge the transition between the device classes. While an expensive option compared to mobile VR HMDs, these standalone headsets offer some of the improved performance of tethered HMDs and remove some of the limitations of mobile based VR.

Tethered HMDs such as the Valve Index, Varjo VR-2, Oculus Rift and HTC Vive Cosmos, have a physical cable connection to a high-capability computer to provide graphical processing for higher fidelity displays. These headsets tend to have excellent resolution and field of view when compared to standalone VR and offer a superior immersive, visual user experience. However, tethering the user to a computer limits potential use cases for medical application development by restricting mobility and introducing snag or trip hazards. For example, use of a tethered VR system in a clinic setting may be quite tenable if a station is set up for users to wear the HMD in that location. In use cases where the mobility is required, this platform would be challenging.

An example of a VR application in medicine is the Stanford Virtual Heart Project [3] in conjunction with Lighthaus, Inc. They have developed a VR application for educating medical students about the complexities of congenital heart disease. In this experience, the user is given handheld controllers to navigate through the cardiac anatomy to better understand the anatomy and the potential surgical repairs.

2.2 Augmented Reality

In augmented reality (AR), the user remains in their natural environment and has the ability to import and anchor digital images into their environment. These digital images enhance, or augment, the environment rather than providing a fully immersive experience akin to the VR HMDs. Google Glass is an example of an AR HMD and has been used in medical applications, including surgical and nonsurgical environments [4, 5]. To date, the results from feasibility, usability and adoption testing has been promising particularly in patient-centric studies and medical education settings [4].

Echopixel was one of the early 3D displays to have clearance from the US Food and Drug Administration of their True 3D system which is integrated into a DICOM workstation to display 3D images of patient radiologic images. The system utilizes a 3D display and polarized glasses with a stylus to manipulate the image. The initial use case in cardiology assessed the pre-procedural use assessment of patients with congenital heart disease for surgical planning [6]. Specifically, cardiologists were asked to evaluate images from nine patients who underwent computed tomography angiography either by using the 3D display or a traditional display to perform interpretation of the imaging.

Interpretation times were faster using the Echopixel True 3D display as compared to traditional display (13 min vs 22 min), with similarly accurate interpretations.

2.3 Mixed Reality

Mixed reality (MxR) allows the user to remain in their natural environment (see Fig. 1), import and anchor digital images to augment their environment with the additional ability to interact with these digital images, predominantly using HMDs. This enhancement to traditional AR displays has been particularly innovative for the medical community, enabling multiple new applications over the past few years [7–9]. Medical applications leveraging MxR has seen the most research and development on the Microsoft HoloLens [10], though there are other available MxR HMDs with medical applications, such as the Magic Leap.

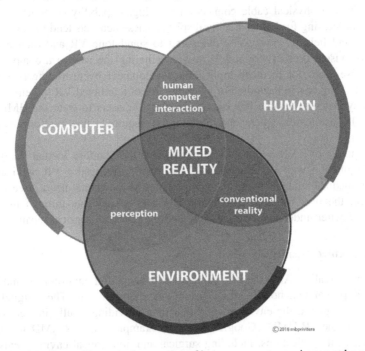

Fig. 1. Mixed Reality resides at the intersection of human-computer-environment by overlaying content in natural environment, or real world [1].

We have been developing a mixed reality system, the Enhanced Electrophysiology Visualization and Interaction System (Project ĒLVIS) [7, 11, 12]. System details are presented below (see Sect. 4).

3   Unique Requirements in Medicine

There are unique considerations when designing and innovating medical devices (see Fig. 2). Early in development, it is critical to identify the end user of the device and understand the current workflow and unmet need(s). For instance, devices that are used by physicians (physician-facing) will have a different set of use requirements than devices that are used by patients (patient-facing). Additionally, devices implemented in sterile versus non-sterile use environments will have different standards to consider. Devices deployed in sterile environments have considerations of disinfection and sanitation prior to use in those environments whereas devices used in a nonsterile space may not need to be tested for these standards. Additionally, devices may be used for diagnostic, therapeutic or combined purposes. For instance, AR devices used in radiologic applications assist the user with visual-spatial relationships to improve interpretation of images [13]. Other devices are used for therapeutic purposes, such as MindMaze's Mindmotion [14] which is used for both inpatient and outpatient neurorehabilitation post stroke. Perhaps one of the most demanding use cases in medicine is the implementation of an AR medical device for use during procedures, including invasive and minimally invasive procedures.

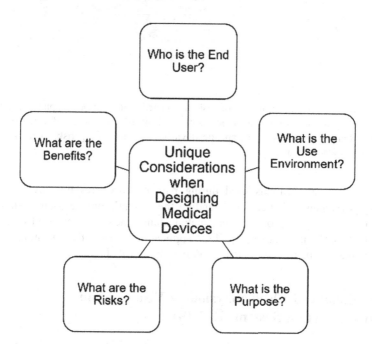

Fig. 2. There are several unique considerations when designing medical devices. Each input requires careful investigation to design a successful tool.

Medical devices for Intraprocedural use inherently pose a higher risk to patients, and are often tied to therapeutic decision making (see Fig. 3). As such, devices that will be used intraprocedurally for therapeutic purposes likely have higher regulatory requirements. Faults in these medical device applications may result in incorrect or incomplete data to the physician, which in turn may result in a negative patient outcome. For these devices where misrepresented or misunderstood data may result in harm to patient, standards surrounding implementation should be high, requiring rigor and reproducibility around the testing of the device.

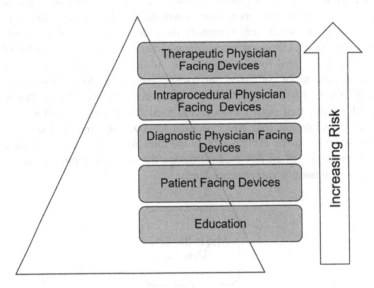

Fig. 3. There are increasing levels of risk associated with various applications. Student education tools pose the least risk, with increasing levels of risk for physician facing devices from diagnostic to intra-procedural to therapeutic devices. With increasing risk, there is increased levels of scrutiny and regulation.

For instance, applications used during patient procedures may assist or guide operating physicians in better understanding the patient's unique 3-dimensional ana-tomies by providing improved visual-spatial communication, improved comprehension, and greater value. Conversely, if the application distracts the operating physician or distorts the geometry, any added value may be negated.

4   The Enhanced Electrophysiology Visualization and Interaction System (ĒLVIS)

We have developed the Enhanced Electrophysiology Visualization and Interaction System (ĒLVIS) which uses a MxR HMD (Microsoft HoloLens) to provide physicians with a real-time 3-dimensional display of patient specific data during minimally invasive cardiac electrophysiology procedures (see Fig. 4). Cardiac electrophysiology studies (EPS) are performed in patients with known or suspected heart rhythm abnormalities. These procedures are performed via catheters that are introduced into the body through blood vessels and navigated into the heart using the vascular system. Once in the heart, these catheters, which have electrodes at the distal end, record the electrical signals in the heart. Using commercially available electroanatomic mapping systems (EAMS), these catheters generate geometries of various cardiac chambers by sweeping the area within the chamber and generating an anatomic shell. The electro-physiologic data is overlaid onto the anatomic shell resulting in electroanatomic maps. These electroanatomic maps have been widely adopted and are used in the majority of EPS [15, 16]. Within these maps, physicians can visualize the electrode tips of the catheters allowing the physician to understand the real-time movement of the catheters and the relationship of the catheters to each other and the cardiac anatomy. Current workflows in the EP laboratory require multiple people positioned at multiple device workstations to control their particular device and data display, including the elec-troanatomic mapping system workstation. These generated electroanatomic maps are displayed on a screen, often in orthogonal views, requiring the electrophysiologist (EP) to mentally recreate a 3-dimensional representation of this data in their mind. In order to reposition the electroanatomic map for the physician to enhance their under-standing, this would occur through coordinated, precise communication between the physician and the technician at the EAMS workstation.

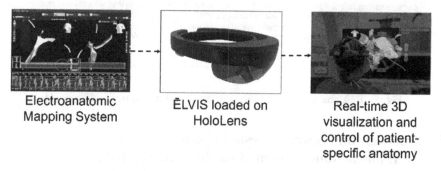

| Electroanatomic Mapping System | ĒLVIS loaded on HoloLens | Real-time 3D visualization and control of patient-specific anatomy |

Fig. 4. Workflow for the Enhanced Electrophysiologic Visualization and Interaction System, or ĒLVIS. Data flows from the electroanatomic mapping system to the ĒLVIS application which runs off a Microsoft HoloLens. From here, the real-time patient specific data is displayed in true 3-dimensions for the physician to visualize and interact with to best understand the data during the procedure to optimize patient outcome.

The ĒLVIS interface provides physicians the ability to see a patient's unique electroanatomic maps in true 3D and allows the physician to have control over the patient data (e.g., projection, rotation, size) using a hands-free, gaze-dwell interface allowing for maintenance of the sterile field during EPS. Thus, the two problems the current ĒLVIS system solves are: 1) current 3D data is compressed to be displayed on a 2D screen, and 2) control of data during the procedure is decentralized from the person performing the procedure.

Throughout the design and development phases, the usability of the ĒLVIS system was carefully analyzed using task analysis, heuristic evaluations, expert reviews and usability studies. This practice meets the requirements for regulatory submission as indicated by FDA Human Factors Guidance (2016) and IEC 62366 (2015). Usability testing of the user interface included formative and summative human factors testing. Feedback from formative human factors testing clarified the needs of the end user specifically regarding the interface method of control. The interface went from a mixed gaze, gaze/gesture, and voice to a more uniform gaze/dwell interface. In addition, users provided feedback on the menu hierarchy, visual balance, legibility, iconography and the identification of potential use errors. Further this testing demonstrated the need to ensure study participants (the end users) were familiar with the underlying technology of the HMD prior to conducting a formal human factors (summative) validation study. The ability for users to become familiar with the hardware prior to the evaluation of interface usability required additional allotment of time in device introduction. Participants required a demonstration of adjustment controls of the hardware as the ability to wear a HMD comfortably might be the difference between acceptance or reluctance in the evaluation (see Fig. 5).

Fig. 5. Best practices for usability assessments of mixed reality devices [1].

5 Practical (and Special) Design Considerations for Implementing Extended Realities in Medicine

Identifying the technology-use case match is the first branch point in decision making when developing XR medical applications. Once the appropriate candidate use case has been identified, the additional hardware and software considerations for the development and testing of XR medical devices can be examined (see Fig. 6).

5.1 Hardware Considerations

XR hardware used in higher-risk medical applications will be subject to unique considerations, as are the majority of tools in these medical environments. The system must balance the user need for immersion, performance and image quality with mobility, battery life and ergonomics. Generally, the more mobile the system, the lower the fidelity of the visualization. Additionally, the number and quality of interaction modes, (e.g. voice, eye, hand) correspond with an increase in cost and complexity. Finally, concerns about biocompatibility, sterilization, and disinfection must be addressed [17].

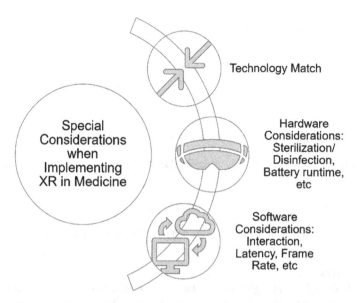

Fig. 6. In addition to the usual considerations when designing a medical device, there are unique considerations when developing an extended reality application in the medical field. In addition to the technology-use case match, there are hardware and software considerations.

5.2   Software Considerations

XR in the medical space require highly testable and stable applications that will behave in predictable ways as they may impact or be directly involved in patient care. Perhaps the most significant software consideration is the interface interaction method. Augmented and mixed reality allow for designing interaction methods that will be comfortable to the end user as they build upon current, widely accepted interaction methods. Various medical contexts (e.g. operating room, emergency room, outpatient clinics) will have special considerations for optimizing interaction methods—gesture, gaze, eye tracking and voice, as mentioned above—and must be considered during the design process (Fig. 3).

For instance, applications used during surgical procedures must consider hands-free methods of interaction as those that require hand gestures may negatively impact workflow. By empowering medical providers through these interaction methods, there can be direct control over data used to inform clinical decision-making. This kind of empowerment, through control mechanisms, may ultimately improve workflows and may ideally contribute to the reduction of medical errors through the improved, accurate and high-quality communication (see Fig. 7).

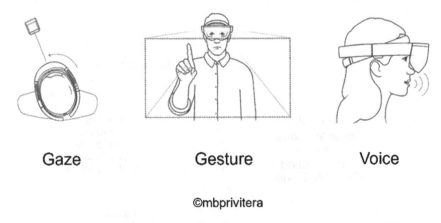

Gaze   Gesture   Voice

©mbprivitera

Fig. 7. Interaction modes for considerations during the design process [1].

Hand Gestures

Implementation of a hand gesture interface has special design considerations. While avoiding some of the pitfalls of the voice interface (see below), hand gesture interfaces must consider the system's ability to see the hand, initiation, mechanics and termination of the gesture. Rigorous testing of the system's interpretation of sudden or jerky movements versus expected movements must be undertaken in various use environments. Gestures must be mechanically distinct enough from other gestures to avoid confusion to the system, but must be easy for adoption by end users. Careful design consideration for gestures that end sessions as inadvertent activation of this may have a significant impact in the use environment. Additionally, hand gesture interfaces are limited to those use cases where the end user's hands are not bring used for other tasks. When implementing an interface for the ĒLVIS system, hand gestures would not be effective as the physician wearing the system is using their hands to guide catheter and perform the procedure. As such, understanding the use environment for the system helped rule out certain interaction methods.

Voice Commands

Seemingly, the implementation of voice commands in AR/MxR should be an intuitive interaction method for the end user, as it closely replicates real world experiences. Voice command interfaces require the end user to verbally express what they would like to happen with the interface. To practically implement such a system, "wake" words need to start the command, notifying the interface that an action is required. Real world examples of this include Amazon's "Alexa," Apple's "Siri" and Microsoft's "Cortana". Notably, these wake words should not be common words in the use environment to minimize inadvertent actions. These words should be easy to remember yet distinctive enough to avoid inadvertent activation (Consider "Alexander" may activate "Alexa"). Additionally, command libraries must be created that use simple, easy to remember commands to increase adoption by the end user. Testing voice command interface must be done with an international user base to account for various accents. When testing the ĒLVIS application, we found that voice commands could be effective for certain users but was not universally reliable due to variability in end user accents, and challenges in achieving an acceptable false positive rate with sufficient sensitivity. To overcome this hurdle will require improvements in vocabulary libraries that these devices are trained on.

Gaze and Gaze Dwell

People often gaze at objects relating to their current task and objects being manipulated. Gaze interactions are an extension of this natural interaction and provide an intuitive interface mode [18]. Gaze refers to looking steadily at an object. This method of interaction provides a potentially faster interaction than a computer mouse when an end user's hands are required for other tasks [18]. Once the user has gazed at an object, the object is selected. There are various methods for "confirmation," including hand gesture (i.e. "tapping" on the object gazed at), voice (i.e. voice command "select" at the object gazed at) or dwell. Gaze-dwell interfaces are completely independent of hand gestures and voice commands, allowing the user to gaze at the object and then hold the gaze (or dwell) over the object for selection. The dwell time for selection of the object varies from milliseconds-seconds and should be tested in the use environment to optimize responsiveness and sensitivity [19]. The gaze-dwell interface was implemented in the ÊLVIS system and was the appropriate fit given the use environment (the electrophysiology laboratory) and end users (Electrophysiologists).

Eye tracking

Recent hardware developments are now allowing for new interaction methods, such as eye tracking. Tracking eye movements is an intuitive mode of interaction for similar reasons to gaze tracking. There may be human eye physiologic variants or certain types of contact lenses or glasses that do not allow for proper calibration prior to implementing eye tracking, requiring careful user screening. Eye tracking does allow for applications to track where the use is looking in real time, opening a wide array of potential future applications. The method of selecting an object should invoke previously mentioned commands, such as voice, hand gesture or dwell. Use of blinking is generally considered not to be an ideal mode of interaction as it is not always a deliberate input and can be a reflexive response of the end user [20].

5.3   Human Computer Interface

Design considerations of the human computer interface are integral for the usability and adoption of these technologies in medicine. Transitioning highly trained and extensively experienced healthcare providers towards adoption of these new technologies requires consideration of existing interfaces which are used daily by the user. As a starting point for the XR application, the User interface (UI) design can build from traditional UI development but must consider the unique advantages of the extended realities. For example, use of familiar icons and symbols with the extended realities will likely increase adoption and decrease learning curves during adoption and implementation. In taking this approach users are eased into the integration of mixed reality technologies in that they in themselves enhance the familiar.

6 Clinical Testing of the ĒLVIS System

6.1 Methods

After approval from the Western Institutional Review Board (IRB), usability of the fully engineered ĒLVIS system was tested prospectively in a first-in-human series performed at Washington University in St Louis/St Louis Children's Hospital in the Cardiac Augmented REality (CARE) Study.

Pediatric patients, ages 6–21 years, with a clinical indication for EP study were eligible for enrollment in the CARE study. Exclusion criteria included: 1) mechanical support, such as ventricular assist device, at time of procedure, 2) age < 6 years, 3) patients in foster care/wards of the state, or 4) pregnancy. Patients underwent a standard EPS as clinically indicated, and physicians had the ability to use ĒLVIS during the procedure per their discretion. During the routine post-ablation waiting phase of the EPS, physicians were asked to complete a series of study tasks under two conditions: 1) using a standard electroanatomic mapping system (EAMS), and 2) using ĒLVIS, in random order. (See Fig. 8) Study tasks included: 1) creation of a single, high-density cardiac chamber, and 2) sequential point navigation within the generated chamber. Physicians were given the option to create any chamber under the abovementioned 2 conditions, given a 5-min time limit per condition. Next, 5 target markers were placed within the chamber and physicians were asked to sequentially navigate to those targets under the 2 conditions, with a time limit of 60 s per target. Physicians were able to move or rotate the geometries, or ask for a mapping technician to move/rotate as needed to enhance their understanding. The number of interactions between the physician and mapping technician were recorded for each study task to determine if use of ĒLVIS changed the communication dynamic n the EP laboratory.

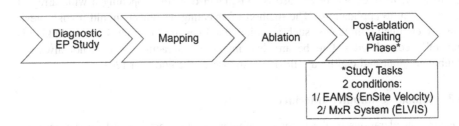

Fig. 8. The Cardiac Augmented REality (CARE) Study workflow.

At the conclusion of the procedure, physician users were asked to complete a 7-question, Likert-based exit survey was specifically designed to better understand the usability of the ĒLVIS system. Additionally, data were collected during study tasks to understand the number of interactions between team members, specifically the physician performing the procedure and the technician controlling the EAMS.

6.2   Results

In total, 16 patients were enrolled in the study with 3 physician end users participating in the studies.

Interactions. Electrophysiology procedures are complex, stressful procedures requiring sustained attention to detail while performing intricate tasks, similar to surgical procedures [21]. Interactions during the EPS occur routinely and can be a source for potential errors [22], particularly during increasingly complicated procedures. To understand how use of the ĒLVIS system affected interactions between the performing electrophysiologist and the mapping technician during the procedure, the number of interactions (quantity) were counted during cardiac chamber creation and point navigation (see Fig. 9) under the 2 study conditions, ĒLVIS and EAMS. During chamber creation, there was no significant difference between the number of interactions under the 2 study conditions (paired student T-test p = 0.5). In contrast, during point navigation, where the physician was given a target in the chamber to navigate to, there was a significantly reduced number of interactions with use of the ĒLVIS system when compared to EAMS (p < 0.05). It was observed that during this portion of the procedure, the physician had the ability to manipulate the geometry and confirm their location rather than relying on another person, the mapping technician, to confirm the catheter location. This reduction in interactions during point navigation may impact efficiency, workflow and team dynamics in the EP laboratory.

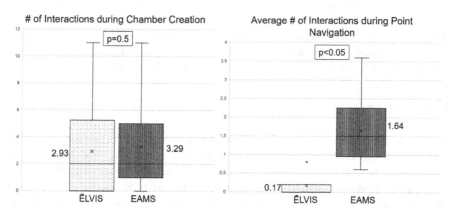

Fig. 9. Interaction data obtained during the first-in-human studies. The number of interactions were recorded when the physician was asked to perform 2 discrete tasks, chamber creation and point navigation, under 2 conditions, using the ĒLVIS system or using standard electroanatomic mapping system (EAMS).

Usability. Results from the physician exit usability survey (see Fig. 10) demonstrated that overwhelmingly, the physicians found the system comfortable (87% agree/strongly agree) and easy to use (100% agree/strongly agree) with readily accessible tools (100% agree/strongly agree). Most physicians (93%) used all the features in the interface and

83% found that the ability to control or manipulate the data was the most important feature of the system. One can reason from this that the power from the ĒLVIS system comes the 3D view of the patient anatomy and catheter locations in conjunction with the ability of the physician to control and manipulate the data to maximize their understanding. Importantly 93% of physicians found that data, when presented in true 3-dimensions and the ability to control the angle of viewing of the data, were easier to interpret than current standard of care, which is displayed on 2-dimensional monitors in orthogonal views. Lastly, 87% of physicians found that they learned something new about the anatomy when viewing the data in 3D.

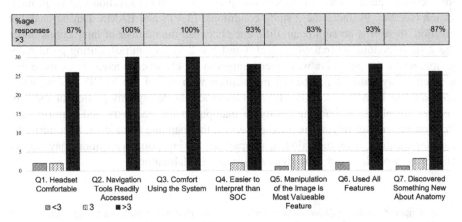

Fig. 10. Results from the physician exit usability survey, based on a Likert scale (1 = strongly disagree, 3 = neutral, 5 = strongly agree). Assessing the percentage of responders who answered >3 on each of the 7 questions is shows in the row above the bar graph.

7   Future Directions

Future hardware development in the XRs will impact application development. With continued testing and increased regulatory guidance for the development of these applications, there will be more applications developed for higher-risk applications, including intra-procedural, intra-surgical, and therapeutic uses. Incorporation of new interaction modalities, such as voice control with natural language processing [23], will allow for a more intuitive, seamless interfaces which will also increase adoption.

Building the electrophysiology laboratory of the future will encompass not only an augmented reality system but also include clinical decision support, including intraprocedural decision support and predictive analytic support, and robotic control which will eventually require minimal assistance of a human operator. By combining machine learning with computer vision algorithms, the entire workflow of the EP lab will change for the benefit of the patient.

8 Conclusion

Overall, the number of medical applications in development utilizing the extended realities are increasing. To best harness the potential of these technologies, an understanding of each use context is necessary in defining the design options to meet those needs. Once technical solutions have been made, design considerations regarding interaction methods of the user interface are critical in the development of high-quality solutions. Medical applications of the extended realities will require intuitive interfaces with seamless interaction methods in order to improve current clinical workflows. Our work with creation of the ĒLVIS system demonstrates that implementation of a mixed reality system can be achieved in the most exacting of settings, to assist intraprocedural use by taking data which is typically a complex cognitive task and translating this to an interactive, exploratory enhanced experience. Ultimately, this system can immediately add value to the medical team and this value will improve patient outcomes.

References

1. Cox, K., Privitera, M.B., Alden, T., Silva, J., Silva, J.: Applied Human Factors in Medical Device Design. Academic Press, Cambridge (2019)
2. ClinicalTrials.gov   (2020).   https://clinicaltrials.gov/ct2/results?cond=&term=virtual+reality&cntry=&state=&city=&dist
3. Stanford Children's Health, Lucile Packard Children's Hospital: The Stanford Virtual Heart - Revolutionizing Education on Congenital Heart Defects (2020). www.stanfordchildrens/org/en/innovation/virtual-reality/stanford-virtual-reality.com
4. Dougherty, B., Badawy, S.M.: Using Google glass in nonsurgical medical settings: systematic review. JMIR Mhealth Uhealth 5, e159 (2017). https://doi.org/10.2196/mhealth.8671
5. Wei, N.J., Dougherty, B., Myers, A., Badawy, S.M.: Using Google glass in surgical settings: systematic review. JMIR Mhealth Uhealth 6, e54 (2018). https://doi.org/10.2196/mhealth.9409
6. Chan, F., Aguirre, S., Bauser-Heaton, H., Hanley, F., Perry, S.: Radiological Society of North America Scientific Assembly and Annul Meeting (2013)
7. Silva, J., Silva, J.: System and method for virtual reality data integration and visualization for 3D imaging and instrument position data. Google Patents (2019)
8. Silva, J.N.A., Southworth, M., Raptis, C., Silva, J.: Emerging applications of virtual reality in cardiovascular medicine. JACC Basic Transl. Sci. 3, 420–430 (2018). https://doi.org/10.1016/j.jacbts.2017.11.009
9. McJunkin, J.L., et al.: Development of a mixed reality platform for lateral skull base anatomy. Otol. Neurotol. 39, e1137–e1142 (2018). https://doi.org/10.1097/MAO.0000000000001995
10. Novarad Corporation: Doug Merrill (ed) (2018)
11. Southworth, M.K., Silva, J.R., Silva, J.N.A.: Use of extended realities in cardiology. Trends Cardiovasc. Med. (2019). https://doi.org/10.1016/j.tcm.2019.04.005
12. Andrews, C., Southworth, M.K., Silva, J.N.A., Silva, J.R.: Extended reality in medical practice. Curr. Treat Options Cardiovasc. Med. 21, 18 (2019). https://doi.org/10.1007/s11936-019-0722-7

13. Molina, C.A. et al.: Augmented reality-assisted pedicle screw insertion: a cadaveric proof-of-concept study. J. Neurosurg. Spine, 1–8 (2019). https://doi.org/10.3171/2018.12.spine181142

14. MindMotion (TM) GO; MindMaze SA: Sylvian Bourriquet (ed) (2018)

15. Pedrote, A., Fontenla, A., Garcia-Fernandez, J.: Spanish catheter ablation. registry. 15th official report of the Spanish society of cardiology working group on electrophysiology and arrhythmias (2015). Rev. Esp. Cardiol. (Engl. Ed.) **69**, 1061–1070 (2016). https://doi.org/10.1016/j.rec.2016.06.009

16. Bhakta, D., Miller, J.M.: Principles of electroanatomic mapping. Indian Pacing Electrophysiol. J. **8**, 32–50 (2008)

17. International Electrotechnical Comission IEC 60601-1:2005/AMD1:2012 Amendment 1 - Medical electrical equipment - Part 1: General Requirements for Basic Safety and Essential Performance. International Electrotechnical Commission (2011)

18. Sibert, L.E., Jacob, R.J.K.: SIGCHI Conference on Human Factors in Computing Systems, pp. 281–288 (2000)

19. Holmqvist, K., Nystrom, M., Andersson, R., Dewhurst, R., Jarodzka, H., de Weijer, J.: Eye tracking: A Comprehensive Guide to Methods and Measures. OUP, Oxford (2011)

20. Virtual Environments and Advanced Interface Design, Oxford University Press, Inc. (1995)

21. Ng, R., Chahine, S., Lanting, B., Howard, J.: Unpacking the literature on stress and resiliency: a narrative review focused on learners in the operating room. J. Surg. Educ. **76**, 343–353 (2019). https://doi.org/10.1016/j.jsurg.2018.07.025

22. Ahmed, Z., Saada, M., Jones, A.M., Al-Hamid, A.M.: Medical errors: healthcare professionals' perspective at a tertiary hospital in Kuwait. Plos One **14**, e0217023 (2019). https://doi.org/10.1371/journal.pone.0217023

23. Sardar, P., et al.: Impact of artificial intelligence on interventional cardiology: from decision-making aid to advanced interventional procedure assistance. JACC Cardiovasc. Interv. **12**, 1293–1303 (2019). https://doi.org/10.1016/j.jcin.2019.04.048

Classifying the Levels of Fear by Means of Machine Learning Techniques and VR in a Holonic-Based System for Treating Phobias. Experiments and Results

Oana Bălan[1]([⊠]), Gabriela Moise[2], Alin Moldoveanu[1], Florica Moldoveanu[1], and Marius Leordeanu[1]

[1] Faculty of Automatic Control and Computers, University POLITEHNICA of Bucharest, 060042 Bucharest, Romania
oana.balan@cs.pub.ro
[2] Department of Computer Science, Information Technology, Mathematics and Physics (ITIMF), Petroleum-Gas University of Ploiesti, 100680 Ploiesti, Romania

Abstract. This paper presents the conceptual design, implementation and evaluation of a VR based system for treating phobias that simulates stress-provoking real-world situations, accompanied by physiological signals monitoring. The element of novelty is the holonic architecture we propose for the real-time adaptation of the virtual environment in response to biophysical data (heart rate (HR), electrodermal activity (EDA) and electroencephalogram (EEG)) recorded from the patients. In order to enhance the impact of the therapy, we propose the use of gamified scenarios. 4 acrophobic patients have been gradually exposed to anxiety generating scenarios (on the ground and at the first, 4th and 6th floors of a building, at different distances from the railing), where EEG, EDA and HR have been recorded. The patients also reported their level of fear on a scale from 0 to 10. The treatment procedure consisted in a VR-based game where the subjects were exposed to the same heights. They had to perform some small quests at various distances from the railing and report the in-game stress level, while biophysical data was recorded. The real-life scenarios have been repeated, with the purpose of assessing the efficiency of the VR treatment plan.

Keywords: Fear classification · Emotional assessment · Affective computing

1 Introduction

This paper presents the conceptual design, development and evaluation of a system for treating phobias, based on gradual exposure to VR simulated real-life situations generating discomfort, accompanied by physiological signals monitoring. The element of novelty in our approach is the holonic architecture we pro-pose and the real-time adaptation of the virtual environment (VE) in response to biophysical data (heart rate, electrodermal activity and electroencephalogram) recorded from the users, which is performed by means of deep learning algorithms and neural networks (NN) solutions.

© Springer Nature Switzerland AG 2020
J. Y. C. Chen and G. Fragomeni (Eds.): HCII 2020, LNCS 12191, pp. 357–372, 2020.
https://doi.org/10.1007/978-3-030-49698-2_24

We designed a prototype for diagnosing and treating acrophobia that includes the corresponding holons operating the input data and system's workflow. The prototype has been tested with 4 users in both the real-world and virtual environments, while biophysical data was recorded. The data collected has been fed to two neural networks (a shallow and a deep one) for fear level classification based on the physiological signals. We obtained a classification accuracy of over 70%. Moreover, even though the training period was short, there were improvements for almost all the studied parameters in the post-treatment phase of the experiment, demonstrating the efficiency of VR based gameplay for relieving acrophobia.

The contributions of the authors are: introducing a holonic architecture for the VR system, designing neural networks as the main machine learning technique used for ensuring system adaptability (stress level estimation and adaptive treatment), acquiring biophysical data and their use in providing the most appropriate treatment. Our VR-based system (PhoVRET – Phobia Virtual Reality Exposure Therapy) is still in development and the results obtained so far allow us to conclude that the conceptual strategy and the chosen machine learning techniques will lead to fulfilling the objective of the system, to be a useful tool in treating various phobias.

2 Related Work - Virtual Reality and Phobia Treatment

Phobia is a type of anxiety disorder manifested through an extreme, uncontrolled and irrational fear, triggered by various stimuli. Phobias are classified as follows: agoraphobia – fear of crowds, social phobias – fear of public speaking and specific phobias – caused by various situations and objects that lead to panic at-tacks [1]. A crisis of phobia causes both physical - high heart rate, sweating, dizziness and emotional symptoms – anxiety, panic, incapacity of controlling one's fear despite a conscious effort. 13% of the world's population suffers from a form of phobia: acrophobia (fear of height) – 7.5%, arachnophobia (fear of spiders) – 3.5% and aerophobia (fear of flying) – 2.6% [2]. Of these, only 20% seek specialized therapy [3].

The treatment indicated in the case of phobias is either medical (pills) or psychological – Cognitive-Behavioral Therapies (CBT) that determine the patient to see in a different way the traumatic experience, through thought and behavior control, gradual exposure in-vivo to anxiety-producing stimuli, in the presence of the therapist who monitors the procedure and adjusts the exposure intensity.

Virtual Reality was used since the 1990s in phobia therapy. VR can train phobic patients in ways that replicate real-world threatening environments on a gradual scale, being immersive, attractive, safe and offering a great variety of environments that can be repeated, with visual and auditory stimuli controlled by the therapist at relatively low costs.

A challenge in the development of VRET environments is to build a system that can be used to treat more specific phobias. For our multi-phobias treatment system we chose a holonic-based approach and for adjusting the exposure level we measure biophysical responses – HR, GSR and EEG. Level adjustment is performed by means of deep learning algorithms and neural network solutions. Furthermore, in order to enhance the impact of the therapy, we propose the use of gamified scenarios. Thus, a diverse, entertaining and engaging gameplay experience will attract and motivate the phobic patients to train and learn how to over-come their fears.

As far as we know there is no VRET system for treating multiple phobias and there is no usage of neural networks-based techniques in phobias treatment. To design such type of system we chose a holonic-based paradigm in order to over-come the complexity of the system and neural networks to estimate the fear level and to generate an adaptive, automatic treatment for the patients, without interference from the therapist.

3   A Holonic-Based Architecture for Phobias VRET System

3.1   The Proposed Architecture

Even if the holon term was proposed by Arthur Koestler in 1967 [4] to highlight the relationship between wholes and parts, the first applications of holonic paradigm were issued in the early 1990s in manufacturing systems. The term holon emerged from the Greek holos = whole and the suffix on, which, as the words "proton" or "neutron", suggests a particle or part, to explain the complexity and the evolution of the biological and social systems. In these types of systems, in general, it is hard to make a distinction between wholes and parts. Often an entity is both a part and a whole. Koestler used the Janus effect to describe a component of a hierarchy: all have two faces looking in opposite directions: the face turned towards the subordinate levels is that of a self-contained whole; the face turned upward towards the apex, that of a dependent part. One is the face of the master, the other the face of the servant [4]. In short, from Koestler's point of view, a holon is a component of a hierarchy that can act intelligently. A hierarchy of holons is called holarchy and a holon can be a holarchy, so a holon has a recursive structure [4].

The Holonic Manufacturing System (HMS) consortium transposed Koestler's concepts in manufacturing systems [5]. A holon is seen as an autonomous and cooperative building block having two parts: an information processing part and a physical processing part [5, 6]. The main attributes of a holon are: autonomy, cooperation, self-organization and re-configurability [5–7]. Autonomy means the capability of a holon to act independently, so it can create its own plans and control their execution [7]. The cooperation refers to the fact that a group of holons develop mutually acceptable plans together and they execute them [6, 7]. The holons' ability to reorganize themselves into the hierarchy in order to achieve the purpose of the system defines the self-organization [7]. A holon can modify its functions to be more flexible, its modular structure allows it to reconfigure itself [7]. In a holarchy the holons cooperate to achieve an objective using a set of rules imposed by holarchy [7, 8].

A reference architecture for HMS, called the Product-Resource-Order-Staff Architecture (PROSA), was proposed by Van Brussel et al. in [8]. PROSA consists of three basic holons: resource holons, product holons and order holons to capture the main concerns in a manufacturer company related to resources, processes and customers' demands. Recently, the Prosa architecture has been refined and became the ARTI – Activity Resource Type Instance – architecture. ARTI focuses on intelligent beings and considers decision making technology as a repository of available tools [9]. The basic holons were transformed as follows: order holons into activity instances, product holons into activity types, and the resource holons are subdivided into instances and types [9].

Another holonic manufacturing paradigm-based architecture is ADACOR (ADAptive holonic COntrol aRchitecture for distributed manufacturing systems) proposed by Leitão and Restivo in [9]. In ADACOR, an adaptive control is introduced, in order to address the agile reaction to unexpected changes and disturbances of the environment. Barbosa extended the ADACOR holonic architecture to ADACOR2, adding self-organizing capabilities [10]. For developing a HMS, it was proposed a multi-agent methodology, called ANEMONA [11, 12].

There are few holonic paradigm-based for medical systems. A medical holarchy is defined in [13] as a system of collaborative medical entities: patients, physicians, medical and sensor devices, etc. There are designed three levels for a Holonic Enterprise in medicine: Inter-Enterprise Level: medical units (hospitals, pharmacies, clinics/ laboratories); Intra-Enterprise Level: units at the enterprise level; Resource Level: medical personnel, physicians, medical assistants, devices for medical tests, information processing resources (medical files, software and hardware resources, databases, decision support systems), etc. Holonic paradigm-based architectures were used for some medical diagnosis or patients' monitoring systems in [14–16] without considering their integration into a unitary medical system.

A holon-based architecture for medical systems seen in its entirety and as a part of a national system, which is part of a continental system is proposed by Moise et al. in [17]. The HMedA architecture (Holonic Medical Architecture) provides the following attributes for medical systems: flexibility, robustness, scalability, quick reaction to unexpected disturbances, modularity, decentralization, auto-configuration.

In the view of developing an integrated VRET system to be used in the treatment of various phobias, we have chosen to use a holonic-based architecture for several reasons:

- We see the phobias treatment system as a part of a medical system;
- We want to design a VRET system for treating multiple phobias, not just one;
- We want to design an easily configurable and flexible system, which can auto-adapt to patients' physiological records.

The architecture proposed for the phobias treatment VRET (PhoVRET) system is adapted from HMedA (see Fig. 1) [17].

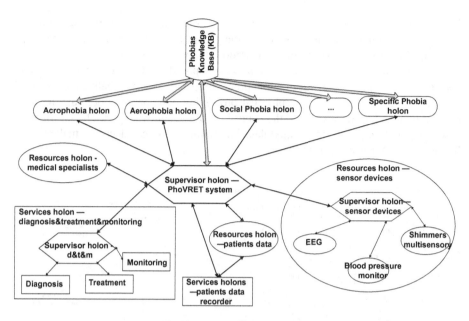

Fig. 1. PhoVRET architecture

We use four classes of holons: supervisor holons (hexagon shapes), services holons (rectangle shapes), resources holons (ellipse shapes), specific phobia holons (rounded rectangle shapes) [12]. The supervisor holons coordinate the entire activities of holons from a holarchy. So, the holon Supervisor holon – PhoVRET system coordinates the entire activities of PhoVRET holons through supervisors of the holarchies. Services holons provide services in a holarchy. The holon Services holon – Diagnosis & Treatment & Monitoring is as well a holarchy composed of four holons: a supervisor and three services holons for phobias diagnosis, treatment and monitoring. The holon Services holon – Patients data recorder deals with the management of the data related to patients. Specific phobias holons are responsible for other resources and services holons of the system: Acrophobia Holon, Aerophobia Holon, Social Phobia Holon, etc. Resources holons deal with the primary resources of the system like patients' data (Resources holon – Patients data), sensor devices (Resources holon – Sensor devices) or medical specialists (Resources holon – Medical specialists). For sensor devices management, we designed a dedicated holarchy (a resource holon) – Resources holon – Sensor devices.

Holons possess social abilities - they cooperate with each other and with the humans. We adopted the concept of cooperation domain from [18] in order to facilitate the communication and cooperation between holons. The cooperation domains can be both dynamically and statically created, and a holon can be simultaneously part of more cooperation domains.

The fixed cooperation domains are associated for each of the next holons: Services holon – Diagnosis & Treatment & Monitoring; Services holon – Patients data recorder; each Specific phobias holon; Resources holon – Sensor devices, Resources holon –

Medical specialists. So, the holons from the same groups interact directly and cooperate in the cooperation domain associated with the group. The holons from different groups interact with each other within the cooperation domain created ad-hoc.

The general architecture for a holon was proposed by Christensen in 1994 and consists of two parts: the information processing part and optionally, the physical processing part (see Fig. 2). The physical processing component is optional and it is divided into the hardware part and the controllers of the hardware part. The information processing part contains three modules: interholon interface, decision making (the holon's kernel) and human interface.

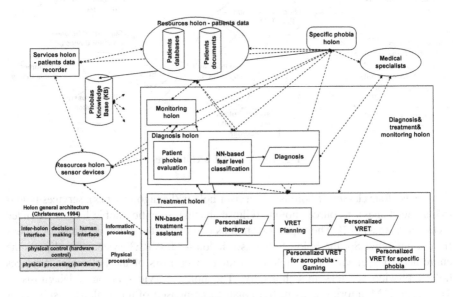

Fig. 2. PhoVRET communication flow

3.2 Implemented Holons in the Current Prototype

In order to validate the holonic-based architecture and the techniques proposed in the system, we chose the most common type of phobia – acrophobia – and designed a prototype to test the applicability of our approach. The holons implicated in the current prototype are: Sensor devices holon, Patients data recorder holon and Diagnose & Treatment & Monitoring holon.

The Sensor devices holon includes the devices employed for recording biophysical data. The recording device we used was the Acticap Express Bundle [19] with 16 dry electrodes, with the ground and reference electrodes attached to the ears. The electrodes have been placed in the following positions, according to the 10/20 system: FP1, FP2, FC5, FC1, FC2, FC6, T7, C3, C4, T8, P3, P1, P2, P4, O1, O2. Electrodermal activity and heart rate were recorded using the Shimmers Multisensory Device [20], particularly the GSR unit. The data has been filtered and the outliers (values too low or too high) have been removed from the analysis. Before the start of the experiment, we waited for the device to connect and to calibrate in order to make sure that it saves correct, uncontaminated and unbiased values. The GSR Unit records Skin Conductance, Skin Resistance, PPG and transforms PPG into HR. In our analysis, we used Skin Conductance, measured in microsiemens and HR, measured in bpm.

The Patients data recorder holon is responsible for data synchronization, recording and storing. All the subjects' activity was synchronized in real-time using timestamps via the Lab Stream Layer (LSL) protocol [21]. A multi-threaded C# application operating both the EEG and game data (events in the game and the players' self-reported level of fear – Subjective Unit of Distress (SUD) at various moments of time) saved the recordings in log files on the computer. The subjects reported their perceived level of fear on the 11-choices-scale. Thus, 0 stands for complete relaxation and 10 for a high level of fear. There are 11 possible fear levels (0–11), this is why we called the scale as the 11-choices-scale.

We recorded the alpha (8–12 Hz), beta (13–30 Hz) and theta (3–8 Hz) log-normalized powers for all channels (the signals have been averaged by applying the typical $\log(1 + X2)$ formula), as well as the ratio of the theta to the beta powers (slow waves/fast waves), segmented into 1-second long epochs. The Shimmer Capture Android application stored the GSR and HR information on a mobile phone that was connected to the Shimmer unit attached to the patient's hand.

The Diagnose & Treatment & Monitoring holon deals with fear level estimation based on the physiological data recorded (the Diagnose part) and treatment using the VR-based game (the Treatment part). The Monitoring subsection of this holon refers to post-treatment evaluation.

The game has been developed using the Unity engine and the C# programming language. For ensuring a full VR experience, it has been integrated with the HTC Vive head-mounted display. In the game, the user had to collect coins of various colors (bronze, silver and gold), situated on the ground floor and on the balconies of a building, at the first, fourth and sixth floor, as well as on the rooftop. The coins have been positioned according to their colors, so that the gold ones were the closest to the balcony's railing, forcing somehow the player to bend over it and catch a glance of the view. Each time the user collected one coin, a virtual panel appeared in from of him, asking for the perceived level of fear (SUD). The virtual panel's choices were disposed on 4 rows, corresponding to the answers: 0 for complete relaxation, 1–3 for low fear, 4–7 for medium stress level and 8–10 for high anxiety. Each patient played the game three times and biophysical data was recorded. The scenes were predefined and presented in the same order across trials. Each subject had to collect $3 \times 5 = 15$ coins across all the 5 floors. In order to finish a level and ascend to the next one, he had to collect all the coins from that level.

The game input was provided by virtual teleportation using the touchpad's center button on the HTC Vive controllers, as we wanted to minimize user movement and prevent noise contamination in the biophysical signals. The player collected the coins by performing a small bending movement towards the ground and by pressing the hair trigger of the controller while raising the coin. The answers to the perceived in-game stress level were provided by pointing the virtual laser towards the panel and pressing the center button of the controller.

In order to automatically adapt the levels of the game based on the player's physiological data, in the Diagnose part of the Diagnose & Treatment & Monitoring holon, we trained two neural networks (a shallow and a deep one), having as inputs the patient's biophysical signals and as output, the perceived level of fear (SUD) on different scales.

Both networks had on the input layer a number of 71 neurons, corresponding to the EEG log-normalized powers in the alpha, beta and theta ranges for each of the 16 channels, the ratio of the theta to the beta powers for each of the 16 electrode positions, differences between the right and left power activations in the pre-frontal (PFaD), frontal (FaD) and fronto-central (FCaD) lobes for the alpha range, beta (bDB) and theta/beta (tbDB) differences from the baseline, GSR and HR values. The data has been pre-processed and noise has been removed prior to analysis. The output layer had only one neuron, corresponding to the perceived level of fear, on a 2, 4 and 11 choices scale.

The ratings from the 11-choices-scale, which range from 0 to 10, have been grouped into 4 clusters in order to create the 4-choices-scale (Table 1):

- 0 (relaxation) - rating 0 in the 11-choices-scale
- 1 (low fear) – ratings 1–3 in the 11-choices-scale
- 2 (medium fear) – ratings 4–7 in the 11-choices scale
- 3 (high fear) – ratings 8–10 in the 11-choices scale

Similarly, the ratings from the 4-choices-scale, which range from 0 to 3, have been grouped into 2 clusters in order to create the 2-choices scale (Table 1):

- 0 (relaxation) – ratings 0–1 in the 4-choices scale
- 1 (fear) – ratings 2–3 in the 4-choices scale

The purpose of this grouping is to improve categorization and classification in the neural networks.

Table 1. Fear level classification scales

11-choices-scale	4-choices-scale	2-choices-scale
0	0 (relaxation)	0 (relaxation)
1	1 (low fear)	
2		
3		
4	2 (medium fear)	1 (fear)
5		
6		
7		
8	3 (high fear)	
9		
10		

The networks have been designed using the scikit-learn library [22] in a Python script and the capabilities of the Tensor Flow framework [23]. The shallow network has one hidden layer with 150 neurons, while the deep one has 3 hidden layers with 150 neurons on each layer. For the hidden layers, we used the "relu" activation function, while for the output layer, the "sigmoid" function for the 2-choices-scale and the "softmax" activation function for the 4-choices and 11-choices scales.

We had a total number of 63 trials for each user. Training and cross-validation have been done using a 10-fold cross-validation procedure, which means that the data was shuffled randomly, split into 10 groups and then each group was hold out as test group, while the rest of 9 groups were kept for training and fitting the model. Both the training and test sets have been also scaled in order to standardize their features. We trained and tested the data in both a user-dependent and user-independent modality. For the user-dependent modality, the model has been trained and cross-validated on each user's data. In the case of the user-independent modality, a model has been computed using the data from 3 subjects and tested on the data of the 4th subject. This modality is less user-specific and allows evaluating the performance of the model in a more general case.

4   The Experiment

We performed an experiment in which 4 adult patients (1 male, 3 females, aged 21–49, mean age 30.75) have been gradually exposed to different heights in both the real-world and in a virtual environment, while biophysical data (EEG, GSR and HR) have been recorded, together with the Subjective Unit of Distress (SUD) value, representing the current level of fear the patient perceived, on a scale from 0 to 10. All subjects gave their consent for participating in the experiment and personally signed a consent form. The experiment was approved by the ethics committee of the UEFISCDI project 1/2018 and UPB CRC Research Grant 2017 and University POLITEHNICA of Bucharest, Faculty of Automatic Control and Computers.

The participants also filled in a demographic and a Visual Height Intolerance questionnaire [24]. The questionnaires can be found on the project's website. According to the results of the latter questionnaire, they have been divided into 3 groups: high level of acrophobia – 1 user (User 1), medium level – 2 users (User 2 and User 3) and low level – 1 user (User 4).

The experiment consists of four stages: baseline, pre-treatment, treatment and post-treatment, performed along a period of 6 consecutive days. In the baseline phase of the experiment, we recorded physiological data in a resting position at the ground floor. In the pre-treatment stage (Diagnose), each patient has been in-vivo exposed to different heights (the first, fourth and sixth floors of a building), at various distances from the railing (4 m, 2 m and 0 m) for approximately 20 s in each position. The physiological and EEG data have been recorded during these 20 s of exposure. The order of the in-vivo exposure was fixed. At this step, each subject performed 3 × 3 = 9 trials. After each trial, the subjects reported the perceived level of fear – the SUD. In the treatment stage, the users have been asked to play the Virtual Reality game for 3 times, in 3 consecutive days, totalizing 3 × 5 × 3 = 45 trials. In the VR game, the physiological and EEG data have been recorded throughout the entire trials, which means from the moment the user moves towards the coin to the moment he collects it. During this time, he can look around, walk at his own pace and interact with the objects from the environment.

In the post-treatment phase of the experiment (Monitoring), we repeated the in-vivo exposure to the first, fourth and sixth floors, at various distances from the railing (4 m, 2 m and 0 m) for approximately 20 s in each position (9 trials). Similarly to the pre-treatment phase, the physiological and EEG data have been recorded during these 20 s of exposure. The reported fear levels have been recorded, together with the corresponding biophysical data. Thus, for each subject, we totalized a number of 9 + 45 + 9 = 63 trials.

5   Results and Validation of the Experiment

As fear is subjective for each patient apart and fear classification is a matter of subjectivism and individualization as well, we present in Table 2 the classification accuracy for each user, for both network types, in the user-dependent modality.

Table 2. Fear level classification accuracy for the user-dependent modality

NN type	Scale type	User 1	User 2	User 3	User 4
Shallow NN	2-choices-scale	67.86%	73.10%	63.81%	86.67%
	4-choices-scale	35.71%	36.43%	36.43%	45%
	11-choices-scale	28.99%	24.54%	24.54%	23.16%
Deep NN	2-choices-scale	66.19%	82.62%	66.90%	90.33%
	4-choices-scale	35.71%	36.43%	36.43%	45%
	11-choices-scale	24.76%	27.14%	26.62%	23%

Table 3 presents the classification accuracy for each user, for both network types, in the user-independent modality.

Table 3. Fear level classification accuracy for the user-independent modality

NN type	Scale type	User 1	User 2	User 3	User 4
Shallow NN	2-choices-scale	70.79%	73.02%	66.67%	90.74%
	4-choices-scale	35.4%	36.51%	36.51%	44.44%
	11-choices-scale	24.3%	27.46%	27.46%	22.64%
Deep NN	2-choices-scale	79.44%	68.89%	73.89%	91%
	4-choices-scale	38.89%	35%	35%	46.35%
	11-choices-scale	28.89%	27.14%	24.54%	25.69%

Fear classification accuracy is comparable for both network types, for both the user-dependent and the user-independent modalities. It is higher for the 2-choices-scale, with values of over 65% (average 72.86% (Shallow NN) and 76.51% (Deep NN) for the user-dependent modality and 75.30% (Shallow NN) and 78.30% (Deep NN) for the user-independent modality), above the "by-chance" threshold of 50%. For the 4-choices scale, the results are higher than the threshold of 25% (average 38.39 (both Shallow NN and Deep NN) for the user-dependent modality and 38.21% (Shallow NN) and 38.81% (Deep NN) for the user-independent modality). Similarly, for the 11-choices scale, we record and average of 25.3% (both Shallow NN and Deep NN) for the user-dependent modality and 25.46% (Shallow NN) and 26.56% (Deep NN) for the user-independent modality. Table 4 presents the classification report for User 3, the user who obtained the lowest classification accuracy for the 2-choices scale, in the user-dependent modality. He has 42 ratings of 0 and 21 ratings of 1. Table 5 presents the confusion matrix.

Table 4. Classification report for User 3, 2-choices scale, user-dependent modality

Rating	Precision	Recall	F1-score	Support
0	0.7	1	0.82	42
1	1	0.14	0.25	21
Average/Total	0.8	0.71	0.63	63

Table 5. Confusion matrix for User 3, 2-choices scale, user-dependent modality

	0	1
0	42	0
1	18	3

Table 6 presents the classification report for User 3, for the 4-choices scale, in the user-dependent modality. He has 18 ratings of 0, 23 ratings of 1 and 22 ratings of 2. Table 7 presents the confusion matrix.

Table 6. Classification report for User 3, 4-choices scale, user-dependent modality

Rating	Precision	Recall	F1-score	Support
0	0	0	0	18
1	0.37	1	0.53	23
2	0	0	0	22
Average/Total	0.13	0.37	0.20	63

Table 7. Confusion matrix for User 3, 4-choices scale, user-dependent modality

	0	1	2
0	0	18	0
1	0	23	0
2	0	22	0

Table 8 presents the distribution of responses for the 2-choices scale. User 1 suffers from a more severe form of acrophobia, User 2 and User 3 from a moderate form of acrophobia, while User 4 has low acrophobia. Table 9 and 10 present the distribution of responses for the 4-choices scale and for the 11-choices scale respectively.

Table 8. Distribution of responses for the 2-choices scale

	0	1
User 1	32	31
User 2	52	11
User 3	42	21
User 4	49	5

Table 9. Distribution of responses for the 4-choices scale

	0	1	2	3
User 1	16	16	19	12
User 2	29	23	8	3
User 3	18	23	22	0
User 4	25	24	5	0

Table 10. Distribution of responses for the 11-choices scale

	0	1	2	3	4	5	6	7	8	9	10
User 1	16	3	8	5	7	5	6	1	5	3	4
User 2	29	11	10	2	4	2	1	2	2	0	0
User 3	18	11	7	6	13	5	2	1	0	0	0
User 4	25	12	8	4	4	4	4	2			

Thus, we conclude that the total number of 63 biophysical recordings obtained during the experiment for each user was enough for a good classification of the fear emotion in the binary range (0 – lack of fear, 1-fear). The classification accuracy in the user-dependent modality is similar to that in the user-independent modality. Thus, in order to have a stronger computational model, we need to train on a larger dataset. In addition, the approach of training on the data collected from more users provides good generalization results. These networks can be successfully used for automatically adapting the game levels (part of the Diagnose & Treatment & Monitoring holon) during a real-time gameplay in our future research.

Another objective that we pursued in our research was to observe how the virtual training sessions affected in-vivo exposure to heights in the post-treatment phase of the experiment. We considered as fear indicators a negative value of the PFaD parameter - mapped to alpha lateralization (high alpha activation in the right prefrontal lobe, corresponding to low alpha power), a large value of bDB (increased value of the beta power compared to the baseline tests), high GSR and HR values.

For each user, we run an ANOVA (ANalysis Of Variance) test to see the significant differences in the post-treatment phase, compared to pre-treatment. We considered that a high HR and an increase in GSR are indicators of fear. When someone is frightened, the heart rate increases in order to pump more blood into the vessels and to generate the "fright or flight" response of the sympathetic nervous system. Similarly, the sweat glands produce more sweat in stressful conditions, fact that has been observed in numerous studies [25].

There are improvements for almost all the parameters, although not all of them are statistically significant at alpha = 0.05. Table 11 presents the average values for the PFaD, bDB, GSR, HR and SUD parameters in the pre- and post-treatment phases. The statistically significant improvements are specified in the corresponding cells.

Table 11. Average values for PFaD, bDB, GSR, HR and SUD in the pre- and post-treatment phases

Parameter	Pre-/Post - treatment	User 1	User 2	User 3	User 4
PFaD (microvolts^2)	Pre	−0.46	−1.26	−0.79	−1.88
	Post	0.34 (0.04)*	−2.09	0.35 (0.002)*	−0.78
bDB (microvolts^2)	Pre	2.83	3.59	8.12	−0.49
	Post	−4.52 (2.09E−7)*	1.28 (0.007)*	1.94 (5.49E−13)*	−3.62 (4.24E−17)*
GSR (microsiemens)	Pre	3.52	1.83	1.96	1.70
	Post	1.97 (0.0002)*	1.78	0.78 (4.14E−5)*	0.24 (6.25E−21)*
HR (bpm)	Pre	80.37	91.33	88.41	88.65
	Post	77.85	86.87	89.68	73.93 (1.96E−11)*
SUD (11-choices-scale)	Pre	5.22	1.66	3.11	1.11
	Post	3.88	1.62	2.33	1.06

value of p for statistical significance in the ANOVA test

For the bDB parameter we recorded the highest improvement, statistically significant for all the users in the post-treatment phase. GSR was situated on the second position, with a significant reduction of its mean value for 3 users, followed by PFaD and HR. The level of fear decreased as well after the VR-based treatment session – with 25% for User 1 (who suffered from the highest level of acrophobia according to the initial questionnaire) and User 2 (medium level of acrophobia). For User 3 and 4 there is a small decrease (2% and 4.5%), but also the initial responses were low (1.66 to 1.62 and 1.11 to 1.06). More information is available on the project's website.

6 Conclusions and Future Directions of Research

The purpose of the current research was to investigate the feasibility of a holonic-based architecture for a system aimed at diagnosing, treating and monitoring multiple phobias. We developed parts of the proposed holons – Sensor devices, Patients data recorder, Diagnose & Treatment & Monitoring holons and performed a series of tests with 4 acrophobic users in both the real-world and virtual environment. The physiological data we collected, together with the Subjective Unit of Distress values, have been fed as training data to two neural networks – a shallow and a deep one – in order to generate a model that would estimate the perceived level of fear based on the individual's biophysical signals. The classification algorithms offered good results, especially for the 2-choices-scale (a binary scale where 0 is associated with relaxation and 1 with fear). These fear level estimation models will be used in our future research for a real-time automatic adaptation of the game levels based on the patient's physiological data. Such, whenever the user is relaxed (level of fear equal to 0), the game level increases (the player is taken to a higher floor) and when he finds himself stressed or anxious (level of fear equal to 1), the game level decreases (for instance, is taken to a lower floor). In order to increase the classification accuracy in the case of the 4-choices and 11-choices scales, we plan to perform further tests, collect more data and increase the number of users participating in the experiment, so that we would have a more robust and stable training database. In addition, we will try to develop other network topologies, vary the number of neurons, the adaptive functions and benefit from the powerful resources of the machine and deep learning techniques.

Another research direction we pursued was to study the effect of VR-based training for reducing the level of fear. Even though the patients played the game only 3 times, they still obtained improvements in the post-treatment phase. For half of the parameters there was a high statistical significance in the results. In the future, we will vary the game levels, add more scenes, increase the interaction complexity and automatically increase or decrease the game's intensity exposure based on the recorded biophysical signals.

To sum up, we conclude that the holonic-based architecture is feasible for designing a phobia diagnosis and treatment system. The holons we designed for the current prototype worked, synchronized and communicated appropriately, so that we can extend their use for any type of phobia treatment, not just acrophobia. Once they are implemented, they can be employed for diagnosing, treating and monitoring agoraphobia, social phobia, claustrophobia or multiple phobias. We have successfully approached the two desired research directions – designing a machine learning model for fear level estimation based on biophysical data and improving the patients' acrophobic condition through VR immersive and interactive gameplay.

Acknowledgements. The work has been funded by the Operational Programme Human Capital of the Ministry of European Funds through the Financial Agreement 51675/09.07.2019, SMIS code 125125, UEFISCDI proiect 1/2018 and UPB CRC Research Grant 2017.

References

1. Arlington: Diagnostic and Statistical Manual of Mental Disorders, American Psychiatric Association (2013)
2. Nation Wide Phobias Statistics. https://blog.nationwide.com/common-phobias-statistics/. Accessed 12 Nov 2019
3. Phobias Statistics. http://www.fearof.net/phobia-statistics-and-surprising-facts-about-our-biggest-fears/. Accessed 12 Nov 2019
4. Koestler, A.: The Ghost in The Machine. Arkana, New York (1967)
5. Garcia-Herreros, E., Christensen, J., Prado, J.M., Tamura, S.: IMS - holonic manufacturing systems: System components of autonomous modules and their distributed control. Technical report, HMS Consortium (1994)
6. Christensen, J.H.: Holonic manufacturing systems: initial architecture and standard directions. In: Proceedings of the First European Conference on Holonic Manufacturing Systems, Hannover (1994)
7. Benaskeur, A., Irandoust, H.: Defence R&D Canada – Valcartier Technical report (2008)
8. Van Brussel, H., Wyns, J., Valckenaers, P., Bongaerts, L., Peeters, P.: Reference architecture for holonic manufacturing systems: PROSA. Comput. Ind. **37**(3), 255–274 (1998)
9. Valckenaers, P.: ARTI reference architecture – PROSA revisited. In: Borangiu, T., Trentesaux, D., Thomas, A., Cavalieri, S. (eds.) SOHOMA 2018. SCI, vol. 803, pp. 1–19. Springer, Cham (2019). https://doi.org/10.1007/978-3-030-03003-2_1
10. Barbosa, J.: Self-organized and evolvable holonic architecture for manufacturing control. Chemical and Process Engineering. Université de Valenciennes et du Hainaut-Cambresis, (2015). https://tel.archives-ouvertes.fr/tel-01137643v2/document
11. Botti, V., Giret, A.: ANEMONA: A Multi-Agent Methodology for Holonic Manufacturing Systems, 1st edn. Springer, London (2008). https://doi.org/10.1007/978-1-84800-310-1_2
12. Giret, A., Botti, V.: J. Intell. Manuf. **15**, 645 (2004). https://doi.org/10.1023/B:JIMS.0000037714.56201.a3
13. Leitão, P., Restivo, R.: ADACOR: a holonic architecture for agile and adaptive manufacturing control. Comput. Ind. **57**(2), 121–130 (2006)
14. Ulieru, M., Geras, A.: Emergent holarchies for e-health applications: a case in glaucoma diagnosis. In: Proceedings of IECON 2002 – 28th Annual Conference of the IEEE Industrial Electronics Society, Seville, Spain, 5–8 November, pp. 2957–2962 (2002)
15. Unland, R.: A holonic multi-agent system for robust, flexible, and reliable medical diagnosis. In: Meersman, R., Tari, Z. (eds.) OTM 2003. LNCS, vol. 2889, pp. 1017–1030. Springer, Heidelberg (2003). https://doi.org/10.1007/978-3-540-39962-9_97
16. Ulieru, M.: Internet-enabled soft computing holarchies for e-health applications - Soft computing enhancing the Internet and the Internet enhancing soft computing-. In: Nikravesh, M., Azvine, B., Yager, R., Zadeh, L.A. (eds.) Enhancing the Power of the Internet. Studies in Fuzziness and Soft Computing, vol. 139, pp. 131–165. Springer, Heidelberg (2004). https://doi.org/10.1007/978-3-540-45218-8_6
17. Akbari, Z., Unland, R.: A holonic multi-agent system approach to differential diagnosis. In: Berndt, J.O., Petta, P., Unland, R. (eds.) MATES 2017. LNCS (LNAI), vol. 10413, pp. 272–290. Springer, Cham (2017). https://doi.org/10.1007/978-3-319-64798-2_17

18. Moise, G., Moise, P.G., Moise, P.S.: Towards holons-based architecture for medical systems. In: Proceedings of 2018 ACM/IEEE International Workshop on Software Engineering in Healthcare Systems SEHS 2018, Gothenburg, Sweden, pp. 26–30 (2018)
19. Acticap Xpress Bundle. https://www.brainproducts.com/productdetails.php?id=66. Accessed 12 Nov 2019
20. Shimmer Sensing. http://www.shimmersensing.com/. Accessed 12 Nov 2019
21. Lab Stream layer. https://github.com/sccn/labstreaminglayer. Accessed 12 Nov 2019
22. Scikit Learn Python Library. http://scikit-learn.org. Accessed 12 Nov 2019
23. Tensor Flow Library. https://www.tensorflow.org/. Accessed 12 Nov 2019
24. Huppert, D., Grill, E., Brandt, T.: A new questionnaire for estimating the severity of visual height intolerance and acrophobia by a metric interval scale. Front. Neurol. **8** (2017). https://doi.org/10.3389/fneur.2017.00211
25. Kometer, H., Luedtke, S., Stanuch, K., Walczuk, S., Wettstein, J.: The effects virtual reality has on physiological responses as compared to two-dimensional video. University of Wisconsin School of Medicine and Public Health, Department of Physiology (2010)

Multi-channel Interaction Design and Implementation of Medical Pendant Based on Virtual Reality Technology

Dini Duan, Zhisheng Zhang[(✉)], Hao Liu, and Zhijie Xia

School of Mechanical Engineering, Southeast University,
Nanjing 211189, China
duandn@foxmail.com, oldbc@seu.edu.cn,
544401457@qq.com, zhijie.xia@gmail.com

Abstract. This paper takes the medical pendant as the research object of virtual reality technology multi-channel interaction design. It expounds the characteristics of multi-channel human-computer interaction in the virtual reality system and discusses the technology realization process of multi-channel human-computer interaction in the virtual reality system. From the aspects of the visual channel, sound channel and haptic channel, the current technical difficulties are analyzed in combination with the principle of human-computer interaction. The significance of multi-channel interaction design research is further verified, and the important principles of interaction design in the virtual reality system are proposed. Simulating the product in a virtual environment improves the sense of use and safety of medical device products. Combined with the user interaction task experiment of the virtual reality system of the medical pendant, the design practice process was verified.

Keywords: Multi-channel interaction · Medical pendant · Virtual Reality (VR)

1 Introduction

Virtual Reality (VR) is the most widely used advanced technology in the field of new digital technologies in recent years and integrates the application of computers, human-computer interaction and other multidisciplinary knowledge [1]. The multi-faceted application of VR technology has great development prospects. VR technology has been applied to medical fields such as surgery simulation, human anatomy virtual platform and VR system operating room. It is the main research direction of this article to be able to directly operate virtual design medical devices in a virtual environment and understand the operation commands. In this paper, the system set up process of a multi-channel medical pendant platform is presented to describe the multi-channel interactive method through virtual input devices.

In recent years, the medical pendant has become more and more important in the application of hospital departments. As an integrated carrier of medical equipment, gas terminal and power supply, medical pendant plays an important role in many hospital scenes. Researchers have proposed that the working efficiency of medical staff was

© Springer Nature Switzerland AG 2020
J. Y. C. Chen and G. Fragomeni (Eds.): HCII 2020, LNCS 12191, pp. 373–384, 2020.
https://doi.org/10.1007/978-3-030-49698-2_25

decreased due to the unreasonable design of the operating mode of medical devices and the unfamiliarity of medical staff with the use process [2]. Researchers have also used data records of medical equipment and cases of medical accidents to analyze the probability of safety accidents caused by medical staff's unfamiliarity with the operation of the medical devices [3]. There is the poor design of medical devices was the main cause of many medical accidents, while many of the causes of these medical events were due to the operation failure of medical devices in use [4]. As a large medical device, the medical pendant is of great value. However, if every medical worker is allowed to operate and learn, the service life of various devices may be greatly lost. Through immersive interactive experience and multi-channel interaction, VR technology helps medical staff to operate and practice freely in the virtual environment.

The application of VR technology to the field of medicine can realize great potential. According to the above problems existing in medical staff using the medical pendant, the combination of VR technology can not only help people solve the problem of medical pendant learning and training, but also bring good interactive experience for medical staff. Some of the researchers have explored the applying of VR technology to medical medicine.

In the current research, however, there is still a lack of relevant theoretical and applied research on how to use VR technology to build a platform for operation learning and training of medical pendants. Therefore, this paper will discuss the construction of virtual multi-interactive channels from the perspective of constructing a medical pendant interactive experience platform suitable for medical staff, put forward the design strategy of the medical pendant interactive experience platform, and provide the design basis for the VR technology to play a better role in the design of the medical pendant interactive experience platform.

2   Multi-channel Interaction of Medical Device

With the support of VR technology, the medical environment is simulated, and virtual operations are mainly performed by introducing real users into the virtual environment through third-party media. The mainstream VR development engine generates general-purpose environments in the virtual world, including three-dimensional environments, three-dimensional sound, natural weather, collision contact, and odor simulation and other general sensing functions, so that operators can directly perceive the virtual environment through the organs. By analyzing and researching the interaction modes in the VR environment, summarizing the characteristics of each interaction mode has important guiding significance for the research of medical simulation systems based on VR technology. Figure 1 shows the common virtual interactive input structural process. After the user enters the virtual scene, various sensors transmit the received data to the background and feedback the sensory information of the corresponding channel to the user to manipulate the object.

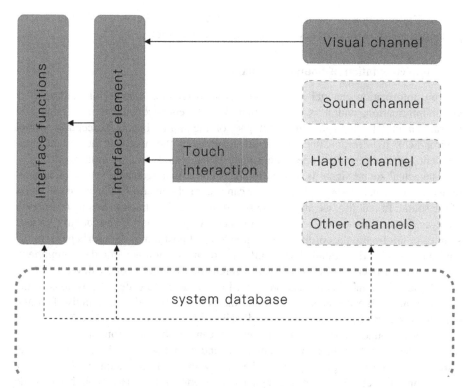

Fig. 1. After the user enters the virtual scene, various sensors transmit the received data to the background and feedback the sensory information of the corresponding channel to the user to manipulate the object.

2.1 Implementation of Visual Interactions

In VR systems, human immersive experiences mainly come from visual perception channels. The technical point of the stereo image display device is to use a computer's high-performance technology to convert a digital signal into a three-dimensional display channel. The parallax of human eyes is the main mechanism for generating stereo perception. Therefore, it is necessary to establish scenes with different visual display effects according to the left and right eyes of the person, and send the screen to the corresponding glasses independently, so that the user can perceive the three-dimensional virtual world [5]. For example, the way 3D movies are presented is based on this principle. When the user wears special glasses, the left and right eyes respectively see the odd-numbered and even-numbered images, and the three-dimensional effect of the picture is generated by the image difference between the odd-numbered and even-numbered frames.

In the process of human-computer interaction of medical devices, the interaction mode of visual channels is mainly displayed through visual information, such as LED display screens and multi-function indicators. When designing visual information interaction, it is necessary to reduce the interference caused by the color and brightness of visual information to the user, taking into account the operating habits of special personnel, and how to read key information more accurately.

2.2 Implementation of Sound Interaction

Hearing information channel is the only second perception channel of humans after visual information, and it is an important way to enhance human immersion and interaction in VR. It is an important part of the multi-channel perception virtual environment. It is responsible for the sound input of the user and the virtual environment and can generate three-dimensional virtual sounds in the virtual world.

The actual sound signal is located to a specific virtual dedicated source in a three-dimensional virtual space, so that the user can accurately determine the precise location of the sound. In real life, we all hear the sound first and then track to this place through the eyes. In the three-dimensional sound system, we can monitor and identify various sources of information according to the direction and position of the user's gaze. In the environment, effective sound channel information interaction is particularly important.

Many researchers have done a lot of research and exploration of the development of sound interaction and made great progress. Lee [6] detected different positions of the sound in the speaker settings and adjusted their output methods accordingly. Through experiments, part of the reason that sound really immerses users in VR is that the sound environment sounds more real. High accuracy can be obtained from speakers 3–4 m apart. In the projection-type VR system, the sound output device is based on the three-dimensional stereo image to provide the user with the information of the auditory perception channel. The electronic signal is converted into stereo through audio file processing, allowing the user to identify the sound source and determine the space of the sound source Orientation. In the head-mounted stereo display device, the earphone can make the user more convenient and truly receive the hearing information, so the earphone is more widely used.

2.3 Implementation of Haptic Interaction

The haptic feedback design makes the user's actions in the virtual scene more realistic. The haptic sense is a very important interactive input channel in reality. Without haptic feedback information, users will feel more troubled about their interactive operation. Researchers have explored how to make haptic feedback more real and natural.

Bovet [7] proposed the importance of passive haptic feedback in making the simulated sensation credible, and experimentally proved that maintaining the consistency of the haptic contact experience will have a huge impact on the realization of virtual sensation because people's experience is more accurate control. Li [8] researched a set of interactive systems based on haptic feedback and found that humans and machines would interfere with each other, then studied how to adjust the posture of the human body in a virtual scene by using a potential collision algorithm interaction, and an optimization scheme is proposed. Xiao [9] proposed in the study of virtual surgery in brain surgery that the introduction of haptic feedback in the VR interactive experience greatly improved the authenticity of the operation, but the operation was unstable. By analyzing the haptic interaction technology in the virtual system, it can be concluded that the main reason is that the force feedback device itself will generate a certain amount of friction and resistance in the virtual environment. Based on the quantitative analysis of friction resistance, the application strategy of haptic devices based on the VR environment is proposed.

The haptic interaction input method based on the determinants of the interaction effect based on the user's key behavior can be divided into different haptic feedback forms such as key combination, key strength, and key duration. In the construction of VR scenes, different haptic feedback combination forms need to be designed according to the characteristics of the environment.

3 Multi-channel Medical Pendant Interactive Platform

3.1 Virtual Medical Environment

A multi-channel medical pendant interactive platform (MMPIP) was built as the specific research object with Unity3D, as shown in Fig. 2. We have conducted market research and human factors engineering analysis on the usage of medical pendants currently used in most hospitals. In the VR environment of MMPIP, the target users are medical staff, so ensuring that the interaction operation maintains a consistent interaction model and operation logic in the real environment is the key to interaction design in the virtual environment. During the interactive operation of the medical device, the operator receives information feedback (visual information, sound information, and haptic information) in the virtual environment, and forming a complete closed-loop of interactive information after the brain processes the information.

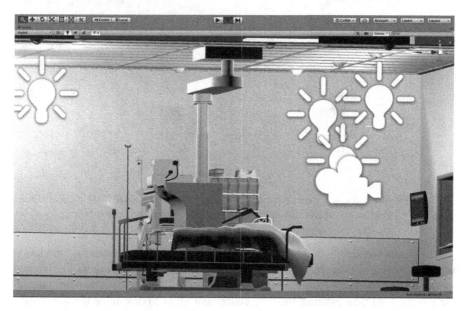

Fig. 2. A multi-channel medical pendant interactive platform (MMPIP) was built as the specific research object with Unity3D.

3.2   Virtual Operation Process

By analyzing the human-computer interaction behavior of existing products, the main interaction channels of users in the MMPIP are determined: visual, auditory and haptic channels. The MMPIP needs to provide reasonable feedback according to the user's operation and predict the user's operation. In addition, the main interaction methods of the visual and sound information channels in the VR system are visual and sound combination, so as to meet the information prompting requirements of medical pendants. The visual information is mainly displayed on the screen, and the sound information prompt belongs to the auditory channel, which is mainly provided by the audio equipment. The main behavioral modes of the haptic channel are switching product selection, controlling the pendant to move up and down, rotating left and right. In the virtual environment, the user receives the information on the perception channel and the effect channel at the same time and interacts with the products in the virtual environment. The multi-channel information is cyclically output in the system, and then the user obtains a more natural interactive experience.

3.3   Visual Modeling Design

The interaction design of three-dimensional objects in the MMPIP is the focus of human-machine interaction in a virtual scene. Through user research and analysis, two models of medical ceiling products have been optimized.

Fig. 3. Before the human-computer interaction simulation of the VR system, the model drawing of the modeling scheme is performed through the three-dimensional model software.

The product modeling design is guided by ergonomics and the aesthetic form law is used to conceive the appearance of the medical pendant. According to the internal operation of the medical suspension, pendant to design the internal structure, interaction process, and then evaluate multiple conceptual plans to determine the appearance color and overall modeling characteristics of the product. Through continuous iteration and modification of the design plan, the final determination two design options. Before the human-computer interaction simulation of the VR system, the model drawing of the modeling scheme is performed through the three-dimensional model software, as shown in Fig. 3 above.

4   Implementation of Multi-channel Interaction

4.1   Visual Stimulus Presentation

There are a number of core Settings that are critical to the multi-channel interactive experience of the MMPIP, including the lighting environment, the sound environment, and the haptic feedback mode of user interaction. One of the most critical is the lighting environment created in a VR environment. Because users receive the most information in the visual channel, if the lighting environment is not set correctly, the virtual medical scene will look very different from the real world, and the user experience of the platform will be affected to some extent. The more realistic lighting environment can make the scene look more realistic, and users can get a more natural sense of immersion in the interactive experience platform of the medical pendant. In the design of the MMPIP, the lighting environment was adjusted according to the lighting characteristics of the hospital ward environment and user comfort.

The lighting environment of the medical pendant was further studied. The environment used by the medical pendant is a variety of different types of the ward, the use of the ward has the most direct impact on the health of patients, lighting environment design should also be paid attention to. The ward environment with sufficient light is more conducive to the work of medical staff, making the operating equipment handier, and bringing a bright, relaxed feeling to people.

In addition, most of the patients in the ward are lying on the bed for treatment or rest. In order to reduce the glare effect caused by direct light to the patients and medical staff, general lamps and lanterns are installed at an upward angle. In the virtual scene, the lighting effect of the ward environment is simulated by adjusting the installation position of lamps and lighting effects of the ward. The following Table 1 gives a summary of illumination standard value of ward lighting in different countries.

Table 1. Illumination standard value of ward lighting in different time periods

	China	UK	Germany	USA	France	Japan
Usually	100	150	80–120	220	70	100–200
Evening	–	5	5–20			–
Late at night	–	0.1		5–15	–	1–2

4.2   Sound Stimulation Presentation

In the MMPIP, considering the sound environment of the medical pendant, it should be presented according to the type and value of the noise actually emitted in the ward.

Through investigation, it is found that in most wards of hospitals, due to the high mobility of personnel, there are generally a variety of noise types, such as the voice of people talking, the sound of instrument running and the sound of patients themselves. The intensive care unit is a special high-risk ward, which requires a low noise environment. Due to the limited access of personnel, the noise value in the ward is relatively low. In the sound environment of the MMPIP, the average of most ward environment sounds should be considered, and different sound sizes should be set for different types of sounds. By monitoring the noise values in the ward, the average data of general noise types in the ward were obtained, as shown in Table 2 [10].

Table 2. Different noise averages in the ward

Noise type	Noise average
Medical instrument sound	65.28
Voice of staff	65.16
Ring tone	63.55
Door bell	58.18

Hearing allows people to identify objects in the world based on the sound they produce, and it allows them to communicate using sound. The dynamic range of human ear hearing ranges from 0 dB to 120–130 dB. All sounds above 90 dB will damage the cochlea of the inner ear, and even irreversible damage will be caused if they exceed 120 dB [11].

There is always sound in the normal environment, there is no absolute quiet space. VR provides users with a highly immersive virtual space, so it is necessary to add a slight noise consistent with the characteristics of the scene to the virtual scene, which makes users feel more real and comfortable [12]. In the operating environment of the medical pendant, some slight sound elements generated by other medical devices are added to the platform, such as the sound of ventilator operation and patient breathing. In the design of the interactive experience platform of the medical pendant, sound elements are added to the Unity3d engine and invoked through relevant sound plug-ins.

It's hard to guess where a sound is coming from with just one ear. The difference in loudness and time between the ears gives people a very good sense of direction on the horizontal plane. With the speaker placed on the left, the sound waves first reach the left ear as the distance decreases, and then around the head to the right ear.

In the virtual interactive platform of the medical pendant, the user can effectively isolate the sound environment in the real environment by wearing the headset, reduce the irrelevant sound interference, and restore the full-dimensional real sound effect for the user as far as possible.

4.3 Haptic Stimulus Presentation

In order to improve users' immersive experience in the virtual system, when users interact with the handle, corresponding haptic feedback is provided for interactive objects in the medical pendant in the virtual system.

In the multi-channel interactive platform of the medical pendant, a vibration feedback module is provided for the user. When the user interacts with the object in the virtual environment, the vibration feedback is provided to prompt the user have touched on the object, which is consistent with the haptic feedback experience of the actual object in the real environment and can effectively guide the user to carry out the next operation. In addition, the vibration mode is adopted to simulate haptic feedback, which is more easily accepted by users than other haptic feedback forms [13].

Haptic perception is not only the passive receiver of information through touch but also the active selection and refinement of feelings according to current goals and concepts [14, 15]. People's fingers, hands, and bodies do not come from outside the world. They take direct action to get the information they need. Therefore, haptic perception cannot simply be regarded as a process to obtain information outwardly but forms a closed "active perception" cycle.

In the virtual interactive experience platform, users conduct an interactive operation in the virtual scene through the handle and provide corresponding haptic vibration feedback. Compared with the previous operation methods such as a mouse, users' hands are liberated to a greater extent, so that users have more "active perception" interaction space. However, compared with the user's flexible hand movements, the handle lacks a lot of haptic experience, and the interaction model also has certain limitations. In addition, in the virtual scene, visual effects stimulate the user's visual senses more strongly. It is easy for the user to ignore the vibration feedback of the handle when operating, and the vibration feedback form is relatively single. When users interact with a variety of sensory channels at the same time, it is difficult for them to understand the prompt meaning of each vibration feedback. Therefore, when designing haptic interaction mode in the virtual scene, visual channel and voice channel should be combined to provide a simple and efficient interaction mode for users. In the multi-channel medical pendant interactive platform, haptic feedback can be designed with two different frequencies: long vibration and short vibration, corresponding to important prompt message and notification message respectively.

5 Feasibility Evaluation

After the MMPIP is completed, the feasibility evaluation of product interaction functions is performed according to the design requirements. First, the mechanical structure of the medical pendant is simulated in the modeling software to evaluate its structural integrity and simulation effect. The mechanical structure can effectively complete functions such as rotation, translation, contraction, and roll. Next, it is necessary to perform operations simulation related tests in the VR environment. The evaluation contains two aspects, one is whether the related functions of the medical pendant product can be fully used, and the function is compared with the real product. The second is whether the product has severe dizziness and unrealism during the simulation operation. This is because of the current limitations of the development of VR technology, a common problem in VR interactive systems.

5.1   Participants

A total of 12 graduate students participated in this experiment (5 males and 7 females). The age and gender were randomly selected to avoid the accidentalness of the experimental data. The subjects did not have experience in operating the VR system, which ensured the objectiveness of the system usability test results sex.

5.2   Experimental Task

This experiment was performed in a laboratory equipped with HTC VIVE. The space size of the Lighthouse base station (3 m × 3 m), including the area for the participants to adjust after completing the experimental tasks. The purpose of the experiment is to observe and record the response during the operation of the participants, to obtain the data of the number of incorrect operations for analysis, and to reflect the problems in the interactive operation and interface design of the platform.

The experiment equipment included an HTC VIVE helmet, a Lighthouse base station, and two configuration handle. The computer equipment used in this test operation system is ASUS FX50JK4710. During the test process, it is necessary to ensure that the Unity3D software can run normally and the helmet display screen runs smoothly. Therefore, the performance of the hardware equipment needs to be kept smooth and stable to ensure the successful completion of the experimental tasks.

Table 3. Different noise averages in the ward

Task sequence	Task content	Mission scenario
1	System environment browsing	Enter the platform through the novice guide page
2	View product Information	Click the device model with the handle
3	Installation of medical equipment	Watch the operation animation in the correct order of the device
4	Scheme switching of medical suspension tower	Select related icon button by handle
5	Back to select other features	Select toolbar back button by handle
6	Shut down the system	Take off system equipment

The task content and task scenario are shown in Table 3 above. The experiment was divided into two parts. First, the design scheme and the operating flow of the platform are explained in detail, and the participants completed all tasks in the table in order. The evaluation criteria of the test results included one-time completion, multiple-time completion, and failure. Secondly, the subjects completed the subjective evaluation scale. The evaluation scale is a subjective evaluation based on the ease of use of the system interface, the sensory experience of the scene environment.

5.3 Results

All 12 subjects in this experiment completed all the experimental tasks, and the task completion rate was 100%. After completing the tasks, 12 subjects scored each item on the subjective evaluation Likert scale. Satisfaction was divided into very satisfied, satisfied, average, op-posed, and strongly opposed, which were recorded as 5, 4, and 3, 2 points, 1 point. The average value is calculated through statistical scores, and the results are shown in Table 4 below.

Table 4. Result of subjective evaluation scale

Task content	Total score	Average score
The overall style of the system design is consistent	54	4.5
Interactive animation loads fast	36	3.0
Product interaction operation conforms to common habits	52	4.3
Reasonable page interaction	52	4.3
Clear classification of navigation page information	52	4.3
Icon is accurate	50	4.2
Timely and clear operation prompt information	54	4.5
Reasonable menu design	56	4.7
Learning content in the system is helpful	56	4.7

The statistical data in the table can reflect that the MMIPP provides users with an effective interactive modality in the virtual environment. The multi-channel interactive design is valid to learn and operate and has good practical value. Multi-channel interaction also helps users more flexibly use multiple sensory channels to operate with the medical pendant in the virtual environment. More importantly, it successfully applied the method of enhancing the user's multi-sensory interaction in a virtual environment, which helped us provide directions for exploring more effective medical device training methods in the future.

6 Future Studies

According to the experimental task availability from the experimental results and the data of the subjective evaluation scale, the design of the multi-channel medical pendant interactive platform can be improved in the following directions:

(1) In the subsequent design process, design optimization needs to be performed to better guide the user to the operation of the choices and allow the user to select the device more quickly.

(2) The loading speed of the interactive animation is too slow due to the excessive loading of files during system development. This is mainly determined by the configuration of the hardware device. The high-configuration computer can be replaced to run the application.

(3) In the design of interactive operation, the fault tolerance of the system is appropriately improved, and appropriate prompts are provided when the user makes an error so that the user feels a more friendly interactive experience.

References

1. Zhang, Y.: The study and application of usability in product design based on VR. Doctoral dissertation (2007)
2. Borsci, S., Buckle, P., Uchegbu, I., Ni, M., Walne, S., Hanna, G.B.: Integrating human factors and health economics to inform the design of medical device: a conceptual framework. EMBEC/NBC-2017. IP, vol. 65, pp. 49–52. Springer, Singapore (2018). https://doi.org/10.1007/978-981-10-5122-7_13
3. Arney, D., Pajic, M., Goldman, J.M., Lee, I., Mangharam, R., Sokolsky, O.: Toward patient safety in closed-loop medical device systems. In: Proceedings of the 1st ACM/IEEE International Conference on Cyber-Physical Systems, Sweden, pp. 139–148. ACM (2010)
4. Lin, L., Vicente, K.J., Doyle, D.J.: Patient safety, potential adverse drug events, and medical device design: a human factors engineering approach. Biomed. Inform. 34(4), 274–284 (2001)
5. Gonzalez, B.G., Medellin, C.H.I., Lim, T.: Development of a haptic virtual reality system for assembly planning and evaluation. Procedia Technol. 7(Complete), 265–272 (2013)
6. Lee, H.C.: Location-aware speakers for the virtual reality environments.. IEEE Access 5, 2636–2640 (2017)
7. Bovet, S., Debarba, H.G., Herbelin, B., Molla, E., Boulic, R.: The critical role of self-contact for embodiment in virtual reality. IEEE Trans. Vis. Comput. Graph. 24, 1428–1436 (2018)
8. Li, C.: Research on human-computer interaction technology in virtual reality system (2017)
9. Xiao, L.: Research on system stability for haptic interaction based on virtual reality. Doctoral dissertation (2015)
10. Yang, D., Song, Y., Zhou, J., Chen, H.: Noise level survey and analysis in ICU. Clin. Med. Pract. 18(24), 191–192 (2014)
11. Human Auditory Range. http://www.cochlea.org/en/hear/human-auditory-range. Accessed 6 June 2018
12. Li, R., Ye, S., He, M., Pan, Y.: Application of film and television VR technology in auditory sound design and case study. Advanced Motion Picture Technology
13. Swapp, D., Pawar, V., Loscos, C.: Interaction with co-located haptic feedback in virtual reality. Virtual Reality 10(1), 24–30 (2006)
14. Gibson, J.J.: Observations on active touch. Psychol. Rev. 69(6), 477–491 (2016)
15. Lin, S.: From haptic to olfactory: how long will it take to truly achieve "virtual reality"? Internet Weekly (11), 14–15 (2017)

A Virtual Reality Dental Anxiety Mitigation Tool Based on Computerized Cognitive Behavioral Therapy

Ting Han[✉], Hanyue Xiao, Tianjia Shen, Yufei Xie, and Zeshi Zhu

School of Design, Shanghai Jiao Tong University, Shanghai, China
{hanting, sarna2018, tianjia.shen,
xyfdesign, zinenviro}@sjtu.edu.cn

Abstract. Dental anxiety has become one of the most important problems affecting patients' timely consultation and visiting experience. The purpose of this study is to help patients who have the emotion of dental anxiety to relieve anxiety by a virtual reality product based on computerized cognitive behavioral therapy. The study collected MDAS, GSR, and HRV data of 24 adults with dental anxiety through experiments to evaluate the degree of dental anxiety, and evaluated the user experience by user experience questionnaire. According to the data analysis, MDAS, GSR, and HRV has been decreased after the intervention, which confirmed the effectiveness of the virtual reality dental anxiety mitigation tool based on computerized cognitive behavioral therapy. At the same time, direct exposure to the virtual dental environment also has certain utility, but the effect is not equal to the former.

Keywords: Virtual reality · Dental anxiety · Serious game · Computerized cognitive behavioral therapy

1 Introduction

Dental anxiety is one of the most important factors influencing the patient's dental experience. Because of the phobia of pain and dental treatment equipment such as dental drills, fear of unknown things, or terrible dental treatment experience in childhood, some people are caught in a negative emotion of dental anxiety. Dental anxiety makes patients unable to cooperate with dentists. Delay treatment or even refuse to see a doctor. Statistically, dental anxiety afflicts a significant proportion as high as 50%, with 6%–20% of patients who have severe dental anxiety [1]. Therefore, reliable and timely management of the negative emotions is necessary to improve oral health and life quality for the people who are experiencing dental anxiety.

© Springer Nature Switzerland AG 2020
J. Y. C. Chen and G. Fragomeni (Eds.): HCII 2020, LNCS 12191, pp. 385–398, 2020.
https://doi.org/10.1007/978-3-030-49698-2_26

2 Literature Review

2.1 Dental Anxiety

A growing number of scholars and dentists are aware of the adverse effects of dental anxiety on oral health, and have carried out a series of researches on dental anxiety. They explore the means of assessing dental anxiety and the factors affecting dental anxiety, with the intention of finding ways to relieve dental anxiety. Those effective ways can be applied in clinical practice. Psychological intervention and drug treatment have proven to be effective in alleviating dental anxiety at present. Psychological intervention such as cognitive behavioral therapy, exposure therapy, music therapy, aromatherapy, relaxation and distraction have been increasingly used in the practice of oral treatment with the advantage of no side effect.

Here comes the overview of some psychological intervention methods and their advantages and disadvantages (Table 1).

Table 1. Overview of some psychological intervention methods.

Methods	Advantages	Disadvantages
Cognitive behavioral therapy [2–5]	Targeted, can be adjusted according to the target users; Wide applicability; Excellent intervention	Traditional cognitive behavioral therapy requires high service and high quality of doctors and nurses
Aromatherapy [6, 7]	Universal	Little correlation with treatment process; Weak interaction; Not suitable for patients with allergic constitution;
Music therapy [8, 9]	Universal; No side effects	Little correlation with treatment process; Weak interaction
Distraction [10, 11]	Excellent intervention on state anxiety	Not suitable for patients with allergic constitution; Poor intervention on trait anxiety
Exposure therapy [12, 13]	Excellent intervention; Targeted	Doctors and nurses are needed traditionally; Some patients may not accept this way
System desensitization [10]	Excellent intervention; Targeted; Milder	Patient's imagination is difficult to control traditionally

2.2 Cognitive Behavioral Therapy

Cognitive behavioral therapy (CBT) is widely used in the practice of dental anxiety through cognitive reorganization, knowledge education, Psychological counseling and relaxation. Mihaela (2014) examined the effectiveness of cognitive behavioral therapy in reducing dental anxiety. Four sessions of cognitive restructuring technique were used in order to reduce the dental anxiety level. Compared with the control group without any intervention, substantial reductions of dental trait anxiety could be obtained through sessions of cognitive restructuring [2]. Tellez (2015) developed a cognitive-behavioral protocol based on psychoeducation, exposure to feared dental procedures, and cognitive restructuring. This computer based tool was confirmed to be efficacious in reducing dental anxiety [5].

However, as a psychological intervention, limitations of cognitive behavioral therapy are also significant. This method requires full follow-up by researchers, dentists or professional psychologists. Moreover, CBT personnel need to undergo rigorous training, which requires a lot of human resources and needs a fixed training location.

Therefore, more auxiliary therapies such as reading therapy and computerized cognitive behavior therapy are developed based on modern technology and resources.

Computerized cognitive behavior therapy can effectively reduce the occupation of professional resources and suggest to be efficacious in alleviating dental anxiety. In recent years, scholars combine cognitive behavior theory with design science furtherly. The interdisciplinary research bridges the deficiencies of traditional cognitive behavior therapy.

2.3 Virtual Reality

With the real-time performance feedback, self-guided exploration and independent practice, low-cost environment that can be duplicated and distributed, virtual reality enables patients to achieve remote self-training in the field of medical, which greatly saves resources. In the field of medical treatment, virtual reality has been widely used in psychotherapy, cognitive rehabilitation, mental disorders and auxiliary training [14–17]. It also has a good effect on relieving anxiety caused by fear. For example, combining exposure therapy and virtual reality can effectively relieve acrophobia, social phobia and preoperative anxiety [18, 19]. On the other hand, it is also an effective way to provide a relaxing environment in virtual reality to help patients escape from the horrible reality [11].

To this end, this study firstly summarized the existing literature, analyzed the characteristics of the people who are experiencing dental anxiety. Then the whole study developed a relief tool for dental anxiety in virtual reality environment based on serious game and cognitive behavioral therapy, and explored a new type of computerized cognitive behavior therapy framework based on virtual reality. The purpose is to help patients with evasion and fear of oral treatment to relieve their negative emotions and improve their treatment experience (Table 2).

Table 2. Literature review about dental anxiety.

Author	Year	Methods	Application	Index	Result	Sample
Di Nasso [8]	2016	Music therapy	The music consisted of 5 tracks composed by Stefano Crespan Shantam which was turned to 432 Hz	DAS; HR; DBP; SBP	Music therapy is a valid nonpharmacologic adjuvant to anxiety perception in endodontic therapies	100
Lehrner [6]	2005	Aromatherapy; Music therapy	Four groups: control/music/orange odor/lavender odor	STAI; MDBF	Both ambient odors of orange and lavender reduced anxiety and improved mood in patients waiting for dental treatment.	200
Haukebø [3]	2008	CBT	Randomized controlled trial: one-session CBT and five-session CBT	DAS; DFS	The five-session treatment did significantly better than the one-session treatment on the self-report measures of dental anxiety	40
Gujjar [12]	2019	VRET	Five different VR scenarios about dental clinics are provided.	MDAS; BAT; DFS; HR	VRET was found to be efficacious in the treatment of dental phobia	30
Neacsu [10]	2014	System desensitization; Relaxation	Randomized controlled trial: Muscle relaxation technique and Systematic desensitization technique	MDAS; DFS	The most effective therapy of dental anxiety will be decided on an individual basis	60
Dumitrache [2]	2014	CBT	Four sessions of cognitive restructuring technique have been used in order to reduce the anxiety level	MDAS; DFS	After using the cognitive technique, the anxiety level decreased significantly both for the global anxiety index and for its components	47

CBT: Cognitive behavioral therapy; C-CBT: Computer cognitive behavioral therapy; VRET: Virtual reality exposure therapy; IVET: In vivo exposure therapy; ET: Exposure therapy; DAS: Dental anxiety scale; HR: Heart rate; DBP: Diastolic blood pressure; SBP: Systolic blood pressure; MDBF: Mehrdimensionale Befindlichkeitsfragebogen; MDAS: Modified dental anxiety scale; BAT: Behavioral avoidance test

3   Materials and Methods

3.1   System Design

Before completing the specific design, the research investigated the reasons of dental anxiety, and determined the horror gradient of the dental clinic scene. It is found that negative associations with dental treatment, insufficient awareness of dental diseases, fear of unknown treatments and barriers to communicate with dentists become the main causes of anxiety. The result will guide subsequent designs.

Four virtual dental treatment scenarios with increasing horror levels are developed according to the research:

1) A dental environment with dental instruments and a virtual dentist surrounding the participant.
2) The virtual dentist with a dental mirror in his hand moves towards to the participant, just like doing an oral examination.
3) The virtual dentist with a dental syringe in his hand moves towards to the participant, just like doing an oral therapy.
4) The virtual dentist with a dental drill in his hand moves towards to the participant, just like doing an oral therapy.

The experiment was performed in a quiet room of 5 m * 3 m. The seat simulates the height and angle of a dental seat. The VR helmet uses HTC VIVE, including a helmet, two handles and two lighthouses. The program is developed by Unity 2018.3.10 and runs in SteamVR.

Experimental Group (VR-CBT). The VR-CBT group will present a narrative and easy-to-understand interpretation of the dentist's upcoming treatment before each scene. Participants can autonomously control the course of treatment according to their own adaptation.

Control Group (VR). The VR group will only be presented in the same 4 virtual scenes as the VR-CBT group (Figs. 1 and 2).

Fig. 1. The virtual reality dental anxiety mitigation product design. (Left: the scene design; Right: the scene from the patient's perspective.)

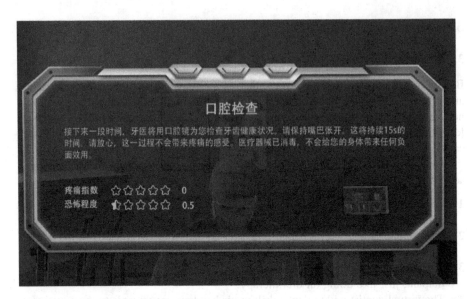

Fig. 2. The introduction to the upcoming virtual treatment in the form of a pop-up window in the experimental group.

3.2   Participants

24 participants who were about to visit a dentist were recruited in order to verify the effectiveness of computerized cognitive-behavioral therapy in virtual reality. All participants were asked to sign a consent and fill out a subjective basic information questionnaire before the experiment. The inclusion criteria are as follow: 1) Participants with a MDAS score ≥ 15; 2) Participants who don't have hearing or visual impairments, known balance disorders, post-traumatic stress disorder, developmental or intellectual disability. 3) Participants have never received any cognitive behavioral therapy treatment for their dental anxiety in the past.

3.3   Procedure

A total of 24 samples were tested in the single-blind experiment, with 12 participants in the experimental group and 12 participants in the control group. First of all, participants should filling the modified dental anxiety scale. Then they were asked to wear the physiological testing equipment in order to get their galvanic skin response and heart rate. After that, a video about tooth extraction was provided to determine their baseline of dental anxiety. Participants both in the experimental group and control group then wore the VR helmet for the text. At the same time, quantitative intervention results were obtained during the text.

After the experiment, participants could remove the physiological testing equipment and the VR helmet, then filled out the modified dental anxiety scale again and filled out the user experience questionnaire.

3.4   Measurements

Modified Dental Anxiety Scale (MDAS). The modified dental anxiety scale is a common measure of dental anxiety which is effective in assessing dental anxiety in an internationally diverse sample. The scale consists of five indicators: 1) If you went to your Dentist for treatment tomorrow, how would you feel? 2) If you were sitting in the waiting room (waiting for treatment), how would you feel? 3) If you were about to have a tooth drilled, how would you feel? 4) If you were about to have your teeth scaled and polished, how would you feel? 5) If you were about to have a local anaesthetic injection in your gum, above an upper back tooth, how would you feel?

Each indicator is divided into five levels with a score from 1 to 5: 1) Not Anxious 2) Slightly Anxious 3) Fairly Anxious 4) Very Anxious 5) Extremely Anxious. The total score ranges from 5 to 25 points, and usually 15 points is the threshold for mid-to-high dental anxiety [20].

Galvanic Skin Response (GSR). GSR measurements work by detecting the changes in electrical ionic activity resulting from changes in sweat gland activity. It is found that galvanic skin response can respond to anxiety. A statistically significant correlation was found between galvanic skin conductance and dental anxiety. Advantageously, combining with GSR measurements during the experiment can quantify patients' anxiety. Caprara measured patients' dental fear scale, GSC and polygraph response to key verbal questions, finally verified that dental anxiety can be measured objectively by skin conductance [21].

Heart Rate (HR). Heart rate can reflect the patient's anxiety during oral treatment. When people feel stress or anxiety, a series of responses come out, such as increased heart rate, blood pressure, blood sugar, and dilated pupils. Heart rate is usually included in the evaluation index when measuring the degree of dental anxiety.

In the study, Brand Psytech were used to collect galvanic skin response and heart rate data.

User Experience Questionnaire (UEQ). User experience questionnaire was used to evaluate a preferably comprehensive impression of the product user experience from the six aspects of attractiveness, perspicuity, efficiency, dependability, stimulation, and novelty.

4   Result

4.1   MDAS

After the F-test, this study used an independent sample T-test to verify whether the baseline levels of dental anxiety in the experimental group and the control group were consistent. The result shows that there is no significant difference in the degree of dental anxiety between the experimental group and the control group ($p = 0.792 > 0.05$). The samples are statistically significant (Fig. 3).

Group Statistics

	組別	N	Mean	Std. Deviation	Std. Error Mean
MDASpretext	1	12	17.7500	3.27872	.94648
	2	12	17.4167	2.81096	.81146

Independent Samples Test

		Levene's Test for Equality of Variances		t-test for Equality of Means						
									95% Confidence Interval of the Difference	
		F	Sig.	t	df	Sig. (2-tailed)	Mean Difference	Std. Error Difference	Lower	Upper
MDASpretext	Equal variances assumed	.591	.450	.267	22	.792	.33333	1.24671	-2.25219	2.91886
	Equal variances not assumed			.267	21.499	.792	.33333	1.24671	-2.25569	2.92236

Fig. 3. Independent samples text of MDAS (group 1: experimental group; group 2: control group).

Moreover, the study used paired-samples T-test to compare the self-reported differences in dental anxiety between the experimental and control groups. There are four sets of MDAS data: the experimental group's pre-text (Mean = 17.75) and post-text (Mean = 14.33), the control group's pre-text (Mean = 17.42) and post-text (Mean = 15.83). The data shows that the degree of self-reported dental anxiety decreased in both groups after the experiment. there is a significant difference between the pre-test and post-test in the experimental group ($p = 0.002 < 0.01$), and there has a difference between the pre-test and post-test in the control group, but the difference was not significant. ($P = 0.027 < 0.05$) The data above proves the effectiveness of the virtual reality dental anxiety mitigation tool based on computerized cognitive behavioral therapy. At the same time, direct exposure to the virtual dental environment also has certain utility (Fig. 4).

Paired Samples Statistics

		Mean	N	Std. Deviation	Std. Error Mean
Pair 1	MDASpretextVRCBT	17.7500	12	3.27872	.94648
	MDASposttextVRCBT	14.3333	12	4.43813	1.28118
Pair 2	MDASpretextVR	17.4167	12	2.81096	.81146
	MDASposttextVR	15.8333	12	3.12856	.90314

Paired Samples Correlations

		N	Correlation	Sig.
Pair 1	MDASpretextVRCBT & MDASposttextVRCBT	12	.737	.006
Pair 2	MDASpretextVR & MDASposttextVR	12	.743	.006

Paired Samples Test

		Paired Differences							
					95% Confidence Interval of the Difference				
		Mean	Std. Deviation	Std. Error Mean	Lower	Upper	t	df	Sig. (2-tailed)
Pair 1	MDASpretextVRCBT - MDASposttextVRCBT	3.41667	2.99874	.86566	1.51136	5.32197	3.947	11	.002
Pair 2	MDASpretextVR - MDASposttextVR	1.58333	2.15146	.62107	.21636	2.95031	2.549	11	.027

Fig. 4. Paired samples text of MDAS.

4.2   SC/GSR

Figure 5 shows one typical participant's GSR, BVP and HR trend which are measured with biosignal recorder during the experiment. It is found that as the experiment progresses, the participant's GSR decreasing gradually.

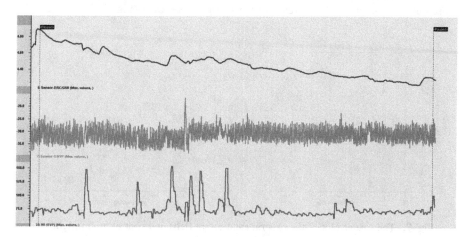

Fig. 5. One typical participant's GSR, BVP and HR trend during the experiment.

Furtherly, the study used paired-samples T-text to analyze the changes between the pre-text and post-text of the experimental group and control group after confirming that there is no significant difference in the degree of the galvanic skin response between the experimental group and the control group before the experiment. The first 30 s of the experiment was selected as the pre-test data, and the last 30 s of the experiment was used as the post-test data. The data shows that both experimental group and control group have a significant difference (experimental group: p = 0.003 < 0.05, control group: p = 0.004 < 0.05) (Fig. 6).

Paired Samples Statistics

		Mean	N	Std. Deviation	Std. Error Mean
Pair 1	1	3.4533	12	1.79302	.51760
	2	2.6933	12	1.60648	.46375
Pair 2	3	2.1617	12	1.44637	.41753
	4	1.7342	12	1.44299	.41655

Paired Samples Correlations

		N	Correlation	Sig.
Pair 1	1 & 2	12	.926	.000
Pair 2	3 & 4	12	.960	.000

Paired Samples Test

		Paired Differences							
					95% Confidence Interval of the Difference				
		Mean	Std. Deviation	Std. Error Mean	Lower	Upper	t	df	Sig. (2–tailed)
Pair 1	1 – 2	.76000	.67956	.19617	.32823	1.19177	3.874	11	.003
Pair 2	3 – 4	.42750	.40930	.11816	.16744	.68756	3.618	11	.004

Fig. 6. Paired samples text of GSR (group 1: experimental group's pre-text; group 2: experimental group's post-text; group 3: control group's pre-text; group 4: control group's post-text).

The research furtherly used a scatter plot to analyze whether the difference is reflected in relieving or increasing anxiety. In the scatter plot, the pre-text is used as the independent variable, and the post-test is used as the dependent variable. According to the chart, most of the scattered points are below the line y = x. The significant difference is reflected in relieving the dental anxiety. Scilicet, the participants in the two groups' dental anxiety level decreased after using the product (Fig. 7).

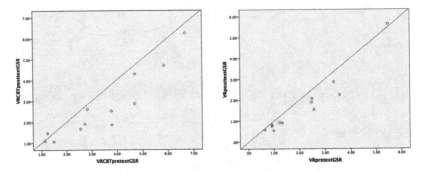

Fig. 7. The scatter plot of the experimental group (left) and control group (right).

Moreover, an independent sample T-test was used to compare the difference of GSR between the experimental group and the control group (p = 0.138 > 0.05). It can be seen that the design of the two groups can alleviate the level of anxiety, but the difference between the two groups is not significant.

4.3   HRV

The study used paired-samples T-test to analyze the differences between the time-domain index RMSD and SDNN of the heart rate variability between the experimental group and the control group (Fig. 8).

Paired Samples Test

		Paired Differences							
					95% Confidence Interval of the Difference				
		Mean	Std. Deviation	Std. Error Mean	Lower	Upper	t	df	Sig. (2-tailed)
Pair 1	VRCBTpretextRMSSD – VRCBTposttextRMSSD	40.36750	50.79827	14.66420	8.09182	72.64318	2.753	11	.019
Pair 2	VRpretextRMSSD – VRposttextRMSSD	21.13417	40.53585	11.70169	−4.62108	46.88942	1.806	11	.098
Pair 3	VRCBTpretextSDNN – VRCBTposttextSDNN	35.97083	31.28349	9.03077	16.09425	55.84741	3.983	11	.002
Pair 4	VRpretextSDNN – VRposttextSDNN	28.06000	57.42069	16.57593	−8.42337	64.54337	1.693	11	.119

Fig. 8. Paired samples text of HRV

In terms of RMSSD, there is a significant difference between the experimental group's pre-text and post-test ($p = 0.019 < 0.05$) while there is no significant difference between the control group's pre-text and post-test ($p = 0.098 > 0.05$). And in terms of SDNN, there is a significant difference between the experimental group's pre-text and post-test ($p = 0.002 < 0.05$) while there is no significant difference between the control group's pre-text and post-test ($p = 0.119 > 0.05$).

4.4   UEQ

The study combines the user experience questionnaire to evaluate the user experience of product design from the six aspects of attractiveness, perspicuity, efficiency, dependability, stimulation, and novelty. In general, the user experience of the experimental group is better than that of the control group. And the product design of the experimental group is more prominent in three aspects of attractiveness, novelty and perspicuity. These three aspects have a significant difference between the two groups (Figs. 9 and 10).

Group Statistics

	组别	N	Mean	Std. Deviation	Std. Error Mean
Attractiveness	1	12	1.8475	.39299	.11345
	2	12	.7925	.30236	.08728
Perspicuity	1	12	1.7500	.81881	.23637
	2	12	1.1250	.37689	.10880
Efficiency	1	12	1.3958	.32784	.09464
	2	12	1.0208	.44541	.12858
Dependability	1	12	1.0625	.44114	.12735
	2	12	.8542	.31003	.08950
Stimulation	1	12	1.5417	.64696	.18676
	2	12	.4375	.62272	.17976
Novelty	1	12	2.0417	.69767	.20140
	2	12	1.0208	.70274	.20286

Independent Samples Test

		Levene's Test for Equality of Variances		t-test for Equality of Means					95% Confidence Interval of the Difference	
		F	Sig.	t	df	Sig. (2–tailed)	Mean Difference	Std. Error Difference	Lower	Upper
Attractiveness	Equal variances assumed	.808	.378	7.371	22	.000	1.05500	.14314	.75815	1.35185
	Equal variances not assumed			7.371	20.644	.000	1.05500	.14314	.75702	1.35298
Perspicuity	Equal variances assumed	4.188	.053	2.402	22	.025	.62500	.26021	.08536	1.16464
	Equal variances not assumed			2.402	15.461	.029	.62500	.26021	.07182	1.17818
Efficiency	Equal variances assumed	3.294	.083	2.349	22	.028	.37500	.15965	.04390	.70610
	Equal variances not assumed			2.349	20.214	.029	.37500	.15965	.04219	.70781
Dependability	Equal variances assumed	.633	.435	1.338	22	.194	.20833	.15565	-.11446	.53113
	Equal variances not assumed			1.338	19.735	.196	.20833	.15565	-.11662	.53329
Stimulation	Equal variances assumed	.014	.908	4.260	22	.000	1.10417	.25922	.56658	1.64176
	Equal variances not assumed			4.260	21.968	.000	1.10417	.25922	.56653	1.64180
Novelty	Equal variances assumed	.014	.907	3.571	22	.002	1.02083	.28586	.42800	1.61367
	Equal variances not assumed			3.571	21.999	.002	1.02083	.28586	.42800	1.61367

Fig. 9. Independent samples text of UEQ (group 1: experimental group; group 2: control group).

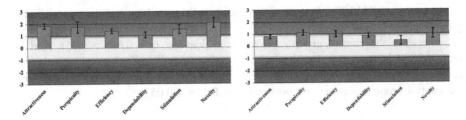

Fig. 10. The mean value and standard deviation of the UEQ's six aspect (experimental group: figure left; control group: figure right).

5   Discussion

It is found that participants had higher levels of dental anxiety before intervention. The anxiety level of experimental group and control group are both decreased after intervention. And the anxiety level of VR-CBT group was significantly lower than that of the control group. This demonstrates the effectiveness of cognitive behavioral therapy combined with virtual reality, while also finding that exposing patients to virtual reality environments directly also plays a role. Compared with exposure therapy under virtual reality, cognitive behavioral therapy in virtual reality environment is obviously more effective, and the result shows that the user experience of the VR-CBT group is better than the control group especially in terms of attractiveness, novelty and perspicuity. In addition, combined with the MDAS and GSR index before and after the experiment, the correlation between the GSR and dental anxiety emotions can be verified.

This study is an interdisciplinary research in the field of health care and industrial design. It provides a virtual reality product design to release dental anxiety that can be used at home. The first advantage of the design lies in the vivid dentistry environment that virtual reality simulated. It can let patients who tend to delay or refuse to see a doctor adjust their mood remotely and seek medical advice timely, and the treatment experience becomes better accordingly. Secondly, computerized cognitive behavioral therapy based on virtual reality can replace oral imparting experience. By the time, it allows patients to control the treatment process autonomously and professional therapists will be no longer needed. This is a new practice of virtual reality in the field of medical, which has certain practical significance and clinical value. The study shows that computerized cognitive behavioral therapy combined with virtual reality is an effective method to alleviate the emotion of anxiety in dental treatment. However, there are still some limitations. The experiment belongs to a short-term experiment, which can only test state anxiety but do not reflect the effects of long-term trait anxiety. In the future, the sample size will be expanded and long-term intervention will be included.

Acknowledgement. The research is supported by National Social Science Fund (Grant No. 18BRK009).

References

1. Kleinknecht, R.A., Klepac, R.K., Alexander, L.D.: Origins and characteristics of fear of dentistry. J. Am. Dent. Assoc. **86**(4), 842–848 (1973)
2. Dumitrache, M.A., Neacsu, V., Sfeatcu, I.R.: Efficiency of cognitive technique in reducing dental anxiety. Procedia Soc. Behav. Sci. **149**, 302–306 (2014). https://doi.org/10.1016/j.sbspro.2014.08.246
3. Haukebø, K., et al.: One- vs. five-session treatment of dental phobia: a randomized controlled study. J. Behav. Ther. Exp. Psychiatry **39**(3), 381–390 (2008). https://doi.org/10.1016/j.jbtep.2007.09.006
4. Matsuoka, H., Chiba, I., Sakano, Y., Toyofuku, A., Abiko, Y.: Cognitive behavioral therapy for psychosomatic problems in dental settings. BioPsychoSocial Med. **11**(1) (2017). Article number: 18. https://doi.org/10.1186/s13030-017-0102-z
5. Tellez, M., et al.: Computerized tool to manage dental anxiety. J. Dent. Res. **94**(9_suppl), 174S–180S (2015). https://doi.org/10.1177/0022034515598134
6. Lehrner, J., Marwinski, G., Lehr, S., Johren, P., Deecke, L.: Ambient odors of orange and lavender reduce anxiety and improve mood in a dental office. Physiol. Behav. **86**(1), 92–95 (2005). https://doi.org/10.1016/j.physbeh.2005.06.031
7. Venkataramana, M., Pratap, K., Padma, M., Kalyan, S., Reddy, A.A., Sandhya, P.: Effect of aromatherapy on dental patient anxiety: a randomized controlled trial. J. Indian Assoc. Public Health Dent. **14**(2), 131 (2016)
8. Di Nasso, L., Nizzardo, A., Pace, R., Pierleoni, F., Pagavino, G., Giuliani, V.: Influences of 432 Hz music on the perception of anxiety during endodontic treatment: a randomized controlled clinical trial. J. Endod. **42**(9), 1338–1343 (2016). https://doi.org/10.1016/j.joen.2016.05.015
9. Mejía-Rubalcava, C., Alanís-Tavira, J., Mendieta-Zerón, H., Sánchez-Pérez, L.: Changes induced by music therapy to physiologic parameters in patients with dental anxiety. Complement. Ther. Clin. Pract. **21**(4), 282–286 (2015). https://doi.org/10.1016/j.ctcp.2015.10.005
10. Neacsu, V., Sfeatcu, I.R., Maru, N., Dumitrache, M.A.: Relaxation and systematic desensitization in reducing dental anxiety. Procedia Soc. Behav. Sci. **127**, 474–478 (2014). https://doi.org/10.1016/j.sbspro.2014.03.293
11. Tanja-Dijkstra, K., et al.: Can virtual nature improve patient experiences and memories of dental treatment? A study protocol for a randomized controlled trial. Trials **15**(1), 90 (2014). https://doi.org/10.1186/1745-6215-15-90
12. Gujjar, K.R., van Wijk, A., Kumar, R., de Jongh, A.: Efficacy of virtual reality exposure therapy for the treatment of dental phobia in adults: a randomized controlled trial. J. Anxiety Disord. **62**, 100–108 (2019). https://doi.org/10.1016/j.janxdis.2018.12.001
13. Gujjar, K.R., van Wijk, A., Kumar, R., de Jongh, A.: Are technology-based interventions effective in reducing dental anxiety in children and adults? A systematic review. J. Evid. Based Dent. Pract. **19**(2), 140–155 (2019). https://doi.org/10.1016/j.jebdp.2019.01.009
14. Pandrangi, V.C., Gaston, B., Appelbaum, N.P., Albuquerque, F.C., Levy, M.M., Larson, R.A.: The application of virtual reality in patient education. Ann. Vasc. Surg. **59**, 184–189 (2019). https://doi.org/10.1016/j.avsg.2019.01.015
15. Scozzari, S., Gamberini, L.: Virtual reality as a tool for cognitive behavioral therapy: a review. In: Brahnam, S., Jain, L.C. (eds.) Advanced Computational Intelligence Paradigms in Healthcare 6. SCI, vol. 337, pp. 63–108. Springer, Heidelberg (2011). https://doi.org/10.1007/978-3-642-17824-5_5

16. Yang, Y.-C.: Role-play in virtual reality game for the senior. Association for Computing Machinery, Aizu-Wakamatsu (2019)

17. Yu, J., Jiang, R., Feng, Y., Yuan, M., Kang, Y.I., Gu, Z.: Mobile VR game design for stroke rehabilitation. In: Rau, P.-L.P. (ed.) CCD 2018. LNCS, vol. 10912, pp. 95–116. Springer, Cham (2018). https://doi.org/10.1007/978-3-319-92252-2_8

18. Sanchez, A.Y.R., Kunze, K.: Flair: towards a therapeutic serious game for social anxiety disorder. Paper Presented at the Proceedings of the 2018 ACM International Joint Conference and 2018 International Symposium on Pervasive and Ubiquitous Computing and Wearable Computers, Singapore (2018)

19. Thanh, V.D.H., Pui, O., Constable, M.: Room VR: a VR therapy game for children who fear the dark. Paper Presented at the SIGGRAPH Asia 2017 Posters, Bangkok, Thailand (2017)

20. Humphris, G.M., Morrison, T., Lindsay, S.: The modified dental anxiety scale: validation and United Kingdom norms. Community Dent. Health 12(3), 143–150 (1995)

21. Caprara, H.J., Eleazer, P.D., Barfield, R.D., Chavers, S.: Objective measurement of patient's dental anxiety by galvanic skin reaction. J. Endod. 29(8), 493–496 (2003). https://doi.org/10.1097/00004770-200308000-00001

Sampling Electrocardiography Confirmation for a Virtual Reality Pain Management Tool

Maria Matsangidou[1]([⊠]) [iD], Alexis R. Mauger[2] [iD],
Chee Siang Ang[1] [iD], and Constantinos S. Pattichis[3,4] [iD]

[1] Department of Engineering and Digital Arts, University of Kent,
Canterbury, Kent, UK
M.Matsangidou@kent.ac.uk
[2] Endurance Research Group, Department of Sport and Exercise Sciences,
University of Kent, Canterbury, UK
[3] Research Centre on Interactive Media,
Smart Systems and Emerging Technologies, Nicosia, Cyprus
[4] University of Cyprus, Nicosia, Cyprus

Abstract. Previous research has shown that Virtual Reality (VR) technology may provide an alternative solution to pain management for clinical applications based on some psychological intervention strategies. Additional research has suggested that Electrocardiography (ECG) can be an objective measure of pain, with evidence showing that as pain increases, ECG signals should also increase. The aim of this study is to examine the effect of VR on naturally occurring pain when no pharmacological analgesics nor psychological intervention strategies are applied. The above statement will be validated via physiological responses, such as ECG and a correlation between subjective and objective measurements of pain will be made. The findings of the present study extend our understanding of the physiological and psychological effects of VR, providing useful insights into the relationship of VR and the levels of pain and discomfort caused by an exhaustive single limb muscle contraction. The main conclusion reached is that the use of VR can reduce physiological and psychological responses associated with negative sensations. Specifically, the results suggested that VR technology can significantly reduce ECG by 6 bmp, and perceived pain and exertion up to 50%, it can also significantly increase pain tolerance up to three minutes, without the use of any pharmacological analgesics and psychological intervention strategies.

Keywords: Virtual Reality · Electrocardiography · Pain perception

1   Introduction

In the treatment of some conditions, patients have to go through painful physical therapies as parts of the recovery process. For instance, patients with burn injuries have to deal with painful physical therapeutic processes. These processes are fundamental components of rehabilitation because they improve functional outcomes and minimize persistent disabilities; however, patients with burns usually neglect to participate fully in physical therapies due to the acute procedural pain [16, 43].

The original version of this chapter was revised: the chapter's title contained a typo. The correction to this chapter is available at https://doi.org/10.1007/978-3-030-49698-2_29

© Springer Nature Switzerland AG 2020
J. Y. C. Chen and G. Fragomeni (Eds.): HCII 2020, LNCS 12191, pp. 399–414, 2020.
https://doi.org/10.1007/978-3-030-49698-2_27

Pain has been defined as "an unpleasant sensory and emotional experience associated with actual or potential tissue damage" [40], which suggests that pain has both a nociceptive and subjective element to its perception. Therefore, whilst the sensory signal of pain for a given therapeutic process is unavoidable, the intensity or quality of pain that one consciously experiences may not always be the same.

Given the key role of pain perception in influencing people's behaviour, it is therefore important to explore techniques which can offset pain perception during physical therapies, as this could result in an increased willingness to engage with the physical therapeutic processes for a sufficient period of time.

In recent years, computer technology and interactive video games such as Dance–Dance Revolution (DDR), Wii Sports, and Wii Fit offer new opportunities for promoting physical activity. Some research has shown that computer technology and interactive video games have increased energy expenditure and physical activity which produces positive health benefits [17, 19, 20, 25, 33, 48, 53]. Research has also looked into using such technologies in rehabilitation. For instance, some specialized robots have been developed which are responsible to assist patients to regain and improve functional abilities after a stroke [30, 51], or motion analysis of human movement which can assist clinicians and patients during physiotherapy through the provision of a detailed representation of movement related to a specific disability [56].

In the past few years, Virtual Reality (VR) has moved beyond research labs into a mainstream consumer electronic device, allowing users to experience a computer-simulated reality based on visual cues, enhanced with auditory and, in due course, tactile and olfactory interactions. VR provides the user with a complete illusion of different senses and creates an immersive experience [29]. Low-cost consumer-facing immersive VR systems have now become widely available (e.g., Google Cardboard, Gear VR, and Oculus Rift), providing a wide range of opportunities for healthcare applications. In the past few years, there have been emerging research looking into using VR and distraction strategy in pain management mostly in dealing with burn pain with promising results [35].

However, and despite the potential benefits of VR technology, there is a gap in the literature with regards to the positive outcomes of VR in physical pain when no psychological intervention strategies, nor pharmacological analgesics are used. This is even more surprising given the growing interest in VR and pain management in recent years.

Although positive results were found in using VR and psychological intervention strategies to manage chronic or experimental pain, little or nothing is known about the pure use of VR and its effect on reducing the naturally occurring pain experienced during strenuous exercise or physiotherapy when no psychological intervention strategy is in place. Such investigation will improve our knowledge about the pure impact of VR technology on the experience of pain. In addition to the above, most of the previous research on VR for pain management supported their results only via subjective measurements, such as pain scales. Therefore, there is a clear need for physiological responses, so as to validate the accuracy of VR on minimizing pain.

Finally, with few exceptions [31, 36, 37] the majority of the previous studies used high-cost immersive VR solutions. Therefore, further research needs to be conducted in order to examine the feasibility of low-cost affordable VR technologies. Using such affordable VR solutions will reduce the cost of equipment maintenance and allow personalized home-based use.

Given the key role of pain perception in influencing people's behaviour, it is therefore important to explore and validate though psychophysiological responses the VR technologies which can offset pain perception during physical training and therapies. With this study, we aim to determine if and how VR technology on its own (without the use of any psychological interventions and pharmacological analgesics) may moderate the experience of pain. This paper will, therefore, provide knowledge for academics and clinicians on the effectiveness of VR for pain management and guidelines for designers, which can turn out to be invaluable in creating virtual environments for reducing exercise pain.

1.1 Electrocardiography and Pain

The significance of pain as human experience can be inferred from the high percentage of people who experience pain, e.g. one out of four US adults experience continuous pain that lasts for a year or even longer [23].

Although the assessment of pain is often based on subjective self-report, research has shown that Electrocardiography (ECG) can be an important, valid and objective physiological signal for the assessment of clinical pain [39, 52]. In addition, there is a highly positive correlation between ECG reports and pain intensity with one shaping the other [5, 7, 8]. This means that as pain level rises, ECG rises accordingly [49]. As such, clinical research often uses ECG to validate self-report of pain [27]. In terms of exercise and physiotherapy, ECG allows recording physiological changes and correlations between exercise intensity [38]. Therefore, ECG is an important measurement to assess pain intensity during exercise and physiotherapy.

It is worth mentioning that, even though the normal ECG differs between people, there is a healthy range of Beats per Minute (bpm), which should be close to resting ECG. In addition, ECG recovery after exercise is generally fast among athletes but much lower among patients with chronic heart failure [24]. Therefore, we hypothesize that if pain perception could be offset during exercise, this could result in a possible decrease in the ECG rates. This decrease in ECG could mean a lower burden to the heart, since the ECG will remain closer to the resting one which will result in a willingness to either intensify exercise or continue the exercise for a longer period of time, without burdening the heart.

To investigate whether VR technology without the use of any specific psychological intervention strategies can have an effect on the experience of pain, we carried out a within-group study involving 20 participants, who were allocated both in the VR and a non-VR groups. The findings of the VR group were then analyzed in relation to the non-VR group and were validated via physiological responses, such as ECG. The findings were further corroborated through subjective scale self-reports. Correlation between the psychophysiological measurements of pain were also made. This was done to determine the effect of VR on naturally occurring pain when no pharmacological analgesics nor psychological intervention strategies are used.

2 Method

2.1 Ethical Considerations

The study was approved by the University of Kent, Research Ethics & Advisory Group (ref. Prop. 77_2016_17). All participants signed a consent form prior to the study and the study was performed in accordance with the Declaration of Helsinki.

2.2 Participants

Twenty healthy participants, equally selected from both genders (10 males and 10 females), with a mean age of 23 years (M = 23.20, SD = 7.54) participated in the study. All 20 participants performed both VR and non-VR intervention in a counter-balanced design. Participants' one-repetition maximum (1RM) for 180° of dominant arm elbow flexion ranged from 4 to 25 kg with a mean of 12.38 kg (SD = 6.91). Approximately 2/3 of the participants reported engaging in no regular, structured resistance or aerobic exercise (no resistance = 70%, no aerobic = 70% during the testing week). Participants who reported engaging in the regular structured exercise had a weekly mean workout time of 3.20 h (SD = 5.06).

All participants were healthy, with normal vision, and no disability that could affect their performance in the exercise task. In addition, no participant reported taking any chronic medication or having any cardiovascular, mental, or brain condition that could affect their performance or pain perception.

2.3 Procedure

The experiment required each participant to pay two separate visits to the laboratory. The first session involved establishing each participant's 1RM (i.e. the heaviest weight they could lift) and carrying out the VR familiarization session. The second session was the main experimental sessions (VR and conventional non-VR). The VR and non-VR sessions were performed in a counterbalanced design, which means that half of the participants performed first the VR session and then rested for 10 min before moving to the non-VR session. The rest of the participants performed first the non-VR session and then, after resting for 10 min, moved to the non-VR session.

2.4 Instruments

During both experimental sessions, the following data were collected:

Electrocardiography (ECG): ECG was continuously measured with a telemetric device, which was a Polar digital ECG monitor and a Polar Wear-link chest strap (with 2 electrodes) (Polar Electro, N2965, Finland). ECG, was found to provide a measure of the psychological pain anticipation of exercise and thus it has been used in several previous studies to assess pain [e.g. 39, 52].

Time to Exhaustion (TTE): TTE was measured based on the amount of time the participants spent holding the dumbbell. TTE has been previously used during continuous pain tasks [13, 52] to assess the effect of exercise pain (EP), on exercise performance [2]. For health and safety reasons, the maximum experimental time was set up to 15.00 min.

Pain Intensity Rates (PIR): Participants were asked to verbally report their level of perceived pain every 60 s, using the 1–10 Cook Scale [12]. Participants were instructed to report their PIR based on the feeling of pain during exercise rather than on other non-exercise type pain (e.g. dental pain).

Rating of Perceived Exertion (RPE): Participants were asked to verbally report their rating of perceived exertion, using the 6–20 Borg Scale [6], every 60 s of the exercise task. Specifically, participants were asked to report how much effort they had to put to keep their arm in a 90° flexion, irrespective to feelings of discomfort.

Immersive Experience: A self-report 7-point Likert scale questionnaire completed after the exercise task in the VR group to assess the immersive experience. The questionnaire referred to several factors such as Presence and Hand Ownership and was based on the individual's impression of realistic experience. The questionnaire also evaluated the system's usability, via assessing whether the exercise task was performed with no difficulties. The questionnaire also examines whether the individual was familiar with the use of VR technology. Finally, the participants' attitudes towards VR training were examined by asking them whether they can see a future where VR will be used on a daily basis for training routines.

2.5 Data Analysis

Data analyses on Electrocardiography (ECG), Pain Intensity Ratings (PIR), and Ratings of Perceived Exertion (RPE) were carried out using ISO time-points (i.e. those time-based data points consistent across all participants). The shortest time to task failure (TTE) across participants and groups was 2 min, and so ISO time analysis was completed on minute 1 and minute 2 of the exercise task (ECG1, PIR1, RPE1 and ECG2, PIR2, RPE2). Participants' ECG was also recorded when they withdrew from the task (finalECG). The mean ECG across the exercise task for each participant were also calculated (meanECG).

Descriptive statistics were performed to identify the levels of Immersive Experience, usability and the users' attitudes toward VR exercise.

An analysis of paired sample t-test and an ANOVA with repeated measures followed by Bonferroni post hoc test was conducted to examine how VR affects ECG, PIR and RPE, based on ISO time points, measured at task failure and mean ECG. All statistical tests were carried out using the Statistical Package for the Social Sciences (SPSS) version 26. Data are reported as mean and SD, and statistical significance was accepted when $p < 0.05$.

2.6 Apparatus

The VR system was developed using Unity3D version 5 to work with Samsung Gear VR and Samsung Galaxy S6 phone. The 3D models (human upper body, the virtual room, and barbells) (Fig. 1) were created in Maya version 2016. The system was developed to allow the researcher to customize the gender of the human body, dominant hand, skin colours, colours of the t-shirt, and the weights of the barbells. In order to create a sense of embodiment, a Microsoft Band's gyroscope was used to animate the virtual arm, reflecting the movement of the participant's arm (rotation X and Y).

Through the Samsung Galaxy Gear HMD device, the participant was able to see the virtual body sitting on a chair in a neutral looking virtual room. The virtual room was void of any distracting visual information since different environmental factors might cause a degree of distraction. A table with a yoga mat on it was present in the virtual room, simulating the conditions of the actual environment (see Fig. 1).

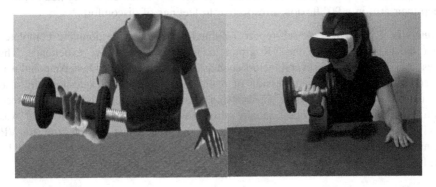

Fig. 1. User's perception: To the left: human 3D model. To the right: representation of the actual environment.

3   Study Results

3.1   Immersive Experience

Most of the participants were not familiar with the use of VR technology. VR technology was a new experience for most of them. Therefore, participants reported moderate to low levels of VR prior use during the VR session (M = 3.00, SD = 2.51).

Overall, the participants reported high rates of Immersion in VR. Based on their ratings, the VR application produced a high degree of Presence and Hand Ownership. In addition, most participants reported that the VR application motivated them positively. The specifics of the results are presented as follows:

During the VR exercise session, the participants reported high levels of presence (M = 5.67, SD = 0.94) and moderate to high levels of hand ownership (M = 4.40, SD = 1.80). In addition, during the VR exercise session, the participants reported high levels of usability, since they found it easy for them to lift the dumbbell and perform the exercise through the VR (M = 5.95, SD = 0.94). Furthermore, we also asked the participants if they can imagine their self to use the VR technology to exercise daily and all the participants (n = 20) responded positively to this query. They also reposed that VR can be a motivational technology for strenuous exercise training (M = 4.90, SD = 2.10).

3.2   Electrocardiography (ECG)

To investigate whether there was a difference in the participants' mean ECG (mean-ECG) between the VR and the conventional non-VR exercise, an analysis of paired sample t-test was conducted. The analysis revealed a significant difference between the ECG and the two sessions (t(19) = 2.63, p < .05), with the participants' ECG showing significant reduction during the VR exercise (M = 85.46, SD = 12.77) in comparison to the conventional non-VR exercise (M = 91.09, SD = 12.02) (see Fig. 2).

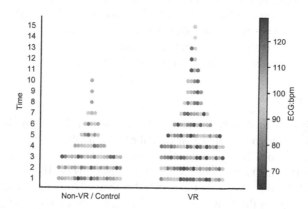

Fig. 2. Sina plot of ECG rates during the conventional non-VR and the VR session.

Additional analysis of an ANOVA with repeated measures followed by Bonferroni post hoc test was conducted to investigate whether there was a difference between the participants' ECG in the two sessions (VR and conventional non-VR) based on the ISO time. The analysis showed a significant difference for the ECG during the two sessions at the first – ECG1 – (F(1, 19) = 4.57, p < .05) and second – ECG2 – (F(1, 19) = 15.31, p < .001) minute. As can be seen in Table 1, the results were in line with the general meanECG, with the participants' ECG being significantly lower during the VR exercise in comparison to the conventional non-VR exercise. Interestingly, as time passed, the data revealed a growing trend for the ECG during the conventional non-VR exercise, in contrast to the VR exercise where the ECG data remained similar for both minutes.

Table 1. ECG: Effects for VR and convectional non-VR exercise during ISO time.

	Intervention	Mean (bpm)	SD
ECG1	VR exercise	82.50	12.67
	Non-VR exercise	87.60	14.06
ECG2	VR exercise	82.50	11.53
	Non-VR exercise	90.25	12.24

The above trend was further supported by the finalECG, with the VR group showing significantly lower (t(19) = 8.22, p < .05) finalECG (M = 88.2, SD = 14.08) in comparison to the conventional non-VR finalECG (M = 95.05, SD = 12.15).

3.3   Time to Exhaustion (TTE)

During the VR exercise, the minimum time to exhaustion for a participant was 3.45 and the maximum 15.00 min, whereas during the conventional non-VR exercise the corresponding minutes were 2.33 and 10.29. therefore, important differences were reported in terms of Time to Exhaustion (TTE) between the VR and the conventional non-VR group (t(19) = −6.54, p < .001). The data indicated that, when the exercise was performed with the use of VR, it lasted significantly longer (M = 7.08, SD = 3.08) in comparison to conventional non-VR exercise (M = 4.23, SD = 1.59).

3.4   Pain Intensity

Additional analysis of an ANOVA with repeated measures followed by Bonferroni post hoc test was conducted to investigate whether there was a difference in the participants' PIR in the two sessions based on the ISO time. The analysis showed a remarkable difference for PIR in the two sessions at the first – PIR1 – (F(1, 19) = 28.36, p < .001) and second – PIR2 – (F(1, 19) = 25.62, p < .001) minute. Further analysis based on the means indicated that, in the conventional non-VR group, at each minute point the PIR ratings given from the participants were significantly; higher PIR1 (M = 3.08, SD = 2.41) and PIR2 (M = 5.95, SD = 3.17), in comparison to the VR group; PIR1 (M = 1.48, SD = 1.83) and PIR2 (M = 3.80, SD = 3.02) (see Fig. 3).

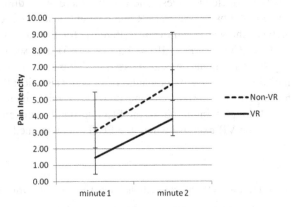

Fig. 3. Mean number of PIR for two sessions, for each ISO minute.

3.5   Rating of Perceived Exertion (RPE)

Additional analysis of an ANOVA with repeated measures followed by Bonferroni post hoc test was conducted to investigate whether there was a difference in the participants' ratings of perceived exertion (RPE) in the two sessions based on the ISO time.

The analysis showed a significant difference for the RPE during the two sessions at the first – RPE1 – (F(1, 19) = 38.97, p < .001) and second – RPE2 – (F(1, 19) = 25.77, p < .001) minute. Further analysis based on the means indicated that exercising with the use of VR can decrease the participants' sensation of how hard they were exerting their arm in order to maintain the muscle contraction (RPE1 (M = 8.05, SD = 2.54) and RPE2 (M = 10.95, SD = 3.75) in comparison to the conventional non-VR group (RPE1 (M = 9.70, SD = 2.90) and RPE2 (M = 14.20, SD = 3.79) (see Fig. 4).

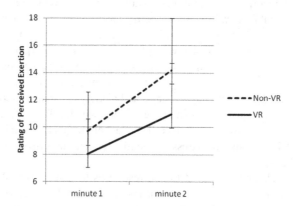

Fig. 4. Mean number of RPE for two sessions, for each ISO minute.

4   Discussion

The results show that VR technology can influence the perception of task difficulty, endurance performance and pain experienced during exercise when no pharmacological analgesics nor psychological intervention strategies are in place. Most importantly, exercising through the use of VR demonstrated a significant decrease in Electrocardiography (ECG), Pain Intensity (PIR) and Perceived Exertion (RPE) reports, and a significant increase in Time to Exhaustion (TTE).

As has been previously explained, ECG increases during exercise [24], but there is a healthy range of bmp, which should be close to resting ECG to be considered as healthy. In addition, ECG recovery after exercise is accelerated in athletes but reduced in patients with chronic heart failure [24]. Our findings suggest that the use of VR technology seems to have helped the individual to exercise for a longer period of time without burdening the heart since the ECG means remained closer to the resting one. This is the first time an application was found to help users to moderate the increase of ECG during exercise without the use of any pharmacological medication or psychological intervention strategies. This is an important finding, because not all pain signals propose a danger to the body, but the experience of it may lead to undesirable behaviour change of the subject. For example, the naturally occurring pain caused by vigorous exercise does not cause physical harm but may moderate exercise behaviour

[38]. This conclusion is a useful starting point towards the identification of effective technologies for subsequent exercise improvement.

In addition to the above, the importance of these findings can be elaborated based on a possible application to individuals with heart disease who could benefit from engaging in exercise. A reduced ECG during exercise could reduce strain on the heart, and therefore exercise in VR could place these individuals at less risk.

The significantly lower ECG might be associated with an observation made in previous research studies, according to which the view of animated cartoons helped to reduce stress and anxiety in clinical environments [11, 28]. The virtual environment used in this study incorporated cartoonish features and representations of the virtual body, hand, and dumbbell, which might be responsible for the reduction of participants' perceived stress and anxiety, which is associated with ECG [47], which is however irrelevant to the personal levels of physical fitness [15]. On the contrary, psychological states, as well as emotional events and processes, can have a dramatic impact on ECG and may result in an increase without an accompanying increase in physical activity [4, 41]. To summarize, stress and anxiety can cause alterations in ECG [18] and their perceived level is an important factor which affects the fluctuations in ECG in response to painful stimuli [see 1]. We believe that the animated cartoon features in our VR encouraged stress reduction, which in turn contributed to the reduction of ECG.

As has been explained above, ECG and responses to painful stimuli increase and decrease in the same direction, which means that when ECG is rising, the pain responses are rising as well [5, 7, 8, 49]. Our findings are in line with the above statement since it was found that when ECG was reduced, the perceived pain and exertion were reduced as well. This effect can be explained by the correlation between ECG and stress. Previous research has shown that stress and anxiety can increase perceived pain [21] and that VR has the ability to decrease situational anxiety related to painful chemotherapy and burn wound care [21] treatments. As a result, the cartoonish representation of the virtual environment might influence the anxiety levels and act as analgesic factors to pain and exertion.

Furthermore, research in psychoanalysis suggests that, unconsciously, individuals recall memories from their childhood and that such memories can shape their mood [10, 42]. Another study has demonstrated that individuals usually regulate negative mood by retrieving positive memories from the past [44]. Therefore, the participants might associate the cartoonish VE with happy childhood memories [see 10, 34], which might, in turn, mitigate the negative emotional experience of pain. This is further supported by a study which demonstrated that viewing an animated cartoon during venepuncture can reduce the levels of perceived pain in comparison to standard treatments [55].

Another possible interpretation of the positive effect VR has on pain intensity and perceived exertion could be offered by Rubber Hand Illusion theory, according to which visual-proprioceptive information allows the individuals to perceive a fake hand as a part of their own body [9]. Research has shown that bodily self-consciousness is generated in the brain by sensory stimulation on a fake hand [50]. Therefore, the Rubber hand illusion theory explains why the user may have the illusive feeling that the fake hand is a part of the real body. Even though the fake hand was perceived as a real part of the body, the presentation of the hand via VR concealed visual stimuli that are perceived by the brain as signals of pain and exertion (e.g., veins swells, skin redness). This visual information might have minimized the perception of pain and exertion the individual felt. Furthermore, the level of interaction during sessions with immersive VR technology can increase participants' pain tolerance [54]. Having in mind that the virtual hand was imitating the real move and tremor, the participants might have felt that the interactivity levels were high, since the VR application produces natural moves, and therefore this might have had an effect on minimizing the perceived pain and exertion.

Finally, a positive relationship was found between VR technology and time to exhaustion (TTE), as it was found that participants using VR exercised for approximately three minutes longer compared to those involved in the conventional non-VR exercise. TTE has been considered to be an important, valid and objective physiological measurement for the assessment of pain. In the past, several studies have used the time for the assessment of pain during a continuous pain task [13, 46] and during a continuous exercise pain task [2].

The positive effect of VR on TTE might also be attributed to the interactive features incorporated by the virtual environment (e.g., hand and dumbbell were imitating the real move). It should be noted that additional interactive actions with the virtual world were not possible since the participant had to remain in a stable condition so as the bicep curl exercise could be performed correctly and no other muscles (e.g. back muscles) should contribute to the resistance exercise. Therefore, the resistance exercise performed in the virtual environment allowed the user to interact with the virtual environment in real-time and perform the exercise. This impacted on the levels of immersion the participants felt. Previous studies showed that the participants' level of interactivity and immersion into the virtual world could affect the perception of time [22, 32, 45]. A comparison between interactive and passive VR technology for individuals experiencing cold pressor pain revealed that the interactive condition was significantly more effective [14]. In addition, it was found that increased levels of immersion can reduce the level of pain reported by participants [22].

4.1 Design Guidelines

Drawing on the findings of this study, it can be claimed that the effectiveness of a virtual environment depends on several factors. Therefore, designers of VR for pain management can derive some guidelines and recommendations from the present study.

Although this study did not compare animated virtual environments to photorealistic ones, the positive findings should not be overlooked; animated virtual environments should be used by designers so that a reduced ECG, PIR and RPE and an increased TTE is achieved during resistance exercise.

In particular, it was found that when interactive virtual environment was void of distracting visual information, but enhanced with cartoonish elements, and incorporated animated elements that did not depict fatigue and pain (e.g. did not depict the swell of veins that normally appear on the limb during exercise), then participants had a reduced ECG, PIR and RPE, and an increased TTE during painful exercise.

Therefore, we suggest for designers of VR, not only to focus on the virtual presentation of material properties that are to be used in exercise and surround the user, but also on the proper design of the virtual human body and the part that will be involved in the performance of the exercise.

4.2   Conclusion, Implications and Future Directions

Given the continuous advances in the usability of VR technologies and accompanying interactive devices, it is now conceivable to use affordable VR technology and low-cost interactivity devices. Our study shows that VR can be used to reduce significantly the naturally occurred pain and effort associated with single limb exercise. Our participants had limited engagement in regular, structured resistance or aerobic exercise (only 30%) and generally low interest in exercise. However, positive attitudes were reported toward the VR exercise. Participants expressed their willingness to use the VR application to exercise on a daily basis. Therefore, an implication of this study is that VR can motivate positively individuals who are reluctant to exercise, and this could potentially result in an increased level of physical activity and thus a healthier lifestyle.

We should not overlook the fact that perceived pain and exertion have been considered to be an obstacle for athletes and professionals during exhaustive training. The results of the study are promising in this respect; perceived pain and exertion can be reduced and this can increase the duration of the exercise. This suggests that VR technologies can be used more widely by athletes and professionals to offset pain and exertion. In such a case, athletes and professionals will increase their durability during training and, by extension, improve their performance. In addition, VR exercise accompanies interactive devices, which have the potential to monitor the user's physiological signals and levels of performance during VR exercise.

The positive implications of this study may well be extended to patients suffering from heart disease. Our results suggest that VR technology can play a significant role in pain perception during endurance performance. In particular, it is shown that the positive outcomes of VR can help to offset the ECG increase. We found that VR can help the individual maintain ECG rates closer to the resting ones. Based on these findings, it can be inferred that VR technology can allow the individual to continue exercising for a longer period of time without burdening the heart. This calls for further research on individuals with heart disease, who could benefit from engaging in exercise but at the same time protected from the risk of an increased ECG that can cause heart failure.

The reported study may also have an implication on stroke patients with arm motor impairments, which need exercise and physiotherapy. Research has shown that a key factor for an effective exercise rehabilitation of stroke patients is the duration and intensity of the exercise performance [26]. The study demonstrated that VR can influence positively PIR and RPE, meaning that the user is able to continue exercising at high intensity for a longer period of time. This potentially results in patients being able to increase the duration and intensity of treatment to promote motor recovery after stroke.

Likewise, given the affordability and ease of use of mobile VR technology, one can imagine a scenario where such a VR intervention can be employed at home with minimal or no clinical supervision. A possible design idea would be to incorporate social interactions into the virtual environment since in many cases patients become homebound for a long period of time and hence lack social interactions. Therefore, in future VR exercise applications could allow patients to carry out daily exercise along with other people virtually.

Another aspect that calls for further investigation is the sustainability of VR in the long term. Although participants reported that they are willing to use the VR application on a regular basis for limb exercise, further research is needed to establish the sustainability of this motivation over a longer period of time. Previous studies, as well as this study, mostly cover short-term effects. Only one study [3] has compared the effect of VR over short- and long-term periods, which found that in the long run, VR is no better than standard interventions. Therefore, whether VR could have long-lasting beneficial effects on pain management remains to be established.

An area which needs to be investigated further relates to the observation that a virtual representation of the body part in pain (e.g., virtual hand) can reduce the perceived pain. Future studies could compare a digital–VR hand to a mixed relativity hand (virtual and augmented reality) in order to identify the most efficient way to represent affected body parts in VR. Moreover, future experiments could also examine whether the perceived immersion of the user is further improved by enhancing the sense of embodiment, via connecting the VR with portable, advanced and low-cost sensors (e.g., leap motion) which can track in higher precision the movement of user's hand and fingers. More precise sensing technologies may increase the sense of presence and hand ownership and this may potentially result in even higher levels of immersion.

The work done in this study provides a basis for future research related to pain management and VR. More importantly, it provides VR designers with innovative ideas to create engaging and effective virtual environments not only for healthy people engaging in regular exercise but also for patients who avoid participating fully in physical therapies due to procedural pain.

Acknowledgements. This works has been carried out by the Lead Researcher, Dr Maria Matsangidou, at the University of Kent, during her PhD studies. Dr Matsangidou is currently a Senior Researcher in the Multidisciplinary Group of Smart, Ubiquitous, and Participatory Technologies for Healthcare Innovation of Research Center on Interactive media, Smart systems and Emerging technologies.

References

1. Arntz, A., Dreessen, L., Merckelbach, H.: Attention, not anxiety, influences pain. Behav. Res. Ther. **29**(1), 41–50 (1991)
2. Astokorki, A.H.Y., Mauger, A.R.: Tolerance of exercise-induced pain at a fixed rating of perceived exertion predicts time trial cycling performance. Scand. J. Med. Sci. Sports **27**(3), 309–317 (2017)
3. Bahat, H.S., Takasaki, H., Chen, X., Bet-Or, Y., Treleaven, J.: Cervical kinematic training with and without interactive VR training for chronic neck pain–a randomized clinical trial. Manual Ther. **20**(1), 68–78 (2015)

4. Berntson, G.G., Cacioppo, J.T.: Heart rate variability: stress and psychiatric conditions. In: Dynamic Electrocardiography, pp. 57–64 (2004)
5. Borg, G.: A ratio scaling method for interindividual comparisons. University of Stockholm, Institute of Applied Psychology (1972)
6. Borg, G.: Borg's Perceived Exertion and Pain Scales. Human Kinetics (1998)
7. Borg, G.A.: Physical performance and perceived exertion. Investigationes XI. Lund, Gleerup (1962)
8. Borg, G., Ljunggren, G., Ceci, R.: The increase of perceived exertion, aches and pain in the legs, heart rate and blood lactate during exercise on a bicycle ergometer. Eur. J. Appl. Physiol. Occup. Physiol. 54(4), 343–349 (1985). https://doi.org/10.1007/BF02337176
9. Botvinick, M., Cohen, J.: Rubber hands 'feel' touch that eyes see. Nature 391(6669), 756 (1998)
10. Bower, G.H.: Mood and memory. Am. Psychol. 36(2), 129–148 (1981)
11. Cohen, L.L., Blount, R.L., Panopoulos, G.: Nurse coaching and cartoon distraction: an effective and practical intervention to reduce child, parent, and nurse distress during immunizations. J. Pediatr. Psychol. 22(3), 355–370 (1997)
12. Cook, D.B., O'Connor, P.J., Eubanks, S.A., Smith, J.C., Lee, M.I.N.G.: Naturally occurring muscle pain during exercise: assessment and experimental evidence. Med. Sci. Sports Exerc. 29(8), 999–1012 (1997)
13. Dahlquist, L.M., Herbert, L.J., Weiss, K.E., Jimeno, M.: Virtual-reality distraction and cold-pressor pain tolerance: does avatar point of view matter? Cyberpsychology Behav. Soc. Network. 13(5), 587–591 (2010)
14. Dahlquist, L.M., McKenna, K.D., Jones, K.K., Dillinger, L., Weiss, K.E., Ackerman, C.S.: Active and passive distraction using a head-mounted display helmet: effects on cold pressor pain in children. Health Psychol. 26(6), 794–801 (2007)
15. Dishman, R.K., Nakamura, Y., Garcia, M.E., Thompson, R.W., Dunn, A.L., Blair, S.N.: Heart rate variability, trait anxiety, and perceived stress among physically fit men and women. Int. J. Psychophysiol. 37(2), 121–133 (2000)
16. Ehde, D.M., Patterson, D.R., Fordyce, W.E.: The quota system in burn rehabilitation. J. Burn Care Res. 19(5), 436–440 (1998)
17. Epstein, L.H., Roemmich, J.N.: Reducing sedentary behavior: role in modifying physical activity. Exerc. Sport Sci. Rev. 29(3), 103–108 (2001)
18. Friedman, B.H., Thayer, J.F.: Autonomic balance revisited: panic anxiety and heart rate variability. J. Psychosom. Res. 44(1), 133–151 (1998)
19. Graves, L.E., Ridgers, N.D., Stratton, G.: The contribution of upper limb and total body movement to adolescents' energy expenditure whilst playing Nintendo Wii. Eur. J. Appl. Physiol. 104(4), 617–624 (2008). https://doi.org/10.1007/s00421-008-0813-8
20. Graves, L., Stratton, G., Ridgers, N.D., Cable, N.T.: Comparison of energy expenditure in adolescents when playing new generation and sedentary computer games: cross sectional study. BMJ 335(7633), 1282–1284 (2007)
21. Hoffman, H.G., Doctor, J.N., Patterson, D.R., Carrougher, G.J., Furness III, T.A.: Virtual reality as an adjunctive pain control during burn wound care in adolescent patients. Pain 85 (1–2), 305–309 (2000)
22. Hoffman, H.G., et al.: Modulation of thermal pain-related brain activity with virtual reality: evidence from fMRI. NeuroReport 15(8), 1245–1248 (2004)
23. Hyattsville, M.D., National Center for Health Statistics: Health, United States, 2006 with Chartbook on Trends in the Health of Americans (2007)
24. Imai, K., et al.: Vagally mediated heart rate recovery after exercise is accelerated in athletes but blunted in patients with chronic heart failure. J. Am. Coll. Cardiol. 24(6), 1529–1535 (1994)

25. Jacobs, K., et al.: Wii health: a preliminary study of the health and wellness benefits of Wii Fit on university students. Br. J. Occup. Ther. **74**(6), 262–268 (2011)
26. Langhorne, P., Coupar, F., Pollock, A.: Motor recovery after stroke: a systematic review. Lancet Neurol. **8**(8), 741–754 (2009)
27. Lechner, D.E., Bradbury, S.F., Bradley, L.A.: Detecting sincerity of effort: a summary of methods and approaches. Phys. Ther. **78**(8), 867–888 (1998)
28. Lee, J., et al.: Cartoon distraction alleviates anxiety in children during induction of anesthesia. Anesth. Analg. **115**(5), 1168–1173 (2012)
29. Li, A., Montaño, Z., Chen, V.J., Gold, J.I.: Virtual reality and pain management: current trends and future directions. Pain Manag. **1**(2), 147–157 (2011)
30. Lum, P.S., Burgar, C.G., Shor, P.C., Majmundar, M., Van der Loos, M.: Robot-assisted movement training compared with conventional therapy techniques for the rehabilitation of upper-limb motor function after stroke. Arch. Phys. Med. Rehabil. **83**(7), 952–959 (2002)
31. Maani, C.V., et al.: Virtual reality pain control during burn wound debridement of combat-related burn injuries using robot-like arm mounted VR goggles. J. Trauma **71**(1), 125–130 (2011)
32. Mahrer, N.E., Gold, J.I.: The use of virtual reality for pain control: a review. Curr. Pain Headache Rep. **13**(2), 100–109 (2009). https://doi.org/10.1007/s11916-009-0019-8
33. Maloney, A.E., Threlkeld, K.A., Cook, W.L.: Comparative effectiveness of a 12-week physical activity intervention for overweight and obese youth: exergaming with "dance dance revolution". Games Health Res. Dev. Clin. Appl. **1**(2), 96–103 (2012)
34. Martin, M.A., Metha, A.: Recall of early childhood memories through musical mood induction. Arts Psychother. **24**(5), 447–454 (1997)
35. Matsangidou, M., Ang, C.S., Sakel, M.: Clinical utility of virtual reality in pain management: a comprehensive research review. Br. J. Neurosci. Nurs. **13**(3), 133–143 (2017)
36. Matsangidou, M., Ang, C.S., Mauger, A.R., Intarasirisawat, J., Otkhmezuri, B., Avraamides, M.N.: Is your virtual self as sensational as your real? Virtual reality: the effect of body consciousness on the experience of exercise sensations. Psychol. Sport Exerc. **41**, 218–224 (2019)
37. Matsangidou, M., Ang, C.S., Mauger, A.R., Otkhmezuri, B., Tabbaa, L.: How real is unreal? In: Bernhaupt, R., Dalvi, G., Joshi, A., K. Balkrishan, D., O'Neill, J., Winckler, M. (eds.) INTERACT 2017. LNCS, vol. 10516, pp. 273–288. Springer, Cham (2017). https://doi.org/10.1007/978-3-319-68059-0_18
38. Mauger, A.R.: Factors affecting the regulation of pacing: current perspectives. Open Access J. Sports Med. **5**, 209–214 (2014)
39. McGrath, P.J., et al.: Core outcome domains and measures for pediatric acute and chronic/recurrent pain clinical trials: PedIMMPACT recommendations. J. Pain **9**(9), 771–783 (2008)
40. Merskey, H., Bogduk, N.: Classification of Chronic Pain, IASP Task Force on Taxonomy. International Association for the Study of Pain, Seattle (1994)
41. Myrtek, M., Brügner, G.: Perception of emotions in everyday life: studies with patients and normals. Biol. Psychol. **42**(1–2), 147–164 (1996)
42. Parrott, W.G., Sabini, J.: Mood and memory under natural conditions: evidence for mood incongruent recall. J. Pers. Soc. Psychol. **59**(2), 321–336 (1990)
43. Patterson, D., Sharar, S.: Burn pain. In: Bonica's Management of Pain, 3rd edn, pp. 780–787 (2001)

44. Rusting, C.L., DeHart, T.: Retrieving positive memories to regulate negative mood: consequences for mood-congruent memory. J. Pers. Soc. Psychol. **78**(4), 737–752 (2000)

45. Sharples, S., Cobb, S., Moody, A., Wilson, J.R.: Virtual reality induced symptoms and effects (VRISE): comparison of head mounted display (HMD), desktop and projection display systems. Displays **29**(2), 58–69 (2008)

46. Sil, S., et al.: The effects of coping style on virtual reality enhanced videogame Distraction in children undergoing cold pressor pain. J. Behav. Med. **37**(1), 156–165 (2014). https://doi.org/10.1007/s10865-012-9479-0

47. Sloan, R.P., et al.: Effect of mental stress throughout the day on cardiac autonomic control. Biol. Psychol. **37**(2), 89–99 (1994)

48. Smith, S.T., Sherrington, C., Studenski, S., Schoene, D., Lord, S.R.: A novel Dance Dance Revolution (DDR) system for in-home training of stepping ability: basic parameters of system use by older adults. Br. J. Sports Med. **45**(5), 441–445 (2011)

49. Tousignant-Laflamme, Y., Rainville, P., Marchand, S.: Establishing a link between heart rate and pain in healthy subjects: a gender effect. J. Pain **6**(6), 341–347 (2005)

50. Tsakiris, M., Hesse, M.D., Boy, C., Haggard, P., Fink, G.R.: Neural signatures of body ownership: a sensory network for bodily self-consciousness. Cereb. Cortex **17**(10), 2235–2244 (2006)

51. Volpe, B.T., Krebs, H.I., Hogan, N., Edelstein, L., Diels, C., Aisen, M.: A novel approach to stroke rehabilitation robot-aided sensorimotor stimulation. Neurology **54**(10), 1938–1944 (2000)

52. von Baeyer, C.L., Spagrud, L.J.: Systematic review of observational (behavioral) measures of pain for children and adolescents aged 3 to 18 years. Pain **127**(1), 140–150 (2007)

53. Warburton, D.E., et al.: The health benefits of interactive video game exercise. Appl. Physiol. Nutr. Metab. **32**(4), 655–663 (2007)

54. Wender, R., Hoffman, H.G., Hunner, H.H., Seibel, E.J., Patterson, D.R., Sharar, S.R.: Interactivity influences the magnitude of virtual reality analgesia. J. Cyber Ther. Rehabil. **2**(1), 27–33 (2009)

55. Yoo, H., Kim, S., Hur, H.K., Kim, H.S.: The effects of an animation distraction intervention on pain response of preschool children during venipuncture. Appl. Nurs. Res. **24**(2), 94–100 (2011)

56. Zhou, H., Hu, H.: Human motion tracking for rehabilitation—a survey. Biomed. Sig. Process. Control **3**(1), 1–18 (2008)

VREye: Exploring Human Visual Acuity Test Using Virtual Reality

Shivang Shekar[1]($\boxtimes$), Pranav Reddy Pesaladinne[2]($\boxtimes$), Sai Anirudh Karre[1]($\boxtimes$), and Y. Raghu Reddy[1]($\boxtimes$)

[1] Software Engineering Research Center, IIIT Hyderabad, Hyderabad, India
{shivang.shekhar,saianirudh.karri}@research.iiit.ac.in,
raghu.reddy@iiit.ac.in
[2] Department of Computer Science, BITS Pilani, Hyderabad, India
bestpranav.16@gmail.com

Abstract. Human Eye is a complex sense organ that allows vision. Vision problems may arise due to various reasons. Vision tests serve us to determine the levels of vision degradation. Early observations can support us to provide appropriate intervention for vision issues. However, one needs an Optometrist (eye specialist) to identify and validate vision issues. Scheduling an eye check-up can be tedious or unaffordable to people across various parts of the world. Acknowledging the real-world challenges on a scale of affordance to laziness, a simplified solution for vision tests can ease understanding the levels of vision issues. Considering this use case, we attempt to build a virtual reality (VR) based vision testing mechanism for studying vision issues for individuals across all age groups called 'VREye'. In this paper, we discuss our journey towards developing a VR based solution for detecting myopic vision. We detail our challenges and insights on building the overall VR scene design, developing a virtual distance scale, and using real-world test subjects for initial validation. We also discuss our plans to extend this application to include more vision problems like hypermetropia and color blindness.

Keywords: Human centered computing · Visual acuity · Virtual reality · Health care

1 Motivation

Indian subcontinent has more than 20% of the world's blind population [13]. Majority of surveys have shown that in India Myopia and Cataract as the most common causes of blindness. Initiatives that deal with prevention of blindness are mainly oriented towards these two significant problems [13]. Considering this health crisis, the World Health Organization (WHO) had come up with a Strategic Plan called VISION 2020 [11] to eliminate avoidable blindness in the South East Asia Region. One of the critical aspects of this strategy is to introduce low-cost tools to detect and operate vision problems in the subcontinent. Recent

© Springer Nature Switzerland AG 2020
J. Y. C. Chen and G. Fragomeni (Eds.): HCII 2020, LNCS 12191, pp. 415–429, 2020.
https://doi.org/10.1007/978-3-030-49698-2_28

studies on the progress of this program have shown excellent results in avoiding blindness. However, the data also warns of emerging threats that, if ignored, could reverse the growth of this initiative that has continued for the past 25 years [7].

With the advent of new technologies, today's society requires new tools and techniques to curb such health challenges. Ophthalmological Studies (branch of study that deals with eye disorders) observed that vergence and accommodation are the two vision stimuli found in the vertebrates. Accommodation is the adjustment of optics of the Eye to keep an object in focus on the retina, when the distance from the Eye varies. Vergence is the simultaneous movement of the pupils of the eyes towards or away from one another during focusing. These two stimuli become the basis for judging the clarity of one's vision. There is also abundant literature available in medicine which talks about standardizing the visual acuity test [4]. Attempts have been made to design visual acuity tests using Software application and few empirical studies have yielded notable results [6]. However, the physical visual acuity test setup is still considered to be tiresome [14].

HCI researchers have explored various approaches to replicate visual acuity test using emerging technologies like Virtual Reality (VR). Stylianos et al. have conducted a comparative study between VR and physical test setup for visual field examination [14]. VR Researchers have explored the effects of visual evoked responses to dichoptic stimulation using VR based apps [5]. Focused studies have been done using VR based apps to explore the Eye and its dimensions of clarity. This includes the Eye-Tracked VR System for remote diagnosis [8]. There are studies to explore the impacts of accommodation and vergence on humans while using HMDs [10]. Study on effects of vision impairments on recognition distances of escape-route signs in buildings has been done using VR based scenes [9]. While studies in the past have tried to explore the complexities involved in the visual capacity of a human eye, there are fairly limited number of studies on conducting visual acuity tests based on VR Systems. These observations motivated us to examine the potential of VR Setup to reproduce a visual acuity test and explore ways to transcend it into a low-cost solution for conducting vision tests for the economically weaker section of the population.

2 Background

We initiated our research by exploring opportunities available in current VR technology to address the standardization of the visual acuity test or vision test of a Human Eye. In this section, we discuss the background of our study that helped us formulate the hypothesis of our work.

Herman Snellen Test - This is a traditional and widely accepted visual acuity test used to judge the human eye vision. The participant is presented with a chart that includes alphabets and numbers placed in a specific order. The alphabets and numbers are organized in multiple rows, as shown in Fig. 1 with decreasing font size (top to bottom). The human participant is made to read these alphabets and numbers from the standardized chart called Snellen chart placed at a distance of 20 ft, i.e., 6 m from the participants' eye. Unique charts are used when the testing distance shorter than 20 ft. Some charts are played as videos on a video monitor showing alphabets or images.

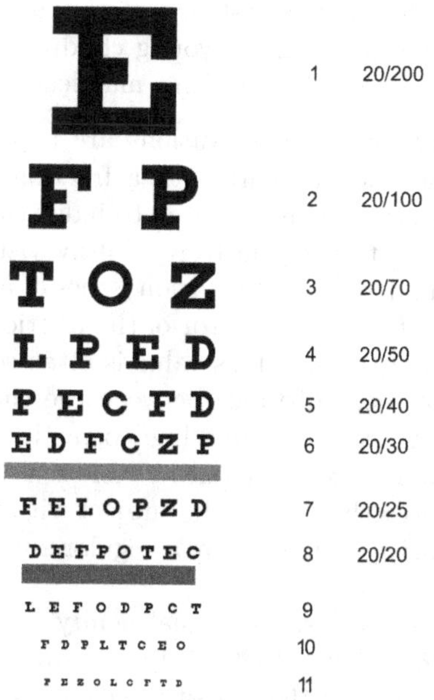

E	1	20/200
F P	2	20/100
T O Z	3	20/70
L P E D	4	20/50
P E C F D	5	20/40
E D F C Z P	6	20/30
F E L O P Z D	7	20/25
D E F P O T E C	8	20/20
L E F O D P C T	9	
F D P L T C E O	10	
P E Z O L C F T D	11	

Fig. 1. Standard Snellen chart

Procedure - Snellen's test is conducted under the supervision of a health care expert irrespective of a test place. It can be set up in an office, school, workplace, or elsewhere. Human participants are required to remove their spectacles or contact lenses, if any, and are allowed to stand or sit in front of the Snellen chart at a minimum distance of 20 ft away from it. At the beginning of the test, the participant is required to close one of their eyes with their hand palm (or) piece of paper (or) a small paddle is allowed to read out loud the smallest of letters they can see on the chart. In the case of participants with illiteracy, numbers (or) lines (or) pictures are used in place of alphabets. This practice is also suitable for young children. The participant is allowed to guess if the alphabet is not clearly visible on the chart. This activity is repeated by closing another eye to complete the test of both the eyes. If required, this activity is repeated while participants are wearing their spectacles or contact lenses. In case of severe difficulties in reading, the participant will be asked to read letters or numbers from a card held 14 in. or 36 cm away. The overall outcome of this procedure will help the health care expert to judge the vision levels of participants. In the case of long-distance vision issues, the participant is considered to be having a myopic vision. Otherwise, he/she is considered to have a hypermetropic vision, i.e., short-distance vision issues. There is no discomfort or hazards or risks to participants involved as part of this test.

Frequency - The visual acuity test can be conducted whenever there is some problem in one's vision. There is no limit on the frequency aspect of this examination. Especially in children, this test is a reasonable means to decide early age vision problems. These problems in young children can often be corrected. When undetected or untreated, the problems may lead to irreparable damage.

Evaluation - Visual acuity test observations are expressed using a fraction scale. Figure 1 shows the Snellen chart with a fraction indicator against each line on the sheet. The fraction scale is defined to judge the vision of an impaired subject concerning a subject with relatively healthy vision. This fraction scale helps health practitioners determine the vision issues of a subject and define the levels of vision impairment. The numerator of the fraction refers to the distance between the subject and the chart. This value is often set to **20 ft i.e., (6 m)**. The denominator indicates the distance between the chart and a subject with normal eyesight (who can read the same line correctly). For example, a 20/20 fraction scale is considered to be a standard visible scale. A 20/40 fraction scale indicates that the line correctly read by the subject with vision problems at 20 ft (6 m) away from the chart can be read by a regular subject with normal vision from 40 ft (12 m) away.

Outside of the United States, the visual acuity is expressed as a decimal number. For example, 20/20 is 1.0, 20/40 is 0.5, 20/80 is 0.25, 20/100 is 0.2, and so on. With the decrease in the size of the characters on the Snellen chart, the fraction scale value decreases concerning normal vision scale grouped by distance. In a given line if one or two letters in the chart are mis-read, the subject is considered to have vision equal to that line's fraction scale. In turn, the respective fraction scale will define the level of their vision issues.

Outcome - Abnormal results may be a sign that the respective subject is in need of a corrected version lens corresponding to the fraction scale value. Alternatively, it may mean that the subject has an eye condition that needs further evaluation by a provider.

3   VR Visual Acuity Test Setup

The major objective of this work is to build a Virtual Reality based prototype called VREye for conducting a simplified Visual Acuity Test, i.e., Vision Test. For this to happen, an experimental setup for calculating vision using a scale (with in VR scene) for judgment of vision impairment needs to be established. The idea is to replicate the Snellen test using VR, utilizing a customized sense to automate the vision test evaluation. We detail our study set up in the following sections.

3.1   Necessary Conditions

We discuss the necessary conditions needed for our work including software and hardware constraints along with the domain-specific standards.

Real-World Distance Vs. Virtual-World Distance - Adapting real-world distance in a virtual environment is a challenge while designing the Snellen test. It isn't straightforward to interpret the real world distance in virtual environments. Almost all the VR Game Engines use object transformation functions to place an object at a distance from the camera in the VR scene. Unity SDK provides an inbuilt library called "Distance Display" which offers transform(x) method. This method can place an object at a given distance from the camera. However, there is lack of clarity on the unit of length in VR Scene and its mapping with a real-world unit of measure for distance. We conducted a sub-experiment to define a scale to address this *'distance unit challenge'*.

Virtual Distance Scale - To address the 'distance unit challenge,' we created a VR Scene with a unit distance scale, which extends to 20 units. The Snellen Chart was positioned on the end of the 20 unit distance scale and about 30 participants were asked to navigate through the virtual scale as shown in Fig. 2 to judge the virtual distance unit in terms of real-world distance units. Based on this sub-experiment, we determined a mapping between real-world distance unit vs. virtual world distance unit. As part of this sub-experiment, we depended on inbuilt depth perception methods in Unity SDK to determine the depth of the VR Scene. We discuss more about this sub-experiment in the following sections.

Snellen Chart Considerations - Snellen charts use alphanumeric symbols on a 5×5 unit grid. This chart has evolved over decades, and it now uses eleven lines of block letters. The first line consists of one huge letter, which may be one of several letters, for example, E, H, or N. Subsequent rows (top to bottom) have increasing numbers of characters with a decrease in size [1]. A person taking the test covers one eye from 6 m or 20 ft away, and reads aloud the letters of each row, beginning at the top. The smallest row that can be read correctly indicates the visual acuity in that specific eye. The symbols on an acuity chart are formally known as "optotypes" [1]. These optotypes have the appearance of block characters and are intended to be seen and read as letters. The thickness of the lines and the thickness of the white spaces between lines are normalized such that the characters are visible [1]. Usually, the height and the width of the optotype (letter) is five times the thickness of the line. Only the ten letters C, D, E, F, L, N, O, P, T, and Z are used in the standard Snellen chart. The perception of five out of six letters (or similar ratio) is judged to be the *"Snellen fraction"*. It is a fraction of distance at which the test is being made, and the distance at which the smallest optotype identified subtends an angle of five arc-minutes [1]. We rely on visual acuity testing standard - BS 4274-1:2003 [1] for all our virtual examinations. Any variation across the test chart shall not exceed 20%. Also, only the letters C, D, E, F, H, K, N, P, R, U, V, and Z are used for the testing of vision-based upon equal legibility of the letters.

Fig. 2. Scale used in VRScene

3.2   Sufficient Conditions

In this sub-section, we discuss the sufficient conditions followed as part of the work, specifically with respect to the study design and test subjects.

Medical History - The optometry history of the participant was captured as part of our study. Other minor details included blood sugar levels, blood pressure levels, as it enabled our study to do minor customization for participants (to make them more comfortable during testing) with glaucoma and other complications related to the eye.

Gender Distribution - We welcomed all the participants from different genders to be part of our study as the physiological differences and the presentation of disease symptoms may give rise to differences in the clinical outcome of medications. Therefore, it was paramount to have diversity in gender in our test trials.

Considerations and Compromises - Our initial study was only limited to the detection of myopic vision in our participants. While designing out study, we didn't consider the effect of fatigue in the participant's eye, as our motive was to demonstrate possibilities of VR as an alternate vision test tool but not as a confirmatory test. As a result some compromises were made on the study design, data set size and population diversity. However, our basic test setup and preamble of the experiment remains constant throughout the future advancements. The effects of hardware refinement are not observed in the present research, which can significantly change in the perception of VR environments.

4 Study Design

About VR Scene - We use the traditional Snellen Chart for our VR Scene based Vision test. We use a VR head-mounted device (HMD) to run the VR Scene. The lenses in the HMD are of zero power magnification. These lenses are adjusted for the generalized audience with no vision issues in general. The HMDs take care of accommodation and the vergence of the human eye. However, when a human eye is exposed to a virtual environment, the accommodation levels of the eye show hurdles. We reviewed contemporary research [3,7] about standard protocols followed for conducting a visual acuity test and observed that the visual acuity test could be conducted using a series of motion-based/action based controls in a Virtual Scene to address this hurdle. However, we found below shortcomings in providing control to the participant in the VR Scene setup.

- Users had to extend/protrude from their respective positions to move around and change their physical position in the scene.
- Buttons that measured scale could not adequately capture the exact values of distance measure.
- A steep learning curve observed in various users who experienced VR for the very first time. Thus the gathered hints of the scene design do not provide confidence to the user.
- *Signifiers*, which aid the user to live in the scene, are not formalized as a standard. It causes challenges to evaluate the '*presence*' metric for a user to access the state of a given scene.

Design Rules for Dynamic Scenes - One way of expressing an object's position in a VR Scene is to refer the X, Y, and Z coordinates in the scene lattice. Despite defining an object in a scene lattice, the position and action i.e., the intentions behind these objects, must be dynamically defined to construct the 3-dimensional scene. When compared to the real-world, a 3-dimensional reconstruction algorithm may not always yield a correct result. The quality of dynamically determining the object's intent is also tricky for virtual reality engines. Thus the real world floors and walls can move and effectively wobble as far as the algorithms are concerned. Considering these challenges involved with scene control and dynamic scene generation, we consider the *signifiers* like *Anchors, Declarative Intentions, Procedural Intentions, Prioritization (each object associated with* *a user or an emitter application)* from the emerging virtual reality taxonomy [2] for describing object placement in our VR Scene. The scene is built considering these signifiers, as it aids us to finalize the focus and navigation settings inside a VR Scene.

Scene Object Placement - In-order to minimize use of motion and variability in participant's tasks and actions, the scene design has only frontal engagement. The scene consists of a pathway with red dots acting as a position index and a Snellen chart at a determined virtual distance. The placement of the Snellen chart object in a VR Scene is critical for the participant as per domain experts.

Color Selection - After obtaining a thorough understanding of the Snellen test, we worked with the domain experts to design the initial experiment setup. We considered the background color to be BLACK and the position index dot color as RED. The BLACK color is darker and aids the participant to draw participant attention towards the Snellen chart. It also helps the participant to determine the position index as a contrast in the scene and determine the locomotion gestures. The position index is the point where the participant can determine the point of presence in the VR Scene space. We considered a less dark color as a contrast for the participant to determine the position in the Snellen test scene, as shown in Fig. 2.

Scene Requirements - Below are our hardware and software considerations for developing the Virtual Reality Scene (Table 1).

Table 1. Scene requirements for VREye

Platform/Hardware	Version	Package
Unity	V 2018f1.1	Oculus VR SDK
Oculus Rift	Rift with touch controllers	Oculus controller SDK

Scene Design Challenges - Calculating Virtual distance, Scene dimensions, and defining spatial limits are few design challenges we faced while replicating the Snellen test. We developed the VR scene in an incremental mode. The scene setup was reviewed with domain experts based on our test requirements in parallel. Our initial scene setup was not consistent and reliable in terms of the above challenges. We incrementally improved the scene by conducting simple pilot studies with participants with no vision issues to replicate the physical test scene inside VR (as-it-is). We observed that the scene should accommodate real-life spatial limits. Thus considering such challenges, we divided the use-cases into the following sub-parts for an enhanced test setup.

- **Scale:** We defined a virtual measurement line (using virtual distance scale) where each point represents a distance value on the virtual Snellen chart. Our incremental pilot study was used to generate a distance scale that mapped to real-world distance.

– **Motion:** A linear motion control was defined over a discreetly divided path for accurate readings based on the scale.
– **Position:** With the incremental pilot study, we identified significant improvements in factors like accuracy on measuring the exact location on the scale and achieved motion stability.

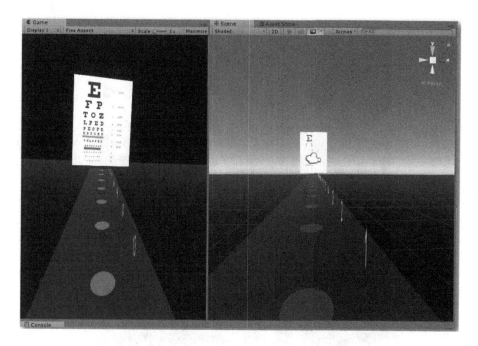

Fig. 3. Recreation of Snellen Test in VR

By addressing the above challenges and issues with Scene design, Fig. 3 is the finalized recreation of a Snellen VR Scene used part of VREye application.

5   Experiment Design

Experiment protocols are vital for data collection and testing tools like VREye. Adherence to protocols are a must before we conduct such tests. The test is divided in to two parts. The following are the few protocols followed as part of first part of the experiment.

– Participants are required to read a standard Snellen chart from 6m (20 ft) physical distance in a well-lit room using a direct eye.
– Participants are later subjected to read the Snellen with their corrected vision or using their spectacles. It is to identify the correlation between vision power and physical distance. It helps us establish a causation relationship.

– Participants are administered with a standard Snellen test process for squinting of eyes so that the data sanctity can be maintained.

In the second part of the experiment, the participants undergo the test using head-mounted-device (using Oculus Rift) as shown in Fig. 4. The participants are subjected to follow the below steps in a sequence listed below.

Fig. 4. Recreation of Snellen Test in VR

– *S1:* The participant's right eye is blindfolded in order to measure the visual reading of the left eye.
– *S2:* The participant is now allowed to read the Snellen chart with the left eye from the top in an invocation position.
– *S3:* In accordance with the Snellen test protocol, if the participant fails to read the 20/20 line in the standard Snellen chart, the test administrator asks the participant to move a unit virtual distance ahead using the locomotion controller.

- *S4:* S2 and S3 are repeated here until the participant fails to read 20/20.
- *S5:* Once the participant is unable to read the 20/20, the unit distance on the scene strip is recorded by the administrator.
- *S6:* Now, the participant is asked to read the 20/15 line as a confirmatory test.
- *S7:* The above steps are repeated for the right eye by blindfolding the left eye to record the visual reading of the right eye.
- *S8:* S1 to S6 is repeated with both the eyes open to record the visual reading of both the eyes.

Participant Selection - Participants were selected on the basis of primary visual confirmation of sight at a physical Snellen Test. To ensure a diverse participant dataset, the subjects are divided into two categories. They are *Control Participant Group* and *Experimenter Participant Group*. Participants from various age groups having no sight were in the Control Participant Group. Participants with myopic vision of various ranges were bucketed in the Experimenter Participant Group. Table 2 shows the test groups further segregated based on age, eyesight last tested, and with and without vision corrections.

Table 2. Participant Pre-test history

Age group	Test history	Corrections(-ive values)
10–15	Earlier than 6 Months	0–1
18–24	6 Months	1–2
25+	More than 6 Months	2–2.5

Implementation - Below were the use-cases considered while designing the experiment of VREye application.

- *Use-Case 1:* Generating an initial test dataset to determine the virtual distance for the virtual Snellen chart for a given participant population. This use-case helped generate the Virtual vision scale as an outcome, as it determines the 20 ft virtual distance for VREye Scene.
- *Use-Case 2:* The outcome of Use-Case 1 is meant to be used to help other instances of the experiment to achieve our overall objective. Use-case 2 is yet to be implemented as it is part of on-going research.

Use-Case Preservations - Children with age < 10 Years have difficulty in understanding the alphabet in English. Hence, it could be challenging to collect data from such test participants. It also holds good for adults who are illiterate and have difficulty in understanding alphabets from the Snellen chart. Also, participants with one eye complications are restricted from being included in our Datasets. We may have to come up with new methods and approaches (including charts in local languages or symbols) to determine visual acuity for such participants as the standard Snellen chart is not a primary base for their vision evaluation.

6   Results and Observations

We collected the results from 39 test participants and built a test data set [12] for our scale analysis, as discussed in Sect. 5. This data set includes various data points like *Gender, Age* to understand the readings across the gender and age group of the subjects. *Previous sight* - is a crucial data point in understanding the history of visual acuity of the test participants. It can help us with a future comparative study between participants with and without visual acuity history. *Family History* - was included in the data set to study acute family diseases of the test participants. *Line Correction* - data point was essential for identifying the confidence of the participants' response to reading the Snellen chart in a VR setup. *First Reading* - is the data point to measure the vision range in a 20 virtual unit scale in the Snellen VR Setup. *Breakpoint* - is the stage in the virtual Snellen test where the participant breaks to read the whole line or a letter from the Snellen chart i.e., it is a state where the Snellen condition is not satisfied by the participant. Beyond this point, the participant would commit more than two mistakes w.r.t the virtual distance unit on a virtual scale in the Snellen VR Scene.

Data - The data collected as part of our dataset [12] was gathered only after the consent of the participants. All participants were subjected to an initial questionnaire which talked about participants not undergoing strenuous eye activities in the experiment. Also, it was clarified if the participants were on any eye medication that could hamper the sanctity of our data.

Primary Observations - As the majority of the data-points are recorded from the age group of 18–24, we observed constant readings across similar participants (For Eg. a constant reading of 10–12 scale points for Left eye-Right eye with/without corrections) was observed. In regards to formalizing the virtual scale, the range 10–13 of virtual units on the scale of VR Scene was found to be the most prominent zone for participants having a clear vision. Most of the participants with corrected values (with spectacles/lenses) had a similar range as with the Control group. Whereas the participants with age groups 35–40 observed values higher in the scale as compared to participants in the age group 18–24.

Secondary Observations - Children (age group 10–15) were examined under the same VR Test setup used for adults. This user group had shown deviation from standard trend and can be considered as potential outliers in the study in our dataset [12]. Participants with corrections had around 50% accuracy in their visual reading at the correction line (20/32) in VR Scene based Snellen test. Overall, Left eye readings were observed to be higher than the right eye, which indicates that the test performed has some percentage of accuracy as this is the natural eye behavior in clinical terms [3]. Though this behavior of eye was never empirically studied but is said to be true in general while performing actual real-world Snellen tests [9].

Outliers - There were few outliers observed in our dataset [12]. It does not conform to the general patterns throughout the data. Data gathered from children did not conform to the tests. Two female participants observed to have a varied set of results for left only, right only, and left-right eye tests, respectively. Some of the participants had physical eyesight ranging above -2.5 dioptres. Our current VREye scene setup may not be able to deal with such data items, which falls under the extreme physical scale. However, we plan to use such data items for our virtual scale refinement in our future versions of VREye Scene.

In future, we plan to collect more data points from a larger population and use it for developing a vision metric in VR Scene. We are in the process of developing a conversion factor to dioptres (traditional vision strength metric) for each scale point in the Snellen VR Scene. It will help us realize the vision metric for VREye. Outlier detection is one of the significant aspects of our future test plan. Once the VR vision metric is developed, the new data from a large population can aid us to normalize the dataset and address outlier issues. Variations in participants' responses are another essential aspect of our future study. Developing a virtual vision metric, the dataset from a large population, and addressing outliers along with data variations can help us address our overall goal Sect. 3. Upon successful completion of this phase, there are high possibilities of making VREye as an authentic and reliable alternative for an eye testing.

7   Conclusion and Future Work

As part of this research, we studied ways to develop a VR based solution for conducting a visual acuity test. We identified various challenges, shortcomings, and benefits of using VR as a way to detect vision issues with individuals. As part of our work, we successfully developed a virtual scale for participants to navigate through a VR scene for Snellen based acuity testing. We formulated a way to conduct the myopic specific test using VREye application. Additionally, we defined a broader scope for our future work. Below are motivations for an end to end VR based eye solution in the near future:

- Improve the current scale of the study and collect vision data from more than 1500 participants from a diverse population for a better scale and data points to conduct efficient myopic testing.
- To bring down the cost of VR hardware by developing a custom domain-specific HMD for conducting a simplified visual acuity testing.
- Include other eye testing methods like color correction test, depth perception test, and measurement of hypermetropia, etc. as part of upcoming versions of VR Eye.

8 Threats to Validity

In this section, we discuss some of the threats to validity of our VREye study.

Conclusion Validity - In our study, we considered the Snellen chart in English only as our base template for testing visual acuity. To start with, it helped us construct a first of its kind VR based test. There is a possibility of other visual acuity methods that can be generalized for a larger participant set. We plan to consider different ways to study visual acuity as part of extending work.

Internal Validity - We worked with respective domain experts from the field of Ophthalmology while constructing our study setup. We received constant feedback from these domain experts who were part of our experiment design and have judged the implementation process through its course of time.

Construct Validity - The review of our observations are directly captured from the participant's results. The review results consider the credibility of the work and design of the VR product or scene developed as part of our research.

External Validity - We have made every attempt to conduct this study under domain-specific constraints. We followed the review protocol by working with respective domain experts. Results may differ if the participant dataset differs for a substantial population.

Acknowledgements. We thank the test participants from IIIT Student, Staff and their families for participating in our study and for helping us build a dataset.

References

1. BS 4274–1:2003 - Visual Acuity Test Types. Test charts for clinical determination of distance visual acuity - Specification. In: British Standards Institution, January 2003
2. Coomans, M., Timmermans, H.: Towards a taxonomy of virtual reality user interfaces. In: Proceedings of the IEEE Conference on Information Visualisation, p. 279. IEEE Computer Society (1997)
3. Lopes-Ferreira, D., Neves, H., Queiros, A., Faria-Ribeiro, M., Peixoto-de-Matos, S.C., Gonzalez-Meijome, J.M.: Ocular dominance and visual function testing. In: BioMed Research International, Clinical & Experimental Optometry Research Laboratory, Center of Physics, University of Minho, Gualtar, Braga, Portugal, vol. 2013, July 2013. https://doi.org/10.1155/2013/238943
4. Ricci, F., Cedrone, C., Cerulli, L.: Standardized measurement of visual acuity. Ophthalmic Epidemiol. 5(1), 41–53 (1998)
5. Arvind, H., Klistorner, A., Graham, S.L.: Multifocal visual evoked responses to dichoptic stimulation using virtual reality goggles: multifocal VER to dichoptic stimulation. Doc. Ophthalmol. 113, 189–199 (2006). https://doi.org/10.1007/s10633-006-0005-y
6. Yu, H., Jiang, T., Wang, C., Zhou, P.: Design and implementation of an automatic visual acuity test software. In: International Conference on Information System and Artificial Intelligence (ISAI), pp. 81–84, June 2016. https://doi.org/10.1109/ISAI.2016.0026

7. Holden, B.A., et al.: Global prevalence of myopia and high myopia and temporal trends from 2000 through 2050. Ophthalmology **123**, 1036–1042 (2016). https://doi.org/10.1016/j.ophtha.2016.01.006

8. Orlosky, J., Itoh, Y., Ranchet, M., Kiyokawa, K., Morgan, J., Devos, H.: Emulation of physician tasks in eye-tracked virtual reality for remote diagnosis of neurodegenerative disease. IEEE Trans. Visual Comput. Graphics **23**(4), 1302–1311 (2017). https://doi.org/10.1109/TVCG.2017.2657018

9. Krösl, K., Bauer, D., Schwärzler, M., Fuchs, H., Suter, G., Wimmer, M.: A VR-based user study on the effects of vision impairments on recognition distances of escape-route signs in buildings. Vis. Comput., 911–923 (2018). https://doi.org/10.1007/s00371-018-1517-7

10. Lee, S.H., Jhung, J., Lee, H., Cha, J., Kim, S.: A technique for matching convergence and accommodation in a fixed screen 3D VR HMD. In: Proceedings of the 20th ACM SIGGRAPH Symposium on Interactive 3D Graphics and Games, I3D 2016, pp. 185–186. ACM, New York (2016). https://doi.org/10.1145/2856400.2876018

11. Pararajasegaram, R.: Strategic plan for vision 2020: the right to sight - elimination of avoidable blindness in the South-East Asia Region (WHO). Am. J. Opthalmol. **128**, 359–360 (2000). https://doi.org/10.1016/S0002-9394(99)00251-2

12. Shekar, S.: DataSet of VREye Empirical Study, November 2019. https://bit.ly/2oMFUQg

13. Thomas, R., Paul, P., Rao, G.N., Muliyil, J.P., Mathai, A.: Present status of eye care in India. Surv. Ophthalmol. (2005). https://doi.org/10.1016/j.survophthal.2004.10.008

14. Tsapakis, S., et al.: Visual field examination method using virtual reality glasses compared with the humphrey perimeter. Clin. Ophthalmol. **11**, 1431–1443 (2017). https://doi.org/10.2147/OPTH.S131160. https://www.ncbi.nlm.nih.gov/pmc/articles/PMC5557117/

Correction to: Virtual, Augmented and Mixed Reality. Industrial and Everyday Life Applications

Jessie Y. C. Chen and Gino Fragomeni

Correction to:
J. Y. C. Chen and G. Fragomeni (Eds.):
Virtual, Augmented and Mixed Reality, **LNCS 12191,**
https://doi.org/10.1007/978-3-030-49698-2

The original version of this chapter 2 was revised. A video was added to help provide clarity and a visual explanation of the paper.

The title of the originally published chapter 27 contained a typo. The title was corrected.

The updated version of these chapters can be found at
https://doi.org/10.1007/978-3-030-49698-2_2
https://doi.org/10.1007/978-3-030-49698-2_27

Author Index

Printed in the United States
By Bookmasters